REAL ESTATE BROKERAGE

5TH EDITION

A MANAGEMENT GUIDE

John E. Cyr • Joan m. Sobeck
Laurel D. McAdams

Dearborn

Real Estate Education

This publication is designed to provide accurate and authoritative information in regard to the subject matter covered. It is sold with the understanding that the publisher is not engaged in rendering legal, accounting or other professional service. If legal advice or other expert assistance is required, the services of a competent professional person should be sought.

Vice President: Carol L. Luitjens
Executive Editor: Diana Faulhaber
Senior Development Editor: Robert A. Porché, Jr.
Managing Editor: Ronald J. Liszkowski
Art Manager: Lucy Jenkins
Cover Design: Salvatore Concialdi

Published by Real Estate Education Company®,
a division of Dearborn Financial Publishing, Inc.®,
a Kaplan Professional Company
155 North Wacker Drive, Chicago, IL 60606-1719
(312) 836-4400
http://www.dearborn.com

Printed in the United States of America.

03 04 05   10   9   8

Library of Congress Cataloging-in-Publication Data

Cyr, John E.
    Real Estate brokerage : a management guide / John E. Cyr, Joan m. Sobeck, Laurel D. McAdams. — 5th ed.
        p.   cm.
    Includes bibliographical references and index.
    ISBN 0-7931-3155-3
    1. Real estate agents—United States.   2. Real estate business—United States.   I. Sobeck, Joan m.   II. McAdams, Laurel D.
    HD278.C95   1999   99-10261
    333.33'068–dc21   CIP

CONTENTS

PREFACE

Being a broker/owner, a member of the senior management team or the manager of a sales office in today's real estate industry can be an exhilarating experience. It also can be unsettling and perhaps even threatening. People who've been in the business for a number of years can feel like they're sitting in the path of a storm as powerful winds threaten to dismantle the familiar landscape. This storm analogy alone may seem intimidating. But we see a valuable message—the force of a storm is akin to the power our organization's leaders have to be the engine that moves the industry in progressive directions. In other words, be at the forefront, rather than a victim in the wake of change.

We hope we got your attention, because otherwise we'd be stating the obvious: our industry is in the midst of an evolution, perhaps a revolution. Every aspect of our business has been altered as we keep pace with the times. Technology has played a major role. It has changed where we work, the way we conduct business and the methods used to communicate and access information. Our consumers also have changed. The age, familial characteristic and cultural background of today's purchaser is quite diverse. New populations, such as generation X (the baby boomers' children), have emerged as forces in the marketplace. Today's consumers are savvy, sophisticated and, because of their fast-paced life styles, demand more efficient ways of doing business. Similarly, our sales staffs demand more efficient, supportive working environments in their brokerage firms.

Returning to the power part of our analogy—as we are confronted by change, we must decide how to deal with it. Change can be empowering, inspiring creativity, unleashing previously untapped talents and causing us to explore exciting new opportunities. Perhaps this means adopting new attitudes, but also this means acquiring new skills. An enormous number of resources are available with which to do this, which brings us to this book, *Real Estate Brokerage: A Management Guide.*

Perhaps the most significant feature of the title is that our book is a *guide.* We don't presume to suggest that every company should fit into the same mold, nor that every manager should be molded into one form. Each organization is unique and each manager is an individual. The purpose of our book is to guide you through a wide range of issues you need to think about. We intend that our guidance will help you make wise decisions that suit your individual circumstances.

This book is directed to anyone who is a *manager*—the person who supervises or directs the conduct of business. You may be the broker/owner, an administrative manager, a sales or office manager or the manager of a department. The principal difference in any of these jobs is the scope of your involvement in the organization and the degree of authority you have. Our goal is to help you manage financial and human resources effectively and cost-efficiently so that an organization can be profitable.

A Guide to Using This Book

Many fine management theorists have studied how companies operate, how managers function and how people become effective leaders. *Real Estate Brokerage: A Management Guide* strives to apply their theories to the operation of a real estate brokerage company. We do this by following one of the generally accepted approaches, which groups a variety of activities into management functions—Planning, Organizing, Staffing, Directing and Controlling. This POSDC model is a useful way for us to explore the activities involved in running a real estate company in a logical fashion.

The first four units are devoted to these management functions. An introduction to each unit explains what the functions intend to accomplish and the activities we will be discussing. Don't overlook these because they set the stage for the chapters that follow. At the beginning of each chapter we've posed some questions to start you thinking about issues related to the chapter material. At the end of each chapter we provide exercises intended to help translate the subject matter into real-life experiences. Finally, the units conclude with a summary that includes a guide about your involvement with each of the functions, depending on your role in the organization. We also provide several real-life experiences or examples under the heading, *The Business, First Hand,* to further inspire you.

Unit Five is devoted to your personal development as a manager. Nothing happens in an organization without people. Your effectiveness in managing these people is directly related to how well you develop your interpersonal and leadership skills. This unit explores how people function in management and leadership roles and communicate effectively. For a sales manager, this may be the most important unit because you directly supervise the salespeople who are responsible for production.

Users of the fourth edition of *Real Estate Brokerage: A Management Guide* have observed that one of its greatest strengths is its futuristic yet timeless value for a wide range of users. While the fundamental management functions don't change, the environment certainly does. Each market place is governed by its own laws, adopts its own customs and at any time can evolve in new, perhaps unpredictable, ways. This book provides a framework to manage in all of those arenas. Whether you first use it for classroom study or a private read in a quite corner, the book will become an indispensable resource in your personal library. In addition, a bibliography of selected publications is provided to further inspire you.

You may be embarking on a new career as a broker/owner or as the manager of a sales office. You may be a novice or an experienced broker/owner or manager. You might be a salesperson, not yet involved in management, but seeking an "inside look" into a brokerage organization. In any case, *Real Estate Brokerage: A Management Guide* will help you. We wish you much success as you seize the opportunities that are on the horizon!

Acknowledgments

Real Estate Brokerage: A Management Guide, fifth edition, is the second edition of the publication formerly known as *Real Estate Brokerage: A Success Guide*. As the title implies, the newer version intends to focus on the management aspects of running a brokerage firm. Although other fine publications addressed various sales activities, few focused on the specific needs of the people who manage a company's operations and its personnel. This publication intends to fill that void by providing a practical manual for managers in today's brokerage firms. The authors are grateful to a number of people who provided valuable input to the latest edition of this publication.

Jack R. Bennett, Gold Coast School of Real Estate, Miami FL

Darryl Bradshaw, Mykut Real Estate School, Lynnwood WA

Larry G. Goodman, Larry Goodman's Continuing Education, Salisbury NC

Ronald M. Guiberson, Bob Hogue School of Real Estate, St. Petersburg FL

Roger A. Harman, North Seattle Community College, Seattle WA

Jo Usry, Education Director, Mississippi REALTOR® Institute, Jackson MS

Reviewers of the fourth edition include Sylvia A. Carver; Jo Ann Cooper, CRB, CRS, GRI; Richard T. Corbett, Esq.; Joyce A. Emory; Richard T. Fryer; Ronald M. Guiberson, CRS, GRI; Patrick J. Keigher; Jim Lawson; Gail G. Lyons; Dick Robert, CRB, CRS, GRI; James P. Skindzier, DREI; Jim Sweetin; Pat Soltys; and Audrey M. Van Vliet-Conti.

The authors also extend their appreciation to Diana Faulhaber, executive editor; Robert A. Porché, Jr., senior developmental editor; and Ronald J. Liszkowski, managing editor, of the Real Estate Education Company for their assistance in the production of *Real Estate Brokerage: A Management Guide*.

We all wish you a rewarding and successful career as you lead your real estate brokerage company into the next millennium.

1 The Challenge of Change

What are the most dramatic changes you have observed in the real estate industry during the past five years? What do you see on the horizon as we begin the new millennium? How well are you prepared to cope with change?

Pick up any newspaper, and you see a front-page story about the latest restructuring of a major corporation. Corporations are merging with others engaged in similar enterprises. Other corporations are merging with dissimilar, but complementary, businesses. Companies are selling off units that no longer fit into their plans for the future. In some cases, the resulting company bears little resemblance to its former self. Some companies are building alliances or partnerships with others in new, perhaps unconventional, ways. The common thread in these stories is that companies are changing to achieve more profitable operations.

You ask, "What place does this introduction have in a brokerage management book?" The message is quite simple: we are surrounded by change in the business world. In fact, the changes that are prevalent in our nation's major corporations are not unlike those we see in the real estate industry.

Real estate companies are merging, divesting themselves of previous affiliations or forging new alliances with other real estate enterprises or related products and services. They are even becoming part of larger corporate structures, drawn under a single corporate umbrella along with other, diverse enterprises.

Real estate companies are moving in directions similar to those of major corporations for the same reason: they are striving to achieve more profitable operations. A salesperson who splits commission with the broker on a 60/40, a 55/45 or even a 50/50 basis is often hard to convince that the company is not reaping a bundle of money. The truth is that the bottom line is very lean. Often it is no more than two percent of earnings after expenses and before taxes. In some firms it's even less. Financial pressures are prompting real estate companies to change the look of our industry in dramatic ways.

The key to success in today's business world, real estate included, is a willingness to shed traditional methods of doing business and adopt new approaches. When strategies that were once successful no longer produce the same benefits, companies must change. At one time the entrepreneurial "change artists" were looked upon as mavericks. Today, they are in the mainstream, leaving those unwilling to change sitting on the sidelines.

While we feel strongly about the strategies that will be explored in later chapters, perhaps the most poignant message to deliver is the one shared in this first chapter. *Today's real estate environment is dynamic, with new trends emerging daily.* These trends affect every aspect of a company's operations and the tasks you perform. To be successful you must be a vigilant observer of the industry, not just locally but globally as well. Then, be willing to seize opportunities to grow your business in new ways.

Look beyond real estate brokerage as you've known it or even as we describe it now. Explore new possibilities and test the limits of your creativity. Regardless of whether you are preparing for a new career as an owner or manager or preparing your business for the coming decade, you will be challenged by change. This chapter looks at some of the most significant trends that have altered the industry and that will change your life as a manager.

CHANGING MODELS

We observed in this book several years ago that the real estate industry had emerged from the land and building business into the information business. We hope you didn't miss this step, because we're on the move again–into the consumer-driven business.

Traditionally, businesses employed a "supplier model," meaning that the supplier controls the selection of products or services offered in the marketplace. The defect in this model, however, is the assumption that consumers will take what is offered. Today's consumers are discriminating shoppers, demanding products and services that are tailored to meet *their* needs. They are driving the market, forcing companies to be responsive or risk losing their patronage. The consumer holds the power.

How does today's consumer-driven business differ from the information business? At one time the real estate industry was the gatekeeper of information, especially with exclusive rights to property listings. Today, consumers can access a wealth of information themselves. They can research and evaluate the market, learn how to be an astute purchaser or seller and take an active role in making their own decisions. Information has given consumers power in the marketplace. This forces the real estate industry to provide products and services that complement, rather than duplicate, those that consumers can access themselves.

Consumers also demand convenience. They want a wide range of services to carry them seamlessly through a transaction. This is frequently referred to as a "one-stop shop." In the past this meant "one stop" for properties, a view of the market through the multiple listing service. Today's "shop" must link the consumer to services associated with a transaction and do so with as little consumer effort as possible. The "shop" may include financing and settlement services. It also may link consumers with other resources, such as job placement for a spouse, daycare for a child or elderly parent, or housecleaning or moving services.

TABLE 1.1   Services Provided to Buyers and Sellers: 1996

	Buyers	Sellers
Group of services at set price	48%*	49%
Menu of services/price per service	22%	19%
Both set price and menu of services	30%	32%

*Percentage reflects the number of firms responding to the survey and the way they structure their provision of services.

SOURCE: *Profile of Real Estate Firms,* 1996, National Association of REALTORS®.

One of the most conspicuous features of our consumer-driven business is that consumers are very price-and-value conscious. Customarily, we have packaged a bundle of services, marketing "one size fits all" to everyone. Then, we charged the seller or landlord a commission-based fee for all the services that we provided to both sides of a transaction. Not only is this "one size" approach hard to sell with the advent of buyer representation, but it fails to accommodate today's price-and-value conscious consumers. They want to choose services that meet their individual needs and pay only for services they use. In response, the industry must unbundle its services and offer a menu from which the consumer can choose. Table 1.1 demonstrates that a number of brokerage firms have begun to restructure the way they deliver services.

CHANGING COMPANIES

Although "changing companies" may look to a salesperson like an invitation to switch brokers, the heading has a much broader, more significant meaning. The change that is altering the basic fiber of our industry is the restructuring of today's real estate firms. Welcome to corporate America!

In some circles, the mere mention of corporate America and the real estate business in the same breath is akin to treason. Those who dare connect the two are seen as traitors to the real estate industry—one that was founded by independent brokers who ran loosely formed organizations that could succeed with relatively unsophisticated business methods. This mode of operation became firmly entrenched in the industry and is a style that some people feel distinguishes us from the rest of the business world.

The reality today is that the landscape of our industry has changed dramatically. Outsiders have entered the business. HFS (originally Hospitality Franchise Systems) acquired Century 21, ERA and Caldwell Banker; a land development company purchased a major Florida real estate company; and an electric utility acquired two large Midwest brokerage companies. These are only a few examples of the moves that corporations which were previously unaffiliated with real estate are making to expand their operations and capture new sources of revenue.

Big brokerage companies continue to capture new sources of revenue. Megabrokers have merged with other megabrokers to strengthen their position in the marketplace or capture a broader, regional market. The country's megabroker brainstorming groups, Masterminds and the Dozen, banded together to form the Realty Alliance to enhance their competitive advantage as independent companies. Large companies continue to expand by assimilating smaller ones into their operations. Midsize companies are often targeted because they command an appealing market share.

To capture the convenience-conscious consumer, real estate brokerage companies are often becoming subsidiaries of corporations that also own mortgage financing, relocation and title or settlement companies. To capture the value-conscious consumer, brokerage companies are forming alliances to offer cross-purchasing benefits, such as with coupons, discounts, shoppers clubs and point programs. Affiliations with these programs, known as **affinity programs** or *cross-purchasing programs*, are the latest attempts by brokerage companies to gain a market edge.

Although consumers are attracted by the benefits of affinity programs, especially because they are prevalent elsewhere in the marketplace, the programs have prompted considerable controversy in the real estate industry. Some licensees question their value in attracting business, especially the cost-versus-benefit equation associated with relinquishing part of their commission. License law regulators are struggling to determine whether commission rebates adversely affect the consumer, particularly because most states' laws contain rebate-prohibiting provisions.

Advocates for the programs maintain that the controversy is largely due to misconceptions about the way the programs work. Nonetheless, regulators in a number of states are enforcing bans on affinity programs.

Your company may have experienced some of the changes we have discussed. Or you may be sitting on the sidelines, either contemplating a move or fearing what the future holds for you. As one of the principals of your company you set the tone for the organization. If you are progressive in your thinking and innovative, you inspire others to be innovative as well. If you cling to the ways of the past, the organization will continue to be a model of the past. There can be no sacred practices if we are to keep pace with the changing needs of our consumers. Companies are far more successful when leadership has a vision for the future and sees change as an opportunity to be creative.

CHANGING TECHNOLOGY

It's impossible at this writing to anticipate what new technology will emerge and how it will change our business after the turn of the century. But based on its dramatic impact during only the past three years, we can safely predict that technology will continue to alter our lives. The Internet alone poses some interesting possibilities.

- According to a report in the June 1998 issue of *PC Computing* magazine, an estimated 75 million people are connected to the Internet. That number will likely grow to 100 million people by the year 2000.

- The amount of online purchases by consumers in 1997 was estimated between $3.3 billion and $4.3 billion. International Data Corporation's Consumer Internet program and RelevantKnowledge Inc. estimate that user spending will increase to more than $54 billion by 2002. The number of Internet users who buy online will grow from 36 percent to almost 50 percent.

- According to Georgia Tech's Graphics, Visualization and Usability Center, 84 percent of users say the Internet is indispensable in their lives.

Consider how our *cyber economy* could affect nearly every aspect of the real estate business as we currently know it. Some people argue that purchasing houses on the Internet is not practical, appropriate or even widely desired. Others suggest that the issue is when, rather than whether, real estate transactions on the Internet will become reality. Regardless of which side of this debate you favor, the fact remains that the Internet will almost certainly alter our transactions in some fashion during the next five years. As indicated in the studies cited above, an increasing number of our potential consumers will be relying on the Internet for more than information. Perhaps they will drive the industry to do more than market listings and promote services.

Obviously, yesterday's "toys," such as cellular telephones, pagers, e-mail, voice mail and the Internet, have become standard equipment today. As consumers become more technologically sophisticated, they will expect the real estate industry to be even more so. The following examples demonstrate how technology has already affected the way today's real estate companies do business.

- The geographic area that we service is expanding, as you will see in Chapter 3. The market place is essentially free of boundaries because of the scope of information we can access about neighboring communities, states and even communities across the country.

- The way we communicate and manage information in our organizations is more efficient, as you will see in Chapter 6. Just about any piece of paper that is generated in an office, from forms, contracts, brochures and listing presentations to reports that track advertising results and the salespeople's production, can originate from a computer.

- People can work almost anywhere they can use their computer modems, fax machines and cellular telephones. An increasing number of people are using technology to work at home. Audio and video conferencing is being used for business meetings and training sessions. In Chapter 6, we discuss how these developments affect office design and equipment.

• Our communications with customers and the marketing of our companies and their services have taken a turn into cyberspace. As we prepare our company to communicate in Chapter 6 and develop our marketing strategies in Chapter 9, we incorporate e-mail and the Internet throughout the organization.

As you delve into the operations of the organization, let your imagination wander into new ways that technology can be used to enhance the way *your* company does business.

CHANGING OPERATIONS

Downsizing and re-engineering are terms commonly heard in corporate boardrooms. In many cases, companies suffer from misaligned structures and bloated workforces as a result of mergers and alterations in the way they manufacture goods and deliver products and services. Technology has played a major role in these changes. Organizations are exploring more effective and cost-efficient ways to do business, especially because of increasing costs of operation. Businesses today are learning to work smarter with more efficient structures, smaller workforces and enhanced technology. In doing so, they enhance their profitability.

Real estate brokerage companies are striving to achieve greater efficiency and enhanced profitability as well. As we introduced the chapter we mentioned the small profit margins on which real estate companies operate. The primary factors that contribute to diminishing bottom lines involve costs to satisfy demands of the sales staff and equip the organization with technology. However, these are the same costs that help brokerage organizations work smarter and enhance their efficiency and productivity. Leaders in our brokerage companies have to shift their priorities and allocate expenditures in new ways.

Staffing

One of the ways today's organizations achieve greater cost-efficiency is by making more effective personnel expenditures. The trend in a number of organizations is to select fewer, but more productive, salespeople. They can then justify the cost of extra support personnel and technology. This is a departure from the customary practice of hiring sizable sales staffs, with the expectation that larger staffs produce comparably larger revenue. Because of the financial commitment brokers are making to attract and retain top producers, it's too costly to support large staffs of marginally productive salespeople.

The industry as a whole is functioning with fewer licensees. An analysis of trends between 1989 and 1996 conducted by the National Association of REALTORS® indicates an average decline of approximately 2.89 percent in the number of licensees each year. Until 1993 the decline correlated with economic conditions and declines in home sales activity. Since that time, however, technology is seen as the most likely contributor. That trend is likely to continue. More long-termers in the business will retire rather than adjust to the changing industry. For prospective licensees, the increased costs to enter the business, especially because of technology, will be a deterrent.

Salespeople as well as companies are striving to work more efficiently. Consequently, the staff in today's real estate companies consists of more than a secretary and perhaps a bookkeeper. Personal assistants, employed by either the salespeople or the broker, and transaction coordinators are performing the non-sales and administrative functions associated with the transactions. Brokers are providing support staff in response to the salespeople's demands, which also enhances the company's ability to recruit top producers. However, these services do add to the financial pressures on the organization.

Sales teams. Salespeople are also enhancing their efficiency. They are working in collaborative efforts with one another, with two or more of them forming a sales team. By dividing sales tasks they can capitalize on one another's strengths and perhaps diverse industry expertise. Ultimately, they can provide better service to the consumer. Often a non-selling person, like a personal assistant, is a member of the team. Frequently, the team is more productive than the salespeople were individually. Team members can work smarter, rather than longer, hours. This also gives them greater freedom in their private lives. The merger of several highly competitive people working together, rather than in competition with one another, also reduces the potential for friction in the office.

Supervising

The job of supervising personnel has also changed. The work force in today's organizations is far more mobile than in the past. For the broker or manager who is accustomed to scrutinizing the salespeople's activities by what they do in the office, this poses a new challenge. Management is also supervising an increasing number of employees in addition to independent contractors. Management styles that are suitable for the culture in today's organizations must be adopted.

- *Home officing.* An increasing number of salespeople are working primarily from home, using the brokerage office only for conferences or meeting customers. Because the manager has fewer contacts with the salespeople, he or she must learn new ways to supervise their activities. Fostering a sense of community and camaraderie and planning group functions, such as sales meetings and training sessions, is more challenging because of the mobility of the sales staff.

- *Employees versus independent contractors.* Brokers are accustomed to hiring staff who are engaged directly in revenue-producing activities—the salespeople. Utilizing salaried staff appropriately and compensating them fairly for their indirect revenue-related activities adds a new dimension to management's job. Because of the tax laws the degree of control management has over the activities of employees, as opposed to independent contractors, differs. Employment and tax costs differ as well. (These issues will be discussed in detail in Chapter 10.)

- *Sales teams.* Sales teams add another dimension to the manager's supervisory responsibilities. While you are managing individual salespeople, you also are managing several of them as a team. This can make a manager's job more difficult. The source of a problem with a transaction, for example, is not immediately clear when a sales team shares responsibilities. Management needs to know how the team members have assigned work responsibilities among themselves and how they intend to share compensation. The company's policy and procedures manual should address the way sales teams are permitted to function, especially because the broker is ultimately responsible for the activities of licensees.

- *Professional growth.* The company's human resources are as valuable, if not more so, than its financial resources. Providing opportunities for personnel to grow professionally and enrich their jobs is an important investment. In brokerage firms this means more education and training for the salespeople. Managers are typically less dictatorial and more likely to create a supportive and energized environment as a way to enhance professional growth and productivity. Salespeople may be involved in collaborative efforts, such as problem solving and brainstorming, and may even have an ownership stake in the company.

Enhancing Revenue

Service businesses, which real estate companies are, have fewer direct means of increasing revenue than manufacturing businesses. We do not have a tangible product for which we can manipulate production and distribution. In real estate we are marketing an intangible commodity: service. Intangibles are difficult to measure in terms of cost, price and value for both consumers and providers of the services. Often consumers and providers have disparate views of these as well. This is especially true when consumers expect to receive more services for the price than the provider intends to deliver. We are on the brink of a revolution over fee structures as the industry wrestles with financial pressures and the consumers' perception of value.

Obviously, many of the changes discussed so far are motivated by the desire to increase revenue and enhance services. Linkage with ancillary services generates revenue directly and indirectly through referral fees. We also mentioned the trend toward unbundling services and the new fee structures that will evolve from that strategy. Companies have also started charging transaction fees. They are attempting to offset the costs of supportive services by charging buyers and sellers administrative fees for processing paperwork. While these fees are rather nominal in some parts of the country, they sometimes amount to several hundred dollars per transaction.

As brokerage companies grapple with profitability issues, the caveat is that they cannot afford to be cavalier about the way they structure their fees. At what point will consumers revolt and eliminate the real estate licensee from the transaction? The challenge at the moment is to keep real estate licensees at the center of a transaction, particularly when they are no longer the gatekeepers of information. To "nickel and dime" the consumer for each task that is performed, while also charging the customary commissions, could eventually raise the ire of consumers. They will then turn to your competitors.

CHANGING YOUR ROLE

If you are changing roles from sales to management, you must be prepared to meet some personal challenges. Perhaps you've always aspired to manage an office or own a brokerage company; being a salesperson was just the first step in a carefully developed career plan. Or you may have fallen into the role because a new opportunity suddenly presented itself. In any case you are changing roles from the person who's being supervised to the person doing the supervising. As you make the transition, there are several points to keep in mind that will affect your success in this new venture.

Be realistic about the role you're assuming. As a salesperson it's natural to speculate about ways you'd do things differently than the broker or manager. These speculations can lead to creative, insightful observations that will be very useful in your new role. It's unrealistic, however, to expect that you can fix all of the things you found objectionable or frustrating in a company. Salespeople rarely see the multitude of issues that confront management when attempting to run a profitable business. The best way to step into your new job with minimal frustration is to arm yourself with information, which is what this book is intended to do.

Be realistic about the financial implications of your move. Do you think that by owning your own firm, you'll make more money because you're not sharing commissions with a broker? In case you haven't already discovered in this chapter, you'll see in subsequent chapters that running a successful, profitable business is far more challenging than may appear on the surface. More is involved than a small office, a desk and a phone and some dollars for advertising and printing. Small businesses are most likely to fail in their first three years. The majority fail because of lack of planning, undercapitalization, unrealistic expectations for the business's success in its early years and the owner's lack of experience in running a business. Your company can be one of the survivors if you avoid these pitfalls.

Consider whether you are personally suited for the job. Do you have the skills to be an effective manager? Do you have the innovative attitude we described earlier? Will your organization and the industry benefit from your being in this position? Once you can answer "yes" to these questions, you're on the right track.

As you contemplate these questions, candidly assess your personal attributes and abilities. You need a healthy sense of self-esteem. But don't let an inflated ego cloud your judgment about your abilities or temperament for the job. The discussion in Unit 5, in which we explore the personal qualities and human resource skills that contribute to your being an effective manager, is useful for assessing strengths and weaknesses. Then you can develop a personal development plan to help prepare you to manage.

Are you prepared to delegate? The manager's job is to empower the salespeople to do their jobs rather than to do the jobs for them. Although we frequently identify potential managers as those from whom other salespeople seek advice or assistance, being a good transaction technician can also hinder your managerial effectiveness. It's difficult to delegate to other people when you're used to being the "doer." But you have to resist the temptation to interject yourself into a transaction, particularly when you feel that you can do the job faster, better or more efficiently. Managers must be willing to adopt a hands-off posture and become a resource for the salespeople. This includes allowing them to make mistakes. Few are fatal, and often mistakes teach valuable lessons.

Are you prepared for a position of authority? By the very nature of the hierarchy in an organization, certain classes of jobs and work groups evolve. Typically these are rooted in the similarity of their tasks and responsibilities. In some organizations the class distinction between workers and supervisors is very subtle; in others it is quite obvious. Much of this depends on the management style or philosophy that prevails in the company (see Chapter 16).

Becoming a supervisor—the owner or manager—involves moving from one class to another. Now you are entrusted with the authority to make certain decisions within the company and affect the lives of the people you supervise or manage. Because we all have preexisting attitudes about authority figures and subordinates, the transition may not be easy. Salespeople, who previously saw you as "one of us," must adjust to seeing you as the manager. The management group must adjust its perception of you as "one of them," to you now being "one of us." You have to gain acceptance in your new role from both groups.

Your success in making the transition will be affected to a large degree by the way you handle yourself and the group dynamics. You can establish credibility and gain respect by approaching this new role with a healthy but modest respect for your new position. If you become bossy or lord your power and authority over your newfound underlings, you will not engender confidence in your ability to use authority responsibly.

Being a manager should not be an adversarial relationship with the salespeople, nor is it a popularity contest. You must not apologize for being the manager or fear jeopardizing your popularity with the salespeople. Yes, you will make unpopular decisions or take steps to correct situations because that's your responsibility to the organization. But there is a distinction between guiding or influencing people and dominating them, as you will see in Unit 5.

Because of group dynamics the transition can be easier if you change companies when you change roles. However, this should not discourage you from taking a promotion within your organization. By recognizing the group dynamics and using authority properly, you can make the transition very effectively.

Management or Sales?

The purists would say that the only way to be an effective manager is to devote 100 percent of your time to management responsibilities. In some firms that is exactly what the broker or office or sales manager do. Others would argue that it is possible for the broker or sales manager to both manage and sell or provide other professional services effectively. In some firms the primary activity of the broker or sales manager is to provide real estate services, with management being only a secondary function. The degree of sales involvement may be determined by financial necessity, especially in new companies or offices. Managers in some companies are even encouraged to sell occasionally, just to stay in touch with the current market.

Strictly management.   When you are responsible for only management activities, your job is very clear: supervise the activities of the salespeople, coach them through their problems and help them reach their production goals. There is no question for you or the salespeople as to exactly where the lines are drawn between who manages and who provides the real estate services. You can focus your energy exclusively on management tasks. Because you are not involved in any sales activities, you are readily available to the salespeople and you are not competing with them for business.

Sales and management.   Successfully blending management and real estate activities is more challenging. Salespeople often criticize "selling managers" for being too busy with their personal sales activities to devote time to them.

Resentment builds when the salespeople think that the manager is grabbing the best leads to fuel his or her own business. Managers may find themselves in a tug-of-war between administrative and supervisory responsibilities and their personal sales.

Managing and selling are separate, demanding jobs. Doing both jobs well, while also keeping the sales staff and upper management content, can be incredibly challenging. No day seems like it's long enough. With proper structure you can undertake both assignments and still preserve your personal life and sanity.

- *Prioritize your responsibilities.* In some companies one job is a primary and the other a secondary assignment. In others the roles are equally important. Be sure that you and the broker (or senior management) clarify exactly what you are expected to do. Otherwise, you may find yourself in that tug-of-war between sales and management responsibilities.

- *Determine the amount of time and effort that must be devoted to each role.* Otherwise, you could find that the amount of effort devoted to some activities creates a priority conflict. This is especially true for a new manager because it's tempting to concentrate on activities that are most familiar (sales) while letting the company and personnel issues slide.

- *Prepare contingency plans.* Unpredictable things happen that demand attention in your personal sales and management jobs. Salespeople need to know how you intend to meet their needs, especially while you are tending to your own sales transactions. If your production is more important to you than your salespeople's, the organization can run aground pretty quickly.

- *Protect harmony in the office.* Competition between selling managers and the salespeople can be highly disruptive. Restricting your sales activities to previous customers and personal referrals rather than taking leads from the office will minimize this possibility. Managers in some companies avoid sales and engage in other real estate activities to eliminate this concern. These could include leasing, property management or property valuation, depending on the provisions of your state's licensing laws.

- *Maximize the use of technology.* Because salespeople are enjoying more efficient and mobile work lives, managers no longer have to be rooted in the office to do their jobs. Pagers, e-mail and computer networks aid both the sales and management functions. Today's technology makes it easier to blend both activities.

CONCLUSION

While reading about changes that are challenging us to adopt new ways of doing business, you may identify other trends that are emerging or that impact the business in your area. The key point to remember is that change is inescapable. Whether you succeed or fail, survive or collapse, is determined by the way you confront change. Astute business people see change as an opportunity rather than a threat. Be open-minded and innovative. No old way is so good that it can't be improved upon. Keep these thoughts in mind as you work through all of the management functions we explore in this book.

DISCUSSION EXERCISES

Discuss changes in the real estate industry that you envision happening after the year 2000.

* * *

What challenges do you envision having the greatest impact on your transition from salesperson to broker/owner or manager? What is your plan for adjusting to the change? If you currently are in one of these positions, what challenges were most significant when you made the transition? What would you do the same or differently if you could start over again?

* * *

What problems have you seen in real estate offices because the manager/broker is also selling? How would you avoid these problems?

UNIT
1

Planning the Organization

Planning is the first management function we discuss. This is the step that sets all of the wheels in motion and guides virtually every decision in an organization. But this step is often the one given the least attention. Typically, people are more oriented to "doing" rather than planning what to do. As Peter Drucker, a popular management theorist, observes, most of us spend more time working at doing things right rather than working at doing the right things. Planning charts the course for doing the right things.

Planning sets priorities and focuses the efforts of the organization to conform with those priorities. It consists of setting goals or objectives and defining activities to accomplish those objectives. Good business plans don't just happen. They evolve from a methodical process that is intended to ensure that a plan is innovative as well as reasonable and attainable. Whether you're starting a new business, reaffirming your current place in the market or planning for expansion, there are several steps you need to take to ensure that your company is doing the right things.

- Study the business environment in your marketplace.

- Analyze the market and identify potential for your company.

- Plan your operations to position the company to succeed.

- Prepare your company to respond to changes in the marketplace.

The planning process begins with what's known as a situational or environmental analysis. This is an information-gathering process that evaluates external factors that impact a company as well as appraises the company's current operations. During this analysis you can identify opportunities for the organization and challenges or barriers that could impede its success. With this information you can develop a plan that positions the organization to be a viable, profitable entity during the coming three or five years. The information you gather will also guide other management decisions, such as personnel requirements, office sites, marketing and advertising strategies and the service that will be delivered. The chapters in this unit will lead you through the planning process.

If you are the broker/owner or a senior manager in a large organization, you will be involved in all aspects of the process as you chart the course for the entire organization. As a manager of a sales office or a department, you will typically be involved in only certain aspects of planning. However, you also need to be familiar with the entire process to understand how your area of responsibility contributes to the accomplishments of the organization.

CHAPTER

2 Analyzing the Business Climate

What factors currently affect the business climate in your area? And real estate companies in particular? How will these factors affect what your company will be doing in the future?

In earlier, simpler days a property owner merely set out a for-sale sign, found a purchaser and sold the property with a minimum of fuss. Today, however, real estate transactions are encumbered by a maze of legal, technical, financial and tax issues. Few people can handle all of their affairs without professional help. Just as we need accountants for our taxes and lawyers for legal matters, people need real estate professionals to lead them through their real estate transactions. As the legal adage says, "The person who represents himself has a fool for a client."

While this observation may be reassuring—we are satisfying a need by being in the real estate business—it doesn't guarantee that a company will succeed as a profitable entity. No real estate firm functions as an island. The economy, the political climate and even the population in the community affect your business. As these factors change, in a sense they manage your business for you. But, *you* need to be in control. This means identifying external factors that affect your business and developing strategies for coping with them. Give your business a sound foun-

21

dation, and you can withstand the down times and maximize the benefit of the good ones.

ECONOMIC FACTORS

A number of key economic indicators give us clues about the climate in which a business functions. The purpose of studying these factors during the planning process is to prepare your company to ride the economic roller coaster. They are valuable for identifying potential opportunities as well as possible future problems.

Keep in mind that economic indicators are just that, indicators. As you peruse the vast amount of information that is available, ranging from the *Wall Street Journal* to online libraries and Web sites, you will discover a range of predictions. Even the most learned experts interpret the meaning of economic indicators differently. But consider what they have to say and "hitch your wagon" to a philosophy that makes sense to you. As you become a student of the economy, you should be able to form reasonably sound educated guesses. Long-range forecasts, however, have to be reviewed periodically to ensure that your assumptions about the future remain valid. Otherwise, your company could be preparing for an economic environment that won't materialize.

The housing industry has been used as a benchmark to indicate the strength of the economy. The number of new housing starts and resold homes is one way to gauge consumers' confidence, their sense of financial security and their demand for other consumer goods. The National Association of REALTORS® has a wealth of useful research for evaluating these trends. When you look at other economic indicators, you can see how the housing industry reflects what's happening in the economy.

Gross Domestic Product

The gross domestic product (GDP) is the broadest indicator of the strength of the economy, showing the economic output and growth. Healthy industrialized economies have an average annual increase of 3 percent. A higher percentage indicates that the economy is overheating. Historically in this country this means that if there's a sharp decline, growth will stagnate. Watch the GDP that is released by the government each quarter and you can see how our economy is faring as the year progresses.

Inflationary Cycles

A healthy economy should generate a low, stable rate of inflation. Since 1991 we have enjoyed a slow, stable growth in the economy, with inflation hovering around 3 percent per year. (Toward the end of the decade the rate has been even lower.) The stock market reached new highs, reflecting the optimism of investors about our corporations' ability to increase profitability and grow their enterprises. The number of new-housing starts and first-time homebuyers reached the highest levels in recent times. According to a Fannie Mae National Housing Survey in 1998, 51 percent of adults expect their family financial situation to be "somewhat better" to "much better" one year from now. How long will this optimism last?

History has shown us that, as trite as it sounds, what goes up eventually comes down. That's the essence of inflationary cycles. For an indicator of where we are in the cycle, look at the spread between short-term interest rates set by the Federal Reserve and the interest rates on long-term bonds.

- If the spread is large or getting larger, the government is trying to fuel the economy by loosening its monetary policy. This encourages people to spend and thereby grow the economy.

- If the spread is small or shrinking, the government is attempting to cool the economy by tightening the money supply. This discourages people from spending and guards against another inflationary spiral.

In recent years the Federal Reserve has managed inflation with gentle, though sufficient, adjustments in interest rates to keep inflation in check. Consequently, during the 1990s we did not experience the extreme peaks and valleys in the inflationary cycle that we saw in previous decades. For example, recall the general recession in 1981–1982. This was the product of strong deflationary measures the Federal Reserve instituted to slow the overheated economy that developed during the late 1970s. One advantage of stable inflation for a business planner is that it provides a relatively predictable indicator for sound planning.

Brokers are challenged to anticipate inflationary cycles, seizing opportunities to expand but without doing so too aggressively. Then, they should be ready to quickly pull in the reins when the economy begins to slow. During the upside of the inflationary cycle, production looks encouraging. The number of transactions increases and, with rising sales prices, the income per transaction increases. But this trend may not endure. The sense of urgency that fuels buyers, feeling they must act before the prices of properties and mortgage funds rise, can wane. Once inflation pushes costs beyond their ability to pay, buyers step out of the market. Soon sellers are frustrated because their properties don't sell. Brokerage firms then struggle to remain profitable as demand for their services and the number of transactions diminish.

Consumer Confidence

The willingness of buyers and sellers to enter the marketplace is tied to their sense of financial security. A number of external factors over which they have little control affect consumer confidence. Employment and job security are issues for many. For others the issue is wage scales coupled with increasing demands on their income. Rising costs of living threaten the financial security of the elderly population and others living on fixed incomes. Although lower interest rates stimulate the housing market, they can negatively affect consumers who support themselves with income from their investments.

Tracking employment and investment trends, costs of living and consumer spending will help you gauge changing levels of consumer confidence. Any of these factors can affect the demand for the types of real estate or the kinds of real estate services you offer. Companies that specialize in a specific type of property or service are especially vulnerable. Remodeling or building an addition may be preferable to purchasing a new home. Investing in discretionary types of real estate, such as vacation or resort properties or second homes, may be less desirable when people feel less financially secure.

The job market is an important gauge for the housing market as well as consumer confidence in your area. The job-growth rate, which the government publishes each month, is more useful than the unemployment rate. This reason is that the housing market is directly affected by your market area's ability to generate new jobs. Your community's economic growth and development efforts contribute to this as well. As employment opportunities wax and wane with businesses expanding, downsizing or moving in and out of the area, the pool of potential sellers and buyers waxes and wanes as well. Watching the job-growth rate for several months will give you a feel for the direction in which the real estate market is headed.

POLITICAL FACTORS

As public policy makers wrestle with the complex problems of society, the solutions they devise are equally complex. Often the solutions have far-reaching implications, many times significantly increasing financial and administrative burdens. Buyers who are struggling to afford a home in today's economy are also affected. Depending on prevailing political ideologies, sympathies and priorities, these problems may or may not get a "sympathetic ear." The role of government and the degree of intervention, as indicated by the volume of new laws and regulations, also fluctuate with the political climate.

Because real estate plays an important role in the economy, the real estate industry customarily identifies several critical issues to promote on the government agenda. Recently, these include the protection of private property rights in government takings, tax reform, revisions of the Real Estate Settlement Procedures Act (RESPA) regulations to address "one-stop shopping" and intellectual property rights and copyright protections on the

Internet. In the past the industry has advocated a balanced budget, reduction in capital gains taxes, preservation of mortgage interest deductions, reduction in regulations and taxes imposed on the business and amendments to IRA rules to permit withdrawals for housing purchases.

Many of the problems our communities face relate to real estate in some fashion. Because your business will be affected, it's important to be attuned to the way communities address their problems. This is also a good argument in favor of getting involved in the decision-making process. Your real estate expertise is a valuable resource that could benefit property owners and the community as well as the industry.

Economic Growth and Development

Preserving the quality of life for a community's residents, revitalizing aging neighborhoods and enhancing the utility of the land and the community's economic base is a balancing act. Residents sometimes fight growth or any other change in their neighborhoods strictly because they want life preserved as they know it. Communities struggling to cope with an influx of people find their infrastructures (sewer, water and road systems) and community services, such as schools, libraries and police and fire services, stressed by new housing developments. Deteriorating inner city neighborhoods struggle to overcome the physical blight, loss in property values and social problems that erode the community. Local municipalities struggle to shore up economies that have been drained by abandoned and obsolete properties.

Bringing the private and public sector together to develop mutually beneficial solutions to these challenges isn't easy. Government sees more regulations and intervention as the answer; the private sector wants less regulatory intervention to allow free enterprise to function. But the private sector also seeks financial commitments from the government as part of the solution. Some communities are successful in developing public-private partnerships. In others, the two sectors seem to hamper one another's efforts.

The fundamental challenge is to plan economically and aesthetically viable ways to use our land. Communities attempt to control growth and land use by adopting comprehensive plans, zoning ordinances and building codes. However, overly restrictive regulations can exacerbate the very problems they intend to solve. If they discourage people from living in the community or discourage businesses from locating or developers from building there, the regulations can hinder rather than enhance the desirability of a community.

Because economic growth and development efforts affect real estate, your business is affected as well. Monitor the way the local, state and federal governments address expanding populations, social problems, increasing land and development costs, the scarcity of land and the use of agricultural land for suburban subdivisions, environmental issues and transportation problems. The future of your business is only as strong as these conditions allow your local real estate market to be.

Environment Issues

As policy makers seek ways to protect public health and safety and the environment, both the property owner and the industry have been saddled with volumes of regulations. Environmental issues—protecting the ecology of our streams, lakes, forests, swamps, deserts and ocean shorelines—have become real estate issues. It is a balancing act to serve the public without unduly infringing on the rights of private owners or eroding the bundle of rights associated with their ownership. Nonetheless, numerous laws have been adopted that restrict the use of real estate. They also impose additional costs for sellers, purchasers and developers plus additional legal liability for all parties involved, including real estate practitioners.

Contamination from pesticides, illicit waste dumping, leaking underground storage tanks and the presence of toxic substances such as asbestos, lead, radon or carbon monoxide are just a few of the problems that confront us.

- Many states and local municipalities require environmental impact reports before any new development of land is approved.

- Banks require a preacquisition site assessment (PSA) or Phase I Environmental Report before loaning money for commercial or industrial properties.

- Owners are responsible for correcting toxic waste conditions.

- In home sale transactions, sellers are responsible for disclosing conditions they know exist.

Identifying and disclosing problems, mitigating or eliminating the problems and properly disposing of toxic substances can be time consuming and expensive.

Because of the current emphasis on environmental and health issues, the list of laws and regulations continues to expand. The Environmental Protection Agency (EPA) and the Occupational Safety and Health Administration (OSHA) are actively monitoring emerging issues and adopting regulations to address problems. State environmental agencies are doing so as well. When forecasting for your business, you must consider the effect of environmental legislation on your customers and clients and the legal liability for your company.

Regulating the Industry

While we are looking at the role public policy makers play in our business, we cannot overlook the most obvious—laws that directly impact the way you deliver your services. Antitrust laws, consumer and licensing laws, the RESPA, the Foreign Investment in Real Property Act (FIRPTA), federal and state fair housing laws, the Americans with Disabilities Act and the Truth-in-Lending Act are a few that directly affect your operations. (See Chapter 14 for a discussion of many of these laws.) All of us are affected by federal laws, but you must also be aware of state and local laws that are unique to your area.

Real estate practices throughout the country have recently been affected by significant changes in state laws, driven in part by a heightened emphasis on consumer rights. In a word—*disclosure*. As the consumer's right to know replaces caveat emptor (let the buyer beware), disclosure of agency relationships and disclosure of property and environmental conditions have become important in today's real estate transactions. Additional responsibilities mean additional paperwork and forms—and additional liability for the broker, especially if the salespeople are careless about complying with these requirements. You know best how these developments affect the practices in your area.

Because the laws impact every aspect of our operations, from the way we provide our services to the way we manage the internal affairs of the organization, legal counsel is essential when planning what the firm will do.

SOCIAL FACTORS

In addition to the economic and political factors that impact your business, you have another very important factor to consider—the population in the community. Although we'll look more closely at your potential clientele in the next chapter, our emphasis at the moment is to look at the general makeup of the community. Consider how the composition of your community, especially the populations we describe, might affect your business.

The Baby Boomer Population and Generation X

The baby boomer generation has been one of the most influential segments of the population, primarily because of its size. We've watched a bulge in the population work its way through various stages of life. It has driven the manufacturers of consumer goods and housing, and impacted our public schools, colleges and universities and employers. Now, the boomers are turning 50, moving into a stage in life that demands goods and services to accommodate their maturing but active lifestyles.

"Gen X" or generation X, as the offspring of the baby boomers are known, is an important population in the market place. They are now entering the work force and becoming financially independent. In fact, they will comprise a significant percentage of the work force; their parents, who will be 45 to 55 years old by the year 2000, will make up slightly less than 22 percent of the work force. The boomers' children, the technology generation, are now in the market for their first homes.

The bulge of baby boomers entering the work force and home ownership has passed. In fact, many are moving out of their large family homes as their children leave the nest. According to a Fannie Mae National Housing Survey in 1998, seven in ten adults, aged 40 to 54, are currently empty nesters or will be in the next 10 years. Slightly less than one in three say they expect to sell their current home and buy a new one.

The Aging Population

A growing segment of our population consists of the parents of the baby boomers, and some of them have parents who are still living as well. Many have been retired for some time. With corporations continuing to encourage early exits as they streamline their operations, the retired population will continue to grow. According to the American Association of Retired Persons, 75 million Americans will be over the age of 50 by 2000.

Add the fact that people are living longer and we have a sizable elderly population that needs suitable housing and senior services. Because today's retirees are healthier and more active than those of previous generations, they also demand social and recreational facilities. Although many can now live independently, an increasing number of people will need assisted living arrangements as they age. Some will reestablish households with their children; others will turn to senior living facilities. These trends will influence the types of real estate they seek.

The Mobile Population

Our population is very mobile, primarily because of employment. Americans change employers and occupations more frequently than do workers in other advanced industrial economies. People are moving from job to job, starting new companies and being promoted or transferred as existing companies grow. Others in the population are seeking new communities for their retirement years. According to the United States Census Bureau, the average American moves 12 times in a lifetime. Developers and businesses are challenged to cope with these shifts in populations.

The International Population

The populations in many communities are also growing in their ethnic diversity, with estimates of one-third of the country's population growth being attributed to immigration. There is also an influx of temporary residents as international corporations move workers from country to country. Figure 2.1 provides an interesting perspective about population trends in citizenry as well as age through 2010.

The most obvious obstacle in serving the international population is language. Seventeen percent of the immigrants in the work force do not speak English. Even if a customer can speak English, that doesn't guarantee that you are communicating. (For example, to the British, a bonnet is the hood of a car; a biscuit is a cookie or cracker. In many other countries their ground floor equates to our first floor.) Subtle nuances in language can get lost, and technical terminology common in real estate transactions can be difficult to translate.

Cultural differences also affect business etiquette and the decisions people make. For example, certain numbers are associated with good or bad luck in some cultures. This may affect the dates appointments or closings are scheduled or the selection of a property because of its street address. Cultural taboos, such as the consumption of alcohol or the consumption of certain kinds of meat, should also be considered, especially when entertaining. There are no "right" cultures, only cultural uniquenesses that must be learned to properly serve an increasingly diverse population.

The real estate industry has begun to recognize the importance of cultural diversity in our business. To help licensees acquire the skills to facilitate homeownership for all persons, especially among minorities and immigrants, the National Association of REALTORS® and the Department of Housing and Urban

FIGURE 2.1 Age of General Population* and Various Types of Citizenry

	25–34 Years Old		35–44 Years Old		45–64 Years Old		65+ Years Old		
	#†	% of Total	#†	% of Total	#†	% of Total	#†	% of Total	Total
General Population*									
1995	42	16	42	16	51.5	20	33.5	13	263
2000	38	14	45	16	60.0	22	35.0	13	276
2005	37	13	43	15	70.0	24	37.0	13	288
2010	38	13	40	13	79.0	26	40.0	13	300
White (Not Hispanic)									
1995	29.50	11.0	31.50	12.0	41.0	15.5	28.75	11.0	
2000	25.75	9.3	32.75	11.9	46.5	16.8	29.50	10.7	
2005	24.00	8.3	30.00	10.4	53.5	18.6	30.25	10.1	
2010	24.50	8.2	26.25	8.8	58.5	19.5	32.25	10.8	
African American									
1995	5.50	2.0	5.00	2.0	5.25	2.0	2.75	1.1	
2000	5.25	1.9	5.50	2.0	6.25	2.2	3.00	1.0	
2005	5.25	1.8	5.50	1.9	7.75	2.7	3.00	1.0	
2010	5.50	1.8	5.25	1.7	9.00	3.0	3.50	1.2	
Hispanics									
1995	5.00	2.0	4.0	1.5	3.75	1.5	1.5	0.5	
2000	5.25	1.9	5.0	1.8	4.75	1.7	2.0	0.7	
2005	5.25	1.8	5.5	1.9	6.25	2.2	2.5	0.9	
2010	5.75	1.9	5.5	1.8	7.75	2.6	3.0	1.0	

* These numbers do not consider people who are younger than 25 years old. Because people under 25 years of age are not included, the numbers do not add up to 100 percent. They are U.S. Census Bureau data estimates.
† Numbers are in millions of people.

Development (HUD) have jointly developed a cultural diversity training and certification program. This program was conceived under President Clinton's One America Initiative.

An important consideration when doing your business planning is the impact of a culturally diverse population on the services your company provides. Foreign language departments at local colleges and universities and local foreign-owned companies are excellent resources in your local community. Not only can you use them to learn about customs in various cultures, but they can also provide assistance to facilitate your communications. Some provide dictionaries of real estate terms in foreign languages.

CONCLUSION

A real estate brokerage company can get buffeted about by a variety of external factors, most of which we cannot control. But we can control how well our company is positioned to withstand these events. Knowledge empowers us to plan our business and position ourselves to function in the prevailing business climate. This means monitoring the economic, political and social factors that affect the business in your community and real estate brokerage firms in particular. A little speculation doesn't hurt, either. Because these factors rarely change significantly overnight, you can identify trends and anticipate future developments. This will enable you to provide vision for your company.

DISCUSSION EXERCISES

Discuss the most dramatic economic, political and social changes in your area that have affected the real estate business recently. How have brokerage firms adjusted to cope with them?

* * *

Have any real estate businesses failed or dramatically changed their operations recently? What do you think were the causes?

* * *

What conditions in the business environment in your area impact other businesses more than they impact real estate companies? Impact real estate companies more than other businesses?

CHAPTER

3 Analyzing the Market

Whom do you expect to be your customers? What services do they really want from you? In what ways have real estate services in your area changed during the past five years? What changes do you see on the horizon?

The first rule for any speaker, teacher or trainer is: learn about your audience. Unless you know something about the people who are going to hear your message, you have no way of knowing if it is appropriate. Speakers often think their message is important or relevant. But if the audience doesn't think so too, you might as well talk to an empty room. Professional speakers take time to learn about an audience and its needs before planning a presentation.

Do the same thing for your business—identify your audience and its needs when you plan what your company is going to do. And go back to your audience from time to time to be sure that your services are still appropriate. People need us in the real estate business to do things for them that they can't or don't want to do for themselves. We can either provide what we think people need and hope they will buy; or find out from them what they need. Our consumer-driven business demands that we listen to them. Otherwise, you could be "talking to an empty room."

Analyzing the market provides the insight needed to design services that "speak" to the audience or audiences you intend to attract—your target market. It's also important to look at what other firms are doing to attract that audience as well. Firms jockey for position in the marketplace, striving to do business a little better or a little differently than their competitors. Even with the appropriate services, you are not guaranteed success unless you can attract the attention of your target market away from the competition.

Examining the market means research! Whether you are evaluating the general business climate, as discussed in the previous chapter, or scrutinizing more specific market conditions in your area, you need information. Census data, the local Chamber of Commerce, banks, utility companies, school districts, even multiple listing services (MLS) are all sources of statistics. These are useful for identifying population and business trends. Also consider your professional and trade associations. They offer valuable research as well as provide opportunities for brokers to learn from one another. Listen to former customers and clients, friends, neighbors and acquaintances; find out what they think about your services. Regardless of whether you are the broker/owner or a manager, the information you gather is invaluable for your job in the organization.

ANALYZING OPPORTUNITIES

Before you can plan suitable goals and activities for the company, you need to consider all of the options available. As was discussed in the first chapter, ours is a consumer-driven business that, because of emerging trends, demands that brokerage organizations adopt contemporary methods of doing business. The purpose of examining the marketplace is to explore all of the who, what, where, how and when possibilities. Because few companies have the financial and human resources needed to take advantage of every business opportunity, you will eventually narrow your focus. However, this is the time to analyze a wide range of alternatives.

Otherwise, you can't be sure that the decisions you make are the ones most likely to get your company where you want to be in three or five years. Your company can also be immobilized by old methods of doing business. After your analysis you may conclude that your current target market or services are most appropriate. You may determine that a modest change is suitable. Or you may decide that the company must target an entirely different market or service to be a successful, profitable entity.

Geographic Markets

Today's brokerage companies operate in much broader geographic areas than in the past, no longer being confined to small, neighborhood markets. Because of the mobility of today's population, brokers can't rely solely on the patronage of local residents. Even where population numbers remain the same, the faces change as the once-loyal customer base moves on to other communities. Brokerage companies are forced to develop new, more regional customer bases and devise ways to retain the patronage of past customers. This focus is driven not only by profit motives but also by the desires of consumers.

Because of technology the geographic market can be as broad as license laws permit. In fact, the market could be free of all boundaries if the nation's regulators achieve license reciprocity. We have already seen how technology has opened the marketplace. It has broadened the MLS's methods of operating; the Internet has moved commerce into cyberspace. As a business planner, your must decide how broad your company's geographic market will be.

Multiple listing services. MLSs have traditionally provided listing inventory for fairly narrow geographic areas, determined primarily by the locale in which their members do business. Today, MLSs have not only adopted a more global view of listing inventory but also have expanded their scope of services.

- Local MLSs are merging to form large, regional systems to expand the geographic area for which listing inventory can be accessed.

- Brokerage firms are banding together to form integrated data bases, essentially structuring their own MLSs.

- MLSs have become information systems, no longer being just listing-inventory systems. Today, they provide members with mortgage loan information, competitive market analysis data, sample contracts, worksheets for qualifying buyers and estimating ownership and closing costs, investment analysis, online mapping and tax records.

- MLSs are linking their listing inventories with Internet sites. Both licensees and consumers can now access inventory for entire states, neighboring states and even the entire country.

Because most of today's MLSs are highly computerized, they have the capability to assemble and distribute a much broader range of timely, useful information. Ultimately, the goal is to provide the resources brokerage companies need to meet the demands of today's consumers. You can see in Figure 3.1 the way today's MLSs are utilizing technology to link their members.

Technology marketplace.   At one time the breadth of the geographic market was tied to the scope of information that was available and our ability to communicate with one another. Today, the marketplace has virtually no borders. The Internet has fostered a cyber economy, delivering information, products and services directly to the desktops and laptops of today's consumers, virtually anywhere in the world. Cable television and satellite networks also deliver information and provide interactive communications.

Consumers can now obtain much of the information they once relied on real estate licensees to provide. They can be interactive in the pursuit and evaluation of information and view property listings located most anywhere—on the other side of town or across the country. Electronically "walking through" a

TABLE 3.1   Type of Computer Access to Principal Multiple Listing Service

	Percentage of Firms	Percentage of Sales Force
No Online access	11*	1
Online access from salespeople's residences	54	85
Online access from office terminals	85	97
Online access from car phones by laptop or portable	6	47

*Percentage reflects the number of firms responding to the survey.

SOURCE: *Profile of Real Estate Firms*, 1996, National Association of REALTORS®.

house in California from your home in New Jersey is today's reality, not yesterday's dream. Just as technology offers a huge number of new opportunities for consumers, it does likewise for licensees. However, this requires that the industry be innovative with, rather than falling victim to, technology.

The Internet has become as commonplace a medium for information as newspapers and television. No longer is it an exotic or curious toy for the hobbyist. The statistics about Internet usage in Chapter One leave little doubt about the importance of the Internet in people's lives, a factor that the real estate industry can't afford to ignore. At present many of the country's major brokerage companies and franchises have Web sites. Individual salespeople are creating their own home pages as well. Commercial online services are courting MLSs to forge alliances for distributing property data. The National Association of REALTORS® has its own Web site, REALTOR.COM™, and connects with its members at One REALTOR Place®.

Referral networks.   One of the tools the industry has used for a number of years to reach broader geographic markets is referral networks. These are formally structured organizations that enable a broker to refer buyers and sellers to another broker. The networks are also a tool for serving customers needing assistance beyond the scope of service a broker customarily provides. Some networks are independent; others are connected with national franchises and corporations. An additional option is to establish an informal referral system within your own company.

FIGURE 3.1 Firms Affiliated with Intercity Referral Networks: 1983–1996

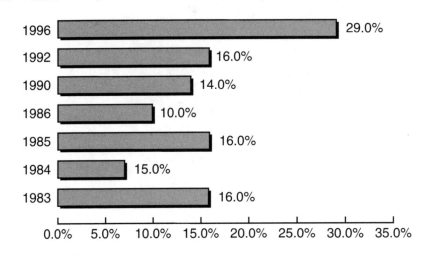

SOURCE: *Profile of Real Estate Firms,* 1996, National Association of REALTORS®.

Consumers appreciate assistance with referrals because it takes the guesswork out of selecting suitable licensees to help them. In Figure 3.1 you can see how the popularity of intercity referral networks has grown, according to the most recent study available.

Referral networks provide a number of benefits. Many offer support for the salespeople, such as training programs. The network may have a regional or national advertising program. This can help you create a local identity for your company that you may not otherwise be able to attain for yourself. Networking with brokers in other communities can also help expedite transactions. If permitted by licensing laws in your state, you may advertise properties listed in other states. For example, a broker from another state could expand the exposure of a unique listing by targeting potential purchasers or investors in your area. Or you could advertise a property located in another state that belongs to a buyer with whom you are currently working. By expediting the sale of your buyer's property, you can expedite the buyer's purchase through you.

As attractive as intercity referral networks are, think about whether network affiliation will actually be beneficial for you. Is there high turnover or a large transferee market in your area? Do you need the affiliation to compete with other firms in your area? Will a national advertising campaign produce significant results for your company? What number of referrals can you expect? What price do you have to pay for membership? Also, do some comparison shopping. An intercity referral network is worthwhile only if the additional benefits justify the cost.

Don't overlook the value of personal contacts—informal networking with potential consumers and other real estate practitioners. Each contact you or anyone in your firm makes is a potential source of business. Most of us value personal recommendations about professionals with whom to do business. A strong informal network with brokers in other specialties and in other geographic areas, even if you belong to a commercial referral network, provides the "personal touch" that gives credibility to the referrals you make.

Relocation networks. These may be part of or in addition to intercity referral networks. Relocation networks can be structured in a number of ways to help people establish residence in another geographic area.

One way is through corporate relocation management companies, otherwise known as third-party equity contractors. These companies enter into agreements with large corporations to handle their employee transfers. Such companies usually team up with reliable local brokerage firms in each community in which their clients have an office or plant.

The downside of these arrangements is that the corporate relocation company may expect you to provide services above and beyond those you normally provide.

- For listings, services could include yard care, plumbing (winterizing), supervising painting and other cosmetic repairs and providing weekly or monthly reports on the status of merchandising efforts.

- For buyers, corporations may expect you to represent the buyers (buyer agency) or provide other assistance to help a family relocate to a new community.

You must be willing to accommodate these demands if you want to attract and retain relocation company business. Your ability to do this reflects on both you and the network. It is advisable to appoint a relocation director who is trained specifically to supervise these transactions and oversee the myriad of details associated with them. This person should not compete as a salesperson with the other associates. Instead, the relocation director should assign listings and buyers to the salespeople and then be responsible for orchestrating the other services that the corporations expect.

Another way to assist employers and their employees is by developing your own contact network and structuring services similar to the corporate relocation companies. Some employers provide their own in-house relocation assistance to current and newly hired employees. In other cases, the company may not provide any organized relocation assistance. Either of these cases presents opportunities for your company to design programs tailored to meet the needs of employers and their transferees.

Any of these relocation arrangements offers the potential to generate additional income. They also can be costly. Again, affiliation is worthwhile only if the additional benefits justify the cost. Additional staff time must be allocated to these services. Further, and perhaps most significant, third-party equity contractors charge brokerage companies numerous fees for handling referral transactions. These are additional costs that must be considered when evaluating potential revenue. A contentious issue as of this writing is the practice of charging "after the fact" fees. These are assessed for servicing a buyer or seller who is the employee of a relocation corporation's client, even though no formal referral was established or disclosed at the time the salesperson began working with the individual.

Service Markets

Are you a generalist or a specialist? That is, do you offer a broad or narrow range of services? In small or rural markets you are more likely to be a generalist, doing such things as selling and leasing residential and commercial properties, brokering industrial or recreational land, appraising real estate and managing property all at once. When deciding the scope of services, consider which ones consumers need in relation to the kinds of properties that are available in your area. Remember that a generalist must be knowledgeable about many things. Unless you have sufficient personal expertise, or can hire it, and can adequately supervise all of these activities, trying to be all things to all people may be unrealistic or even disastrous.

Specialization has become as common in the real estate industry as it is elsewhere in business. Because of the enormous liability brokers face today, it is advisable to practice within the limits of your expertise. Even if you are specializing in residential sales, for example, you must decide which transaction services you will provide. You may limit your services to marketing properties and following the transactions through to settlement. You could add mortgage brokerage and title or escrow services. Or you also may provide the services of an auctioneer.

Niche marketing. The ultimate in specialization is *niche marketing,* or targeting very specific or narrow segments of the market with specialized, focused services. Niche marketing appeals to consumers by satisfying their demand for very specialized knowledge or service. It also offers some exciting opportunities to be innovative and to distinguish yourself from the competition.

Study the demographics of the population, profile of land-uses in your area and the competitions' target markets to identify niche opportunities. Table 3.2 provides some interesting national demographics to start you thinking about market opportunities. Also think about an area of considerable expertise or a distinctive skill that can be promoted to a target market.

Your niche might be related to specific kinds of property, such as condominiums, resort, vacation or waterfront

TABLE 3.2 Homeowners in the Year 2000

Age	Number of People Who Will Be Homeowners in the Year 2000
25–34	17.4 million
35–44	24.0 million
45–64	35.0 million
65–74	11.7 million
75 and over	10.7 million

SOURCE: Joint Center for Housing Studies.

properties, ranches, farms, prestige properties or new construction. Or you might select a specific consumer population.
Perhaps it is one that is underserved or one with whom you have
unique commonality or are particularly sympathetic. The most
obvious niches to consider are the populations we discussed in
the previous chapter, such as senior citizens, baby boomers and
their children or international buyers. Or you may target singles,
people with disabilities or first-time buyers. Be careful that,
when you target certain populations and ignore others, you do
not violate the fair housing laws. Niche marketing must be done
carefully to avoid discriminating against people in the protected
classes.

There can be drawbacks to niche marketing. Putting all of
your eggs in one basket is not without risk. If the market is too
specialized, there may not be enough business to sustain a profitable operation, especially as populations shift or the economy
changes. You could select several niches to minimize the effect
of these changes. Also, be sure you have the credibility to gain a
niche's patronage. If you are targeting a specific type of
property, learn all you can about its ownership, use, transfer and
any special laws that affect it. If you are targeting a specific population, learn its uniqueness, identify its needs and sharpen your
skills related to the services that are appropriate.

Beyond residential brokerage. You may decide to specialize in investment properties, commercial sales or leasing,

industrial properties, commercial farming, real estate development or exchanges. Depending on your state's licensing requirements, you may consider brokering businesses. Engaging in any of these specialties requires more than real estate expertise. The practitioner must be knowledgeable about a wide range of issues that affect the use and operation of a property, including government restrictions and tax laws.

For example, real estate investors require sophisticated expertise. A broad scope of knowledge about tax laws and real estate is necessary to help people make wise decisions about acquiring, managing and disposing of their investments. In addition to buying and selling, investors need assistance with leasing and property management. Instead of brokering investment properties, you may decide to specialize as a real estate counselor. In this case you are engaged to analyze and offer objective and educated advice about real estate investment problems.

Agency Services

What kind of help do you think consumers want from you? What kind of assistance do your state's licensing laws require or permit you to provide? Because these are policy decisions, the broker/owner is responsible for determining the services the company will provide according to prevailing laws. At the risk of dating our discussion, we'll venture into one of the most hotly debated issues in recent years—how real estate licensees should provide customer and/or client services.

Traditionally, our states' license laws have been rooted in the common law of agency. Simply, an agent serves the principal and has fiduciary obligations to that client. When the client was the seller and the customer was the buyer, the licensee's fiduciary obligations to the seller were very clear. (Some people would argue that licensees treated buyers more like clients than customers, anyway.)

Then buyer-agency emerged. Brokers wanted to preserve their client relationships with sellers while also adding buyers to their client list. This created a dilemma for the broker when acting as the agent of a client/seller and client/buyer in the same transaction. The legal community has argued for years that it is impossible to properly represent both sides of the transaction, even when the dual agency is disclosed. Add to the controversy the fact that consumers, regardless of which side of the transaction they're on, have typically thought they were being represented by the licensee. In the meantime the real estate business became increasingly litigious, creating liability at nearly every turn of the transaction.

Our states' regulators face the challenge of protecting consumers while also responding to the industry's desire to preserve all of a broker's business options and minimize liability. Real estate licensing laws have been amended and even completely overhauled in an attempt to resolve the dilemma. The passage of new laws has not silenced the debate, however. In some cases the laws did not accomplish the goals that were anticipated, which necessitated additional amendments. In other states the new laws have been questioned in their entirety, with the possible reversion to prior procedures.

The debate continues, which forces you to carefully monitor the legal developments. In the meantime the broker/owner must determine policy for the company and develop services and systems to support that policy. The broker must also consider how that policy responds to the demands of the consumer.

- If your state's law relieves licensees from all fiduciary obligations, this is a significant deviation from the customary practices under the law of agency. In this case the licensee's role is to facilitate or bring the parties together to effect a transaction without being an advocate for or representing any party in the process. The challenge is to ensure that consumers understand that you are not representing anyone. If they want representation in a transaction, they will need to consult a lawyer.

- If your state's law permits both agency and nonagency relationships, the broker must decide which way the company is going to serve the consumers. It's likely that consumers have some preconceived notions about what licensees do. If you're going to depart from the norm or the traditional services that consumers expect, you'll need to be sure they understand whether you are providing client-based or customer-based services.

- In states where the laws permit the full range of agency relationships, there are more complicated decisions to make. Does the firm represent buyers/tenants or sellers/landlords or both in the same transaction? Will you act as a subagent or permit other brokers to be your subagents? What do consumers need or expect?

- If your state's law permits *designated agency*, how will this be implemented in your company? In an attempt to resolve concerns about dual agency, some states permit the broker to designate agents within the firm so that one represents a buyer and another represents a seller in the same transaction. Unless your state's law permits designated agency, however, remember that salespeople are not entitled to independently represent clients.

Once you've determined what services you are going to provide, it is essential to develop clear, detailed policies and procedures for the salespeople. (See Chapter 8 about policy and procedures manuals.) Remember that the broker makes these important decisions for the organization.

Listing agreements. What do sellers want? Typically, they want their property sold and for it to be sold at the best possible price; they want maximum market exposure and minimum hassle; they want to pay a low fee for this service; and they want to be represented throughout the transaction.

Each type of listing agreement offers advantages and disadvantages for both you and the owner. Although you need to decide whether to enter into an open listing or one of the two types of exclusive listings, as the member of an MLS your decision may already have been made for you. It's not uncommon for MLSs to require that any property inventoried in the system be listed on an exclusive agency or exclusive-right-to-sell listing agreement.

Open listings are rarely satisfactory for either the owner or the broker. They create considerable controversy over procuring cause and, in the case of multiple brokers showing the property, who is entitled to a commission. Frequently the owner misses out on the amount of marketing or services that the broker would typically provide under an exclusive arrangement. This objection can be mitigated to some extent when these listings are promoted to buyer or tenant representatives. This provides exposure of the property to prospects for whom it is suitable.

Each market has customs regarding the type of listing agreement commonly used for various types of properties. The needs and preferences of the owners as well as the practices of the other brokers should guide your decision. You may decide that your company policy is to enter into only exclusive-right-to-sell agreements or to provide alternatives in selected, unique situations. Even exclusive agency agreements do not eliminate controversy, but they may be tolerable in certain cases.

Buyer agency agreements.   What do buyers want? Typically, they want maximum service to help select a suitable property and guide them seamlessly through all aspects of their purchasing transactions. Most of all they want an advocate, someone to look out for their interests and provide advice and counsel in their decision-making. Because real estate licensees rarely provided this service to residential purchasers, buyers had to seek the counsel of attorneys. Today, an overwhelming majority of the brokerage firms have associates who work as buyer-agents (Table 3.3).

Just as there are various types of listing agreements, there are also various types of buyer agency contracts.

- Open agreements—similar to open listings, the buyer can work with more than one agent as well as locate properties without any assistance. These also may be used when the buyer wants your representation for the purchase of a specifically named property.

- Exclusive agency buyer agency agreement—similar to an exclusive agency listing, this contract relieves the buyer of any obligation to you if the buyer finds a suitable property without your assistance.

TABLE 3.3   Firms Having Buyer's Agents

	1992	1996
All Firms Responding	46%*	75%
Size of Sales Staff		
Five or less	40%	65%
6–10	42%	82%
11–20	50%	90%
21–50	64%	92%
More than 50	64%	98%

*Percentage reflects the percentage of the number of firms responding to the survey

SOURCE: *Profile of Real Estate Firms,* 1996, National Association of REALTORS®.

- **Exclusive buyer agency contracts**—similar to exclusive-right-to-sell listings, the buyer owes you 100 percent loyalty, regardless of whether you locate or the buyer locates the property.

Again, the broker must make these policy decisions about the type(s) of buyer agency agreements the company will use and under what situations. The needs and preferences of the buyers as well as the practices of the other brokers should guide your decision.

Defining *Your* Market

Having looked at a wide variety of opportunities, you can now begin narrowing your choices. Before finalizing decisions about which market segment(s) you are going to target, several questions must be answered to be sure that your endeavor will be profitable.

- How many potential users of your services are there?

- How many can you reasonably expect to capture? (You are not likely to be the only real estate brokerage firm in the area.)

- How many properties of specific types are there in your area?

- How many of those properties are likely to sell during the next three or five years?

- How many of those can you reasonably expect to be your company's transactions?

One of the most useful resources for answering some of these questions is demographic data. With this data you learn about the demographics–the profile of the population in the area. The age, education level, income and employment statistics, household structures and the number of people who rent and own homes will tell you a lot more about the business potential of possible target markets than simply population density. As you look at this data you also can see how choosing broader or narrower geographic areas can affect your business potential.

Demographic information is available from a variety of sources. Although you can engage your own study to identify potential markets for your products or services, this is a costly venture. At least initially, information that is readily available in the public domain, such as census data, will serve your purposes. Local municipalities and school districts, utility companies, public and private social service agencies and collegiate institutions are also good sources for information. Often these groups have studied demographics for their own forecasting; this information can be very useful for you as well. In addition, communities often have Internet Web sites where you can find useful data.

Study land uses. Zoning maps, community development officers and collegiate institutions are all resources for analyzing the number of properties in various land-use classifications. Consider this data in relationship to the needs of various segments of the population. The most useful data for identifying potential in the marketplace are the trends that develop over time. Track the changes in the demographics of the population and how the land use accommodates those changes. If one segment is growing more rapidly than the supply of suitable

FIGURE 3.2   Analyzing Potential in the Market

$$\frac{\text{Total prices of properties sold in an area}}{\text{Total number of sales}} = \text{Average sales price in an area}$$

$$\text{Average sale price} \times \text{Number of sales transactions for one brokerage company} = \text{Gross sales volume}$$

$$\frac{\text{Number of sales transactions for one brokerage company}}{\text{Total number of sales in the market}} = \text{Percentage of the market}$$

Using these simple calculations, you can analyze the sales data by the types of properties being sold and the percentage of the market you or your competitors command by type of property or total volume. You can then begin forecasting goals for your company.

property, for example, you know there will be greater demand than there is supply. Also consider the reverse situation.

Finally, look at sales data. By researching the register of deeds (or the office in your area where real property transfers are recorded) or MLS statistics, you can determine the number of various types of properties that have transferred. You also can gather sales price data. By adding the sales prices of the properties and dividing that total by the number of transactions, you can determine the average price of a transaction. If you separate the data by brokerage company, you can compare the number, average price and types of properties that each company, including yours, handled. Look at several years' data, considering the economic conditions that prevailed at the time, before forecasting average prices and numbers of transactions. (See Figure 3.2.)

The purpose of working through this process is to help you identify target markets that offer sufficient business potential. Your organization will become obsolete (and unprofitable) if it depends on a market that has shrunk or no longer exists. Because the profile of the population changes, the assumptions you make now are not necessarily valid over time. Periodically review this same process to be sure that the organization is tuned into the marketplace. Once you have identified your target market, you can give more thought to the business strategies that are suitable for meeting its needs. In addition to the services we've already discussed, pay attention to the following discussions in which we look more closely at the competition and the things your company has done in the past.

ANALYZING YOUR COMPETITION

Astute business managers look at what their competitors are doing. Just because you may be more knowledgeable, more ethical or more likable doesn't necessarily mean that you'll rise above all the other brokers in the area. Competition is a cleansing process, survival of the fittest. The market leaders have learned how to take maximum advantage of the opportunities that their competitors create for them. By constantly monitoring the competition and then adjusting your business strategies accordingly, you can be a contender. You can learn a lot from your competitors: profit from their successes and avoid their mistakes.

The way consumers see the competition is different from the way we see our competitors. Often consumers see little distinction between the services each of our firms provides. The absence of a service is more noticeable than the particular services you *do* offer. On the other hand, we in the industry see more differences than similarities. Perhaps this is because we attach more importance to certain aspects of a company and its services than the consumer does. The challenge is to differentiate between your company and the competition in ways that are meaningful to the consumer.

Market Share

Earlier, when we discussed your target market, we posed several questions relating to the competition that must be answered. Once you know what the competition is doing and have identified possible target markets, you can decide where to position yourself in the marketplace. Figure 3.2 contains several formulas to help you do this.

You can't be successful by specializing in condominiums, for example, if there are only a few developments in the area and one broker is very competent and successful in that specialty. This is not to suggest that you have to avoid markets that are already being served. But it's much easier to succeed, at least initially, by targeting a market in which there are ample opportunities. After you are established, you can pursue smaller or very specialized markets.

Monitoring market share is an ongoing activity for most brokers. Tracking the market share you command in relation to the competition's provides a key piece of information about how your firm is faring during the year. You can adjust business strategies if you are losing ground or when you see new opportunities.

Competitive Edge

Many of the decisions you make about what your company does to serve its target markets are affected by what the competition does. Should you join a franchise or a referral or relocation network? Where should your office be located? Should you buy billboard advertising or sponsor a TV listing show? Before answering these or other similar questions, you need to look at your competitors. Pay closest attention to firms that are similar to yours in size and target markets. There's little point in trying to go head-to-head with the largest firm in your area, for example, if you're a new, small company.

Here is another cost-versus-benefit analysis. Franchises and national or regional networks try to attract your affiliation with many appealing advantages. At professional conferences or conventions and in trade publications, vendors promote a wide variety of tools, such as home warranty programs, guaranteed buy-back programs and telephone hot line services. It's tempting to buy into every affiliation and new program or gadget. But they can be expensive, especially if they have little value to your customers or contribute little to your competitive position. Decide which ones are absolutely necessary to keep you in the running with your competitors. Then defer those that would be nice enhancements to your operation until you have discretionary dollars.

Affiliations.   Begin by looking at your competitors' affiliations. Are the majority connected with franchises, national corporations or networks? How many are independent? Is MLS membership necessary? You don't have to do what everyone else does, but don't eliminate options that would make you competitive. Most of these organizations have production statistics and cost comparisons from other similar markets to use in your analysis. Also, talk to brokers in your area who have relinquished their affiliations with organizations you are considering. Their experiences could be valuable when making your decisions.

Location.   Study the locations of other offices. There's more method than madness in the selection of office sites. Cheap office space may be available off the beaten path. But, your competitors will benefit from your being in business more than you will if they are more accessible to or within the travel patterns of the customers you intend to attract. Is the area saturated with offices, particularly in relation to the number of potential customers in a certain target market? Again the statistics you gathered about the market segments will be useful when analyzing locations.

Marketing strategies.   Study the advertising and marketing strategies of other firms. Advertising and promotional strategies are designed to promote not only you and your services but also to promote you above the competition. As you strive for exposure and visibility, consider the impact you can make in light of the competition. But just because someone else has a billboard doesn't necessarily mean that's the tool for you. It is too costly to "buy" the market, so you have to make wise choices. The services of a public relations or advertising professional are invaluable when assessing the competition and developing your strategies.

Consumer services.   Look at the services the competition provides to its buyers and sellers. Consider the types of agency representation and listing contracts being offered. Also, look at services such as home warranty or guaranteed buy-back programs, decoration or furnishing allowances, cross-purchasing programs or closing cost credits, to name a few. Before you follow suit, evaluate how prevalent the services are in your area and the benefits you can derive from the expenditures. Some services may be necessary to keep you competitive and others are frills you can bypass in favor of more productive expenditures.

You also need to be innovative—think about the latest creative tools and techniques you've learned about at conventions or in professional publications. It's great to bring new ideas and approaches into your marketplace. But as you do, consider if they are suitable for your target market. Also consider how receptive consumers in your area are to new ideas. If you're contemplating a very unconventional approach, think about why no one else is doing it. The approach may have been tried before, but with disastrous results. Or it may have been an idea that was ahead of its time, which means the time could be right for you now. You'll never know unless you research the idea.

Recruiting advantages. Although our analysis has focused on the marketplace, we can't overlook what the competition offers its salespeople. Earlier we said that consumers perceive that all of our firms' services are fairly similar. However, one of the greatest competitive advantages any firm has is its sales associates. Because the majority of transactions result from personal referrals, you need to attract the salespeople who bring strength to the organization because of their personal networks.

Your ability to recruit salespeople is directly related to the quality of work life you can offer them. When analyzing competitors, look at the tools and support services they provide salespeople, the size of their staffs and turnover, their commission structures and the general working conditions in their offices. As brokers respond to increasing demands of the salespeople, they face diminishing profitability. You have to weigh whether offering a higher commission split or providing a transaction coordinator, for example, will attract enough high-quality new hires to merit the additional costs.

ANALYZING YOUR ORGANIZATION

There's one more factor in the market that needs to be scrutinized: your company. The information that you've gathered so far is not particularly meaningful until you look at how your company stacks up by comparison. Before developing new plans, you need to take an objective, candid look at your current organization. Ask yourself the following questions:

- How do my services compare with the competition? Which services generate profits for me and which ones do not? What services should I consider adding or eliminating?

- Is my current organization structure appropriate? Are there staff services that should be added or eliminated? Are there divisions or departments that should be added or eliminated? Are there internal procedures that need to be revised that can be less burdensome or will make my organization more efficient?

- What is the physical condition of my offices and equipment? Are there improvements that will increase the efficiency of my operation or enhance its image?

- How do my salespeople perform? What are their strengths and weaknesses? What should I be doing to enhance their performance?

- What is my "head count?" Have I gained or lost salespeople? How are my recruiting efforts working? What changes are needed to attract the salespeople I want? Why do salespeople leave?

- Have I met my previously stated objectives? Have I met my production forecasts? What is my market share and am I on target with my projections? Have I gained or lost ground? What situations contributed to or inhibited my meeting objectives?

These are some of the most critical questions you need to answer before you can decide what to do next. Later in this book, we discuss ways to use information to monitor what the firm is doing. That data will help you answer many of the questions we posed. Also, involve your salespeople. Because they are on the front line, their experiences in the marketplace can tell you a lot about the way you do business and the services your company provides. The salespeople can provide valuable insight that statistics can't.

CONCLUSION

In the first two chapters of this unit, we analyzed the environment in which you do business. This chapter has focused on a wide range of issues in the marketplace that could affect a brokerage company. Your task is to make decisions about how *your* organization should respond, to seize opportunities and prepare for the challenges that could arise in the future.

From your analysis of the business climate and the marketplace, you are now armed with a considerable amount of information. Use it to guide your decisions about the target markets you intend to serve, the services you will offer and the ways you will position the company to cope with competition. Virtually every decision, from the development of your business plan and financial projections to the development of your marketing and advertising programs, will be impacted by the information you have gathered during this process.

DISCUSSION EXERCISES

Discuss the methodology you would use to analyze the marketplace. What do you already know about the consumers and the real estate in your area that affect your services?

* * *

Discuss the methodology you would use to analyze your competition. What do you already know about the firms and their services that affect your company?

* * *

What innovative services or business strategies do you think will work in your area?

* * *

Discuss the methodology you would use to analyze your company. What procedures already exist to gather the information you need? What systems should your company implement to give you the quality, reliable data that you need?

4 Developing a Plan

Why is a business plan important for your company? In what way, if any, will the mission of your organization change in the coming years? What goals should be included in your business plan to seize the opportunities that will arise and overcome the barriers that could challenge your company in the future?

You can form some notions about what your organization should be doing while analyzing the business climate and the marketplace. But notions are vague and don't provide sufficient guidance for a company. It's like embarking on a trip without a specific destination in mind. Even when you have a destination, you need a map to get you there. A plan identifies a specific destination for your company and the methodology for reaching that destination.

Recall the point we made in the introduction to this unit: planning will chart the course for doing the right things. Those who plan succeed; those who don't, won't. One of the reasons businesses fail is that they haven't utilized their financial and human resources properly. If you avoid planning entirely, you must be willing to suffer the consequences. Yes, something will happen in your organization. But that doesn't necessarily mean that the *right* things will happen to *keep* you in business. People will work, but they may not produce the results your company needs to grow and be profitable. The time and money that you invest in developing a plan, initially, pays enormous rewards in the long run, especially if you avoid financial calamity.

To plan the "right things" you need information, which is what we've been gathering in the situational analysis. Now, use this information to forecast the future and develop a plan. As a student of the business climate and the marketplace, you should be able to plan a futuristic as well as realistic course. The object is to direct the organization's resources in focused ways, things the organization needs to be doing to accomplish its goals. You may discover that the way the company has been operating is no longer "right." Be willing to restructure operations or plan new ventures. A company that is bound to the past can lose while its competitors take the lead.

Developing sound business plans takes time and perhaps skills that you do not currently possess. In this chapter we present a framework for developing a plan. In addition, the advice and counsel from others can be very valuable. Accountants, business-savvy friends or consultants are useful resources as you conduct your situational analysis and develop your plan.

PLANNING RATIONALE

Several general concepts about planning are important to keep in mind. They affect the way plans are developed as well as the way plans impact the organization.

- The *purpose* of a plan is to direct the organization's financial and human resources to those selected activities that will yield the greatest return on investment. Conversely, plans prevent the organization from diverting its resources to activities, regardless of tradition or popularity, that produce meager results. (While we're discussing this concept, consider how beneficial planning is for salespeople.) A plan tells the organization how to "work smart."

- A properly constructed plan tells the organization *what* it wants to accomplish and provides a general framework for *how* the organization intends to do this. Plans turn aspirations into concrete expectations. Plans contain specific, measurable goals, and provide a methodology, including timeframes, to tell the organization how to accomplish them. Specificity tells the organization precisely what goals it must pursue and provides benchmarks for determining whether it's accomplishing what it set out to do. The methodology guides the pursuit of the goals. Otherwise, you have a destination but no road map.

- A plan helps the organization to be *flexible*. Organizations must be responsive, but they also must resist the temptation to abandon course at the sight of each intimidating change. With thoughtful forecasting you should be able to develop a plan that empowers the organization to function in the contemporary environment. By anticipating changes and restructuring activities, if necessary, you can keep the organization on course which also prepares it to weather turbulent periods.

- Planning activities must be *integrated* throughout your organization. This means that planning must occur at all levels of the organization. After upper management defines the long-range plan, lower levels of management must plan activities around the goals and objectives for which they are responsible. A business plan is of little value unless all units of the organization are working in concert with one another.

- Planning requires *commitment* from everyone in the organization. This means you need people to buy into the plan. Otherwise, they will stride off on their own paths, which defeats the purpose of having a plan. Commitment is achieved when people see that a plan evolved from a deliberate, logical decision-making process. Engage people at various levels in the organization in the planning process. Not only do you gain multiple perspectives, but also you give people a sense of ownership. People are more likely to be committed to a plan they've had an opportunity to influence.

- A plan must be *implemented*. Unfortunately, the planning documents in some organizations are stowed a file drawer as soon as they are typed, never to see the light of day again. Some organizations use the documents for awhile and then stray off on some other path. Because considerable time and effort are involved in developing a plan, the organization cannot afford to squander its resources on projects that are not utilized.

- Planning is the most fundamental management activity. Virtually every business decision is guided by the plan. You can identify how to structure your organization, determine staffing requirements and measure the effectiveness of the organization. A business plan is also useful for building credibility with others outside your organization. Lenders, suppliers and potential business affiliates will commonly review your plan in their decision-making processes.

- A business plan is only a management tool. It should not take the fun out of being in business nor stifle your enthusiasm or creativity. In fact, a properly designed and implemented plan should have a positive effect on you and the people who work for you. Be flexible! If your plans don't materialize as expected during the first year, don't give up on your business venture. (This is where your entrepreneurial spirit is an asset.) Because a plan is reviewed each year, you can make adjustments if necessary and set more realistic or achievable goals. It's difficult to anticipate, especially for a new business venture, how long it will take to reach certain plateaus.

YOUR BUSINESS PLAN

Now we're ready to develop a business plan. Although there are various levels of planning, you have to begin with a long-range blueprint for the organization. A typical long-range plan spans five years, though a three-year plan may be more feasible if the dynamics in the market place are volatile.

Some organizations resist planning for more than one or two years. But few endeavors blossom in a short period of time. It takes time to solidify your position with a particular target market or to reap the benefits of a franchise affiliation, for example. Without a long-range plan, the temptation is far too great to shift course each year if you do not see instant results. Valuable human and financial resources could be expended in one direction, only to be diverted in another direction and then another. Although organizations must be responsive to change, these must be deliberate and thoughtful responses.

Would you rather push a rope or pull a rope to get it from one place to another? It takes little effort to push one end of the rope. But when you do, where does it go; and how many turns does it take? Isn't it more productive to take hold of one end and pull it? In doing so, you can control where it goes. But you have to know in which direction to move. And the longer the rope, the longer it takes for the tail to line up behind the leader. A long-range plan, as opposed to a short-range plan, provides the map and enables all facets of the organization to line up on the same course.

Mission

The development of the long-range plan begins with the answers to several important questions about your organization.

- What is your purpose for being in business?

- What does your business specifically do?

- Where do you want your business to be in the future that is different from where it is today?

Your responses to these questions help define the company's **mission**. Determining a mission is a thought-provoking exercise. It requires that you critically assess the organization and validate your reason for being in business. Most important, it requires that you provide vision for the organization. Solidify these thoughts into one or several sentences to form the **mission**

statement. This provides focus for the organization. Everything that follows in the business plan must support its mission.

Next, expand on the mission statement by identifying several **general objectives** for your organization. These crystallize how the organization expects to accomplish its mission. In a brokerage organization these may refer to target markets or major services. An analysis of your human and financial resources will help you determine the number of general objectives that can be effectively accomplished. If the organization is fairly small, you may identify two general objectives. Most larger organizations don't chose more than four. If the organization is diversified, with a number of divisions or departments, and has sufficient human and financial resources, it can be more ambitious. Often, in this case, a general objective is related to the nature of the activity within each division or department.

The mission statement and the general objectives tell what the company aspires to do. But you need specific guidance, a precise course to turn those aspirations into reality. Think about planning the same way you would describe a sports game. First you identify the game and the general theme of the game; these are your mission statement and general objectives. Now you have to tell people what the object of the game is; these are the goals of your company. Then describe a series of plays that will get the team to the goal; these are the strategies your organization will use to reach its goals.

The following discussion concentrates on how to define the goals and strategies. The terminology, or what you call these components of a plan (strategic planners have individual preferences in terminology), is not nearly as important as understanding what each component should tell you.

Goals

Each general objective for your company is supported by a number of specific **goals** or *objectives*. These are the end results you want to achieve. They break down the aspirational or futuristic nature of the general objectives into manageable, short-term accomplishments and show how the organization intends to achieve its general objectives.

Goals or objectives must be translated into specific words that tell precisely how to focus the organization's resources. They have four characteristics. These are

1. specific or identifiable,

2. measurable (quantitative),

3. attainable, and

4. framed in time (beginning and completion dates).

Using words like *increase, maximize, decrease,* or *minimize,* with nothing more specific or measurable, does not provide a way to determine whether the organization is on target. Specific goals would say "increase by 100 transactions," "increase by 25 percent" or "earn $225,000 in gross commissions." You may hesitate to make such precise statements because they represent a commitment that is easily scrutinized; failure is obvious. But specificity is needed to give the organization readily identifiable *outcomes* for measuring the results of its efforts.

Providing time frames adds to the specificity of a goal. If you want to increase your activity in a particular service by 100 transactions, do you mean in 1 year, 2 years or 6 months? A time frame serves as a benchmark for determining achievements. Goals that lack time frames can leave the organization floundering just as badly as they can without any goals. If an accomplishment is so significant that it is a goal, the organization depends on it being achieved in a timely fashion.

Goals must be challenging but also attainable. There may be many things you would like to do, but you do not have endless resources. Focus your resources on the most productive activities and de-emphasize those that are less rewarding. Don't be too ambitious—that can be frustrating and confusing—but don't underestimate what you can accomplish. One of the best ways to determine realistic goals is to assess the organization's capabilities and past performance (which is the reason for the company analysis described in the previous chapter).

For example, before setting a goal related to revenue or number of transactions, evaluate the past listing or sales figures. Then decide the amount of gross revenue you want to generate.

Convert this figure to a number of transactions by determining the previous average commission and dividing the new gross figure by that amount. Now decide the distribution of listings and sales; compare these figures with previous activity. This way you can determine whether your gross income or transaction projections are realistic.

Using other historical data, you can set goals relating to such achievements as the percentage of the market share you want to capture, the volume of business generated by various types of properties, or the volume of business generated from rentals and sales or other services.

As you review your plan periodically during its three-year or five-year life, you have the verifiable, measurable data with which to assess the organization's accomplishments. If you've been unrealistic when you developed the plan or if there are unanticipated changes in the marketplace, you may have to revise the quantitative measures and the time frames in subsequent years. But don't change the numbers in the plan just to make your organization look better. The harsh reality may be that the organization is really straying off course. Face the facts and do something about it.

Strategies

Each of the goals is supported by strategies, which prescribe the methodology you will use to accomplish that specific goal or objective. Long-range planning is otherwise known as *strategic planning* because it provides not just goals but also the strategic methodology for accomplishing them. Goals are not particularly useful unless you provide guidance for achieving them. Remember the game analogy: people need to know what steps to take to score. Strategies provide that guidance.

When formulating strategies, consider the obstacles or barriers you may encounter and the amount of human and financial resources that are available. Strategies can include things you need to do to overcome any obstacles or enhance your resources. Strategies also help weed out nonproductive activities, those that won't help you reach your goals. If certain customary activities no longer contribute to the achievement of an objective,

---

FIGURE 4.1   Goals and Strategies

General Objective—To provide real estate services relating to vacation properties and second homes.

Goal—To obtain 48 listings of properties suitable as vacation properties or second homes within the next 24 months. (Now you need to define strategies to get these listings.)

Strategy—Assemble the professional knowledge necessary to identify suitable properties, including buyer's preferences, lifestyles and desirable amenities.

Strategy—Train the sales associates to identify and list suitable properties.

Strategy—Develop a network with developers of these properties.

Goal—To close 36 sales transactions within the next 24 months. (Now you need to define strategies to acquire the sales.)

Strategy—Train the sales associates to work with potential buyers.

Strategy—Develop marketing and advertising programs to promote these properties to the target population.

Strategy—Develop an outreach program to target potential buyers in other geographic areas.

Goal—To increase vacation property and second-home market share to 40 percent of the company's total sales production within three years.

Strategy—Establish a business unit within the organization to provide a wide variety of services to people who own or desire vacation properties or second homes.

---

they should be discontinued. This is how organizations maximize the effectiveness of their resources.

Figure 4.1 shows how goals and strategies support a general objective. If you have decided that one of the company's niche markets is vacation properties and second homes, for example, a portion of your business plan could be developed following this format.

The sample format can be used to develop goals and strategies around any general objective your firm intends to achieve. Not all goals may be production-related. You may set a goal to establish a new business unit, such as a relocation department, or to open a branch office by a certain target date. Define strategies to make the necessary preparations and plan the allocation of resources to that end. Or you may set a goal to trim back a certain operation. Strategies define how you will assimilate those activities and personnel elsewhere in the organization.

A business plan is unique for each organization. Plans are not packaged programs that someone else has developed. Nor can you borrow another organization's and make it yours. There are, however, computer software programs that will guide you in developing a business plan that is tailored to meet your needs. A plan must support *your* company's mission. The goals, strategies and time frames or measurements must be suitable for *your* organization in *your* marketplace. The measurements in our illustration, for example, may be understated or overly ambitious for you. Perhaps the general objective is entirely inappropriate for your organization or market area.

Contingency Plans

Because planning involves forecasting, the more futuristic the forecast, the fewer variables there are that can be predicted with great certainty. Changes in laws or economic conditions or actions by competitors can send you scurrying to adjust. If you're monitoring the industry, the legal environment and the marketplace, you are less likely to be surprised. Most situations don't arise without some warning.

If you anticipate that certain events are possible, though are not yet evident, you can incorporate **contingency plans** into your business plan. These plans establish alternative goals and strategies that will be implemented to cope with an event. This prevents the organization from being thrown for a loop and protects against knee-jerk reactions that could divert resources in careless or uncontrolled ways.

For example, a major employer may be contemplating a merger, which could result in a sizable loss of jobs in your market. A mass exodus of employees with no incoming replacements could increase the number of properties on the market for sale and the cost and effort to get the properties sold. If the employer is one on whom you depend for a lot of business, you could lose a key source of revenue. Although the merger may not materialize, the prudent manager is prepared to take advantage of increased relocation business and prepare for the long-term impact on the market. It takes a little extra time and effort to wander down the "what if" path, but the preparation pays enormous dividends if a contingency plan is needed. You can rejoice if the scenario never materializes.

Reviewing Your Plan

Unfortunately, many people think that with a three-year or five-year plan in hand, there's nothing left to do until it's time to write a new plan three or five years later. Just as you check a road map, counting miles that have been traveled and studying the route to the next stop on your journey, you need to review your plan. The business plan is a tool for monitoring an organization's progress, including that of each office or department.

Some of your goals will be short-term accomplishments, while others will take longer to reach fruition. By reviewing your plan each year, you can monitor your short-term progress and reconsider the validity of the long-range forecasts. You either validate that you're on the right course or revise your plan to respond to changes within your organization and the marketplace. In doing so, each year you develop a new three-year or five-year plan. This way your organization can be flexible and responsive to change without getting jerked off course on a whim.

ACTIVITY PLANNING

This phase of the process implements your long-range or strategic plan by designing activities or tactics. Again, what you do is more important than the terminology used to describe it. The long-range or strategic plan is only a skeleton. Referring to the game analogy, activity planning tells the team each "play of the game."

In the strategies illustrated in Figure 4.1, there is still more we need to know about what to do. For example, in the strategy relating to training, what is the plan for developing and implementing the training the sales associates may need? In the strategy relating to marketing and advertising, what specific marketing and promotional activities are needed? If you are going to establish a new business unit, what must be done to assemble the necessary money and personnel and define the work for the department? And when do these strategies need to be accomplished? Activity planning answers these questions.

If you are just starting your own business, you're the one who will identify the activities for the company. Then you have to answer the question, "If I don't perform these activities myself, who will?" Unless you have sufficient human resources or can obtain assistance from external sources, you may find that your plan is more ambitious than you can manage by yourself.

In larger organizations, this planning phase involves the people who will be responsible for implementing the strategies and accomplishing the goals. Earlier we mentioned that planning should be done throughout the organization. One of the manager's responsibilities involves planning the related activities. For example, a goal relating to sales production is delegated to the sales manager of the office.

Depending on your management philosophy (discussed in a later chapter), activity planning could be conducted in an autocratic manner or a participatory manner. The manager of a sales office, for example, may involve the salespeople in planning activities. This participatory approach can help obtain their commitment to performing these activities. In an autocratic environment the manager defines the activities, then directs the salespeople to perform. In either case, the manager has the responsibility for ultimately achieving the desired outcomes. As activities are defined, the manager is responsible for seeing that financial resources are not diverted to activities that are counterproductive.

SHORT-RANGE PLAN

With a short-range plan you can tell the company what it should be doing in the coming year. That becomes this year's business plan. This plan should be relatively easy to assemble because you already have a blueprint in the long-range plan, along with activities that are necessary to accomplish it. A short-range plan is simply an extrapolation of goals and strategies that will be accomplished during the year, with some refinements.

Even though there are time frames specified in the goals in the long-range plan, the achievements may be rather futuristic (3 years, 24 months, in Figure 4.1). If you wait until the 23rd month to determine how you're doing, you've wasted valuable time, and perhaps resources, in the meantime. Most companies develop yearly projections, using the same methodology we described when forecasting long-range goals. Because you're dealing with only a one-year time frame, you should be able to forecast with a greater certainty. There are more "knowns" in the business climate and the marketplace. You also know about transactions that are pending for closing and your progress on strategies that were prescribed.

The short-range plan becomes the working document for managers at all levels in the organization to monitor progress. You can devise a variety of barometers to review the activities of the staff periodically. For example, a production goal can be segmented by quarters of the year, by sales associate, by branch office or by any other measure that is appropriate for your operation. As managers review the activities of their staffs, they also can determine whether the activities that were defined are productive. For example, if you are the manager of a sales office, you can identify activities that should be restructured or new strategies that could be recommended for the next plan as you review the salespeople's production.

CONCLUSION

Whether you are starting a new business, embarking on a new venture within your company or setting a course for profitability, the long-range plan is the critical starting point. It's tempting to just get on with "doing business" rather than planning, but that compromises the organization's survival in the long run. Planning does not need to be a burdensome process. With some thoughtful design and practice, planning will become as routine as any other activity in the company. True, resources are devoted to the task, but this is one of the most valuable expenditures of time and effort.

The other phases of planning simply embellish the long-range plan by defining activities that are needed to implement the plan and provide the "marching orders" for the coming year. You can also make contingency plans so that the company is prepared to cope with a significant change that could occur. As you review the long-range plan each year, basing your review on the previous year's accomplishments, you are constantly providing the vision for the organization that will keep it on course for the long term.

DISCUSSION EXERCISES

Practice writing good objectives. Are they identifiable, measurable, attainable and framed in time?

* * *

Prepare several strategies that could be implemented around these objectives.

* * *

As the manager who's been assigned one of your objectives (with accompanying strategies), what activities are appropriate?

In Conclusion of This Unit

Armed with a business plan, you are prepared to move on to the other management functions. You should be able to do so with some assurance that you're on the right track, particularly because of the amount of research that went into the development of your plan. You know your target markets and how you intend to serve them, and you are prepared to assign the resources necessary to implement the plans.

Throughout this unit we have developed the various stages involved in the planning process. Depending on whether you are the broker/owner, a senior manager in a large organization, a sales manager or a department manager, your involvement in these phases will probably be different. As a guide for understanding your function in the process, the following summary is provided.

➤ Analyzing the business climate:

- The broker/owner along with senior management conducts the analysis and may use outside resources.
- Other managers could be invited by the broker/owner to participate. Beyond that they need to understand how the analysis impacts the planning process.

➤ Analyzing the market:

- The responsibilities are similar to those described above.
- Other levels of management, such as a sales manager, can provide valuable insight about the marketplace, the competition and the current state of the company.

➤ Developing the plan:

- Business Plan

  The broker/owner and senior management are primarily responsible for developing the long-range plan and any contingency plans. Though other levels of management may be invited to participate in the development of the long-range plan, they are primarily responsible for implementing the plan.

- Activity Planning

  All levels of management may be involved in planning the activities that are needed to address the strategies prescribed in the long-range plan.

- Short-Range Plan

  The broker/owner and senior management are primarily responsible for developing the short-range plan. All levels of management are responsible for monitoring their areas of responsibility to accomplish the short-range plan.

THE
BUSINESS, FIRST HAND

Many people in the real estate business today can share experiences about how their careers have changed as our industry evolves. The good news is that, while the names and numbers change, many of the faces are still the same. We share first-hand experiences that demonstrate two different approaches to confronting the challenges of an evolving industry. The first one relates how changing demographics and changing competition caused a company to shed its traditional way of doing business and forge a new alliance to carry it into the future. In this case it was a very special tradition: a family-run business.

One of our authors, Joan m. Sobeck, founded a real estate company in 1968. During 30 years in business it developed into a successful "boutique" type office in the Pascack Valley area of Bergen County, New Jersey. Most of its business came from personal referrals and a loyal following of repeat business, including family and friends of former buyers and sellers. With an equally loyal staff, a number of whom had been with the company for over 15 years, this family-owned real estate company gained a major share of the market.

Eventually, most of the network of customers, who were by now senior citizens, left the area. As they left, so did a major source of business, as well as their referrals. Though the company had a prominent reputation and name recognition in the area, it was unknown to the incoming population of "yuppies." The major share of the market held by the company's 12 salespeople, who had previously outsold the large companies by four to one, was diminishing.

Competing with the major New Jersey real estate companies was increasingly challenging. Joan m. Sobeck REALTORS® could not afford to "buy" the market to overcome the "big is better" mentality and compete with their competitors' full-page ads to attract the new population. It was difficult to attract new salespeople, especially when many of the larger companies owned real estate licensing schools. These companies also offered training and managerial opportunities.

The broker and her son, Peter j. Sobeck, decided it was time to chart a new course. Their company could expand, but it wasn't able to recruit. Or it could downsize to two or three people, but the problems would be the same, only on a smaller scale. They did not want to relinquish control and sell out to one of the big companies. Their primary objectives were to retain an ownership position and utilize their experience to effect policy. These objectives were especially important to them because they were accustomed to working in a highly professional, ethical organization and prided themselves on their reputation for personal service.

The solution was to buy ownership in a RE/MAX organization. Now merged with an existing company, they accomplished their primary objectives. In addition, they enjoy the benefits of an international referral organization, the latest technology and a national identity. They are quick to say that this has been a bit of an adjustment, but they firmly state that the move was the "shot in the arm" they and their sales associates needed—a strategic decision that ensures their longevity as viable competitors into the next century.

This second experience demonstrates another approach to meeting the challenges of an evolving industry. In this case the company moved out of the residential business and into an entirely new real estate field. In fact it provides a variety of specialized services.

Another of our authors, John E. Cyr, has been in the real estate business for approximately 40 years. At one time he owned a residential real estate firm comprised of over 20 salespeople in three offices. The company boasted that it was "Numero Uno" in Stockton, a city of approximately 250,000 in the Central Valley of California.

Two significant factors altered the course of his firm. Franchises began taking hold in the industry, which diminished the company's share of the market and reduced its sales staff to about a half-dozen salespeople. The market relocated, moving north and away from the downtown area where the firm was located. As the market moved, new companies also located to the north. The firm could have followed the competition by joining a franchise and relocating the office.

Instead, the principal identified an exciting new opportunity for his company—the downtown market. The movement of real estate companies away from the area left a void in that market. At about the same time, several large national and statewide commercial and industrial franchised firms were getting established in the downtown area. However, those companies were primarily interested in dealing with large chains rather than the small service business around the downtown area. This unserved market created additional opportunities. Another niche developed as old-time farm brokers left the business or retired. Although there was not a lot of farm brokerage business, it was sufficient for a firm that didn't have to depend solely on that activity.

John Cyr, REALTORS®, Inc., evolved into an new entity, devoted entirely to county-wide sales, leasing, exchanging and appraising industrial, commercial and agricultural properties. Appraisal activities came about as a result of a shortage of qualified individuals when the state began licensing appraisers. Today it is the only real estate office offering comprehensive, though specialized, services in the downtown area of Stockton.

Because of the varied expertise needed to perform all of the company's activities, it needed a different approach to staffing to ensure it had the proper talent. Cyr calls the approach "The Professional Team." This is a staff comprised of individuals with specialized skills who work together in handling specific aspects of the company's services. Now, rather than competing with residential practitioners, this company is a complementary companion, handling referrals for specialized services their firms are not equipped to provide. A willingness to change, seek new opportunities and acquire new skills has enabled this company to endure with a promising future.

UNIT
2

Organizing the Organization

Remember, "Here's the desk; here's the phone; good luck, you're on your own?" This brings back memories for both brokers and salespeople of the simpler, less-sophisticated times in real estate. Handing a business plan to a broker is like giving a desk and a phone to a salesperson and expecting wonderful things to happen. This assumes we know what to do or that we have the necessary tools to perform the job.

While we have emphasized the importance of planning, equally important decisions are involved in the next management function—organizing. You have to decide who, what, where and how your business is going to meet the challenges set forth in your plan. As you revise your business plan, you have to reevaluate your organization and reconsider the same decisions.

Organizing creates structure for the company and its operating systems so that the company can deliver on the business plan. Whether you are starting a new business, or revising or expanding your operations, the company needs to be prepared to operate effectively and efficiently. The organizing function gives the company the tools with which to do this. The company needs

- structure for its ownership, business alliances and human resources;
- physical facilities equipped with communications and information systems;
- a financial structure to manage the company's financial resources;
- policies and procedures to prescribe how business is conducted; and
- a marketing and advertising program with which to generate business.

This is the management function that brings the company to life, following the blueprint outlined in the business plan. You allocate money and personnel and give the company its own personality. Its individuality is reflected in your facilities, your policies and procedures and your marketing and advertising program. The structure of your operations must reflect contemporary ways of doing business. Technology plays a major role in the structure of a company's communications and information management systems. It also affects office space requirements. Today's business environment is also inundated with laws and litigation which affect a company's policies and procedures. The chapters in this unit are devoted to organizing the company, that is, preparing the company to accomplish its mission.

If you are the broker/owner or a senior manager in a large organization, you will be responsible for the major legal and financial decisions. This will also include company policy. If you are a sales office or department manager, you most likely will have some authority to make financial decisions and to develop operating systems within your office or department.

5 Structuring Your Organization

How are you going to organize your company to do business? What is the legal form of ownership? Is your company independent or affiliated with other organizations? What are your personnel requirements— staff people and sales associates?

The first step in implementing your business plan is to develop a framework for your organization. If you are starting up a new company, you have to make some basic decisions about the legal form of ownership, your mode of operation and the internal structure of your organization. For existing organizations, these decisions must be revisited periodically to ensure that the structure supports their business plans.

As plans change, organization structures change. Operating structures must evolve in contemporary ways to enhance effectiveness and efficiency. Ownership may be reconfigured, adding new owners or severing relationships with current ones. Business affiliations may change, adopting new alliances or discontinuing existing ones. A company's operations may expand to include new business sectors or scale back to reduce the number of services. Operating strategies must empower the organization to function in the contemporary environment.

LEGAL OWNERSHIP

The broker may be the sole owner of the business or join forces with other owners. The salespeople may even have an ownership position in the company. In any case, if you are the broker, you must decide the most suitable form of legal ownership. If you are the lone worker or employ only one or two salespeople, you may feel comfortable being a sole proprietor-doing business under your own name. However, you may decide that other forms of ownership are preferable. Because these decisions have serious legal and tax implications, you should seek the counsel of a lawyer and an accountant. The licensing laws in your state may specify certain ownership positions for the responsible broker and officers of a corporation, which must also be considered. Table 5.1 shows the trends in the broker's ownership role in the firm since 1978, according to NAR's most recent study.

Sole Proprietorship

In a sole proprietorship the broker is the sole owner. If you are the broker, hang out your shingle and you're in business. You personally reap all of the rewards of your business's efforts. But you also bear sole responsibility and personal liability for its losses.

As the sole owner, not incorporated, your business is more dependent on you than you think. If you die or are unable for some other reason to run the business, it's unlikely that your business will survive, especially if it is a legacy to family members. According to Deloitte & Touche, accountants, statistics show that only 35 percent of family businesses survive under the leadership of the second generation. Using the help of a lawyer and a tax accountant, plan how your business will run if you are incapacitated, and develop a succession plan in the event of your death. Your state's licensing laws may also include provisions for succession.

TABLE 5.1 Broker's Ownership Role In The Firm: 1978–1996

	1978	1981	1984	1987	1993	1996
Partner In A Partnership	9%	8%	10%	7%	5%	3%
No Ownership Interest	25	37	43	47	54	79
Individual Proprietor	48	38	34	31	26	5
Stockholder/Corporate Officer	18	18	14	15	15	11
Other	NA	NA	NA	NA	NA	2

NA = not asked on previous surveys

SOURCE: *Profile of Real Estate Firms,* 1996, National Association of REALTORS®.

Corporations

A corporation is a sole legal entity created under state law. Although it is an association of one or more individuals, a corporation is regarded as having an existence and personality of its own. A corporation is treated as a single individual, despite the fact that a number of stockholders own shares in the corporation. The corporation has legal capacity to contract and conduct its affairs under its articles of incorporation. Closely held corporations are owned by relatively few people, all or most of whom are directly involved in the business of the corporation. There are several advantages that may make this form of ownership appealing.

- *Limited liability.* Liability incurred by the corporation becomes an obligation of the corporation and not of the individual owners. Unless a shareholder has signed a personal guarantee for the corporation's obligations, actions for damages, judgments or bankruptcies will not affect the person's assets. Only the amount of the stockholder's investment in the corporation is at risk.

- *Perpetual existence.* Because a corporation is a legal entity that exists indefinitely (until and unless it is properly dissolved by legal proceedings), it technically never dies. Any officer who dies, retires or resigns can be replaced.

- *Centralized management.* The stockholders elect a board of directors that, in turn, elects a slate of officers. The officers are responsible for the general affairs of the corporation. At least one of the officers, the licensed broker, is directly responsible for the real estate brokerage operations under state license law.

- *Transferability.* The corporate stock may be transferred freely from one stockholder to another.

- *Lack of income limitations.* A corporation may have an unlimited number of stockholders and is permitted to earn an unlimited amount of income.

One of the major disadvantages of a corporation is that profits are taxed twice: once at the corporate level, before dividends are distributed, and again as the dividends are distributed to the stockholders. Salaries paid to the officers are not considered profits, so they are taxable only to the individuals who receive them. Losses may not be passed on to the stockholders but may be applied to the corporation's future earnings. If the corporation realizes any capital gains, these are passed on to the stockholders as ordinary income.

Your lawyer and your accountant can advise you whether this form of ownership is suitable for your situation. Because the tax laws are constantly changing, your accountant can evaluate the advantages and disadvantages according to prevailing laws.

S Corporation

The S corporation offers the same first four advantages described for a corporation and overcomes one of the disadvantages. The double taxation is eliminated by passing the income, losses and capital gains directly to the stockholders. They, rather than the corporation, pay taxes or deduct losses on their personal tax returns.

There are restrictions on an S corporation. The number of shareholders is limited to no more than 35 owners. Not more than 20 percent of the income may be generated from passive investments, such as stock dividends, rental of investment properties and interest from money deposits. If the S corporation is engaged primarily in real estate brokerage activities, these restrictions may not be burdensome. But it is easy to make mistakes, jeopardizing the S corporation status. Again, consult a lawyer and an accountant for advice.

General Partnership

A partnership is an organization formed under the state's Uniform Partnership Act in which two or more co-owners engage in business for a profit. All of the owners are general partners and share full liability for the debts or other obligations of the partnership. The partnership itself does not pay taxes, although it does file an information return, reporting the amount of income it distributed to each partner. The partners are responsible for paying their own individual taxes. Losses or capital gains also are passed along to the partners.

A partnership can maintain a real estate broker's license, provided each partner who is engaged in the real estate business is also a licensed broker. Because the partnership does not enjoy status as a sole legal entity like a corporation, it does not have a life of its own. It can be dissolved by the death, withdrawal, bankruptcy or legal disability of any of the general partners. It is advisable to seek counsel before forming a general partnership, including assistance in writing a partnership agreement.

Limited Partnership

In a limited partnership agreement one or more people, the general partner(s), organize and operate a partnership venture. Other members of the partnership, the limited partners, are merely investors. These individuals do not have responsibility for or say in the direction or operation of the partnership. They share in the profits from the efforts of the general partner and are liable for losses only to the extent of their investment. The general partners, however, have unlimited liability. Limited partnerships are closely regulated by state and federal agencies. Again, your legal counsel can advise whether this is a suitable form of ownership for your real estate brokerage business.

Limited Liability Companies

Personal liability and corporate income taxes are the two most persuasive issues that affect your choice of ownership structure. Many states have laws that enable businesses to operate as limited liability companies (LLCs). The investors are members rather than partners or shareholders, holding membership interests rather than stock in the company.

LLCs may be an appealing alternative to S corporations or limited partnerships. You can avoid some of the restrictions that are imposed on an S corporation. You also can partially limit the liability that otherwise exists in a limited partnership, provided you take the appropriate steps to accomplish this. Regulations and fees for establishing LLCs vary considerably from state to state. Again, you need the guidance of a lawyer and/or tax consultant as you consider this form of ownership.

MODE OF OPERATION

Once you've determined the most desirable form of ownership, you need to decide your mode of operation, that is, whether your business is going to be independent or affiliated in some fashion with other organizations. Your competitive advantage or disadvantage will likely influence this decision. Weigh the benefits and drawbacks both for you as a business person and for your company as you choose a mode of operation.

Independent

An independent business appeals both to owners, who want maximum freedom to conduct their affairs, and to customers, who want to do business with people who totally own and operate their own companies. In this mode of operation you can be totally self-reliant and enjoy being in total control. Successes are yours alone, but so are the struggles. You do not have the benefit of the support that is available when brokers are affiliated with one another.

FIGURE 5.1   Franchise Affiliations

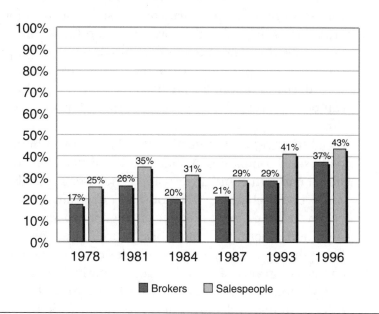

SOURCE: *Profile of Real Estate Firms,* 1996, National Association of REALTORS®.

Franchise

Franchising is a popular mode of operation for many types of businesses. In real estate, for example, approximately 37 percent of the broker-members of the National Association of REALTORS® are associated with franchised firms according to a survey conducted by the organization in 1997. Figure 5.1 shows how franchise affiliation has grown in popularity.

Franchisees are independent business owners who, at the same time, are affiliated with other similar businesses. Franchises provide a packaged program for running a business, including operating strategies and a product or service. This is attractive, especially for a start-up company, because it is a relatively risk-free way to engage in business. Franchisees expect that the product or service has been market-tested and is accepted in the marketplace. Because the reputation of the franchise (and its revenue) are affected by the success or failure of its franchisees, they normally provide technical support to the business owner.

The primary focus of the national real estate franchises varies. Some offer primarily advertising and promotional benefits, including referral networks. Some focus on services that target specific consumers; others provide specific approaches to the internal operations of a brokerage firm. Carefully weigh your decision to join a franchise. As good a franchise sounds, it can be expensive. Be sure the benefits will justify the costs.

Marketing and advertising. The most common reason real estate companies affiliate with a franchise is for its professional marketing and advertising expertise. Typically, franchises offer comprehensive promotional programs, including television, radio or print media campaigns, brochures, newsletters, signs and other marketing tools. National franchises also are utilizing their purchasing power to offer coupon and merchant-discount programs and other cross-marketing strategies that today's consumers find attractive. In addition, franchises often offer training and motivational programs for the salespeople and business development programs for the brokers.

Affiliating with a national franchise gives you name recognition in your local market. This can be a blessing or a curse. It's not uncommon for consumers to remember the name of the franchise rather than the name of the individual firm. Some franchises grant exclusivity or limit the number of franchisees in geographic areas. However, others do not, which means you may not achieve the power in the marketplace you expected. Additional efforts are needed to promote your individual identity while also linking you with the franchise.

A franchisee's affiliation with other franchisees around the country provides a natural connection for referrals. However, you also can be adversely affected by this association. If customers or clients had an unsatisfactory experience with one franchisee, they may resist referrals to other franchisees. Get acquainted with other franchisees to decide whether this is a group with whom you want to be affiliated. It's advantageous, though not a necessity, to share similar philosophies of doing business. Remember, too, that an unsatisfactory experience can be an isolated event rather than indicative of customary practices.

Once you evaluate the benefits of a franchise, decide if you need or can afford the affiliation. Initial franchise fees can be very expensive. For an established company, additional costs are also involved to convert signs and other signature materials. Once you've joined, you are obligated to pay the franchise additional fees during the term of your contract. In some cases these fees are collected monthly, regardless of your production activity. In other cases the fees are based on transactions, collected either periodically or out of each transaction. If you are convinced the benefits warrant the additional expense, you have to decide how to foot the bill—by yourself or collect it from the salespeople.

Target market services.   Some franchises design their services to capture specific consumer populations. Your affiliation with one of these franchises is suitable when its target market is the same as one identified in your business plan. Some franchises target owners by providing counseling services to people who want to sell their properties themselves. There are franchises that target buyers, providing the various services associated with buyer agency. The primary advantage with consumer-service-oriented franchises is the technical expertise they offer. Again, cost versus benefit must be considered.

Internal operations.   There are franchises that offer a structure for your internal operations as well as the marketing and advertising programs that were previously discussed. The best known of these franchises provides an operating strategy for setting up a 100 percent commission business. Each licensee affiliated with the company pays a stipulated monthly fee to cover office expenses such as housing, staffing and equipment. Essentially, the licensees are leasing office space from the company. In addition, the licensees are responsible for other expenses, such as advertising, telephone and postage, plus the typical costs associated with franchise membership. These franchises also provide national marketing programs, referral systems and training and motivational programs.

National Corporations

A number of national corporations have been attracted to the real estate business in recent years. Often the goal is to strengthen their operations by engaging in diverse but compatible enterprises. The ability to link the products and services of these enterprises in cross-marketing programs is an additional enticement. National corporations typically purchase existing local real estate brokerage firms, selecting those that meet certain criteria for size or market share. The terms of the agreement you make with the corporation will determine the structure of your business under the corporate umbrella, your role and responsibilities within the organization and the degree of financial independence (or dependence) your brokerage operation will have.

Once the business is sold to a national corporation, the broker/owner essentially becomes a manager. While you relinquish some decision-making authority, the power of corporation affiliation may be an attractive trade-off. Benefits include corporate name recognition, along with advertising and promotional programs and strategies to enhance the internal operations of your company. Depending on the financial terms, you may have an infusion of cash with which to enhance your brokerage activities. As attractive as these benefits may be, you need to consider whether you can relinquish the control and prestige you enjoyed as an independent business owner.

Local Affiliations

In recent years, local brokerage firms have sought ways to strengthen their competitive advantage and achieve cost-efficiencies. By forming an association, corporation or local franchise, they can pool their resources to cover expenses such as training, marketing and advertising programs and secretarial and accounting services. They also can pool talent or expertise as professional sales teams to offer complementary services such as land development, commercial leasing and property management. Collectively, brokers can increase their power in the market by capitalizing on the market share of each firm and creating local name recognition for new affiliates. Because each of these ventures is structured individually, there is no standard financial arrangement.

As you consider the costs versus the benefits of these ventures, you also need to consider the image and success of the firms with whom you will be associated. If you're the rising star, you may be providing greater benefits to the weaker firms than they will provide to you. On the other hand, joint sharing of a larger share of the market benefits everyone.

An informal way brokers may band together is by sharing office space and housing their independent operations under one roof. By sharing rent, common facilities such as conference rooms, and secretarial and accounting staff, they can achieve cost-efficiencies. Before aligning yourself with other brokers in this way, consider that sharing office space may also mean sharing liability. One broker's unpaid bills may become the responsibility of the other brokers.

Because several brokers are working out of the same physical location, consumers may not see the businesses as distinctly separate entities. In addition to compromising market identity, conflicts over entitlement to customers can arise. In the event of litigation between a consumer and one of the other brokers, you could unexpectedly be drawn into the proceedings simply by virtue of your affiliation. If you are considering an informal alliance with other brokers, consult your legal advisor. Also, review your state's license law regarding office requirements.

Controlled Business Arrangements

If the strategies in your business plan include ancillary services for your real estate transactions, you may consider a controlled business arrangement (CBA). A CBA is a network of interrelated companies, owned by one holding corporation, that offers services tied to a real estate transaction. The most obvious service is the acquisition of a mortgage loan, though acquisition of title insurance, settlement services or property inspections are also possibilities.

For years real estate brokers have sought ways to enhance the services they offer consumers. Today, this strategy is even more important to satisfy the consumers' quest for seamless transactions. CBAs provide the related services consumers desire and provide the operational structure real estate brokerage companies covet to coordinate and control a transaction. The linkage of services through CBAs also links sources of revenue.

In a CBA your mode of operation becomes more complex, requiring additional supervision, expertise and capital to set up and operate separate companies. There are complex legal considerations as well because of antitrust laws and the Real Estate Settlement Procedures Act (RESPA) (see Chapter 14).

Multiple Listing Services

Our discussion of affiliations would be incomplete without once again mentioning multiple listing services (MLSs). Whether you are independent, a franchisee or part of a national corporation, MLS membership may be an important facet of your mode of operation. In Chapter 3 when we analyzed the market, we explored the role MLSs play in serving the needs of today's consumers. Depending on the strategies in your business plan, MLS membership may be important not only for serving your customers and clients, but also for your competitive position in the marketplace.

MERGERS AND ACQUISITIONS

Mergers and acquisitions among brokerage companies have become quite common in many areas. Although you may debate whether "big is better," the fact is that corporate America has found that combining forces offers cost-efficiencies in their companies' internal operations and strengthens their power in the marketplace. Essentially, companies can accomplish "more with less" by forging alliances. Real estate companies have made a similar discovery.

The distinction between a merger and an acquisition is more academic than practical. In reality, companies combine operations in very individual ways, constructing legal arrangements that suit their specific situations. Your company may be the one searching for an alliance or yours may be the company being courted by another. In either case, the goal should be to combine forces in ways that provide a win-win situation for both organizations.

If yours is the company being pursued—joining forces with another company may not be as dramatic a departure from your original business plan as it first appears. Depending on the financial arrangement, additional resources may be available to aggressively pursue selected objectives in your plan. Depending on the role the broker/owner would have in the new organization, this may be an opportunity to relinquish some management responsibilities and concentrate on activities in which she or he has particular expertise or interest. Or this may be the most suitable way to phase into retirement. While these could be attractive advantages for the broker/owner or upper management, the staff may not be quite as receptive. Any change is unsettling, even though it could be beneficial in the long run. The staff must be reassured that the merger or acquisition is a positive step.

If yours is the company doing the pursuing—joining forces with another company may be the most suitable way to expand your operations. If your business plan calls for adding new products or services or increasing your geographic territory, purchasing an existing operation that offers these features is one way to accomplish your goals. While you could start your own enterprise from scratch, buying an existing business offers a number of advantages. It has an established presence in the marketplace, experienced personnel, a physical office site, complete with furnishings and equipment, and possibly a franchise affiliation. All of these assets take time and money to establish. The business also has a proven cash flow, which is an advantage if you need financing to acquire it.

Although the acquisition of an existing business eliminates some of the less predictable variables associated with starting a new enterprise or opening a branch office, this strategy is not without risk. The market position you thought you bought may quickly deteriorate if you lose the principal asset, the sales staff. In fact, this newly created company is ripe for recruiting. Upheaval is frequently viewed as a prime opportunity for other firms to court top producers. Another risk is that you may have bought more than you bargained for. You may now own worn-out equipment, a staff of malcontents, a franchise affiliation that is more costly than benefits warrant, an office location that is no longer viable or more debt or other liability than you anticipated.

Be an astute purchaser when buying a business. Be alert to the hidden problems you might be buying. Why is the business for sale? Are the current owners just ready to retire or are they unloading their frustrations. How much is the business really worth? Without carefully scrutinizing the company's financial operations, you can't be sure whether the profit is overstated or understated. If the owner has deferred expenditures that should have been made, the profit will look better than it really should. If the business is incurring expenses, including salary and compensation programs, that should be trimmed, the profit won't look as good as it could.

Evaluating a Business

Appraising the value of a business is a difficult task. Many factors must be evaluated, some of which involve more subjective than quantitative measures. The unique circumstances surrounding the sale of a business could prevent you from determining exactly how much a business is really worth. Just as in a real estate transaction, there is value and there is price. We know that these are not necessarily the same, depending on the motivations of the parties. As a real estate broker or appraiser, you may have experience evaluating businesses. Unless you do, don't venture into a merger or acquisition without the help of an accountant who can lead you through a financial analysis.

Return on investment (ROI) is the most widely accepted valuation approach. It is expressed as present value returned on investment, internal rate of return or financial rate of return. In any case, these theoretical approaches to value use a large amount of financial data to produce the numbers with which to analyze an investment. As your accountant helps you work through the analysis, remember that the business being analyzed may not continue to be the same business after the sale.

As you work through the financial analysis of a business, look closely at individual aspects of the organization, especially those that attracted you to the acquisition in the first place. Determine the value of that which you are buying—the name, current listings, pending sales, all or some of the company's services (property management or mortgage business), office equipment (or leases), employees or salespeople, contracts (such as advertising, franchise or multiple listing service), or office location. Sometimes all a purchaser wants is the salespeople, leaving the seller with the rest of the business assets and liabilities.

Any of these could be worth either more or less under your ownership. Depending on the length of time the company has been in business and the way you intend to integrate its name with yours, the value of the name and goodwill will vary. The quality of the listings and the volume of sales transactions may improve or decrease. Because the salespeople have a significant bearing on these aspects of the business, a mass exodus can seriously jeopardize the value of the business.

Because business cultures and management philosophies differ, consider how your leadership will affect the overall operation of the current firm. Look at the

- planning philosophy,

- organizational structure,

- staffing or personnel assignments and supervisory responsibilities,

- training and professional development programs, and

- financial management of the current firm.

You may run a more structured operation, you may direct your financial resources differently (maybe you place greater emphasis on staff services and less on advertising) or you may expect staff or salespeople to perform activities other than those to which they are accustomed. These differences can affect how well the two organizations will merge.

Buying an existing business can be a very expensive way to recruit new salespeople, especially if they don't fit into your

organization's culture. A considerable amount of retraining may
be needed (and the staff still may resist your way of doing
things). If you're depending on the current salespeople to make
your venture a success, you can't underestimate their value.

Transition

You will be either assuming the existing operation, hanging
your sign on the building and keeping the basic company
structure intact, or folding the operation into yours. If the latter
is your intention, you may plan to close the office you purchased
and incorporate the sales staff into one of your existing offices.
In either case, you need to define in your purchase agreement
the legal ownership structure, the working relationship between
you and the previous owner and compensation arrangements.

Rumors are the biggest enemy of mergers. Unfortunately,
they start even before the closing. You can't wait until you own
the company to map out how you're going to kick off the new
venture. You need to keep the staff intact and assure others with
whom you do business that all is well during the transition.
Although some salespeople may look forward to a change in
ownership, more will react to the uncertainty of the unknown
and seek other employers, especially if you are a new broker.

Launching a business is like launching a new product in the
marketplace. It takes considerable planning and a good marketing strategy. You need the obvious items—signs, business
cards and promotional literature—ready for the first day of the
company's "new life." Kick it off with an exciting event for the
company staff that day. Then introduce the new company in the
community several days later, launching your new signs and an
advertising campaign. Because current clients and customers
should hear about the change from you, time their receipt of a
personal letter before the public promotion. The initial kickoff
is a fast-paced, high-energy time.

The pace of the next phase in the transition is slower and
more methodical. During the next two weeks, introduce the
salespeople to the company's programs and services and its
internal policies and procedures. The sooner you do this, the
better. A new name is exciting, but uncertainty can torpedo the

acceptance of this new venture. Remember, too, that existing cultures don't change overnight. Some changes in policies and procedures can be gradually implemented once you're assured the sales staff is settled into the new company.

INTERNAL STRUCTURE

You have one more decision to make about the general operation of your organization: its internal structure. This reflects the way work is organized. If you are a single-person organization, the structure is readily apparent—you are the organization. You are responsible for all facets of its operation. As the scope of work in your business plan grows, the structure of the organization grows more complex as well.

The internal structure must be constructed to help the organization work efficiently. Begin by identifying the work that needs to be done to accomplish the goals or objectives in the business plan. Then bundle interrelated tasks and assign them to work groups. Groups may be organized according to property type (residential, commercial, etc.) or services (brokerage, property management, appraising, etc.). You may have a business unit that acquires and develops land. There also may be groups that provide administrative support. As your operation grows larger or more decentralized, these work groups become increasingly important to keep the organization running efficiently.

Once you identify and arrange the work, determine the personnel that are required. You can't define staffing needs before you know what work needs to be done and the amount of time and effort that will be involved. How many salespeople are needed? Should the staff be expanded or streamlined? What are the capabilities of the current personnel, their strengths and weaknesses? Should some workers be reassigned to different jobs within your organization? Would a current salesperson be a good relocation director or transaction coordinator? Once you've answered these questions you can determine your recruiting, hiring and training needs.

One-Person Organization

If you are a one-person business, you are the broker, salesperson and manager. We've been raised on the theory that the bigger a company is, the better it must be. But there are advantages to being the sole contributor to the organization. You are most likely to target your services to a very narrow market segment. In doing so, you can be very attentive to the needs of your customers and clients and provide personalized service.

Because you have no one to supervise but yourself, your only other responsibility is to manage the financial affairs of your business. The amount of time you devote to your enterprise is motivated solely by the amount of income you need and how hard you want to work. If you decide to take time off, you can close the office without restricting anyone else's livelihood. The initial investment is relatively small, unless you decide to incur the expenses of franchise or MLS affiliation.

There are drawbacks to this type of operation. Because you are the firm, no business is transacted when you're not available. Your capacity for growth is limited to the amount you can personally produce. You also don't have the resource of other salespeople to whom you can refer business if you have a personality clash with a customer or client.

One-Agent to Ten-Agent Organization

A one-agent to ten-agent organization is a small, centralized operation. In this organization the broker/owner role changes to include supervisory responsibilities (see Figure 5.2). As soon as you hire one salesperson, you become a sales manager. Typically, one-tenth of your time will be devoted to this activity. With each additional salesperson, another tenth of your time is added to sales management activities. As your sales staff grows, you have less time to devote to your own sales activities. Eventually you will find yourself being a full-time sales manager, unless you decide to hire one. You also need the services of a secretary-receptionist.

Your capacity for doing business grows as the size of your organization grows. Your personal efforts in the marketplace are supported by those of your salespeople. The firm can sustain

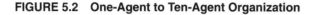

FIGURE 5.2   One-Agent to Ten-Agent Organization

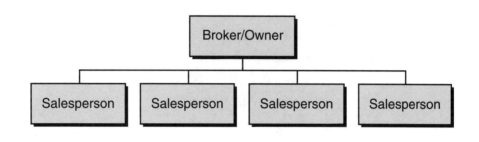

more consistent operations and provide a steadier stream of revenue than when it is totally dependent on one person's efforts. You also have the satisfaction of watching your company become a substantial business in the community.

There is a downside to this growth, however. Just because you have more people producing transactions doesn't necessarily mean you will have proportionate increases in revenue. Your cost of doing business will increase as the need for office space, equipment and supplies grows. Your management responsibilities increase and unless you are attentive to your financial affairs, growth will cost rather than make money. Regardless of whether you are the sales manager or you hire one, you are still ultimately responsible for the activities of your salespeople. In today's litigious climate this is not a responsibility you can afford to take lightly.

As you do your financial planning (discussed in detail in Chapter 7), you can thoroughly analyze the relationship of costs, revenue and the size of the sales staff. Often, though, brokers use desk cost as a simple rule of thumb to guide hiring decisions. **Desk cost** is calculated by dividing the expenses of the firm by the number of salespeople. For example, if your annual expenses are $20,000 and there are two salespeople, the desk cost for each is $10,000 annually. If there are four salespeople, the desk cost is $5,000 for each one. On a 50/50 split, for example, each of the four salespeople begins to earn a profit only after each has brought in a total of $10,000 gross commis-

FIGURE 5.3   Monolithic Organization

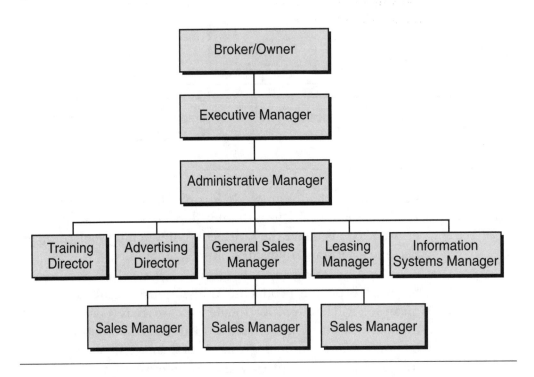

sions for the year. There's no profit for the company built into this calculation, so you have to plan carefully if you want to do more than break even.

Monolithic Organization

A monolithic organization is a highly centralized operation. It functions as a single (mono-) unit, though it normally consists of a number of work groups. You can see in Figure 5.3 that there are a number of departments or offices. Each is responsible for accomplishing various goals in the business plan. Some of the departments are directly responsible for delivering a firm's services. Others are responsible for administrative services that support the salespeople and the internal operation of the company.

The distinguishing characteristic of a monolithic organization is that there is one single source of authority at the top of the organization. This is normally the broker, owner or president. Authority flows from this position to the next level of senior management, then from senior management to department or division managers. The managers at each level are responsible for directing the activities related to their positions or departments. However, they do this only within the scope of authority or limits that are authorized by the immediate superior. Decision-making is highly controlled by one or only a few individuals in upper management. Lower levels in the organization normally have little authority to make decisions.

Depending on financial resources, all departments may be housed under one roof or in several locations. If the company is housed in one location, you can the make most efficient use of your office costs, spreading them among a number of departments. This arrangement also reduces the cost per agent (refer to desk cost). Because of their physical proximity to one another, the potential also exists for enhanced communications and coordination of activities among departments. However, this close proximity can cause problems. The roles and responsibilities of everyone must be clearly understood and enforced.

Selecting an office site can be tricky. One geographic location may not be best for all of your departments, especially if they are not located in proximity to the market segments they serve. The physical space must be adequate to comfortably house the current scope of work. But unless the space can be reconfigured, you may be unable to accommodate additional work if the organization grows. Not only is it difficult to work efficiently in overcrowded conditions, but morale suffers as well.

You may decide that the best way to carry out your business plan is in multiple office sites, locating work units according to their function. Branch or neighborhood offices may be located where you can serve your target markets most effectively. This offers convenience to both customers and salespeople. Administrative offices need to be located where they can support the sales offices most efficiently. In a monolithic organization, the path that authority travels is the same, regardless of the number of office locations.

FIGURE 5.4 **Decentralized Organization**

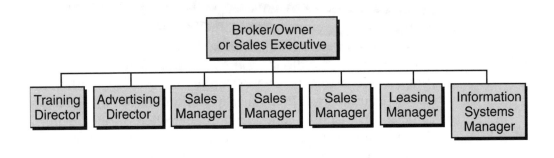

Decentralized Organization

A decentralized organization is characterized by the way authority is delegated. It is similar to a monolithic organization because it normally consists of a number of work groups or departments. But as you can see in Figure 5.4, it is dissimilar because of the path that authority travels. Once authority is delegated from the top of the organization, the next management level has greater authority and control over the activities of its departments or divisions. In a decentralized organization, there are usually fewer levels of management, thus giving the managers the decision-making authority to operate essentially as individual business units.

The trend today is to configure more streamlined and decentralized organizations. With fewer layers of management, people have greater freedom to control the work for which they are responsible. Consequently, they have greater flexibility to determine how the work should be accomplished. Each sales office or department, for example, usually becomes its own **profit center**. This means that each work unit must produce enough income to cover its cost of operation plus make a profit for the firm. Otherwise, other operating units will have to support them.

The challenge in a decentralized organization is to achieve the proper balance between autonomy and control. Each work unit must be able to function independently while at the same time work as a team to achieve the organization's goals. All units must also adhere to the business policies established by the firm. The selection of the appropriate people to manage each business unit is critical for achieving this balance. They must not only have professional skills that are appropriate for the work being done in the business unit, but they must also be able to demonstrate good judgment and the prudent use of authority.

It's not uncommon in a decentralized organization to centralize certain administrative functions. Rather than each unit setting up separate accounting, training or marketing functions, for example, dedicated departments handle this work for the entire organization. This is often the most effective and cost-efficient way to accomplish certain activities. However, these activities must be coordinated throughout the organization. Each business unit or sales office must have the administrative support it needs so that its ability to function is not restricted.

CHAIN OF COMMAND

As we discussed the structure of the organization, we mentioned the path of authority. You can see in the organization charts that each of the various business units, divisions or departments within the firm is directed by a manager. This person is responsible for seeing that the goals or objectives of that unit are accomplished. Each manager is given authority over this work, which is the fundamental right to make decisions, issue instructions and expect that the work will be done. As each manager exercises this authority, a chain of command within the organization evolves. The chain is the order of authority, beginning at the top and filtering down through the organization.

In real estate organizations there are typically two types of authority: staff authority and line authority.

- *Staff authority* is given to the people who are responsible for support services—the work groups providing administrative support. These groups contribute *indirectly* to the achievement of the company's objectives. They provide services such as accounting, marketing and advertising, training, purchasing (materials for the operation of the business) and maintenance.

- *Line authority* is given to the people who are responsible for contributing *directly* to the achievement of the company's objectives. These include work groups such as the sales offices or the property management, leasing or new construction departments.

The organization charts indicate very clearly the route that authority travels–the chain of command. You can see exactly who is accountable to whom and how the activities within the organization are coordinated with one another. The organization's structure sets up clear lines of communication. Your job is to enforce the chain of command. People need to know who their immediate boss is. They also need to know from which work units they are permitted to seek direction or support outside the formal lines of communication.

One way to maintain order within the organization is to ensure that people know exactly what to do. This is done by preparing a **job description** for each position. A job description defines the responsibilities of a position and the activities that are involved. The tendency is to list a variety of tasks that are associated with a position. But that doesn't really tell people what they need to know to help you maintain order. A job description should tell people where they fit into the big picture of the firm: to whom they are to report; the positions that report to them; and exactly what their responsibilities are versus the responsibilities of others. Describe the activities for which people are accountable, rather than a litany of chores or tasks associated with those activities.

It's tempting to say, in the case of salespeople, "They already know what to do . . . get sales and listings." But that is not a suitable job description. Are they responsible for meeting production goals or complying with the law or company policies, for example? Don't *assume* people know what a job entails. Furthermore, you can't chastise a person for failing to discharge his or her responsibilities if you haven't been explicit about what they are.

Informal Organization

Despite the way positions appear on a chart, most organizations have an informal structure. Work overlaps and doesn't always fit neatly into a chart. Everyone in the organization needs to understand the situations in which they are authorized to work outside the formal organization structure.

For example, the relocation director may be responsible for all aspects of servicing a listing funneled through the relocation network. The manager of a sales office may control the advertising budget for listings generated in that office. Now a salesperson has two separate directives for advertising a listing, depending on its source: one is to submit a request to the office manager for general listings; the other is to seek authorization from the relocation director to advertise that department's listing.

Sometimes people create their own order for your organization, regardless of the formal or informal structure you conceive. Look at some examples of how people circumvent the chain of command and disrupt your organization:

- A salesperson may seek a decision from a person whom he or she expects will give a desirable answer, regardless of whether that person has the authority to make the decision.

- Some people want to exercise more authority than they've been granted, so they take matters in their own hands and render decisions they don't have authority to make.

- When people don't agree with a company policy or procedure, they may make decisions or give directions that are beyond their scope of authority, thereby derailing your policies or procedures.

Consider this scenario. As the broker of a small company, you've hired a sales manager. A salesperson with whom you previously had a close working relationship feels that you will be responsive to a plea for a referral. However, the sales manager is responsible for referral assignments. How do you respond when the salesperson approaches *you* for a referral? If you intervene and grant the request, you undermine the authority of the sales manager. You also give the appearance that you are siding with the salesperson against the manager. Ultimately, the chain of command can unravel because you've authorized the salesperson to ignore it.

How could you handle this situation to preserve order?

- You could ask the salesperson to raise the issue with the manager (and if the salesperson doesn't, it could be that the salesperson was seeking preferential treatment from you); or

- You could approach the manager along with the salesperson and inquire about the status of referral assignments.

With either approach you demonstrate to both the manager and the salesperson that you are responsive and that you respect the authority that has been delegated to the manager. By your intervention you have also addressed an issue that, if ignored, could mushroom into a major problem. A disgruntled salesperson could turn other salespeople against the company's referral system. (Repeated queries about referrals, however, could indicate a more serious problem that should be addressed with the manager.)

There are other reasons why people work outside the formal structure of the organization. Perhaps they have found better ways to organize work. This should be your call to action, that some changes are needed. Either the work is not organized properly or you have the wrong people in positions of authority.

CONCLUSION

Giving structure to an organization gives it the orderly form it needs to execute the business plan. The broker (and other owners, if there are any) must decide the most suitable form of legal ownership and appropriate business affiliations. These involve decisions about the degree of independence or interdependence the company and its principals will have with other organizations.

As the scope of work grows or becomes more complex, the company can get disorganized or even become dysfunctional. Organizations need an internal structure that groups work in a logical, efficient order and a chain of command that clearly defines the path of decision-making authority. Job descriptions tell people the scope and limits of what they are expected to do. Just as the business plan provides a blueprint around which the company is organized, the structure of the organization provides a road map for assembling the tools for the business and allocating its resources.

DISCUSSION EXERCISES

Chart your current organization. What is its formal structure? What activities are each work unit responsible for accomplishing? What personnel are assigned to each work group and who is the supervisor?

* * *

What is the informal structure of your current organization? How does this differ from the formal organization? What problems, if any, arise from people working within the informal rather than the formal structure of the company?

* * *

Prepare job descriptions for various positions in your organization.

6 Structuring Your Business Systems

Where should your office be located? How will it be designed? What technology will you use to make your sales office a communications and information center?

The first impression you make on the public, the people who work for you and others in the industry begins at the front door. Once people cross the threshold, they should see a professional, efficient operation. Many successful companies grow from humble beginnings to new state-of-the-art office facilities. Whether you are in the humble beginnings stage or the state-of-the-art phase, you need to create an image for your company that inspires today's consumers to do business with you.

Once you showcase your firm in its offices, don't disappoint either the people who work for you or your customers with out-dated or inefficient systems and equipment. Technology has revolutionized virtually every activity within an office. Unless you are maximizing its use, you will be frustrated trying to keep pace with the competition and the demands of today's consumers. Remember that for them, as well as an increasing number of our employees and salespeople, technology has become a daily part of life. You can't afford to operate with 20th century systems when the 21st century is on the horizon.

Before you go shopping for office space or get carried away on a buying spree for furniture, telephones and computers, remember that your decisions must be guided by the scope and complexity of work the company does and the number of personnel that must be accommodated. In the previous chapter we outlined a structure for your company. Now you must assemble the facilities and equipment to support that operation.

Because significant financial resources are committed to setting up your systems, it's best to be a smart shopper. Investigate the wide range of office goods that are available and compare prices. This will help you make astute decisions about the expenditures you budget to ensure that they will contribute to the effective and efficient operation of the business. (Chapter 7, Structuring Your Finances, covers budgeting in detail.) Many resources are available to assist in designing the physical layout and automating your business. Think about these expenditures as an investment in the productivity, recruitment and retention of your staff, as well as an investment that benefits your customers and clients.

YOUR OFFICE

Your office is more than a place to house furniture and equipment. It reflects what you think about your company and creates an image. Choose the geographic area, the site and the physical layout of the facility with that image in mind. Consider, too, that your needs today may not be your needs tomorrow. The office space should be flexible so that you can accommodate change, particularly if you expect to increase the size of your staff or add office equipment. Otherwise you could incur greater costs, falling victim to the "penny-wise, pound-foolish" trap. The cheapest choice in the beginning could be more expensive in the long run.

Location

The selection of a location must be guided by the nature of the work that will be done in that office. If this is a sales office, use the analysis of the marketplace to determine the location of your target markets. The office should be located within a convenient traffic pattern in which these customers are likely to travel. The salespeople will also appreciate being in close proximity to the customers, even if this means they have to travel greater distances from home. If the work is primarily administrative, consider the office's proximity to other aspects of your company's operations and the convenience of the people who work in those business units.

The choice of location for a sales office also will be influenced by the location of your competition. Again from your analysis of the market, you have identified the location of your competitors and the amount of potential business that exists in that area. There's a common fear that if you're not where the competition is, you'll lose. But if there's not enough business to support everyone, you're better off charting new territory. On the other hand, if there's a concentration of other brokerage firms in an area, it could be that they have identified an area with great potential.

Site

Having determined a general location, select a specific site. Do you need to be in a high-traffic (vehicular or pedestrian) area? Do you expect walk-in trade? Does the staff work primarily in the office or elsewhere? Should you be in a free-standing building or a shopping center, mall or office building? To capture your target market you must consider its needs and buying habits.

Office and sign visibility are important if you expect the public to visit your office. A free-standing building may provide visibility, greatest flexibility for growth and, perhaps, ownership if you are interested in purchasing an office site. Depending on where the available space is located, shopping centers, malls or office buildings may or may not offer the visibility you need. Your signage can get lost among that of other merchants or tenants. In any case, a site that is easy to spot and get to through traffic may be just as satisfactory as one that is on the main road.

Unfortunately, when we're office shopping, most of us don't see the same things that a customer sees, particularly if we're familiar with the area. There's nothing so frustrating as a barrier in the middle of a four-lane highway that precludes access from the opposite side of the road. But if you rarely travel that route, this may not occur to you until it's too late. Anticipate how your customers will get to you from a variety of directions. If you are in a rather out-of-the-way location, consider whether you can provide adequate directions so that a person unfamiliar with the area can find you.

How important is parking? Even if you are a commercial broker in a central business district, customers will be frustrated if they can't locate parking easily. Suburban sites, especially in malls and office complexes, can be equally frustrating. Before you sign a lease or purchase a building, visit the site at various times of day and on different days of the week. You need adequate space for both customers and staff. If parking is limited, you may become a parking lot attendant trying to keep spaces intended for customers free from salespeople who "just stop by for a minute" and take those spaces.

If you're shopping for a branch office site, consider the value of your name recognition in the area. If you stray too far from where you're known, you have to anticipate greater marketing and advertising costs. (Don't expect salespeople to bear the entire cost of self-promotion when you relocate them to a new office.)

Size

While you're shopping for sites, consider the amount of floor space you need. We'll address the physical layout shortly, but for the moment consider the number of salespeople and support staff you'll be supervising, the number of salespeople for whom you intend to provide work space and the activities that must be accommodated in the office.

Trends in today's work environments greatly affect the size of an office. Because of technology such as laptop computers, cellular telephones, beepers, facsimile machines, electronic mail and computer networks, people can work virtually anywhere.

This is known today as a **virtual office,** meaning that the office exists anywhere people can use technology. An increasing number of people are taking advantage of the convenience and efficiency by working primarily from their homes, that is **home officing.** Using today's communications systems they can telecommute with nearly anyone, including your real estate office. Ultimately, the amount of work space a company provides for workers in an office is greatly reduced.

A real estate sales office today is primarily an information and support center. As such, it must accommodate management and support staff and office and telecommunications equipment. Only minimal desk space is needed for the salespeople if a number of them are home officing. For them your office is their official place of business, in accord with licensing requirements, and primarily a place for meeting with customers and clients. Attractive and comfortable conference rooms become a priority.

The amount of office space you need and the costs increase when you provide a working headquarters for the sales staff. A rule of thumb is approximately 100 square feet of floor space per salesperson. Of course this will vary depending on how you configure the space. Partitioning single offices will require more space than an open or bull-pen arrangement.

By calculating desk cost you can see how many salespeople you need to cover the anticipated overhead plus make a profit. Keep in mind, though, that increasing the number of salespeople to reduce desk cost creates other situations. One manager will have a difficult time supervising more than 30 salespeople, regardless of whether the primary work site is the office or the home. Also, the size of the support staff will have to increase to serve a larger sales staff.

Use the checklist in Table 6.1 to identify which areas are essential for your operation and those that are desirable or optional. Don't overlook the importance of public areas such as reception areas, conference rooms, restroom facilities and refreshment centers. These contribute greatly to your company's image. Think about how the "back office" space for staff, equipment and supplies will contribute to the efficiency of your operation.

TABLE 6.1   Space Area Checklist

	Essential	Desirable	Optional
Reception Area			
Customer			
Receptionist			
Display Area			
Desk Space			
Management			
Salespeople			
Personal Assistants			
Secretarial			
Accounting/Bookkeeping			
Advertising/Promotions			
Research/Data Collection			
Others			
Work/Equipment Area(s)			
Computer(s)			
Fax Machine(s)			
Copy/Duplicating			
Telecommunications			
Conference Area(s)			
Filing			
Storage			
Office Supplies			
Signs, Promotional Materials, etc.			
Records			
Coat Closets			
Rest Room(s)			
Coffee Bar/Kitchen			
Training/Audiovisual			
Library			
Children's Play Area			

Consider where you will conduct training programs and sales meetings. You need an atmosphere that is free of distractions, which means that the salespeople's desk area is not appropriate. You also need the electronic capability to incorporate audio and video conferencing and satellite delivery in your programs. Renting outside facilities as needed may be more cost-efficient than setting aside space that will be used infrequently.

Unless you are skilled in designing offices, consider using the services of a professional. A space planner can help you select the most efficient and cost-effective space. This person also has the design expertise to help build flexibility into a space, identifying areas that can be used for multiple purposes and providing for future staffing and equipment needs. Frequently the person from whom you're leasing or purchasing an office has a professional who can help you.

Legal issues.   Before you settle on an office site, there are several legal issues to consider. The first is your state's licensing law. It may specify requirements for an office. In most jurisdictions, even if the requirements are minimal, you still must have the facility inspected before you can conduct business from that location. Also investigate local zoning ordinances. Be sure that your intended use does not violate these ordinances. Obtain any necessary occupancy permits or certificates of occupancy.

Another law to consider is the Americans with Disabilities Act (ADA). Because you are offering services to the public, the office (regardless of whether you own or lease) must be accessible to people with disabilities. Or you must provide accommodations that will enable a person with a disability to access your company's services. As an employer you also have certain obligations under ADA. Consider ADA before you select your office space rather than after you move in. Some sites may be readily accessible; others may require considerable retrofitting, which can be quite costly. Engage the services of an architect or someone versed in the law to review the facility and recommend the most suitable ways to comply with ADA.

Structural barriers pose the greatest challenge. Accessibility can be accomplished by either modifying the existing premises or by providing other accommodations to ensure equal access to your services. ADA provides alternatives that are acceptable in the event that making certain alterations poses an undue hardship. For example, if the installation of a handicap-accessible door is an undue hardship, the installation of a call button at a suitable height for a person using a wheelchair would be acceptable. If you customarily provide client and customer access to rest rooms, refreshments and other comforts in your office, you must do likewise for people with disabilities. (See Chapter 14 for more information on ADA.)

Design and Decor

Your next task is to design and decorate the office space–from the entry door to the back door. Figures 6.1 and 6.2 give you some ideas with which to begin designing a floor plan. Table 6.2 provides a checklist of things to consider as you remodel or decorate and furnish the office. Again, the help of a space planner or designer is valuable. Some companies use similar floor plans and decor, including the company's signature color scheme, in all of their offices. This reinforces their image and provides added efficiency for people who have occasion to work in several offices. The design of the office should provide both the public and the people who work for you with maximum comfort and convenience.

Public areas.   The reception area is the first place people see, and is often where they form their first impression of your firm. The atmosphere should be calm and inviting and reflect the professional image of your company. Provide a work area for a receptionist and a comfortable sitting area for visitors, stocked with informative or promotional material. Some companies use video displays to entertain waiting customers. And don't overlook what people hear as they enter your place of business. A paging system that echoes throughout the office may be useful, but it destroys the atmosphere you want to create for your visitors.

Conference rooms are as important as the reception area for showcasing your firm. They should be designed to serve customers with minimum distraction and maximum comfort.

FIGURE 6.1   Sample Office Arrangement

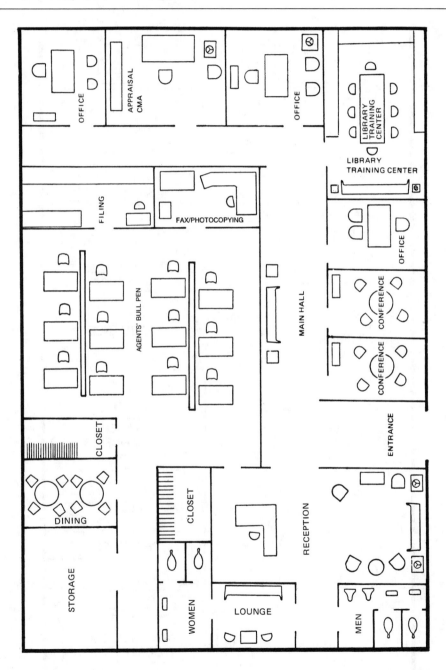

FIGURE 6.2 Additional Office Layout

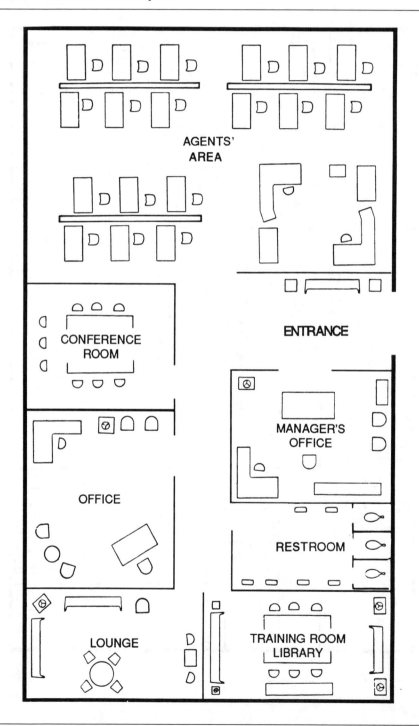

TABLE 6.2   Remodeling, Decorating and Furnishing Checklist

Carpentry
Partitions, Paneling, Shelving, Doors
Electrical Service
Lighting and Switches, Outlets for Equipment
Painting and Wallpaper
Walls, Ceilings, Moldings
Plumbing
Rest Rooms, Kitchen
Heating and Air Conditioning
Communications
Telephones, Fax Machines, Modems
Floor Coverings
Carpeting, Tile
Window Coverings
Blinds, Drapes
Furnishings
Desks and Chairs
Vinyl Floor Mats
Credenzas and Filing Cabinets
Typewriter and Computer Stands
Conference Room Chairs and Tables
Reception Area Seating and Receptionist Unit
Pictures, Plaques, Clocks and Bulletin Boards
Lamps and Wastebaskets
Workroom Table/Counter, Supply Cabinet

Salespeople should not entertain customers at their desks. You will commit a larger portion of the floor space to conference areas than to desk space if the majority of your salespeople work primarily at home. It's ideal if you have the financial resources to equip conference rooms with items like telephones, computers and video facilities. This maximizes efficiency for both the sales staff and a person conducting a closing or settlement.

While you are planning the decor, think about wear and tear and maintenance. Very cheap could be very expensive in the long run. If carpeting, paint, wall coverings and upholstery can't withstand use, abuse and repeated cleaning, you will be replacing or refurbishing long before you planned. Think about safety as well. You can't afford to have people fall on slick or wet floors or trip on mats or torn carpeting. The beautiful tiled entry, for example, can lead to catastrophe on a rainy day. Anticipate the worst weather, soil, spills and tears and plan accordingly.

Work areas.   The work areas should be separate from the public areas of the office. Areas used by the salespeople and support staff, such as the work or equipment room, supply areas and kitchen, should be easily accessed from their work stations. The sales support staff should be easily accessed by the salespeople, while the administrative support staff should be accessible to the broker or manager. The broker's and/or manager's office(s) should be private and accessible to both the staff and the public. Areas that are used by workers and customers, such as rest rooms, should be accessible by both without infringing on each other's space.

Mapping a floor plan for the office is easy compared to the decisions involved when designing desk space. The trend in design, even in the corporate world, is toward "open offices." These resemble the corral or bull pen arrangement that has commonly been used in the real estate industry. This design creates an environment that fosters teamwork and interaction because workers are less isolated. With virtual officing this is especially important because the entire staff is rarely in the office at the same time. With work-station partitions, the floor space can be configured efficiently and reconfigured as needs change.

Although the bull pen arrangement is not as innovative in our real estate offices as it is in other businesses, it is not without drawbacks. Salespeople may not think kindly about this arrangement if they've had negative experiences working in a communal environment in the past. The lack of privacy and the inability to protect business leads, client confidences (especially important if you permit designated agents) and personal belongings can foster problems rather than teamwork. Also, shared office space is a step down for top producers who see private offices as a status symbol.

When planning desk space, consider the work habits of the salespeople and challenges of managing the atmosphere in your office. Provide an inviting and efficient place for people to work, but don't spend lavishly on workspace that salespeople will rarely use. (Though an uncomfortable work environment should not be used to motivate people to get out of the office to work harder.) As you evaluate costs, consider how efficiently you can use floor space and the costs of investing in quality work station partitions as opposed to the costs to outfit separate offices.

Equipment and furnishings. Because today's offices are technology centers, the design of an office must accommodate a wide range of equipment. Later in this chapter we discuss communications and information systems. But we mention equipment at this point because you not only have to allocate space for the equipment, but also plan where it will be used. Telecommunications, computers and other office equipment require special wiring. It's also important to anticipate future needs so that you can build flexibility into the installation of utilities for these systems.

Furniture is available in a variety of qualities for a variety of prices. Often better quality, used furniture is available for less cost than new, inexpensive furniture. As you select furniture, also think about the office equipment you will be using. Small desks are less expensive, but they are unsatisfactory if most of the work surface is occupied by a large phone set and a computer. With the help of a professional designer, you can incorporate the efficient use of furnishings in imaginative ways, such as using lateral file cabinets for dividers, to create an appealing decor.

Security in the Office

A fact of life today is that no place is 100 percent secure from a determined intruder. But you must take steps to protect your facilities, your staff and your customers and clients. You may not see your office as a warehouse of salable equipment, nor that your office provides an accessible route through which a person can easily escape with that equipment. If a collection of keys to your listings (including the addresses!) is readily accessible to your staff, they also are readily accessible to anyone else. A professional security firm can audit your facilities and help you secure your property.

Beginning with the exterior of the building, make sure that the exterior, the parking lot and all entrances are well lighted. Trim shrubbery away from windows to eliminate hiding places. Windows should be double paned and double locked. Exterior doors should be metal or thick wood and have double-side keyed dead-bolt locks. Change the locks or alarm codes periodically to protect against lost keys and unauthorized entry. Don't overlook the roof; be sure that there are no hiding places or possible entry sites.

Protect your listings. Code the addresses on keys and lock them in a secure location. Keep track of lockboxes so that you know the properties on which they are installed. Lockboxes have improved considerably, making them less vulnerable to vandalism or unauthorized entry. Some have a system that tracks the entry each time the box is opened. Nevertheless, keys, key pads and combinations do fall into the hands of unauthorized people on occasion.

Establish security procedures to keep the staff out of harm's way. Protect salespeople in the field by using sign-out sheets and call-in systems so their whereabouts are known and a threatening encounter can be detected. Establish a code or warning system so that a person can summon help and alert others to danger. Identify a secure location in the office where personnel can go.

Plan an escape route so they can get out in case of a problem. Encourage salespeople to think about their personal safety as they schedule appointments. Also, caution them about the amount of personal information they distribute in their promotional materials.

Safety in the Office

Provide a safe environment for your staff and the public who does business with you. Their safety is not just a matter of legal liability, but is a practical consideration as well. Take steps to prevent accidents and minimize the likelihood of problems. Prepare to respond to a fire or medical emergency.

- As soon as you install phones, program them with emergency numbers and be sure everyone knows how to use them.

- Be sure you have smoke detectors installed in all the appropriate places. If you are in a building with a sprinkler system, be sure it works properly.

- Purchase a first-aid kit and fire extinguishers, particularly for the workroom. Instruct everyone about how these items are to be used so that they don't create more problems than they solve.

- Familiarize people with safety procedures. More injuries and loss of life occur when people ignore the alarms that were intended to protect them. Consider having fire and disaster drills. Don't overlook weather-related emergencies.

- Secure handrails. Clear walks and stairways of obstacles.

- Make certain the electrical service is adequate to accommodate the computers and other office equipment and appliances.

- Familiarize yourself with the labor laws in your state to be sure you comply with any safety requirements that are specified.

COMMUNICATIONS SYSTEMS

While you are provisioning your office to do business, consider the systems your company needs to communicate. Today's businesses can't function without telephones, fax machines and computer modems. Because the tools with which you communicate are so important, you need to make wise choices about the equipment and services your company will use.

Begin with the help of a consultant. Someone familiar with all of the available technology can analyze your needs and help you choose the most suitable, cost-effective and efficient systems. (Telecommunications and business equipment companies usually have consultants who can assist you.) The answers to several questions will guide your decisions. Do you need an office intercom or internal paging equipment? Is automatic dialing, audio or video conferencing or a hands-free speaker phone worth the expense? What about a diverter for evening or after-hours calls, or are you better off with an answering service or voice mail? How will the use of a computer affect your telephone lines? What future needs can you anticipate?

In many cases spending more initially will offer considerable savings in the long run. Inexpensive or used systems and equipment may be available. But if the technology is outdated or inappropriate for your needs, you could fall victim to the "penny-wise, pound-foolish" trap again. The following discussion includes some things to consider when making your decisions.

Voice Messaging

Call almost any place of business today and you will encounter a voice messaging system. Automated attendants field calls and direct you to the appropriate party or funnel your call to the party's mailbox. A call may be directed to a pager service, adding to the ways you can contact a person through the company's voice messaging system. If you're seeking information the company routinely disseminates, your call may be linked to a prerecorded outgoing message. As a last resort, you reach a human being with whom you can communicate.

Voice messaging systems have become popular because they are efficient.

- Directing phone traffic electronically relieves staff so time can be devoted to more urgent calls or more productive activities.

- Because many calls simply relay information or seek responses that require preparation, immediate human interaction is not necessary.

- "Telephone tag" can be minimized with messages to confirm dates for conversations.

- When calls are recorded in a mailbox, you eliminate problems with lost and inaccurate messages and phone numbers.

- Because only the intended receiver has access to a message, the confidences of the caller are protected (an important consideration when dealing with clients).

- These systems also eliminate the need for after-hour answering services.

From the callers' point of view, voice messaging systems can be frustrating. If they are accustomed to talking to a human being or they need immediate attention, these systems seem very impersonal. If calls are not returned more promptly or people are no more successful in reaching someone than before the automated system was installed, the systems do more harm than good. Workers are also more tempted to hide from the phone or to screen calls. You can minimize these problems by monitoring the callers' responses to your system or using a staff person to field incoming calls during business hours. Also, you can establish procedures to ensure that salespeople are responsive to their messages.

Several features can be incorporated in your voice messaging systems that are especially appealing for real estate companies. In a multioffice organization you can network all of your offices through one central message center. This eliminates the need for a person to make a number of calls to communicate with several offices. That's a great advantage in large metropolitan areas where toll calls could deter people from communicating with you. Audio-text features can be used to disseminate information. A caller can access information about a property simply by punching in the code number of a listing on a Touch-Tone phone. Or you could design the system to disseminate information about the real estate market, mortgage interest rates, your company or a career in real estate.

Facsimile Machines

A facsimile machine is as much a necessity as a telephone in today's office. It's faster, easier and cheaper to fax documents than to send them through the mail. With the wide range of computer software available, cover sheets can be designed to make your faxes look as professional as your letterhead. Because a fax is a print rather than voice transmission, you can be sure that a message is communicated exactly as you intend. Plain-paper fax machines are more cost-efficient because, although they are slightly more expensive to purchase than thermal-paper machines, they eliminate the added time and expense of photo-copying thermal-paper faxes.

Combining fax technology with other systems increases your ability to communicate electronically and satisfy the consumers' quest for instant information. By using a fax modem with your computer, you can send documents prepared in or scanned into your computer. (Depending on your computer software, however, this may not replace a stand-alone machine for receiving incoming faxes.) By linking your voice messaging system with your computer you can set up a "fax-back" system. Callers can access descriptions of listings and other information, such as floor plans and photos, by punching in a code on a Touch-Tone phone. Your computer then faxes the requested information to the caller's fax machine.

You may also consider purchasing multifunction machines. Combining telephone, fax modem, computer printers and scanners into one machine takes up less equipment space and efficiently links communications through one unit. This may be a more cost-efficient expenditure than purchasing separate pieces of equipment. The trade-off, however, may be that one of the functions may not produce the same quality product as its single-function counterpart.

Because faxes and modems use telephone lines, you can achieve some cost efficiencies by installing separate, no-frill lines that are dedicated for their use (unless they are linked to your voice messaging system). Call forwarding, call waiting, multiple numbers and other phone services are not necessary. You can also reduce costs by purchasing a rapid transmission modem, which minimizes "line time."

E-mail and the Internet

Communicating in cyberspace has become as critical in business as communicating by phone or fax. In fact, because people are spending an increasing amount of time at their computers, e-mail and the Internet are often preferred over the telephone. People can access information and communicate on their own time, which is a great convenience considering people's varied and hectic schedules. Often communications do not require interaction between the sender and receiver, for the same reasons we mentioned about voice messaging. If you do care to interact, many of the online Internet service providers offer the ability to chat in real time.

E-mail addresses are as important as phone numbers. Often e-mail is used for the same messaging purposes–simple communiqués, requests for information, or setting times for meetings or phone conversations. E-mail is a useful tool for communicating with your staff by eliminating paper memos and posted notices that often get lost or ignored. If your software permits, you can import documents from other computer programs to your e-mail account to distribute more lengthy communications. Assemble a list of your customers' and clients' e-mail addresses and you can distribute broad-based messages, informing them about market trends, a new service or an upcoming seminar.

Just as customers and clients have discovered the wealth of information they can access through their online service providers and the Internet, real estate companies have discovered the value of establishing their presence there too. It's not uncommon for salespeople to establish their own home pages on the Internet as well. The promotional information you commonly distributed in print can be shared on a Web site. We'll discuss in later chapters how you can integrate the Internet into your promotion and marketing programs and explore some of the legal and procedural issues you must consider.

To get into cyberspace you need a computer with a modem, a telephone line and the appropriate software. You can access the Internet through online service providers, such as America On-line, CompuServe or Microsoft Network, who have assembled their own content in addition to that which you can access on the Internet. Or you can access the Internet more directly through Internet Service Providers (ISPs). In either case you can establish an e-mail account. There are also independent e-mail programs that can be used separately from either an online service or ISP.

The costs, features, ease of use, time to navigate and state of the technology are all considerations when choosing a path to the Internet. Often people find the online services easier to use, especially as novices, and are attracted to the proprietary content and additional features the services provide. Many resources, including your Internet-savvy friends and professional computer advisors, are available to help you learn about the Internet and the options and opportunities that are available.

Communicating with People Who Are Deaf

People who are deaf or hearing-impaired need to be able to access your services as well as communicate during the transaction of business. Their first challenge is trying to communicate with your office. Text Telephones (TTs), formerly known as TDDs, are typewriter-like units that display conversation on a screen that can be read. TTs "talk" to other text telephones or computers. If there is sufficient need to warrant installing a TT in one or more of your offices, you are encouraged to do so. Otherwise you need alternative ways for people to contact you. Your local phone company may have a service that can be used, or a local organization that serves this population can provide suggestions.

You also need to provide accommodations that a person who is hearing-impaired might request during a transaction. (See ADA in Chapter 14.) This normally requires the use of oral or sign language interpreters. Again, consult a local organization that services this population for assistance.

Communicating with People Who Are Blind

People who are blind or have limited vision need to be able to not only evaluate the property but also to review the written documents that are used. They rely on auditory and tactile communications. Numerous options are available, particularly because of technology. Large-print or raised-print publications can easily be provided with the aid of today's computer and copier technology. Our real estate documents can be converted to audiocassettes to provide an easy way for people to review contracts and other materials before signing them. A local organization that services this population can help you provide accommodations.

Multilingual Communications

People of all cultures and language need to be able to access your services as well as communicate during a transaction. As we mentioned in Chapter 2, this is increasingly important because our population is becoming more culturally diverse. Be prepared to provide accommodations for people for whom English is not the first language. Someone on your staff may have proficiency in another language, or perhaps you can find translators at a local college or university. Multilingual materials can also be accessed on the Internet. If you plan to promote your services to the international population, be sure that you do so according to the fair housing laws. (See Chapter 14 for further information.)

INFORMATION SYSTEMS

Today's offices are information centers. This means that companies must find ways to assemble, manage, retrieve and store a vast amount of data. Because of today's technology, information management is easier and more efficient than in the past. Although we've heard predictions that electronic data management would eliminate paper in our offices, we've not yet reached that point. However, there are those who suggest that we are rapidly approaching a time even when printed forms will no longer be used in our real estate transactions.

Information is a powerful tool for managing your company and serving consumers. Using the wide variety of software that is available, you can analyze financial data and business activity. You can expedite communications and the dissemination of information. The possibilities for enhancing your operations are limited only by the technology that is available. And that is probably more plentiful than you imagine. The more familiar you become with computerized information systems, the more you will depend on them.

Computerization

Most residential real estate offices who are members of MLSs were introduced to electronic information systems when MLS data was converted from the cumbersome print-and-paper format to computers. Although many brokers for years would not embrace technology beyond that point, attitudes have changed. Today, according to the 1997 National Association of REALTORS® profile of real estate firms, 94 percent use computer technology in some facet of their operations.

Obviously, today's firms have computerized their operations in some fashion. Perhaps there are advantages that had not occurred to you. Or perhaps you have experienced some of the glitches that are inherent in the use of technology. Shortly we will explore software and hardware options in greater detail. But for the moment our point is to discuss some basic issues to consider when computerizing your organization.

Storage and retrieval. Offices are overrun with paper. This problem only gets worse after you've been in business for awhile, even to the point of costing you money to store years' worth of paper. Computerization provides more efficient filing, storage and retrieval. Address files can be stored in the computer rather than sitting on desks. Memos and messages can be stored and retrieved in the computer. Quarterly financial statements don't have to be filed because they can be accessed in the computer. There's no need to make a paper copy of a letter; it's stored in the computer. Data is not only accessible but it's also portable, which is especially important for today's mobile work force.

Networking. Perhaps one of the greatest advantages of computerization is the ability of the users to connect to data. This is a critical feature, considering the mobility of today's workforce and the number of business units operating from various sites in many firms. A number of options for networking can be considered. Perhaps you are interested in providing telecommuting access to a limited range of data. Or you can interconnect all of your offices to one central database. Again, a consultant can introduce you to the range of options and help select the hardware and software needed to support your choice.

Protecting data. Computers are not infallible. As advantageous as it is to store all the company's data and documents on a computer, you can be temporarily out of business if something happens to the hardware or the software. An essential element of any computerized information system is a plan for routinely backing up or preserving data. This can be done on disk or tape so there's no need to add to your paper files.

Y2K problem. At the risk of dating our discussion, we mention the Y2K problem. Hopefully, you're not reading this while your business is paralyzed by computers that think the year is 1900 rather than 2000 or later. The problem arises when software and internal hardware configurations aren't programmed to recognize four-digit field codes for dates. Consequently, two-digit fields can't distinguish "00" as being 1900 or 2000. Your system must be programmed for the new millennium so that you can continue to function.

Also, you must look outside the organization. Everyone with whom you come in contact must have protected their systems as well. Otherwise, you could be in business but be immobilized because a funder can't distribute money, a supplier can't process or ship an order, or a title company can't access records to prepare for settlement. You may also find that the computer-operated heating and air conditioning system in your office shuts down.

Technical support. You'll see in Chapter 7, when we develop the general operating budget, that we budget for a computer consultant. Unless you're a computer junkie, these people can spare you enormous headaches in the long run. They can help you select the hardware (the equipment) and the software (the computer programs) that suit your needs and level of computer expertise. A consultant can also help you set up procedures to manage your system and protect data. Ongoing support to help unravel the inevitable software or hardware glitches is essential. Depending on the size of your organization, you may also consider providing an in-house computer support person to the users of your systems.

Software

It is best to select your software before making a decision about the hardware. That way you can be sure that the hardware you select is appropriate for the software you intend to run. Although you can have software designed specifically for you, this is rarely cost-efficient for a small operation. You could wind up with a program that is friendly only to the designer.

The good news is that with the wide variety of available software, even novices can enjoy the benefits of computerization. Your consultant can help evaluate your information management needs so that you select suitable software. Also talk to other users of software you are considering before you leap into a purchase. Sometimes they see products differently than an experienced computer person does. Also evaluate the technical support a software manufacturer offers. How readily accessible and affordable is it? The person who's responsible for using the software will greatly appreciate this resource.

TABLE 6.3   Computer Software Currently Used by Firm Size

			Size of Sales Force			
	All Firms	Five or less	6–10	11–20	21–50	More than 50
Accounting/ Payroll/ Financial	61%	56%	60%	69%	80%	90%
Communications	43	40	43	45	53	60
Property Management	26	25	26	25	33	30
Spreadsheets	51	49	49	53	54	67
Time Management	14	11	15	20	15	22
Graphics/ Presentation Software	40	30	43	55	60	77
Loan Analysis	36	28	41	45	49	52
Multiple Listing Software	77	69	81	90	93	95
Comparative Market Analysis	54	40	61	69	81	92
Contact Management	22	15	23	30	40	57
Desktop Publishing	43	36	45	50	63	75
Word Processing	89	88	91	90	95	95
Mapping Software/ Geographic Information Systems (GIS)	15	11	15	20	21	37
Other	23	25	20	25	20	20

SOURCE: *Profile of Real Estate Firms*, 1996, National Associaton of REALTORS®.

Table 6.3 shows the kinds of software being used in today's real estate firms. Note that the larger the organization, the more inclined they are to use various types of software applications.

Management software. The most obvious activities to computerize in your business are the accounting functions. But the data that is compiled for financial purposes can be used to perform a wide variety of other management functions as well. You could monitor transactions and pending closings; track listings about to expire; track business by region, office or salesperson; project cash flow for the coming months; and monitor the performance of salespeople at any given time. You can even track real estate trends in the area. When a property sells you can prepare, print and mail cards announcing the sale and promoting the salesperson and your company to homeowners in the neighborhood. Some programs offer as many as 38 assessments of your operation.

Task-specific and complete programs designed specifically for real estate brokerage operations are available (see Appendix A). You also could consider general software like spreadsheet, word processing, desktop publishing and money-manager programs to perform these functions.

Word-processing software. Unless all of the forms or contracts that you use are available for the computer, you still need a typewriter. But the computer offers so many more options and is far more efficient. The obvious advantage of word processing is that you can edit and correct a document before printing. In addition, you can do such things as design form letters, generate mailing lists, merge correspondence with mailing lists, prepare professional reports complete with charts and graphs, and prepare standard contract contingencies that the company will use.

A closely related but more sophisticated type of software to consider is a desktop publishing program. This offers additional options for preparing professional brochures, newsletters and fax cover sheets. Typically it has more powerful and sophisticated graphics capabilities than word-processing programs. If you have a staff person who can use a desktop publishing program to its best advantage, you can prepare many outstanding marketing and promotional tools in-house.

Transaction software. Don't overlook your customers and clients and the salespeople. Customers and clients thrive on information and salespeople need the tools to respond. The list of available options is lengthy, but consider how useful loan qualifying, comparative market analysis, mortgage analysis, contact management, transaction management, mapping or listing management programs can be. Although some of these are available from the more sophisticated MLSs, many more options are available in the growing software market.

Survey your salespeople to determine what software they want to use. Otherwise you'll make a purchase that takes up space on your computer and is never used. Make sure the software is user-friendly as well. And remember that these are copyrighted programs; don't risk violations by allowing salespeople to download them onto their personal computers. Establish clear policies about company-owned software being available for use only in-house.

Online software.   In the discussion about communications systems, we mentioned e-mail and the Internet. While these are important tools for communicating, they are also important for gathering information. You can access databases, newsgroups and other resources around the country. This information is useful for managing your business, including your planning activities, and for serving customers and clients.

In order to take advantage of the Internet, you need software. Many of the online services promote themselves by distributing disks or CDs, which include an introductory period of free connection time. Taking advantage of these offers is a relatively risk-free way to familiarize yourself with the services, especially because novices can use a lot of connect time just learning and exploring. To get beyond the on-line service's site, you also need an Internet browser, such as Netscape or Internet Explorer. This software may be included in your computer's operating system. Or it can be downloaded from an online service or installed separately.

Providing online access also introduces you to another aspect of your organization you have to manage–connection time and expenses. Each of the online services offers a number of membership plans. Consider the number of people in your company who will be users when determining the most suitable program. Because additional fees are charged for visiting premium sites and charges are incurred for ordering services or products online, you need rules for covering these expenses. Regarding telephone-line charges, most Internet services can be accessed via local or 800 phone numbers rather than long-distance numbers. However, you will incur costs on a business telephone line for usage. Connecting during off-peak hours and using the fastest modem available can minimize expenses.

Hardware

Once you decide what you want the computer to do and who the users will be, you can identify your hardware needs—the number of monitors and keyboards, the capacity of the central processing unit and the number of work stations that will be connected. A computer consultant can guide the selection of your hardware system and design its installation. Remember that both hardware and software are constantly improving so you need to select a system that can be upgraded. Even today's state-of-the-art hardware is likely to be outdated in three years.

Next, you go shopping. You may be able to locate used hardware, but purchasing a system that's two or three generations old could be another penny-wise, pound-foolish exercise. You may not be able to upgrade the system sufficiently to make the software you intend to use work efficiently, if at all. Because today's new hardware systems are considerably less expensive than they were several years ago, new hardware would be a wiser purchase. Where you buy is as important as what you buy. You need technical support as well as warranties, which are worth a few extra dollars. If support is available by phone, determine the hours of availability, whether an 800 phone number can be used and any charges for the service. And find out how busy the phone lines are.

Before you start wiring for computers, phones and duplicating equipment, be sure that you're satisfied with the office layout. Earlier we mentioned space planners. With their help you can move furniture around and determine the most efficient traffic flow for the comfort of the staff and the customers. Each time you rearrange furniture and work stations you have to move equipment, and that can be expensive. Be sure you don't have plugs and cables that people can trip over. That's liability you don't need.

CONCLUSION

The office site and equipment can be a significant part of your initial investment and operating budget. But you can help or hinder the image and efficiency of your business, depending on where you spend and scrimp. We tend to put money into things the public sees, beginning with the office, and that's not bad. But you also should look at the environment in which you expect people to work. It does not need to be a designer facility, but it does need to be efficient and comfortable.

Because the office design and the communications and information systems are interrelated, you need to do some planning before making an investment. As you select an office site that will help you in the marketplace and provide for safe and secure working conditions, consider how you will use technology to give you a competitive edge and make your office the communications and information center that the salespeople need to be most productive.

DISCUSSION EXERCISES

Critique a real estate office with which you are familiar, considering its general location, its site and its design or layout.

* * *

What communications and information systems do you consider to be essential for your business to run efficiently and effectively? Which are desirable and optional?

* * *

Outline the steps you would take to open a branch office.

7 Structuring Your Finances

If you are starting a business, how much money do you need? If you are developing a budget for the coming year, how can you project realistic income? What expenses should you anticipate?

Running a profitable business and at the same time remaining competitive is a major challenge for today's broker. Consumers are pressuring us to provide additional services; salespeople are doing so as well. This forces the broker to provide the latest in office technology and increased staff and administrative support. Communications and information systems, such as those discussed in the previous chapter, and staff support can be costly. It's difficult to quantify the amount these expenditures contribute to the production of revenue. However, they do contribute to the efficiency of the company and the salespeople, which is reflected in the bottom line and the company's ability to recruit salespeople.

Organizing or structuring your financial resources is one of management's most important activities. In the beginning you need start-up capital. Once you're up and running, you need to manage the revenue and expenses to make your operation profitable. A financial plan or budget sets goals for your financial management, just as the business plan sets goals for the organization. A budget also provides a mechanism with which you can monitor and control revenue and expenses throughout the year.

FINANCIAL RESOURCES

One of the reasons new businesses often fail is that they are undercapitalized. Drive and motivation or a desire to see your name on a business will help you succeed only to a point. Aspirations don't convert into hard cash, particularly when you're trying to convince a loan officer that you are a worthy businessperson.

As in other aspects of our discussions so far, we come back to planning. It's important to determine the amount of money you need to get started and then to plan a strategy for gathering these funds. A number of resources, such as accountants, lawyers and your business-savvy friends, can help with financial planning and assist in preparing documents needed to apply for a loan. You may also have a branch of the Service Core of Retired Executives (SCORE) in your area that can provide assistance.

Capital Requirements

How much money will you need to get started? Depending on how you've structured your organization and the affiliations and services you need to compete in the marketplace, the list will vary. The basic necessities include

- legal fees (establish the business);
- accounting fees (advice and setup books);
- telephones and installation;
- initial fees for affiliations (MLS, franchise, etc.) and professional associations;
- office space (deposit, remodeling);
- office equipment (computers, facsimile machines, duplicating equipment, desks, chairs, file cabinets, etc.);

- office supplies;

- graphics (logo, signs, stationery);

- promotion and advertising (initial entry into the market-place); and

- signage (office and yard signs).

Compare the total cost of these items with the amount of money you've saved plus the amount you can gather from other sources. Depending on how closely these figures are aligned, you could consider additional expenditures, such as an automobile, or you may have to find more cost-efficient ways to provide the basic necessities. As you comparison shop, you can determine whether renting or purchasing items such as office space, telephone systems or duplicating equipment is more feasible.

Your capital requirements must also include *at least* six months of monthly expenses to carry you, or more if the economy is slow. If you figure three months will elapse before the first transaction occurs plus two months for it to close, you cannot anticipate any income for five months. You need enough capital to cover operating losses for this period plus several months or more thereafter until income catches up with expenses. *Be conservative when estimating income and generous when estimating expenses.* Too often brokers are overly optimistic when estimating cash flow. (See "General Operating Budget" later in this chapter.)

Obtaining a Loan

Ideally, you've had time to work on a conscientious savings plan before you start or expand your business. Most likely, though, you will need other resources in addition to your savings. You could join forces with other brokers or find private investors, but you will probably also need to borrow money. From your days as a salesperson you should have a network of contacts with lenders. Granted, most of these involve mortgage lending. But in the banking world any connection is valuable for getting you networked with the person who can help finance your real estate operation. Other business owners also can make introductions. And don't overlook the Small Business Administration as a resource for funding a new venture.

Just as banks will not grant a mortgage loan without collateral and some evidence that it can be repaid, banks will not grant a business loan without similar guarantees. Because there's no collateral in a business that doesn't yet exist, you need some form of guarantee that you can repay a loan. Lenders are interested in financing only ventures that appear to be viable. You will need a professional loan application portfolio that provides the information lenders need to make this determination. The portfolio should be easy to read, concise and should stand out on the pile of other applications on a lender's desk.

The things that should be included in your application portfolio include the following:

- *a letter of introduction* that states the amount of money you want, what you want it for and who you are. All of this should be composed on one side of a single sheet of paper, in about three paragraphs. The following exhibits support your request.

- *a proposal* that itemizes how you plan to use the money you are requesting.

- *a personal financial statement* that lists your cash on hand, investments (including your personally owned real estate) and indebtedness (including mortgages on your real estate, credit cards, etc.) to show your total net worth. It also includes your gross annual income.

- *a business plan* that explains what you expect to accomplish by being in business.

- *a budget* that includes both income and expense projections (which we will discuss shortly), as well as the capital requirements previously discussed.

- *a personal résumé* that includes your education, work experience and qualifications for embarking on your business venture.

- *recommendations* that list individuals (including contact information) who can vouch for your abilities and credit-worthiness.

GENERAL OPERATING BUDGET

Preparing a budget is an essential management function, regardless of whether you're just starting out or are preparing for the coming year. Most salespeople have had the experience of living from commission check to commission check, hoping that the income would cover the bills at the end of the month. But you can't run your business on hope. While there are a few isolated success stories of companies who succeed without budgets, many more fail because of a lack of financial planning.

A general operating budget is a road map for directing the financial resources to support your business plan. It is a forecast of anticipated income and expenses, normally for a one-year time frame. If you evaluate the marketplace and the abilities of the salespeople carefully, the income projections should be fairly realistic and attainable. In planning your expenses you need to find the most cost-effective way to run the business. But as we've mentioned in previous chapters, the least costly expenditures may not give you the best value for the dollar in the long run.

Gross Income

Begin preparing the budget by estimating gross income. Consider the following as possible sources of income.

- *Commissions*—This will likely be the most substantial source of income, including both commissions that are generated by your salespeople and those received from cooperating brokers. If you have unbundled your services, offering a menu of services from which a client or customer can choose, the income will be calculated on a fee-for-service basis.

- *Additional services your firm offers*—These could include fees for activities such as appraising or property management.

Depending on your operating structure, you may generate income from referral fees to other business units providing services like insurance, title or escrow and mortgage lending. (Fees generated from these sources must be structured in accordance with all applicable laws.)

- *Transaction fees*–These are charges, assessed per transaction, to cover administrative functions associated with each sales transaction. Although these fees have been controversial, they are one of the ways brokers have recently attempted to increase their profitability. Their justification is that these fees are necessary to cover increasing costs, especially to cover salaries of support staff.

Unless your income projections are realistic, your budget will not be a useful guide. In Chapter 3 we presented calculations with which to evaluate the company's sales activity in comparison to the total sales activity in the marketplace. Our purpose was to identify reasonable production goals for the business plan. These goals now can be used to forecast gross income. Multiplying the average sale price of a home by the number of transactions gives you gross sales volume. Be realistic about the average price and number of transactions you project so that the projected gross sales volume will be realistic. Finally, calculate the income you expect to earn on the gross sales volume.

Before making this final calculation, the broker must determine policies regarding compensation. The company could charge a percentage of the price of a transaction. Or the company could be compensated on some type of a fee-for-service basis, which could be an hourly rate, a flat fee or fees for individual services. Keep in mind the antitrust implications involved when making these decisions. (See Chapter 14 for a discussion of antitrust laws.) Even when the broker decides to base compensation on a percentage of the price of a transaction, this calculation is not as straightforward as it appears. Different rates may be charged according to the type of property, the total value of a transaction or concessions the company may make in certain circumstances. All of these issues must be considered when forecasting transaction-based income.

Fee-for-service. Some brokers, particularly those with sophisticated specialties or buyer/tenant representation, favor fee-for-service pricing. Because other professionals sell their time and expertise, the notion is that real estate licensees should, too. These charges are normally hourly or contingency fees, though these decisions are the broker's to make. When charging by the hour, you could cap the amount charged for a month's service. With contingency fees, you could collect a specified amount when an agency agreement is signed. Then include a performance clause that requires the return of this initial fee if the company is unable to perform the stated service within a certain time period. In addition, you may charge for expenses. If you're intrigued with this method of compensation, check your state's licensing laws to be sure that a licensee is not prohibited from charging an advance fee or being reimbursed for expenses.

Consumers pressing real estate companies to unbundle their services so they can select only those which they feel they need adds another dimension to fee-for-service pricing. Brokers will be challenged to determine suitable fees for each of their services or perhaps offer attractive prices for packages of services. Because consumers expect fee-for-service pricing to be more cost-effective for them, brokers will be expected to charge realistic prices. The brokers who blaze the trail into this venture will have an additional challenge: forecasting income without a track record or historical data to guide their projections. Transaction fees, which we mentioned earlier, are just the beginning of the fee-for-service trend. However, these fees are typically charged in addition to, rather than instead of, commission.

Operating Expenses

The gross income forecast at this point is not the actual amount of money the company can use for its operations. You frequently hear the term *company dollar.* This is the amount remaining from gross income after the cost of sales has been deducted. The cost of sales includes

- the commissions paid to your salespeople and other brokers cooperating in the transactions;

- overrides paid to the manager; and

- sales fees, such as MLS, franchise and referral or relocation fees.

Even if the broker does not draw commissions but keeps them in the business account, they should be deducted for the purpose of calculating the company dollar. The theory behind this calculation is that the cost of sales is inescapable, so this is not money you have for operating expenses. By taking this cost off the top, you know exactly what's left with which to run the business.

While the company dollar approach has been the common accounting procedure used in the real estate industry, more companies now are using the **income statement**. This is otherwise known as the *profit-and-loss* statement. (See Figure 7.1 for a sample form.) The cost of sales appears on the statement as an operating expense because that's, in fact, what it is.

Operating expenses fall into two categories: *fixed expenses*, such as rent, dues and fees, salaries, taxes and license fees, insurance and depreciation (funding for depreciation on equipment, buildings and automobiles the company owns); and *variable expenses*, such as advertising and promotion, utilities, equipment and supplies, and cost of sales. It's easy to forecast fixed expenses because these are already known. The variable expenses are more difficult to forecast and also require the most management to control.

Cost of sales, being a *variable* expense, fluctuates according to the volume of production (the number or amount of sales); the number of transactions that are attributed to each individual salesperson and their commission splits; the number of transactions that involve cooperating brokers; and the number of transactions in which other sales costs, such as referral, relocation fees and MLS fees, are incurred. Cost of sales can be controlled with the compensation arrangements you make with the salespeople, managers and cooperating brokers and by increasing

FIGURE 7.1   Income and Operating Expense Budget

GROSS INCOME

Commissions on in-house sales	$_____
Commission received from cooperating transactions	$_____
Referral fees	$_____
Other fees for service	$_____
Total Gross Income	$_____

GENERAL OPERATING EXPENSES

Commissions paid to salespeople	$_____
Commissions paid to cooperating brokers	$_____
Overrides paid to managers	$_____
Relocation and referral fees	$_____
MLS fees	$_____
Franchise fees	$_____
Other	$_____
Total Cost of Sales	$_____
Marketing and advertising consultant	$_____
Classified advertising	$_____
Institutional advertising	$_____
Direct mail	$_____
Brochures	$_____
Television/radio	$_____
Signs	$_____
Telephone directories	$_____
Other	$_____
Total Marketing and Advertising	$_____
Rent	$_____
Utilities	$_____
Janitorial services	$_____
Trash/recycling removal	$_____
Other	$_____

[handwritten note: allocating this as an expense item is different than from the "company dollar" approach]

FIGURE 7.1 Income and Operating Expense Budget *(Continued)*

Total Occupancy		$__________
Equipment maintenance/supplies	$__________	
Office supplies	$__________	
Postage and overnight delivery	$__________	
Packaging and shipping	$__________	
Bulk mail permits	$__________	
Printing	$__________	
Lock boxes	$__________	
Kitchen/beverage	$__________	
Other	$__________	
Total Equipment and Supplies		$__________
Professional dues	$__________	
Membership fees	$__________	
Subscriptions	$__________	
Total Dues and Publications		$__________
Accounting services	$__________	
Legal services	$__________	
Computer consultant *14 YR. OLD*	$__________	
Communications services	$__________	
Telephone *4-5 PEOPLE $1000/MO.*	$__________	
Paging services	$__________	
Computer information networks	$__________	
Insurance	$__________	
Comprehensive business policy	$__________	
Workers' compensation	$__________	
Errors and omissions	$__________	
Credit bureau	$__________	
Total Services and Fees		$__________
Managerial salaries	$__________	
Secretarial and clerical salaries	$__________	

CONSIDER $50-100/MO. CREDIT TO AGENT FOR CELL PHONES FOR LOCAL CALLS OR LONG DISTANT

GOOD SECRETARY IS WORTH $35,000/YR.

FIGURE 7.1   Income and Operating Expense Budget (Continued)

Other	$_____	
Fringe benefits	$_____	
Total Salaries		$_____
Real estate licenses	$_____	
Business licenses	$_____	
Taxes *Cr. for Business Privilege Taxes*	$_____	
Income taxes	$_____	
Social security	$_____	
Unemployment	$_____	
Other	$_____	
Total Taxes and Licenses		$_____
Awards	$_____	
Incentive programs and contests	$_____	
Education	$_____	
Conferences and conventions	$_____	
Travel and entertainment	$_____	
Auto expenses *Sometimes Better for Co. to own Car*	$_____	
Petty cash	$_____	
Other	$_____	
Total Miscellaneous		$_____
Interest on loans *If Handling Escrow Acc't Ask for Waiver of Bank Fees, etc.*	$_____	
Bank account charges	$_____	
Total Bank Charges		$_____
Total Operating Expenses		$_____
NET INCOME		
Total Gross Income	$_____	
Less Total Operating Expenses	$_____	
NET INCOME		$_____

production in transactions for which the company incurs less cost.

Because each company's business plan is different, your other operating expenses will reflect expenditures needed to implement your plan. Although the way these expenses are categorized may differ from our examples, depending on your accountant's design or that of your computer software, typical expenses for which you should budget are described below.

Marketing and advertising expenses.   These include costs to develop marketing and advertising strategies and design the materials. Costs also include the placement or distribution of classified, institutional, listing and recruiting advertising and signs (for sale, sold and open house); advertising on television and/or radio; and listings in telephone directories.

Occupancy.   These are your housing costs, which include rent, utilities, janitorial services and trash/recycling removal. Depending on the terms of your lease, some of these expenses may be included in your rent. If you own your building, you need to budget for the mortgage payment, even though it is not considered a pure expense.

Equipment and supplies.   These include the rental or maintenance of, as well as the purchase of supplies for, equipment such as typewriters, computers, duplicating equipment, fax machines and audiovisual aids. This category also includes postage (including overnight delivery service) and packaging, shipping, bulk-mail permits, printing, office supplies, lockboxes and kitchen and restroom supplies.

Dues and publications.   These include the broker's and the company's dues in professional and industry organizations and MLS and franchise fees; subscriptions for directories, newspapers and magazines; and other dues for organizations such as the credit bureau and chamber of commerce.

Services and fees.   These expenses include accounting and bookkeeping services, insurance (comprehensive business policy, workers' compensation and errors and omissions policies), legal services, credit reports, computer consultant and communications services, including basic, local and long-distance telephone service, fax and computer lines, Internet services and paging services.

Salaries. These are salaries for the broker (unless the broker doesn't take one), managers, secretarial and clerical personnel, and other employees, including the training director, relocation director and transaction coordinator. Also included are employee-related costs such as medical and dental insurance and other fringe benefits.

Taxes and licenses. This includes real estate licenses for the broker and the company; business licenses; and taxes, including payroll taxes (income taxes, social security and unemployment taxes).

Miscellaneous expenses. These include awards, incentives and contests, education, conferences and conventions, travel and entertainment, auto expenses and petty cash.

Bank charges. This includes payments on debt and service charges on bank accounts.

Transaction expenses. These are the costs of sales that were previously mentioned, including commissions paid to your salespeople and other brokers; overrides for the managers and various service fees, such as relocation and referral fees; and expenditures the broker may make to assist a transaction to settlement, such as minor repairs or the purchase of an appliance.

Repairs and replacements. These include the repair and replacement of equipment you own, which are expenses that must be budgeted for even though, in strict accounting terms, they are asset expenditures that are depreciated. (Consider the inconvenience if the copy machine breaks down and you can't pay the repair bill.)

Reserve for contingencies. This is an amount you set aside for unexpected expenses or opportunities that present themselves during the year. A budget is only an estimate or a financial road map. Regardless of how carefully you forecast income and expenses, there can be detours. An actual expenditure could exceed the budgeted amount, without an offsetting amount in another item to keep the budget balanced. It's tempting to eliminate the reserve line in the budget. But unless you've already funded a substantial reserve account to carry you through the unexpected or hard times, you can't afford to overlook this item. When you have the greatest need is often also when you have the least resources.

Net Income

After projecting the income and deducting the anticipated expenses, the difference is your anticipated net income for the year. This can be a sobering moment if you discover there's no profit. Or worse, there's a deficit, especially if there's no salary or commission allocated for the broker/owner. Maybe the net income does not look as substantial as you would like, which could mean delaying or eliminating a major expenditure you were planning. Before you adopt the budget, reevaluate the projections to see if there are better ways to allocate your financial resources.

You can do a number of things to improve the net income. You can minimize certain expenses if the salespeople share in some of those expenditures. In advertising, for example, your salespeople could purchase signs or pay a sign fee; pay some of the costs to advertise their listings; or, if you sponsor a TV listing program or use cable TV advertising, pay a fee to have their listings promoted in this media. You could charge the salespeople for the use of the copier, office supplies, promotional brochures or coffee. They could pay some of the postage, overnight delivery or telephone or fax costs. Or they can pay some of the franchise or MLS fees.

Any of these options could improve your budget, but they could also have a negative effect on your ability to attract or retain salespeople. Unless you charge them a desk cost and pay them 100 percent commission, you could find that they resent being "nickel-and-dimed." This will be especially true if carried to extremes with each three-cent charge for an envelope, 50-cent charge for a cup of coffee, or a dollar to the secretary for typing a sales contract. Although it's common in most areas for salespeople to be responsible for some advertising, franchise, postage or brochure expenses, if your compensation and expense structure is seriously out of line with the competition, the salespeople will leave to work elsewhere.

Profit Centers

Certain aspects of the general operating budget can be budgeted in greater detail. This is similar to what you did in the planning function: you developed the business plan for the entire organization and then developed more detailed plans at lower levels in the organization. Each work unit, such as a department or sales office, can be its own profit center. This means that each unit is charged with the responsibility for generating a portion of the net income in the general budget. An office or department must go through the same process that was used in developing the general operating budget. It forecasts the gross income and expenses to produce its share of the net income.

Variable Expense Budgets

Note that in a general operating budget specific categories of expenses are allocated for specific purposes (see Figure 7.1). To guide the use of these funds, variable expense budgets are needed to identify individual expenditures. For example, an amount is designated for marketing and advertising. To make the most efficient use of these dollars, it's necessary to decide how to allocate these funds among various marketing and advertising activities. In large firms it's not uncommon to delegate budgeting responsibility to the marketing director. This person becomes responsible for deciding the best way to use the funds allocated for marketing and advertising. These specific budgets provide a good tool with which to monitor your expenditures throughout the year, giving you greater control over your financial operation.

Monthly Operating Budgets

With your annual operating budget in hand, your next task is to give yourself benchmarks throughout the year. This can be done simply by dividing the anticipated gross income and operating expenses by twelve, giving you monthly projections. You can do the same with the specific budgets for variable expenses. As you monitor the income and production of your salespeople and review your expense ledgers at the end of each month, you can monitor the financial status of your organization every 30 days. Prudent financial management demands that you review income and expenses periodically throughout the year.

Because a budget is only a road map or a forecast, the *actual* monthly totals may be ahead on certain lines and behind on others, particularly because income and many expenses vary each month. Next month the numbers may shift. The most important things to monitor are the "bottom line" and net income and expenses that appear to be exceeding projections.

It's best not to change the budget during the year. You might feel better, but the status of the organization won't change just because you maneuvered figures on a piece of paper. Any expenses that seem to be getting out of control after three months should be evaluated (some may be seasonal), and damage-control measures should be planned. You may not decide to implement them as long as it appears that you are at a break-even point, that is, generating the minimum income necessary to cover the expenses. But at least you have a battle plan.

ACCOUNTING

Managing a company's financial data involves a variety of bookkeeping functions. Typically these include income and expense ledgers, accounts payable and accounts receivable ledgers, commission and payroll records, plus bank and escrow account statements. Because of the critical nature of this information, companies need specific procedures for collecting, posting, maintaining and verifying financial data. These procedures are needed to create an information database with which management can prudently monitor and control many aspects of a company's operation.

Once upon a time accounting or bookkeeping functions were labor intensive tasks. Today even the smallest brokerage company can streamline this operation with automation. However, automation is only a tool. Management is still accountable for the financial affairs of the organization. Financial data systems must be structured according to generally accepted accounting principles. In addition, many states' licensing laws provide very specific procedures that govern these functions.

Electronic Data Management

With the wealth of computer software that's available, it's possible to structure a financial database that provides meaningful management information. These programs set up the general ledgers, accounts payable, accounts receivable, payroll records, commission records, property management accounts and bank accounts. You can balance the books, issue checks and bill accounts at the same time. Your accountant can help you make wise selections of software that will suit your operation.

Automation saves staff time and provides more timely information. With a keystroke the bookkeeper can produce information about any aspect of your financial operation, rather than labor for several weeks to generate a report. Management and the accountant can access current information to review periodically. When it's time for a general audit of the company's books or to file taxes, the preparation can be done with minimal aggravation.

License Law Requirements

While you're wandering through the maze of available software, consider the requirements of your licensing laws when making a selection. Many states have very specific requirements relating to financial management, particularly the administration of escrow accounts. Separate accounts must be established for escrow money so that it is never commingled with the firm's general operating funds. In addition, the laws establish procedures for making deposits and withdrawals to escrow accounts. Because the proper management of escrow accounts is extremely important, be sure that your procedures comply with your state's laws.

The laws usually specify detailed record-keeping procedures. Certain information relating to a transaction must be posted with each deposit to the escrow account. In some states the manner in which bank statements for escrow accounts are reconciled is quite specific. Companies must also be prepared to produce records as required for inspections by regulatory agencies. (See Figure 7.2 for a sample trust/escrow ledger.)

Security Procedures

As grand as computers are, they can create problems unless you take steps to protect and preserve your data. This is especially important when your computer system is networked throughout the company. Only upper management and the accountant should be able to access information about the company's financial affairs. Fortunately, there are ways to limit access to certain computer functions to prevent tampering with data and guard against confidential information falling into the hands of unauthorized persons within the firm or of a competitor.

Unfortunately, anything of value can tempt unscrupulous people. You can hope that you've hired honest and trustworthy people, but real estate companies are not immune to internal theft or embezzlement. Internal controls are needed to ensure that escrow money, security deposits, rent checks or other funds relating to transactions, as well as general operating funds, are properly handled. Transaction monies should be tracked beginning at the time they are received by anyone, including a salesperson, to the time they are deposited and then disbursed. The fewer people who handle money, the fewer opportunities there are to divert funds. This is an argument in favor of centralizing these activities. The company should have zero tolerance

FIGURE 7.2   Trust/Escrow Ledger

TRUST/ESCROW LEDGER

Street Address	Town	County	State	Zip Code	❏ Sale ❏ Rental

Seller/Landlord	Purchaser/Tenant
Name _____	Name _____
Address_____	Address_____
City_____State ____ Zip_____	City_____State ____ Zip_____
Telephone (Home) _____ (Work)_____	Telephone (Home) _____ (Work)_____

Miscellaneous Comments

Date	Received from/on Behalf of or Paid to	Amount Received	Received By	Check No.	Amount Paid	Balance

for mishandling funds and develop specific termination policies for people who do.

Protect your company's assets as well. Prepare an inventory of equipment, listing locations and serial numbers. Also, develop security procedures to protect access to checkbooks and certain files. The company with whom you have your business insurance can advise about proper procedures. The goal is to protect your assets from the people who work for you, as well as from outsiders.

COMPENSATION MANAGEMENT

Managing the compensation of the people who work for you is one of a broker's most challenging tasks. People must be fairly compensated for their efforts and earn a decent living. Compensation programs must be affordable so companies can stay in business. More personnel in today's firms are wage or salaried workers. Consequently, brokers have to revise their approaches to compensation, which means structuring appropriate pay scales and planning for other costs associated with hiring employees as opposed to independent contractors.

Because salespeople have been demanding better compensation arrangements and more transaction support services, brokers have been watching their bottom lines shrink in the process. A survey by The National Association of REALTORS® research group in 1997 revealed that 37 percent of the reporting firms had financial losses; only 20 percent reported profit margins between zero and five percent, with 1.9 percent profit on gross revenue being typical. Increasing profitability while also attracting and retaining productive salespeople has become a balancing act.

When developing compensation programs, consider the following issues:

- *Parity with the competition*—The compensation programs offered by other real estate brokerage firms in the area impact your ability to recruit and retain personnel. This is especially true for the sales staff. Compensation should be commensurate with that paid by similar organizations to people working in similar classes of jobs.

- *The company's financial position*—Wages, salaries, benefit plans and costs of sales for transactions are major expenditures. Compensation programs must be competitive, but they also must be structured within the company's ability to pay. If a company is unable to stay in business, it won't matter how generously the firm plans to compensate people.

- *Internal equity*—People have to feel that they are being fairly compensated in relation to the work they and others do. Although a company can establish a variety of wage and salary scales, benefit plans and commission structures, people in similar classes of jobs must be compensated similarly.

Equity with the Competition

Each firm can structure its own individual compensation programs. However, the market or your competitors influence these decisions. Salespeople, especially, go comparison shopping. While *you* may think your compensation structure is fair, what's most important is that the *salespeople* think it's fair. If they don't, they grow resentful or feel taken for granted and start looking at your competitors who may offer a better deal. Although compensation is not the only reason salespeople leave, it does have a significant bearing on the their decisions.

The assumption in the industry has been that money is the greatest motivator to encourage production. The rationale behind commission programs is that because salespeople are being compensated for the work they do, they will be motivated to work harder to earn more money. The failure in this assumption is that money is not always the motivator we expect it to be. The salesperson who's embarked on a second career after retirement takes off to see the grandchildren after receiving the commission check. The person who is working for tuition money for a child's schooling turns to other activities once the tuition bill is paid. Obviously, there are aspects about work that are equally important as, or more so than, money.

Today, salespeople are demanding more from their brokers than attractive commission programs. They desire supportive services, technology and other benefits. A number of companies are now offering insurance, retirement or profit-sharing plans as well as generous commission structures to recruit salespeople. However, these programs can be costly. Unless the salespeople are employees, fringe benefit programs must be structured meticulously to preserve the independent contractor status. All of these issues affect your competitive position, but you must

TABLE 7.1 Compensation Structure of REALTORS®

	All* REALTORS®† %	Brokers/Broker Associates %	Sales Agents %
Percentage Commission Split	74	65	80
100% Commission	17	22	15
Straight Salary	2	2	2
Salary Plus Share of Profits	2	3	1
Commission Plus Share of Profits	3	6	2
Share of Profits Only	1	1	1
Mean Starting Percentage Commission Split	57	60	56
Median Starting Percentage Commission Split	55	60	50
Mean Year End Commission Split	63	68	61
Median Year End Commission Split	63	70	60

* Because of rounding error, columns may not add to 100%.
† REALTOR® identifies only those people who are members of the National Association of REALTORS®.

SOURCE: *An Executive's Guide to REALTORS®: NAR Membership Profile,* 1996, National Association of REALTORS®.

consider the benefits in relationship to the costs and how the company can realistically cover the increased expenses. Tables 7.1 and 7.2 provide some insight about trends in compensation and fringe benefit structures.

Commission programs. Companies today typically compensate salespeople on graduated rather than fixed commission splits. Graduated splits intend to increase the company's income by increasing productivity. Salespeople will be motivated to increase their production in order to earn a higher percentage of the commission. (Of course, this assumes that money is the motivator.) Newly licensed salespeople are likely to be offered a lower split until their production reaches a certain level. More experienced salespeople are likely to be offered higher graduated scales or even the option to pay a desk cost and receive 100 percent commission.

A staff comprised of a large number of more experienced or productive salespeople will stabilize revenue, but the cost of sales increases. On the other hand, a sales staff of less

TABLE 7.2   Fringe Benefits Offered by Real Estate Firms

			AGENTS IN FIRM			
	All Firms %	5 or less %	6–10 %	11–20 %	21–50 %	51+ %
Group Term Life						
Independent Contractor	2	2	1	0	2	2
Employed Licensees	3	3	1	3	4	12
Administrative Staff	5	3	4	5	6	17
Profit Sharing						
Independent Contractor	2	2	3	2	3	7
Employed Licensees	3	2	2	2	2	12
Administrative Staff	4	3	4	3	6	23
Pension Plan						
Independent Contractor	1	1	3	1	0	0
Employed Licensees	2	2	2	2	0	5
Administrative Staff	3	2	5	3	4	10
Health Insurance						
Independent Contractor	19	15	20	24	28	48
Employed Licensees	15	11	13	17	24	48
Administrative Staff	21	14	18	27	39	67
Errors and Omission Insurance						
All Sales Staff	62	45	73	83	88	95

SOURCE: *Profile of Real Estate Firms,* 1996, National Association of REALTORS®.

experienced people, whose commission splits are typically smaller, saves on the cost of sales. But production can suffer and ultimately threaten the company's financial position.

Some companies play numbers games with commission splits. They offer the salesperson an attractive percentage. But the company deducts a variety of expenses from the salesperson's share to recover some of its costs before actually paying that amount. On the surface it appears that the salesperson is benefiting, maybe doing better even than they would with a company's competitors. But in reality they are earning less. If you bait salespeople with attractive percentages and services to recruit them and then tack on numerous charges, you still can lose salespeople to the competition.

Internal Equity

Internal equity means that all people who work in the same class of jobs are compensated at the same pay scale. People with greater experience, productivity or responsibilities or who have specialized expertise are compensated at higher scales. Once the scales are determined, they must be applied uniformly to all persons within a class to achieve internal equity. Especially when dealing with employees, a lack of equity can raise questions about whether the company has adopted equal employment practices.

The internal commission or pay schedules should be published, which can be done in the company's policy and procedures manual. Secrecy and favoritism lead to feelings of deception, which also threatens management's credibility. Furthermore, management should not favor some salespeople over others with similar experience or production, nor should it bend the rules to recruit someone. The compensation of one salesperson must be commensurate with the pay that another salesperson with similar experience, production or working relationship receives. Salespeople who work primarily at home and do not use as many of the company's support services may get a different split. It's also possible to offer some compensation programs in only selected offices of the firm.

There are several other compensation plans to consider. Some are more commonly used in isolated situations; a few have fallen out of favor in recent years.

- *Provide a bonus plan.* In addition to a commission, the salesperson is paid a bonus based on his or her contribution to net income. If you're considering this arrangement, consult a lawyer to be sure that the way a bonus is structured doesn't violate the salesperson's independent contractor status.

- *Treat the salesperson as an employee and pay a salary.* This practice has not been widely embraced in the real estate industry in the past, especially in the residential business. However, today a number of real estate firms around the country are pursuing employee relationships with their salespeople. The broker has greater ability to control their activities as employees rather than independent contractors. Benefits such as insurance and retirement programs can be more easily structured for employees as well.

- *Pay a salesperson a draw against future commissions.* Unless this is done very carefully, it could violate the independent contractor status. As a practical matter, the company could also get stuck paying money in advance for commissions that never materialize.

Compensating Managers

Real estate brokers who have been groomed under the independent contractor philosophy are accustomed to compensating people based on their contribution to production. Every dollar of compensation is directly related to the dollars produced for the company. But managers (as well as staff employees) contribute *indirectly* to the productivity of the organization. It is more difficult to quantify the relationship between the activities of management and staff and the dollar produced for the company. Consequently, these brokers usually struggle to define fair and equitable compensation programs for people who are not front-line salespeople.

The issues a broker must consider when developing compensation programs for management are similar to those for the salespeople.

- *Financial position of the company*—The compensation of a manager is an operating cost, regardless of whether it is a salary, an override (which is a cost of sales) or a combination of both. These expenses affect the net income, so the overall financial condition of the organization must be considered. *The manager should also be able to earn a decent living.*

- *The responsibilities of the manager*—The primary job of managers is to supervise the people who work in their departments or offices and to administer the activities in these work units to achieve the goals for which the unit is responsible. Compensation should be related to the work managers are expected to do, the level of authority they have and the amount of time they are expected to devote to these activities.

- *The expertise of the manager*—The compensation of managers should relate to their levels of competency, the sophistication of their expertise and their experience.

- *Internal equity*—Because the expertise and responsibilities may vary widely from manager to manager, the compensation program for each may be quite different. A manager's responsibilities when getting a new sales office up and running, for example, are different from those in an established office. Consequently, the compensation program may be structured differently. There should, however, be parity among managers with similar expertise and responsibilities.

- *Parity with the competition*—Compensation programs offered by competitors may not affect recruitment and retention of managers as dramatically as they do salespeople; however, the company could lose a valuable asset if a manager feels undercompensated for the job he or she is expected to do.

The title of *manager* implies that this person is likely to be an employee. Later in this book we discuss the independent contractor and employee relationships in greater detail. But consider for the moment that when the way a person performs his or her job is controlled by the employer, the IRS considers this person to be an employee, not an independent contractor. Often the design of a manager's job includes supervisory and administrative responsibilities and a level of accountability to senior management or the broker that is not suitable for an independent relationship. Companies also assume obligations for withholding taxes and social security and paying workers' compensation for these individuals as employees.

The following discussion addresses a variety of compensation programs for managers of sales offices without regard to their IRS status. Just because a manager's compensation is based on the production of a sales office, for example, does not mean the person is an independent contractor.

Salary. Managers can be paid a straight salary. For brokers who operate in the compensation-for-production mindset, paying a salary appears to offer little incentive for a sales manager to increase production. Before you discount this compensation plan, however, look at the manager's job description. If the manager is expected to devote undivided attention to administration of all activities in the office and supervise all of the people who work in the office, both support staff and salespeople, the manager should be paid for being an administrator. The effectiveness of the manager will be reflected in the sales volume of the office. A manager with valuable expertise as an administrator and effective supervisory skills is an asset to the office and should be compensated accordingly.

Override. Managers can be paid strictly an override on the salespeople's commissions. This could be based on a percentage of the gross commission (before the salespeople's shares are deducted), a percentage of commission after the sales and listing commissions are deducted or a percentage of the office's net profits. If the manager has authority for making financial decisions and authorizing expenditures, it's preferable to base the override on a percentage of the net profits. This is an incentive to control expenses as well as build sales volume. Otherwise, a manager who is expected only to build volume without regard to net profits might, for example, incur astronomical advertising expenses in the process.

Here's how an override plan works. If the broker pays 5 percent of $250,000, the sales manager would earn $12,500. If the override is 10 percent of the company dollar and the broker is on a 50/50 split, the compensation would be based on one-half of $250,000, that is, 10 percent of $125,000, or $12,500. The type of override usually depends on the commission arrangements with the salespeople. In any case, as the office productivity increases, the sales manager's compensation increases as well.

Salary plus override.   In this case the sales manager enjoys the best of both worlds, a stable salary plus an obvious reward for increasing production in the office. If the manager has a variety of administrative responsibilities and is expected to participate in managers' meetings and other management level activities, a salary plus override is the fairest compensation arrangement.

Sales commission plus percentage.   In the case in which a sales manager must also sell, which may be the situation in a small office or one that is just opening, the manager is compensated according to the commission program for the salespeople. In addition, the manager receives a percentage similar to an override.

CONCLUSION

One of management's most important responsibilities is to organize a profitable organization. A financial plan helps the company use its resources in the most cost-effective and efficient ways to accomplish its goals and objectives. As the company forecasts revenue and allocates expenses in the general operating budget, it sets financial goals for the coming year.

A budget is only as good as the research and analysis that precede its development. Knowledge of the marketplace and the company's capacity for generating revenue help the company formulate realistic income projections. Any company has limited resources, so it must use its revenue wisely. Knowledge of the costs of doing business and a careful analysis of the expenditures that are necessary help the company identify the best ways to utilize its resources.

Budgets for the general operation of the business and its profit centers or departments and sales offices are valuable only if the company uses them. They give the company tools with which to control expenditures and monitor income during the year. In Chapter 13 we discuss ways to streamline or enhance where necessary to keep your company on track, using the operating budget as the road map.

DISCUSSION EXERCISES

Discuss issues relating to the marketplace and your organization that affect the development of a general operating budget for your company or a budget for your office or department.

* * *

Discuss the financial management procedures that are required by your state's license law, particularly those that address the management of an escrow account.

* * *

Discuss the advantages and disadvantages of various ways to compensate salespeople and managers.

CHAPTER

8 Business Policies and Procedures

What are your company's ethical policies? What business policies and procedures has your company adopted? How effective are they?

Everyone in the organization needs to know exactly how to conduct themselves—the rules of the game. Let's return to the game analogy that was used in previous chapters. In planning we told the team the object of the game (the mission statement), the goal of the game (the goals for the organization) and the plays that the team will use to score the goals (the strategies the organization will use to achieve its goals). Unless you tell the team the rules of the game, you're fielding a team that may execute plays in ways that could be inconsistent with your philosophy or policies.

The broker makes the rules by first establishing a philosophy for doing business. This creates the culture for the organization—the rules of fair play and ethical conduct. Then the broker establishes policies and procedures that support the organization's culture and the particular nature of the company's business. After the broker makes these decisions, (s)he must be sure that everyone knows them. A published rule book—the policy and procedures manual—tells people how they are to conduct business for your company.

A policy and procedures manual is a valuable management tool. It provides authoritative guidance about how the company functions, which also avoids the "nobody told me" problem. By addressing potentially problematic situations, along with solutions, the manual minimizes the amount of time management must devote to solving problems and resolving controversies. Essentially, people can govern themselves in most situations. By setting up rules ahead of time, it's much easier for management and fairer for the workers when managers do not have to make up the rules as they go along. Sports events have referees who assess penalties for infractions, but we hope that the analogy ends here. Management should be coaching rather than refereeing the game, but management must also be willing to penalize the offenders.

How do you formulate a business philosophy and policies and procedures?

- Only the principal(s) of the company, whether the broker/owner or senior management, can determine the business philosophy, because it reflects the values and ethics this person sets for the organization. The culture in which people work and the company's policies, rules and procedures rise from that philosophy.

- This project takes time. Don't rush to publish a manual just because a management book says the organization should have one. This project requires careful planning, particularly because a number of situations must be contemplated to ensure that the document addresses all of the critical issues. Developing a manual is not necessarily a cumbersome exercise. After all, certain policies and procedures have evolved over time and are already in practice; they just need to be committed to paper. As you do this you also can identify inconsistencies or improvements that should be addressed.

- It's not advisable to copy someone else's manual. The philosophy of the company and the policies and procedures that support it are specific to that organization. Those that are suitable for one firm may not be suitable for another. A number of issues that should be addressed are suggested below, but the specifics of how they should be handled must be determined by the individual company. The purpose of this chapter is to present some points to ponder as the manual is prepared.

BUSINESS ETHICS

Ethics involves morality and a set of beliefs that guide a person's actions. Behavior is defined as good or bad, right or wrong, morally approved or disapproved, according to the ethics of various groups or cultures. Individuals as well have developed their own definitions and consequently, their own beliefs about what is right, wrong, good, bad and so forth.

In the business world there needs to be a guide by which words and deeds can be measured to determine ethical conduct. But there cannot be different sets of values that govern different parts of our lives or one standard that governs our personal lives and one that governs business. One standard must govern all areas of our lives. Peter Drucker, in his book *Management: Tasks, Responsibilities, Practices,* argues that there is no such thing as separate ethics for business. All professionals should have one fundamental ethical principle that guides them: "Above all, do no harm."

The Heart of Ethics

Before we explore an ethical code for your company, we need to make several points about human behavior. Our country seems to be in the midst of an ethical dilemma, with reports of scandals in government, cheating on college campuses and resignations of corporate officials. Recent studies also indicate that consumers rank the ethics of real estate practitioners fairly low. (Various accounts list them sixth or lower from the bottom of a list of 25 business practitioners.) When you hear these reports, you may think, "Don't these people know any better?" Other people might say, "I'd do the same thing they did," "They must have had a good reason," or "I'll not likely get caught." Isn't it interesting that not all of us size up situations the same way?

Why don't we? One reason is that each of us has developed our own personal set of values that guide our behavior. Ask a group of people what they value in their lives and you'll get a variety of responses. For some it may be money; for others it may be such things as freedom, health, family, prestige, respect or loyalty. Certainly, there are others as well. The point is that people prioritize those values for themselves. The passion that burns within them guides their decisions and, therefore, their behavior.

We could expand this discussion into the root of values and the theories noted authorities have developed about value systems. But for our purposes we leave with the point that our past experiences, family upbringing, cultural influences and traditions and the lessons we learn about fundamental principles that guide morality all contribute the formation of individual value systems. Because all of us don't come out of the same mold, the challenge is to blend us together and provide order for the group.

Society does this with laws, codes to live by, including codes of ethics, and rules. These work with varying degrees of success because personal values may be different than those established for the group. Each of our heads gets into the act, too, as we think through the rules of the group. Some people comply because they decide to avoid undesirable consequences they would incur if they don't. Others may see the rules as inherently flawed and therefore discount them as worthy of being followed. (Not all laws are "right" in everyone's mind.) Some people are less motivated by the legality of an issue and more persuaded by how a rule affects an individual situation or the group as a whole.

These rules that are intended to guide behavior of the group, be it your company, the industry or the community, fall into two general categories: laws and ethics. Laws are established by government along with consequences for violators; conduct can then be described as legal or illegal. Ethics are driven by morality, the values and principles of individuals in the group as well as the group as a whole; conduct can then be described as ethical or unethical. Some laws may appear to be unethical, which is the reason that ethics often impose a higher standard for conduct.

To conclude this brief lesson, we turn our attention to the real estate industry and your company in particular. We practice under an expanding body of law, which is intended to enhance the protections afforded to the consumers with whom we do business. Repeatedly in this text we mention compliance with certain laws because the consequences for violations can be quite damaging to the organization. But laws alone are not sufficient. We need ethics, the higher standard, to enhance the conduct of our business. Our professional organizations have codes of ethics. Companies need to adopt policies or codes for ethical behavior as well. It's even more important that people practice what is preached and that the policies are enforced.

Code of Ethics

One firm can't take responsibility for the entire industry, but it can be responsible for the professionalism and ethical conduct within that organization. A company needs a code of ethics to define its moral principles, rules and standards of conduct. Begin by determining a general philosophy that guides the ethics within your organization. Then provide specific rules and standards for conduct.

A number of real estate licensees belong to professional organizations whose basic philosophy is the Golden Rule: "Do unto others as you would have others do unto you." This provides a guide for ethical conduct as the question is posed, "Would I want someone to act in this manner toward me?" This is one philosophy the firm could adopt as the foundation for its code of ethics.

You may recognize this philosophy as the one adopted by the National Association of REALTORS® in its Code of Ethics. You could say, "There's already a code for the industry, so why does my company need one, too?" According to NAR's 1996 analysis, 41 percent of the real estate licensees in the country were REALTORS®. Regardless of how notable a standard their code sets, the fact is that not everyone in the industry is practicing on the "same page." Professional organizations' codes are useful for their members and also can be incorporated in your company's code if you choose. But the purpose of a code of ethics for your company is to go a step farther by providing guidance for *your* personnel, not just the salespeople, and set ethical standards for your organization.

Once you set those standards, the organization must make a commitment to *following* its code of ethics. This requires the active participation of everyone at all levels of the organization. People must focus not only on the *results* but also on the *process* to achieve those results. Ethical practices occur when the process is not compromised or bypassed to achieve a result.

If a company's attitude is "I don't care how you do it, just get it done," this says that the result is more important than how the result was achieved. The ethical code of an organization can become meaningless if upper management tolerates or ignores behavior that is contrary to the values it has established. Although businesses need to survive financially, they need to decide the price they are willing to pay while pursuing a dollar. A commitment to ethical conduct is one of your firm's most valuable assets. Doing what's right is not always the easiest course of action, nor does it always produce immediate financial rewards. But *there is simply no right way to do the wrong thing.*

Institutionalizing Ethics

Institutionalizing ethics means integrating ethics throughout the organization: 1) clearly state what you expect in ethical conduct; 2) establish systems within the organization to ensure that the behavior is consistent with the words; and 3) provide penalties for people who deviate from your code of ethics. You can institutionalize your company's commitment to a code of ethics in several ways.

- *Commit your ethics to writing.* While you can identify values or ethical standards for your organization, they are meaningless unless they are cast in print. Intangibles are elusive and difficult to enforce. Written statements show a commitment and leave no room for ambiguity, as long as they are specific. For example, it's not sufficient to state that "integrity is expected of every salesperson." You must identify specific behavior that exemplifies integrity. A code of ethics that is too vague becomes a public relations document rather than a meaningful script for the organization.

- *Communicate your code of ethics.* Once the values are identified, they must be communicated to everyone in your organization. This can be done through training and orientation programs, pamphlets, letters and, most important, by personal example. The firm also should communicate its commitment to the public. This can be accomplished in brochures, contracts and advertising. The behavior of the people who work for you, however, is the firm's most powerful communication.

- *Get actively involved.* The broker/owner and all levels of management must lead by example to gain commitment from others in the organization. Make ethics an integral part of every aspect of the organization. Clearly communicate that unethical conduct will not be tolerated, regardless of the financial gain that would result. Do not impose expectations for production that will compromise the value systems of the people who work for you or the organization.

   Sales or office managers play a significant role in implementing the company's code of ethics. These are the people who work directly with the staff who interact with customers and clients. The institutionalization of ethics is measured not only by actual behavior but also by how employees, customers and clients *perceive* the ethics of the company. Because the managers are responsible for creating an ethical environment in the office, they can take a lot of the credit or share some of the blame for this perception.

- *Enforce the code of ethics.* The most powerful way to institutionalize ethics is to confront violations. One of the reasons unethical behavior persists is because organizations do not aggressively pursue enforcement. You must remove barriers that discourage people from stepping forward and informing upper management about unethical conduct. Otherwise, the organization is functioning with a code of silence rather than a code of ethics. Provide directives about ways suspected unethical behavior is to be reported. Establish an investigatory process and a series of penalties that will be assessed for violations. Then do it!

- *Reinforce the code of ethics.* Constant exposure to and reinforcement of the code is essential. It should be addressed in workshops and seminars on an ongoing basis. Ethics training will not produce the desired behavior without case examples to illustrate the code of ethics in action. People should understand the factors that must be considered in ethical decision making, the dilemmas they could encounter that might discourage ethical behavior and develop possible solutions to these dilemmas.

You can either manage or mismanage ethics. Some simply ignore the issue, but those who do could suffer unintended and undesirable consequences. Because some unethical conduct is also illegal, the company's legal liability is significant and the penalties can be costly.

POLICIES AND PROCEDURES

Earlier we mentioned the rule book—the policy and procedures manual. This is a handbook that tells people "the way we work" in the organization. Often that is explained in the introductory statement in the manual. With specific procedures related to your firm's services, a manual reinforces practices that are consistent with your business objectives. We cannot overstate the value of a policy and procedures manual for

- providing ready answers for many of the dilemmas people face during the course of daily operations;

- setting rules by which everyone shall play;

- helping to resolve conflicts before they arise; and

- providing a risk-management tool for both the company and its staff.

Policy and procedures manuals are worthless if they aren't used. Provide everyone in the organization with a personal copy. This is also a good orientation tool for new staff. Make it a living document by encouraging them to refer to the manual. (This also spares a manager the aggravation of repeating answers to questions that already have been addressed.) Management must stand behind the policies and procedures and adhere to them consistently. Once you start playing favorites and allowing some people to circumvent the rules, you create many of the conflicts the manual was intended to prevent.

A policy and procedures manual is also a public declaration about certain policies that have legal implications. If you are involved in litigation, it can be your ally by supporting the company with a written statement about the way the firm works. Or it can be your enemy if you don't adhere to the established guidelines. The manual also should clearly differentiate between working procedures for employees and independent contractors. Involve legal counsel in the preparation and use of the manual to be sure you are managing rather than creating risk for the organization.

As was mentioned earlier, the manual contains *your* company's philosophy, policies and procedures and supports your company's business ethics. What you say about various procedures will determine the standards by which people are expected to perform their jobs and by which the company delivers its services. Also be sure to provide sanctions or enforcement procedures. The following is a discussion of issues that should be addressed when constructing the manual. Because your company may hire employees as well as independent contractors, some issues will apply to all personnel and others will apply only to independent contractor/salespeople or to employees.

General Business Policies

Begin with general statements about your organization. These tell who the company is and what it does: the mission statement, a brief history of the organization and a description of its target markets by geographic area and types of properties or services. This is also where you state the company's general philosophy of doing business and its ethical code. At this point you are making pronouncements that affect everyone who works for the company, as well as telling the public who you are.

There also are a number of policy decisions that the company must make which relate to its real estate services. These identify the specific services the company provides and define the conduct of the people who work for you, according to the multitude of laws that affect your business. The company has the right to expect that all workers, including independent contractors, conduct themselves in a legal and ethical manner.

Agency.   The broker must clearly define the company's policy, in accordance with state law, regarding law of agency relationships. The policy must state whether the firm represents buyers/tenants, sellers/landlords or both as disclosed dual agents or as designated agents, and state a position about subagency. Procedures must be outlined to explain how fiduciary obligations are to be discharged, including agency disclosures. Detailed procedures, especially those that preserve confidentiality and loyalty, are essential if you are practicing designated agency. If your state's law permits nonagency relationships, the broker must define policies and procedures accordingly. (Sample office policies about agency relationships are available from the National Association of REALTORS®.)

Antitrust.   Because practices in our industry are constantly being scrutinized for antitrust violations, the broker must be very specific in explaining the rationale for the company's charges and the various fee structures for its services. Equally important are procedures that provide guidance to the salespeople about protecting the company from antitrust violations. (See Chapter 14 about antitrust laws.)

Equal opportunity in housing. The real estate industry must comply with all applicable fair housing laws. The company should express its commitment to equal opportunity and establish procedures to ensure that everyone in the organization serves all customers and clients properly under federal, state and local fair housing, civil rights and disability laws.

The company also could participate in affirmative action programs. As an example, the National Association of REALTORS® and the Department of Housing and Urban Development have entered into the Fair Housing Partnership Agreement. This is a voluntary program in which participants can further equal opportunity in housing by engaging in certain advertising practices and outreach programs in the community.

Real estate licensing laws and regulations. A policy should state that all of the activities in the organization must comply with your state's licensing laws. Any procedure that is defined in the manual should support this policy. Because the company must not permit unlicensed employees to engage in activities for which licensure is required, procedures should address what unlicensed people can and cannot do.

General Policies for All Workers

Whether you are writing a policy and procedures manual for independent contractors or personnel policies for employees, several general policies will apply to *all* of your workers. These normally address the following issues:

- Equal employment opportunity (including a culturally diverse workplace)

- Sexual harassment (between staff members, management and staff and employees/independent contractors and customers and clients–see NAR's sample policy)

- Substance abuse (what, where and procedures for violations of policy)

- Smoking (in the workplace and outside with customers and clients)

- Personal safety and security in the workplace (including procedures to protect personnel and precautions for sales-people)

- Standards of conduct (including issues such as theft, conflict of interest and violations of laws, ethics and policies)

- Worker relations (general working environment and climate for professional development)

- Confidentiality (company matters as well as clients)

- Public relations (image of the organization)

- Actions on behalf of the organization (only authorized individuals permitted to make legal commitments on behalf of your firm)

- Solicitation (prevent disruption in the workplace)

About the work day:

- Office hours (including procedures for salespeople being in the office after hours)

- Holidays (including accommodations for cultural and religious preferences)

- Personal phone calls (including emergency procedures and reimbursement of charges)

- Dress policy (general professional appearance)

Procedures for Independent Contractors/Salespeople

Although salespeople will enter into independent contractor agreements with the company (unless they are employees), their working status should be reaffirmed in the policy and procedures manual. As the procedures are detailed, they should be carefully worded to avoid violating the independent status (another important reason why the manual should be reviewed by counsel). The manual should address the following issues:

- Personal assistants (their role in your company, whether they are employees of the salesperson or the company; licensed and unlicensed activities)

- Sales teams (the way they are accommodated in your company, including notification to management about how the team has structured its relationship)

- Part-time agents, full-time agents and home officing (hiring policies and the way they work)

- Referrals (procedures for distributing in-house leads and referrals between salespeople and referrals to other companies)

- Agent cooperation (in-house, including sharing customers and clients)

- Standards for servicing customers and clients (listings and sales)

- Open house procedures (including sales procedures and safety precautions)

- Transactions:

  Listing and agency agreements (types; situations in which each are used; policy on written versus oral agreements)

  Forms and contracts (policy for written and oral contracts, written disclosures, contingency forms, transmittal forms, record keeping)

  Escrow money (tracking procedures, deposits and withdrawals, cobrokerage procedures, disputes)

  Litigation and legal expenses

  Settlement or escrow procedures

- Commission programs

- Insurance (coinsurance on autos, errors and omissions)

- Dues and fees (professional association, MLS, franchise)

- Education and designations

- Advertising and marketing procedures (who pays and for what, which publications are used, frequency, content and approval of copy even when salesperson is paying the bill and solicitation)

- Internet policy (representing broker affiliation, copyright and trademark infringement, defamation, sexual harassment and racial discrimination, wire fraud)

- Telephone procedures (personal and business calls, phone log, who gets the lead on an inquiry, expectations for returning messages)

- Dissemination of information (about the company and its listings, including the nature of information to be discussed on the phone and who is permitted to disseminate what information)

- Keys and lock boxes (procedures, who pays)

- Signs (procedures, who pays)

- Office equipment (use of supplies, fax, copier, computer and Internet connections and company-owned computer software)

- Postage, printing and direct mail (who pays, limits, review of copy)

- Attendance (*recommendations* for floor time, sales meetings, training sessions)

- Parking at the office

- Salespeople's selling and purchasing real estate for themselves

- Handling disputes (between salespeople, with customers and clients, with licensees in other firms)

- Termination (grounds, procedures, disposition of listings, leads and pending closings)

Employee Personnel Policies

In addition to the items listed under General Policies for All Workers, a number of issues are addressed in personnel policies that relate specifically to employees.

- Categories of employment and related fringe benefits
- Pay procedures
- Travel/expense accounts (if any)
- Overtime
- Attendance and punctuality
- Employment procedures (including recruiting, selecting, hiring, performance reviews)
- Layoffs
- Disciplinary actions
- Resignation and discharge
- Vacation and leave:

  Personal days

  Vacation time

  Sick time

  Court duty

  Bereavement leave

  Military leave

  Family leave (check requirements under the federal Family and Medical Leave Act of 1993)

A number of state and federal laws exist to protect employees and govern their working conditions. Because many brokers are unaccustomed to hiring employees, you need to become familiar with these laws. Seek legal advice to be sure that the policies, employment procedures and conditions in the workplace are in compliance with these laws.

CONCLUSION

If your policy and procedures manual includes the scope of information we've discussed, it provides a fairly complete picture of your organization—its general business policies and ethics, and its rules for the way business is done and how people conduct themselves with one another in the company, with their customers and clients and with other professionals. The company makes a commitment to these policies and procedures by putting all of them in writing. Management then becomes responsible for implementing them throughout the organization. As with any other document that guides the organization, the manual should be flexible and change as the company changes (which is why assembling the manual in a loose-leaf binder is a good idea).

DISCUSSION EXERCISES

Discuss your company's code of ethics. Are there conflicts between what the company preaches and the way it practices?

* * *

Discuss typical ethical dilemmas that you encounter in daily practice.

* * *

Discuss typical problems that arise in your company and how these could be resolved in the company's policy and procedures manual.

CHAPTER

9 Marketing and Advertising

What is a marketing plan intended to do for your company? What media attract today's consumers? What tools can you use to promote your company? To promote your services or listings?

The traditional focus of marketing in real estate has been the promotion of listings. Although this is an important activity and one the property owner expects us to perform with the utmost skill, it is only one aspect of a total marketing program. As our industry expands its services, the focus of a firm's marketing program must shift.

Today, marketing efforts must promote the firm, all of its services and the people who provide these services. Consumers do business with *people* more so than a firm. They are looking for salespeople who can be their trusted advisers or helpmates, not just order takers. Consumers *don't* want to be the means to the end—the sale or rental of a property. Showcasing the salespeople and their services is an important effort for the success of the firm's marketing program.

Marketing is image making for the purpose of generating business. It showcases your company in everything it does, whether you are advertising a listing, promoting a relocation service or sponsoring a Little League team. Presenting the company to the public is not without risk. People form impressions based on what they see, read and hear about you. A powerful message can get lost if it's not well presented. The goal of marketing is to cause people to react to you. That reaction should be favorable so they want to do business with you. Professional "image makers" are invaluable in helping you elicit the desired reaction.

MARKET IDENTITY

Make a statement about who you are. You do this with the name you choose for the company, the design of its logo and the selection of a slogan. Just as people give themselves a "handle," or a shorthand code, by which they can be recognized, you do the same for the company. Words, graphics and colors become the company's signature; they give it identity everywhere the signature appears—the sign on the office, yard signs, business cards, letterhead, brochures and Web sites. That signature makes an even more powerful statement when affiliated companies are recognized under the same banner.

The design of the signature is critical, which is a persuasive reason to use a professional graphics designer. Think about how the signature will look in a variety of formats. One that looks good on a billboard may not look good reproduced on a business card. Striking colors or screens may not look good in black-and-white reproduction. If the design or size of your logo isn't suitable for use in a classified ad (or if it will be expensive to use), you'll regret it every time you run an ad. Also think about how your signature will look on a Web page.

What's in a Name?

The name of the company tells a story about your firm. Because real estate brokerage is a personalized service, some brokers feel they can communicate that personal touch by using their own names for the company name. If the broker has a high profile in the community, name recognition can be a powerful draw for the business.

A fictitious name can be just as powerful. It may identify a specialty, a geographic area or other special characteristic that distinguishes the firm from the competition. Even if you're affiliated with a franchise, you need your own identity as well. Some people even consider the alphabetical position of the name in a phone directory. If you're choosing a fictitious name, clever and compelling is fine. But be sure it doesn't sound frivolous or unprofessional. Get the reactions of your friends before filing for the fictitious business name (FBN).

FBNs, which are registered in the state where you do business, must first be approved before they can be used. Words like *Bank, Insurance, Escrow, Trust, Federal, National, State, United States, Reserve* or *Deposit Insurance* may be questioned if they appear in the FBN. Names that are already in use or names that imply the existence of nonexistent partnerships or corporations are unacceptable. Some states require a certificate of fictitious name to be recorded in the city or county where the entity will do business. The name is usually advertised in a local general circulation newspaper for a period of time before the certificate is issued. In most cases, a corporation is not required to file a certificate because the corporation as a legal entity is entitled to use its own name. Check your real estate licensing laws to determine whether both the broker and the FBN must be jointly licensed.

THE COMPANY'S MARKETING PLAN

Now that the company has a signature or identity, the next step is to prepare a plan to promote it. Before you can develop this plan, you need to identify what you are promoting, whether it's the company's expertise or services, and the needs of the consumers in the marketplace. This probably sounds like a familiar exercise because that's what we did in the planning process. The target market you identified for your services is now the market you target with your promotions and advertising. As you develop your marketing strategies, consider what your competition does. You don't have to mimic the competition, but you should be aware of the strategies they use. Figure 9.1 shows the results of a national survey that could be useful.

FIGURE 9.1   **Business Derived from Marketing Promotions**

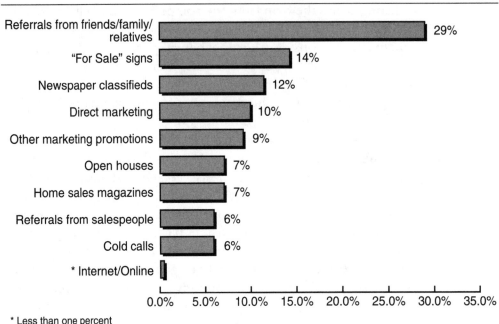

* Less than one percent

A marketing plan integrates a variety of tools or advertising vehicles into a coordinated program. You cannot afford to advertise in every medium, nor can you afford to waste money on a message that misses the mark. You must make a powerful statement that appeals to the consumers you want to target, using promotional methods that will reach that audience. Your analysis of your consumers should help you tailor an appropriate message and select the appropriate tools. Then develop a plan for using them.

Advertising can be costly, so you want to get maximum benefit from the expenditure (which is one of a franchise's persuasive selling points). One of the basic rules in marketing is repetition. This means making public appearances on a number of fronts to reinforce your message. While some tools are most useful for promoting the company and others for promoting services or listings, in either case you are reinforcing identity for the company. This is especially important for marketing buyer-agency services. A short but intense campaign, rather than one that is drawn out over a longer period of time (with less frequent appearances), provides greater benefit for the same amount of money. Let's discuss the tools that can be included in a plan to market a firm and its services.

Mass Media

Mass media include television, radio and newspapers. Usually they are used as institutional advertising, that is, to promote the firm. But they may be used to launch a new service or even to market your listings.

Radio and television.   With today's fast-paced lifestyles radio and television are major sources of information for consumers. A significant drawback is that there's no tangible, printed literature to put into the consumer's hands. The secret is to capture the audience's attention in 30 seconds and then introduce or reinforce your message elsewhere. Professional media consultants can help tailor a radio or TV message to capture the audience's attention. Because this can be an expensive way to promote your company, you want to make a strong impact in a short time.

Select radio and television stations that reach your target market. Stations compile audience profiles, sometimes providing demographics according to zip code, which are useful in selecting suitable stations and identifying the number of consumers you can reach. Don't overlook cable TV stations. Their audiences may be more localized, which is particularly true with community stations, but the stations are useful for reaching very specific target markets. Some have bulletin board services that are good for promoting listings as well as other services. If the primary audience of a radio or television station is not a cross-section of the population, be sure to include media that reach the general population so you do not violate the fair housing laws. (See the section in Chapter 14 about the fair housing laws.)

The cost of air time is a good indicator of the size of the audience and its value as consumers. Inexpensive time slots are available in both radio and TV, but look at the station's statistics to see if that's a worthwhile expenditure. For example, how many people hear your message between midnight and 5 A.M.? Other than health care and other night-shift workers, your audience may be pretty slim. But the time is cheap! A 60-second spot could equal, or be less than, the cost of a 30-second spot in prime time. Radio is generally less expensive than commercial TV at any time of the day. Some stations offer packaged timeslots that include preferred time as well as off hours, which may be a good deal.

You could also consider producing and sponsoring an interactive TV or radio program. These are ambitious projects because you are responsible for preparing a program every week. Hosting a talk show can be fun as you plan programs and interview guests. But if you start to run out of creative ideas and tire of the amount of time these projects take, the fun can wear thin after several months. Even with a listing magazine show, where there's no "talk," you have production time and costs to consider. There isn't much lead time either, because the listings must be current. A public relations consultant can provide invaluable assistance for production of any of these programs.

Print media.   Evaluate print media, such as newspapers, the same way you do electronic media. Most publications track circulation and profile their readers. You can determine whether you will reach the desired audience and how to tailor your message for maximum benefit. Consider local weekly and shopper newspapers and magazines in addition to metropolitan and regional daily publications. Compare the costs and the number of people in your target audience you will reach. When looking at publications that are free to the reader, remember that while they may have a wide distribution, they may not get read. Investigate the actual results advertisers get from these publications.

Newspapers can be used for several kinds of promotions. Display ads can be used to promote your company or a particular service. Your public relations or marketing consultant can design an appealing message and layout to maximize the impact of these ads. Consider a paid advertisement that appears as an editorial column. Provide timely and informative news the consumer can use. Because the column is prepared by the company, rather than the publisher, you can include a commercial for your firm. Publishers rarely include this information from press releases or interviews. Even when you use classified advertising for your listings (which will be discussed in detail later), you are also advertising your company.

Internet

One of the fastest growing ways to reach your audience is through the Internet. According to NAR's 1996 membership profile, at least 50 percent of their respondents had company home pages. That number is increasing daily, with the Internet becoming as commonplace a medium as newspapers. Some people suggest that the Internet will be the most cost-efficient way to reach an audience because consumers are turning to the Internet for information in staggering numbers.

With the explosion in the number of Web sites, the challenge is to make yours stand out above all the others. You can develop your own Web site with do-it-yourself software. Or you may find that the company will benefit from using the services of a professional designer. You need an attractive, captivating presence on the Internet, one that will encourage visitors or "hits," but you also need to be easily found. See Figure 9.2 for an example of a real estate Web page.

- Choose an Internet service provider that will give you high traffic and is easily accessible via the popular search engines.

- Help the search engine, which acts like a librarian, locate your site by selecting key words that people who are searching for information are likely to use.

- Place your key words or phrases on your page where the search engines are likely to find them–in the first several words on the page title. Note "Ft. Pierce Florida Waterfront Homes – Ft. Pierce Real Estate" in Figure 9.2. Don't lead off with an individual's or company's name, copyright notice or welcome message. The general viewer won't find you.

FIGURE 9.2   Sample Web Page

Ft. Pierce Florida Waterfront Homes — Ft. Pierce Real Estate

Beautiful Florida Homes in VR

Rays Real Estate on the cutting edge!

Waterfront homes are the some of the most beautiful homes in the world. Lets face it, it just doesn't get any better than Waterfront homes in Sunny Florida.

Rays Real Estate is on the cutting edge of marketing some of the most beautiful homes in the world in

Virtual Reality. Tour exquisite waterfront

About Rays

Tell us what you want

Relocation Services

Tour our Homes

Ray's Chat Room

Listings   Waterfront   Dream Homes   Fla. Information   Local Info

Ray's Real Estate
2140 N. Federal Highway
Ft. Pierce, Florida
raysre@floridawaterfront.com

Click Here For More Virtual Reality

Phone: 561-460-1601
Fax: 561-460-1603
Cell Phone: 561-595-2613
Pager: 561-785-1431

Courtesy of Ray's Real Estate, Ft. Pierce, Florida.

- Provide descriptive information, or metatags, to describe your site in a search engine's index. The viewer of your page won't see these, but they help the search engines respond to the viewer.

- Register your site with the search engine's index and consider ways to link your site with others (with their permission) to maximize your exposure.

Because consumers browse the Internet for information, your Web site will be most satisfying to them if it is informative. Some of the tools we discuss later in this chapter, such as newsletters, that are geared to educating consumers, are also useful for your Web site. Take advantage of the online services' "favorite site" features by making yours one of the browser's favorites. What better way is there to institutionalize your company's signature?

The Internet poses as many challenges as it does opportunities. A Web site requires constant monitoring. The information on your site, like any printed piece, has limited shelf life. You can't just post it and forget it. Someone has to be in charge of constantly updating the site. This is especially true if it includes time-sensitive information or listings. Remember that MLSs have a routine for revising the status of listings; now you have the same chore. You could be in violation of license law with the posting of an expired listing. Also, because Web pages are not tamper-proof, you need to monitor your site to be sure that the message you so carefully crafted has not been altered.

One of the most significant, and potentially litigious, challenges on the Internet is the ownership of information. Not all information is considered public domain. Domain names and content of sites are assets, or *intellectual property,* that the owners frequently protect by copyright and trademark. As such, you must ensure that you do not violate ownership with the unauthorized use of another's property. If you intend to retain control over your original work, learn to use copyrights and trademarks to protect it. Post only those listings that are yours to control and check whether you or the Webmaster own the assets.

Newsletters

Although newsletters can serve many purposes, one of the most useful from the consumer's point of view is one that educates. Today's consumers thirst for information, so you can perform a public service and promote your company at the same time. These informative newsletters are a great tool for the salespeople as well as for the company's marketing campaign. You also can post a newsletter on your Internet Web site.

A newsletter is an ideal vehicle for providing information about emerging trends, changes in the law, recent court cases and government regulations that affect ownership, leasing and development. The information must be stated in a precise, factual manner. If you're including interpretations of legal findings or applications of laws, be accurate and also include a disclaimer. If you choose to editorialize, indicate that the comments are your personal views. Certain views may alienate some readers, so think about the risk you are taking before expressing your opinions.

Because a lot of time is involved in writing good copy, it's tempting to use other people's work. Or you may find a captivating article somewhere that your readers would like. But, you can't just duplicate these pieces in your newsletter without violating copyright laws. Be sure to get the author's and/or publisher's permission to use a work. Otherwise, don't include it.

Press Releases

Press releases are another tool for educating the public. The media want material they perceive as having a direct impact on their audiences. Information that is timely (recent changes in laws or government regulations) or controversial, and information that announces an innovative service or a community service project are appealing. Because the media are bombarded with press releases, they are selective about the ones they use (which is an argument for using a public relations specialist to help prepare effective releases). Many newspapers and TV and radio stations, particularly in large metropolitan markets, will not use ones that are primarily sales talks or commercials for your company. However, they may use a release that announces a major event in your company, such as a merger, the opening of a new office or a public information seminar.

If your local newspapers have columns in which they spotlight local business people, take advantage of the opportunity to promote your salespeople and their professional accomplishments. An example of this kind of press release appears in Figure 9.3. Notice the form that it follows. Catch the reader's eye by presenting the most important information at the outset, including who, what, where, how and when. Do so in a factual manner and without editorializing. Some publications edit the copy in the press releases, so catch the editor's eye at the very beginning of the release, because that could be the information the editor chooses to use.

Brochures

Brochures can be one of the best, most professional ways to tell consumers what they need to know about doing business with you and, most important, the *benefits* they will derive from such an association. A general brochure about the company should explain why it's in business and its business philosophy, and then concentrate on specific services and expertise. You also can do a brochure about a single aspect of your business or one that promotes a real estate career with your company. Salespeople should be encouraged to do their own self-promotion brochures as well.

Most consumers don't want to be subjected to information that does not appear to be relevant to them. A "brag sheet" tends to reinforce the stereotype that business people are self-centered. While you're preparing the copy, think about how the reader will react to the story you tell. Remember that readers may not be familiar with industry jargon or our organizations or designations. These mean more to other real estate professionals than they do to the general public. If you're going to list your professional accomplishments, show how these will help the consumer. Be truthful and realistic about what you are able to do to avoid setting unrealistic expectations.

It's discouraging to spend a lot of money on beautiful brochures that don't get used. So use them generously. Once you

FIGURE 9.3   Sample Press Release

FOR IMMEDIATE RELEASE WITH PHOTO

_____ Date _____

_____ Address of paper _____

To: _____ Name of paper _____

Attention: _____

Photo Caption: Peter Jay, president of ABC REALTORS®, is shown presenting plaques to each of the top three winners for 1999. From left to right are: Jay, Wendy Lewis, William Eltee and Doris Moore.

ABC REALTORS® HONORS TOP THREE AGENTS FOR 1999

HOMETOWN: Wendy Lewis, Willam Eltee and Doris Moore recently were honored at the ABC REALTORS® annual staff awards ceremony as the top three producers in the firm for 1995. The winners were announced by ABC REALTORS® president, Peter Jay, at a dinner held in their honor at the Hillswood Country Club in Hometown.

Lewis attained the firm's highest sales volume,more than $6,000,000, and first place in selling the most company listings. Lewis, who joined the firm in 1977, has consistently been a top producer in the company. She has served as a director of the Hometown Board of REALTORS® since 1988 and was elected as the 1998 treasurer of the board.

Eltee has been with the ABC firm almost two years. His production for 1999 neared the $3,500,000 mark. A graduate of Weston High School, Eltee attended Emerson State College where he majored in business administration and finance. He also has extensive experience in general contracting and new construction.

Moore, a seven-year member of ABC, achieved close to $5,000,000 in sales volume and was recognized as having the most closed listings for the year. Active in the Hometown board, she has chaired the Grievance Committee since 1993 and serves on the REALTORS® Community Service Committee.

In presenting each of the recipients with a plaque, Jay said, "I congratulate the three winners and want to extend ABC's thanks for their efforts and dedication over the years. We are very proud to have them on our staff."

# # #

prepare the copy and do the design, layout and the first print run, it's relatively inexpensive to order another supply. Because the per-piece cost drops as the size of the print run increases, it may be even better to print a larger supply in the first place. But it's even more discouraging to find many unused brochures that are out of date, so try to gauge the usage and prepare copy that has a long shelf life.

If brochures are going to be distributed to people's homes, use the mail service properly. Don't leave any personally delivered materials in a mailbox or other receptacle intended to receive delivery from the U.S. Postal Service. The offender can be subjected to the amount of first-class postage for the entire postal route in which the material was hand delivered, can be fined or can jeopardize the firm's bulk-mail permit. If you plan to use bulk mail, investigate the regulations. Obtain the necessary permits and follow the correct procedures to preserve the company's bulk-mail privileges.

Videos

Another way to tell consumers what they need to know about doing business with you is with a video. This is essentially a high-tech version of a brochure, but it makes a statement about your company that print does not. You make a strong impression on the viewer with the script and music that accompany the visual story. It's possible to tell more about the company and your people in a 10-minute video than is normally provided in a short brochure. You can appeal to the high-tech generation whose members are accustomed to accessing information on their TVs and VCRs. A video can be such a powerful showpiece for your company that the production should be as fine as possible, which means using professionals to assist in its production.

As with any promotional tool, the investment is only worthwhile if it is used. You might provide the video in the reception or conference area for waiting visitors to preview or distribute it to potential transferees or their employers. Have salespeople personalize the video by adding material to the company's video for their self-promotion. Or consider adding listings at the end of the video that could be updated from time to time.

Telephone Directories

The real estate section of the Yellow Pages is one of the most frequently referenced headings; as many as 30 to 50 percent of the customers use this publication to locate a broker. (Wonder what happened to the business cards you distribute?) Although a listing or display ad in a telephone directory is not a sole promotional tool, it is a vehicle that should be considered in your total marketing plan. Because some directories are published infrequently (and many of us do not replace old editions), protect your credibility by avoiding information that could date your listing, particularly in display ads.

Outdoor Advertising

Billboards, taxi, bus and automobile signs, and yard signs fall into this category. Your message can become a fixture in the landscape because these usually provide long exposure. (Your yard signs should provide long exposure because they appear on many listings, not on the same one.) Because they are eye catching, these tools are good for reinforcing the company's signature. But they are not suitable for lengthy messages because people must be able to grasp what you're saying in about four seconds.

Novelties

There are literally hundreds of items on which you can imprint your name, from combs and sponges to calendars, balloons, rulers and bottle caps. It is possible to imprint many of these items with your logo and lettering style rather than plain type. If you have a company theme, select an item that reflects that image. These are useful items for recruiting programs or public seminars or for your salespeople to use as handouts.

Solicitation

One of the most effective marketing tools is personal contact with the public. Most salespeople strive to present themselves in a professional, competent manner. But some consumers have a different view of salespeople in general and solicitors in particular. Any solicitation that is done on behalf of your company must be conducted in ways that are not offensive and in ways that comply with the laws and the ethics that govern these activities.

Telephone Consumer Protection Act. The Federal Communications Commission has issued regulations relating to the Telephone Consumer Protection Act of 1991. These regulations, which became effective on December 20, 1992, govern the use of telephone lines for commercial solicitation and advertisement. The legislation is intended to protect telephone subscribers who do not wish to receive unsolicited live "cold called," autodialed, prerecorded or artificial voice messages and fax machine solicitations. The regulations prohibit contacts with 911, health care facilities, physicians, poison control and fire or law enforcement emergency lines. Also prohibited are contacts with telephone lines in hospitals, health care facilities and retirement home guest or patient rooms as well as paging services, cellular telephones or any other service for which the consumer is charged a fee.

According to the procedures in the regulations, the soliciting company

- may not telephone a residence before 8 A.M. nor after 9 P.M.;

- must identify the business name and telephone number and the name of the person making the call;

- must adopt a written policy and maintain a "do not call list" of residences requesting that they not be called;

- must advise and train all personnel and independent contractors engaged in any aspect of telephone solicitation regarding the "do not call list" maintenance and procedures;

- must share the "do not call list" with an affiliated entity (one that a consumer reasonably would expect to be affiliated with the soliciting company based on the company's name);

- may not use an automatic telephone dialing system in such a way that two or more telephone lines of a multiple-line business are engaged simultaneously; and

- may not use a telephone, computer or other electronic/mechanical fax machine device to send unsolicited advertisements to another telephone, computer or electronic/mechanical receiver.

Company solicitors can be sued for up to $500 in damages for violations. If you have established written policies regarding these procedures, they may be used for defending alleged violations. Note that these rules apply when the caller has no prior business relationship with or permission or invitation from the consumer to make contact. Consult your lawyer for further information and advice regarding compliance with the Telephone Consumer Protection Act.

Salespeople should carefully choose whom they solicit. It is considered unethical to attempt to disrupt an agency relationship that a person has with another licensee. If, for example, an owner has an exclusive listing with another firm, the salesperson should not solicit the listing until it has expired. The licensee should not engage in discussions regarding a future agency relationship unless invited to do so by the owner. General solicitations to a geographic area or group, which may include individuals who are already clients of other firms, are not unethical. But targeting solicitations to another licensee's client promoting the same services that are already being provided by the other licensee is a problem.

Harassment.   Salespeople must use common sense about how aggressively they pursue prospective customers and clients. If people are alienated by their actions, the firm's reputation suffers. Be sure the salespeople obey any state or local laws regarding soliciting and obtain any solicitation permits that may be required.

Blockbusting/panic selling.   Any discussion of solicitation would be incomplete without a mention of blockbusting or panic selling. This consists of frequent efforts to sell real estate in a neighborhood by generating fear that people in the protected classes are moving into or out of a neighborhood. The fair housing laws further define these actions as ones that include representations that real estate values are declining because of these transactions, which in fact have nothing to do with the intrinsic value of the real estate. Blockbusting or panic selling violates the fair housing laws.

News Columns

One of the best ways to showcase your expertise, and the company in the process, is by writing a news or real estate column. You may publish in a local general circulation newspaper, a weekly or shopper's newspaper or a business or professional magazine or newsletter. Depending on the publication, you may or may not have to pay for the column. Figure 9.4 is a sample news column that was printed free as a public service.

These columns are intended to be informative, providing substantive content that is useful for the consuming public. When you (or a professional writer working on your behalf) prepare an article, be sure it is an accurate, objective discussion of an issue. Otherwise, your credibility as an expert can be threatened. A major advantage of news columns is that you control the content. Often newspaper reporters are looking for controversy to sell headlines or a slant that can distort the story and mislead readers. As the expert author, you can ensure the accuracy of the content. (Be sure to clarify the editorial policies with the publisher. Otherwise you may find that your carefully prepared words have been edited.)

Letters to the Editor

Observe current events in local communities, in city council chambers or state government; listen to the topics of conversation on the radio or television; and read the newspapers. You may get sufficiently stirred up to make a public comment. A letter to the editor is a natural outlet. Not only do you create visibility for yourself by stepping forward, but also you might influence public thinking with your comments. Don't make your

FIGURE 9.4   A Sample News Column

Real Estate

John Cyr

Foothills sprout subdivisions

A few years ago, when land developers subdivided many thousand acres of homesites in the Valley Springs area and sold them to buyers from other parts of the state, we in the real estate business marvelled at their success.

Unfortunately, many of the lots would not sustain septic tanks. (For a homesite to qualify for a septic tank disposal system it must pass what is called a "percolation (perc) test," which means that the effluent from the leach lines must be absorbable to a depth of at least the first four feet of ground area.)

It turned out to be true that many of the lots sold could not pass such tests and, consequently, at last count, many owners hold lots they can't build on using the conventional septic tank systems.

Many of us think the reason the developers were so successful in selling so many lots is probably because they met the needs and desires of people from all parts of the state who wish to escape traffic congestion, smog, drugs and crime. They would go almost anywhere within reason to get away from it all. That's why the hill

country looked so good to them, and still does.

The market for hill country property is still strong but the local authorities are now wise to the septic problems and have taken measures to protect buyers from buying unusable lots. Enter the subdividers who have solved the problem by installing sewer plants that meet all county specifications.

La Contenta Golf and Country Club near Valley Springs was one of the first to provide such facilities and it sold out in just a year or two. Now several experienced Stockton developers have followed suit and are offering homesites in hill country subdivisions that offer "state of the art" community sewer systems.

Tony Meath of Lockeford is one who has installed such a system in his Gayla Manor Subdivision located on Highway 88 just about 5 miles east of Pine Grove. Gayla Manor not only has one of the first modern sewer plants outside of a city plant to be built in Amador County, it also offers community water service, paved streets, street lights, and protective restrictions, among other ameneties. Although on the market for only a month or so Tony reports that over half of the 56 lots are already sold.

Another enterprising developer, Jimmy Winchell of G. M. Winchell & Sons has just finished improvements on Wallace Lake Estates, a subdivision adjacent to the small community of Wallace on Highway 12. (Next to Rossetti's Restaurant).

Wallace Lake Estates is a more ambitious project with its own sewer and water system to serve 300 lots but also offers paved

streets, TV cable, telephone, security gates, street lights and propane piped to each homesite. Also, they have reserved a 14½-acre site for a future shopping center.

The lots are a minimum of 10,000 sq. ft. and surrounded by 240 acres of scenic oak-studded hills with it's own private lake. Jimmy already reports sales of over 39 lots with little or no advertising. The prices of the lots range from $50,000 to $80,000 with no bonds.

Other, smaller subdivisions, for people who want more land around them are coming on the market in the Valley Springs-Burson area offering 3 to 5 acres in size with guaranteed percolation for septic tanks. Rosemarie Realty (Rosemary Mendonca of Lodi) is one of the developers and a group of investors from Northern California are putting together another subdivision tentatively named Shangri-La Valley Estates, which will be selling 5 acres and larger homesites.

Such subdivisions make good sense because instead of using up valuable high-production agricultural land in the valley, they use land that has little value for other uses. The only drawback to such developments is the distance factor. But for those people who can carry on much of their work out of their homes, they might just as well live in a more pleasant, less stressful environment.

John Cyr is a Stockton real estate broker, author and owner of John Cyr Realtors. Questions can be submitted to a rotating panel of experts by writing BusinessMonday, The Stockton Record, Box 900, Stockton, CA 95201.

letter too long and think about what message will be communicated if the letter is edited (if that's the paper's policy). Before you mail the letter, think about how the public will react to the viewpoint or position you express. If you will be alienating potential customers, you may be better off keeping your opinions to yourself.

Media Resource

Consumers in your local real estate market can be affected by both current events and specific developments in the industry. The local newspapers and radio and television stations may not be particularly attuned to real estate issues. By developing relationships with local reporters, broadcasters and real estate editors, you can become a resource on whom they rely when it's time to do a story. This can be a two-way relationship. They may contact you for information or a viewpoint; or, once you have an established relationship, they will be receptive to you contacting them. Because the media is bombarded with press releases, phone calls and letters, your message is more likely to be heard because of this relationship.

Learn how to become a good spokesperson or interviewee. People who are quotable because of their stature, their expertise or their provocative or insightful comments appeal to the media. Many brokers welcome the opportunity to make an impact on the community, which media exposure provides. The media look for "sound bites" or short comments they can use in limited space or air time. If you can provide concise and effective comments, you make a desirable interviewee. If the media are looking for an official position, be sure that only the person who is authorized to speak on behalf of the company provides these comments.

You could be surprised by what appears in print or on the air unless you are properly prepared for an interview. First find out the nature of the story. Before you start answering questions or volunteering information (especially personal viewpoints), determine whether you are providing an expert's quote or background information. Any comments you make could be aired or printed unless you clearly establish that you are speaking "off the record."

The media normally work on very tight deadlines. Consequently, they want immediate access to you. If you're unavailable they'll move on to someone else. But don't let yourself be rushed. Normally you can return a phone call in several minutes, which gives you time to gather statistics or other specific information that is relevant to a story. You also can use this time to collect your thoughts so you speak directly to the points you want to make. This minimizes the likelihood that you will make unintentional or offensive comments or that your comments will be reported inaccurately or taken out of context.

MARKETING PROPERTIES

A strategy for marketing listings is an significant part of your company's marketing plan unless your company is exclusively representing buyers. Owners generally have a number of concerns when they decide to sell their properties. They turn to real estate licensees with the expectation that we have the tools and expertise to calm these concerns. Now it's time to fulfill those expectations.

According to a 1998 National Association of REALTORS® survey on the Home Buying and Selling Process, the most frequent concern cited by sellers was getting a sales price high enough to recover what they put into the property. Keeping their homes in showcase condition during the selling process, closing on time for a relocation deadline and selling in time to buy the house they want were three other major concerns.

Unfortunately, too many salespeople see the signature on a listing contract as the end of their responsibility to the company, rather than the beginning of their responsibility to the property owners. Some of that is the company's fault if it focuses on quotas rather than on service. A property worth listing is worth marketing. Figure 9.5 demonstrates what sellers want real estate licensees to help them do.

The marketing plan for listings involves as much common sense as advertising skill and knowledge of the laws that govern advertising practices. One rule of thumb you can use is: If this were my property, how would I want to see it showcased? In the

FIGURE 9.5   What Sellers Most Want Their Real Estate Agents to Help Them Do

Help with paperwork, inspections, settlements
5%

Price competitively
28%

Find a buyer
30%

Help find another home to buy
1%

Negotiate/deal with buyer
5%

Sell within timeframe
26%

Advise on fixing up home to help it sell
5%

SOURCE: *The Home Buying and Selling Process,* 1998, National Association of REALTORS®.

best light, of course. You need flattering pictures of the listing, a property that is really ready for show, and a realistic listing price before aggressively marketing it. Otherwise a new relationship with the owner can get off on the wrong foot, and you will incur expense that would yield greater benefit elsewhere. You also don't want to turn away potential buyers with overpriced listings.

A variety of marketing tools are commonly used to promote your listings. The things you do to promote the listings also reflect on your company. How well you do this is as important as what you do. You can keep your own statistics to determine which strategies are most effective for your company. The following tools, as well as those discussed when we set up the company's communications system in Chapter 6, can be considered in the marketing plan for your listings. Regardless of whether you are marketing your listings on the Internet, in the newspaper or on TV, the rules about pictures and copy apply.

Pictures

Advertising includes words and pictures to create an impression and cause people to act. Consider the pictorial representation of your listings. The picture of a tree instead of the front door or a brown hillside instead of the house won't present a pleasing or useful image of a new listing. Even though there are obstacles to overcome, you must still capture a flattering, yet accurate, image of the property. It takes time and good equipment to compose a worthwhile picture. Today's digital cameras produce outstanding photographs, which are also useful for computer and Internet distribution. But if the salespeople can't take good pictures, you may be better off hiring a professional. We should provide better pictorial representations than the property owners can produce themselves.

Still photographs compiled on video tape and strolling videos have become popular tools for showcasing listings. The quality of these productions, however, is critical. They can look amateurish unless you use the proper camera and lighting equipment and have the technical know-how, particularly for taking interior shots. These are great tools for marketing as long as they look professional. Also consider other technology to showcase your listings, such as interactive videos.

Once the listings are captured on film, the pictures are useful for many purposes. The most obvious are photo listing magazines, Web sites, MLS books, brochures and fliers. When a salesperson shares the pictures with the property owner, this is a tactful way to persuade the owner to do maintenance or repairs. Pictures also make nice memory gifts at closing or postcards that can be used for marketing purposes.

Advertising Copy

Whether you are preparing copy for classified advertising or a Web site or writing a script for a TV promotion, the story you tell about a property is critical. The listing salesperson is most familiar with the property and thus is presumably the one best suited to write the ad. However, writing truly effective ads requires some skill. You must decide whether the salespeople (or their personal assistants) have the necessary expertise, or whether to use a copy specialist to prepare the ad. Figure 9.6 is a form on which a salesperson can prepare notes for the copy specialist to use. You can enhance the effectiveness of your ads

FIGURE 9.6   Ad Copy Form

		WHAT MAKES THIS HOUSE DIFFERENT FROM ALL OTHER HOUSES ON THE MARKET AT THIS TIME? (USP—UNIQUE SELLING PROPOSITION)
CLIENT'S NAME:	SP.:	
ADDRESS:	LED NO.:	
TOWN:	AGE:	
LIST PRICE:	LIST DATE:	
STYLE:	EXT.:	WHO DO YOU SEE BUYING THIS HOUSE?:
ROOMS:	DR:	FAM. RM.:
BR:		E-I-KIT:
BATH:	FULL:	HALF:	LIST AN INDIVIDUAL FEATURE AND DESCRIBE THE BENEFIT OF THAT FEATURE TO A BUYER
FINISHED BASE:		
FPLC:	WHERE:	TYPE:	SPECIAL FEATURE: BENEFIT:
# GARAGE:		CENT. AIR:
POOL:		DESCRIBE:
PROP. SIZE:		
ITEMS INCLUDED:		
WALL TO WALL: ____	SELF CLEAN OVEN: ____	
REFRIG: ____	CENT. VAC.: ____	
WASHER: ____	INTERCOM: ____	
DRYER: ____	OTHER: ____	
SPECIAL INSTRUCTIONS AS TO ADVERTISING COMMITTMENTS:		
		1-Year Homeowner's Warranty Included: ____ Yes ____ No

by conducting classes or seminars in ad writing. There is also computer software that is helpful.

Salespeople, not ads, sell properties. The purpose of an ad is to get the readers' attention and develop their interest in and desire for the property so that they will take some action to pursue the property with a salesperson. This is the AIDA approach (Attention, Interest, Desire and Action). The first five to eight words should capture the readers' attention so that they will read the balance of the copy. Then an ad should say just enough to pique the readers' curiosity and spur them to action, without saying so much that there is no reason to pursue the property.

The language in an advertisement either communicates a message about a property or creates a word picture. Numerous studies indicate that the three most important factors to buyers are the neighborhood (location), the size of the property and the price. Ads that don't provide the information a buyer is looking for are less likely to be read. And as a practical matter, while abbreviations are common, does everyone understand our shorthand? A 4BR, 2B, hse w/EIK, FR and 2 FPs can be a real puzzle. Read the ad aloud to see if it makes sense and conveys the message you intended.

Legal issues.   Ultimately the responsibility for the quality, accuracy and legality of an ad is the broker's. Monitoring the advertising copy, including those ads paid for and submitted by the salespeople, is a critical activity for management. *Monitoring advertising on Web sites, including the salespeople's own, is an especially important risk-management responsibility today.*

The property must be accurately represented. There's a difference between highlighting a property's best features and misrepresenting the property. Superlative comments or opinions are permissible; misrepresentations of facts are not. If a house is described as "energy efficient," the typical reader is going to expect that the house has superior insulation or cost-saving features, not just ordinary construction. Brand names, such as Thermopane®, should not be used unless the named product is actually used. A typographical error is untruthful regardless of who made the mistake or how it occurred. The licensee is responsible even if a secretary typed "3 bedrooms" instead of "2" in the ad copy.

An ad also should be an accurate representation of the owner's position. Prices should be stated according to the terms authorized by the listing contract or the seller. You have no authority to publish a price or reduction without the owner's consent. Nor should you publish any information that compromises the owner's negotiating position or violates the broker's fiduciary responsibility to the owner.

Your state's licensing laws may include provisions that affect the contents of your ads. Several important issues are revealed as you answer these questions.

- Does the advertisement of a listing have to include the licensed name of the firm? The phone number? In the case of multiple offices, which phone number?

- What conditions or restrictions are imposed when salespeople include their names and phone numbers? What about personal voice mail and pager numbers?

- What are the procedures for advertising on the Internet?

- What are the requirements if the broker or a salesperson advertises property that is personally owned?

If there are financing terms for the listing that are appealing, they must be presented properly. According to the Truth in Lending laws, general expressions, such as "owner will finance" or "liberal terms available," are permissible. But consider how misleading "only $1,000 down" can be, especially when a low down payment means higher monthly payments and closing costs. You must be specific about the amount of the loan, amount of the down payment, amount of the monthly payments and length of the loan when specific loan terms are advertised.

Is the language nondiscriminatory? The fair housing laws prohibit making, printing or publishing any statement that indicates any preference, limitation or discrimination based on race, color, religion, sex, familial status, handicap or national origin. If you're unsure about the language, consult the Fair Housing

Advertising Regulations (Federal Register/Vol. 54. No. 13/ Monday, January 23, 1989/Rules and Regulations).

For example, language such as *whites only, Hispanic neighborhood, Christian home, adults only, adults preferred* or *older neighborhood, singles, no children, walking distance to the synagogue, one block from the Italian club* and *good parish schools* are considered discriminatory. It is permissible to say *mother-in-law quarters, family room, walk to bus stop, bachelor pad, great view* or *wheelchair ramp.* These are federal guidelines, so be sure to consult your local or state human relations commission for advice. (See Chapter 14 for more detail about the fair housing laws.)

Classified Advertising

Why do you use classified advertising? To promote your firm or to locate a purchaser or tenant for the property? The property owner and the broker may see classified advertising differently. Owners do not expect to be used by the firm for its own promotional purposes. They hire you to showcase their properties. Salespeople should be trained to present a total promotional plan for the owner's property at the time it is listed. This should help assure the owner that the company has his or her best interest in mind.

One of the owners' most common criticisms involves the amount of advertising devoted to their listings. It may be that promises were made just to get the listing. Or perhaps no amount of advertising would be acceptable to an owner who's frustrated, waiting for a property to sell. Regardless of the reason, a discussion of the company's advertising policies should avoid unrealistic expectations. Then provide periodic reports to substantiate the advertising. Compiling these reports is a relatively simple task with today's computer software.

Multiple Listing Services

One of the most common marketing activities in residential sales is the promotion of our listings to other licensees. Though most of us don't think about MLSs in a marketing sense, they are, in fact, one of the most useful and effective tools for exposing the property to potential buyers. Traditionally MLSs have promoted properties through other licensees. But as MLSs turn to the Internet, their inventory can be promoted directly to consumers.

Many of the legal issues that have been discussed also affect promotions in the MLS. Inaccurate information about the property not only creates an unfavorable impression of the listing salesperson, but also creates liability for both the listing and the selling firms. Whether misrepresentation is the result of a mistake or carelessness, it still amounts to a misrepresentation of the property. This could start a chain of events that jeopardizes a settlement. You should monitor the copy the salespeople provide the MLS to ensure that it does not violate the fair housing laws or their duty to protect the confidential information of their principals.

Brochures and Fliers

A brochure is another tool for marketing a listing. It may be as elaborate or expensive a publication as you desire. Some firms chose to produce these only for unique, boutique or high-priced properties because of their expense. The owner should not be led to expect a brochure unless such a piece is part of the promotional plan for that property. Because MLS printouts and Web sites typically contain limited information, a less elaborate flier may be used to explain additional features. Fliers are useful for other salespeople as well as prospective purchasers and tenants. Again, management should monitor the content of brochures and fliers to ensure they do not create legal problems.

Open Houses

Open houses appeal to our natural curiosity. We want to see and feel for ourselves. Incorporating open houses into a marketing plan can increase the exposure of the listing as well as create opportunities for the salesperson to talk about the property. Property owners sometimes measure the attentiveness of salespeople by their willingness to conduct open houses. Conversely, some owners need to be convinced that open houses have the merit.

A recent survey by Texas A&M University's Real Estate Center disclosed that 59 percent of the responding real estate practitioners didn't think open houses helped to locate buyers for the properties. Forty-one percent of the respondents indicated that they hold open houses to appease sellers. Others who have studied the results of open houses suggest that the salesperson, rather than the seller, is the principal beneficiary, suggesting that open houses are great for self-promotion. It may be that your decision to offer open houses is driven by the competition or results of open houses in your area.

Be realistic with the owner about the results that can be expected. Owners don't mind sacrificing their time and effort, but they get upset (as do salespeople) when open houses do not produce any visitors. Picking a good day and time for a public open house is a critical, maybe even a mystical, exercise. Strategies work differently in different markets. In some a weekday evening during daylight savings time may work; in others it may not. A decorated holiday tour of your company's listings may be appealing. Track attendance to determine the best strategy.

Open houses are joint projects between the owner and the salesperson and require careful planning and execution, regardless of whether they are conducted for other salespeople or the public. Owners hesitate to authorize open houses when they expect to be inconvenienced. They may be uneasy about opening their homes to strangers. The salesperson should discuss preparations for the property and arrangements for the owner's comfort during the event. An open-house checklist that the salespeople could use is provided in Figure 9.7.

Safety of the salesperson.   Unfortunately, real estate salespeople have recently been victims of violent crimes while on the job. They should not take chances with their personal safety at open houses. Establish procedures for tracking the salespeople's whereabouts and their intended schedules. Also insist they have the ability to summon help if needed. They should determine several routes of escape from the property—into a fenced yard does no good—and park their vehicles where they can get away quickly

FIGURE 9.7   Open House Checklist

TWO WEEKS BEFORE:

_____ 1. Discuss and coordinate open-house plans with owners to get informed consent and cooperation.

_____ 2. Arrange for owners to be away from premises during open house.

_____ 3. Set up an advertising schedule at least ten days before open house to ensure meeting newspaper deadlines.

_____ 4. Prepare ads and submit to newspapers.

_____ 5. Schedule personnel. For security reasons, two salespeople should cover an open house whenever possible.

_____ 6. Mail invitations to neighbors (an excellent source of leads).

NIGHT BEFORE:

_____ 7. Confirm arrival time and responsiblities with accompanying salespeople.

_____ 8. Pack:

    a. a guest book, properly headed with listing salesperson's name, address and telephone number _____

    b. pens for signing in guests _____

    c. flags (optional) _____

    d. signs (open house and for sale) _____

    e. tackers and directional signs _____

    f. alternate listings to discuss with guests not interested in subject property _____

    g. offer-to-purchase agreements _____

    h. mortgage payment book _____

    i. a sufficient supply of company brochures _____

    j. souvenirs or giveaways (if available) _____

    k. business cards to hand to prospects _____

    l. key to house _____

    m. deodorant spray or scented candles to eliminate odors _____

MORNING OF OPEN HOUSE:

_____ 9. En route to property, post directional signs along main roads and roads leading to the house.

_____ 10. On arrival, park away from best parking; leave plenty of convenient space for guests.

_____ 11. Make sure flags and signs are in place in front of house.

_____ 12. Turn on lights and open shades and drapes.

_____ 13. Say good-bye to owners, reassuring them if necessary.

FIGURE 9.7   Open House Checklist *(Continued)*

_____ 14. Arrange soft background music.

_____ 15. Prepare fireplace and light fire or turn on air conditioner.

_____ 16. Prepare refreshments, if appropriate.

_____ 17. Assemble any available information concerning warranties on appliances, utility bills, disclosure notices, if required, schools and transportation on a coffee table.

_____ 18. Place a picture of the house in alternate season on display.

DURING OPEN HOUSE:

_____ 19. Make sure only real estate material is available for reading.

_____ 20. Keep TV turned off.

_____ 21. Greet people at the door when possible.

_____ 22. Accompany people through the house. Do not leave them.

_____ 23. If guests want to see any other house suggested by you, call your office and arrange for another agent to meet them and take them or to replace you at your position while you take them. Make sure your replacement is there before you leave.

_____ 24. Have each guest sign the guest book

_____ 25. Treat every guest as a listing prospect.

IMMEDIATELY AFTER OPEN HOUSE:

_____ 26. Turn off all lights and any air conditioners or check fireplace before you leave, unless owners have instructed otherwise.

_____ 27. Lock all doors and close all windows.

_____ 28. Remove all signs, guest book and all items not previously on property.

_____ 29. Tidy up; empty ashtrays (if smoking was permitted) and wash coffee cups and utensils.

WITHIN 24 HOURS AFTER OPEN HOUSE:

_____ 30. Return all items—signs, brochures and other printed material—to office.

_____ 31. Record all names of prospects in prospect book. Indicate if source was newspaper ad, sign or invitation sent to neighbors.

_____ 32. Report activity to owner by telephone call or in person.

_____ 33. Send owner photocopy of guest book page with cover letter of explanation.

_____ 34. Send thank-you note to everyone who attended.

_____ 35. Follow up all prospects according to normal procedure.

if necessary. There's safety in numbers, which is an argument for using several salespeople to host an open house, especially if the structure is large. Use a sign-in/sign-out register for the visiting public and licensees. Although attendance records are not foolproof for identifying those with questionable intentions, they just might encourage an ill-intentioned person to leave.

Safety of the seller. No one should be allowed to freely wander through a property unattended. Although sellers should be encouraged to tuck valuables out of sight, this does not guarantee that the owner's belongings are secure. Nor can the salespeople, for that matter, but they must be vigilant observers and be guided by proper procedures to safely handle suspicious situations. Think about the artful thief whose hands are quicker than the eye or an unscrupulous visitor who's surveying the premises for future reference. At the conclusion of the open house, the salesperson should account for every visitor (the reason for sign-out entries) to be sure no one is still lurking in or around the property.

Safety of the visitor. Make sure that your salespeople pay attention to any potentially dangerous conditions at the property. Although we know that property defects are an important issue in our transactions, property conditions are also a consideration at open houses. For example, as the result of a case filed against a broker in New Jersey, the state's supreme court determined that agents have a legal duty to conduct a reasonable inspection of the property and warn visitors of discoverable physical conditions that may be dangerous. Although this case set a precedent in New Jersey, it also provided evidence that could be used by courts elsewhere.

The court ruled that the salesperson has some degree of responsibility to protect the invitees from harm because the property, during an open house, is being used as a place of business. People attend an open house as the invitees of the principal as well as of the brokerage firm. To protect all concerned, the salesperson should walk through the property, identify any dangerous conditions and take precautionary steps, such as posting signs or colored tape or verbally warning visitors of these conditions.

Yard Signs

Yard signs promote the fact that a property is for sale and, as indicated in Figure 9.1, were determined to be the origin of approximately 14 percent of sales transactions. This may not seem like a large percentage, but every avenue is important to attract buyers for the property. Granted, there are some properties, such as condominiums, where signs may not be permitted. There also are ongoing controversies in some municipalities about the use of for sale signs. But they are a valuable tool that the owner should be encouraged to allow you to use. Some signs have mounted holders for fliers or listing sheets, so people can help themselves to detailed information. Or you might consider "talking signs," which transmit information on a limited radio frequency that people can listen to while parked in their cars in front of the property.

PROTECTING YOUR IMAGE

The best-designed marketing plan isn't worth the expenditure if you cause problems for yourself in the process. You don't want to tarnish your image or, worse, create legal problems. Earlier we mentioned some legal issues that affect both what you say and do. The following are some additional items to contemplate.

- If you're going to promote yourself as an expert, remember that consumers have grown weary and wary of the hollow representations that are occasionally made in this business. You should be able to substantiate your claims.

- Targeting a message to the wrong audience is not only a waste of time and money but also can damage your reputation. Have you ever received a mailing and wondered why? Perhaps it was addressed to a party who has long since moved from your address, or its subject matter was totally irrelevant to you. Don't embarrass yourself or invite questions about your attentiveness to details by being careless when distributing materials.

- Do you claim to be "number one?" Number one in what? We're all number one in something, but unless you're specific, this claim can be misleading. Do you mean sales volume, market position or number of offices? Can you substantiate this claim? A point to ponder—what are the actual *benefits* to a consumer for doing business with "number one?" The consumer is really interested in benefits, not claims.

- Use care when making comparisons between you and the competition. False or misleading statements about competitors are unethical. Knocking the competition can make you look desperate or unprofessional, neither of which will enhance your reputation.

- Be *truthful* and *realistic* in your claims. Stating that you provide a "free service" when the service is contingent on some business benefit to you, such as a listing or commission, is not only unethical but also a flagrant misrepresentation. Offers of premiums, prizes or merchandise discounts may be regulated by your state's licensing laws.

- Do you have an affiliation with a professional organization or trade group? We work hard to promote our associations and professional designations. The use of trademarks, trade names or insignia of organizations by individuals who are not members is unauthorized by these organizations. This also may violate your state's license law.

- Promote the company as an equal opportunity firm that serves people regardless of their race, color, religion, sex, familial status, handicap or national origin. Display the equal opportunity slogan and logo in *all* of your printed material and publications. When using pictorial or graphic representations of people in a community, neighborhood or housing development, be sure that the human models represent a cross section of the population.

- Selective use of media (print or electronic) could lead someone to conclude that your services are available only to certain populations. You can use publications whose audience profile is a population protected by the fair housing laws only as long as you also use publications that have general circulation.

- Can you select publications that target specific audiences by, for example, nationality, language or religion? Yes, provided you also advertise in a publication with general circulation. For example, if you are fluent in another language, you may want to use this skill to assist individuals who speak that language. You are permitted to advertise in a foreign language or ethnic publication as long as you also advertise in a publication that reaches the general population.

MANAGING YOUR MARKETING

Advertising is your largest expense (25 percent or more in some firms) after cost of sales. Add other costs associated with marketing and you have a sizable expenditure that must be carefully managed. Because a marketing program combines a variety of tools that are intended to complement one another, you have to look at the total program to determine its effectiveness.

The effectiveness of some tools will be more apparent than others. A radio spot, for example, may cause a person to seek out your newspaper ad or Internet site. You can't say which vehicle ultimately caused a consumer to do business with you. Furthermore, some tools produce results faster than others so you have to assess their effectiveness on a long-term basis. People may not act on or respond to one ad, but they will respond after a number of repetitions.

The primary data with which you evaluate the program is collected from the consumers. The quality of that data is affected by their perceptions. A person may indicate that he or she was referred by a friend, but the person's decision to contact your firm may have been reinforced by your advertising. Nonetheless, companies should establish procedures to gather data about the source of phone calls and other inquiries. Then back this up with a line on the transaction report so that you can identify the source of contact that actually resulted in a transaction. Your public relations counsel can help set up procedures for evaluating your marketing program and decipher the data.

Advertising registers are very important for determining the effectiveness of classified advertising. Look at the number of calls and the total cost of the classified advertising for the same period. You can determine how much each of those calls cost simply by dividing the cost by the number of calls. As you monitor the per-call cost over the course of several months and look at the conversion to transactions, you get some idea of the effectiveness of each of the classified advertising vehicles you're using. Follow the same process to evaluate your Internet site.

No matter how much advertising you do or where you do it, you may not satisfy the salespeople. You have choices—spend more, argue with them or involve them in a solution. People are more likely to complain when they don't understand your advertising strategy. All they see is that you cut the amount of advertising in a certain publication or that you never advertise in a publication that other brokers use. Share your advertising strategy so the salespeople can see how it fits into the entire plan and how the expenditures are distributed for best results. Also invite their input. Because they're the ones in the field, they may have some valid observations about ways your marketing program should be designed to help them.

CONCLUSION

Marketing is a total program, with advertising being just one piece of the plan. Any broker who's weathered a newspaper strike knows the frustration when a major contact with the public is temporarily out of circulation, especially when sellers want their properties advertised and the listings take a bit longer to sell. But the company still survives, and buyers buy and listings sell. We tend to place a great deal of emphasis on the power of classified advertising. But we can't overlook the value of all of the other marketing outlets we have, especially with the growing popularity of the Internet.

Perhaps the most powerful marketing tool you have is the people who work for you, from the salespeople to the receptionist and the person who removes the "sold" signs from the properties. They are the ones who provide your services and really contribute to the image of your firm. The marketing plan incorporates a wide range of tools to promote your firm, your services and your listings, all designed to get the public to meet your people.

DISCUSSION EXERCISES

What marketing strategies have been most effective in promoting your firm in your area? What did you try that didn't prove to be very effective?

* * *

What marketing strategies have you found to be most effective in promoting your listings? What ways have you found to control the cost of advertising listings?

* * *

What, if any, legal problems have you observed in the way companies and listings have been promoted in your area?

In Conclusion of This Unit

Now that the organization has assembled the necessary tools, it is prepared to conduct business. The ownership and affiliations are established; the structure of the organization and staffing requirements are identified; the financial resources are planned, considering the income potential and the anticipated expenditures; the company's policies and procedures are established; and the company has a marketing plan with which to generate business. The company has a plan and is organized so that it's prepared to work with its most important asset, the people who provide the company's services.

Depending on whether you are the broker/owner, a senior manager in a large organization, a sales manager or a department manager, your involvement in the various decisions and tasks involved in the organizing function of management will probably be different. As a guide for understanding where you participate in the process, the following summary is provided.

➤ *Structuring the ownership, business affiliations* and *human resources*:

- The broker/owner must decide the most suitable legal structure for the ownership and, perhaps with the assistance of senior management, decide the business affiliations for the company, chart the organization and make preliminary decisions about manpower requirements.

- Other levels of management need to be familiar with the decisions that the broker/owner and senior management make and understand specifically where their authority or chain of command fits within the entire organization.

➤ *Structuring the business systems,* which include the company's physical facilities and communications and information systems:

- The ultimate responsibility for deciding the location of offices and the design of the company's communications and information systems rests with the owners and perhaps senior management.

- Lower levels of management may be invited to provide input into these decisions.

- Depending on the scope of authority, a sales or department manager may be authorized to purchase office equipment and furnishings and design the physical layout of the office.

➤ *Structuring the finances* of the organization:

- The development of the general operating budget, including the compensation programs, is the responsibility of the broker/owner and senior management. They may, however, solicit input from other managers.

- Lower levels of management are normally responsible for the budgets for their departments or offices.

➤ *Developing policies and procedures* for the company:

- The broker/owner decides the general business philosophy and ethics for the organization.

- All levels of management are typically involved in developing the policies and procedures to define the rules people are expected to follow in the general conduct of business.

➤ *Marketing and advertising* programs:

- The chain of command in the organization determines the management level at which the major decisions about the company's general marketing plan are made and the level that is responsible for individual marketing strategies.

THE
BUSINESS, FIRST HAND

With millions of people turning to the Internet for information and consumer purchasing, this media has become one of the most powerful tools in any marketing plan. The growth of the Internet provides tremendous opportunities for real estate companies to reach contemporary purchasers in innovative ways. Although many large or megabrokerage firms have hopped on the Internet in recent years, as one small, single-office company has found, an organization simply has to be creative, not large, to embrace this medium. As enticing as the Internet is, however, its benefits will not materialize unless companies learn to develop and manage effective Web sites. The lessons in our example are valuable for any firm and demonstrate how, with some inventiveness, a company can use the Internet not only for marketing but also for enhancing business relationships.

Ray's Real Estate, whose Web page appears in Figure 9.2, began exploring the Internet in 1994. Today, the company has five Web sites, with another soon to appear. Each day the sites attract approximately 25,000 hits and 35 to 50 inquiries for properties. Approximately 25 of those convert to viable inquiries to pursue. The Internet is not only an outlet for property listings but is also a tool for linking viewers to a wide variety of resources. The Web sites are designed to connect people to other information and services that are key to purchasing decisions.

This small real estate company, with nine to ten sales associates plus a network of fifteen licensees scattered throughout Florida to handle referrals, has attracted a worldwide audience for its waterfront properties. Inquiries come from as far as England, Germany, Spain, South America and Canada, as well as stateside. In some cases people purchase properties based solely on information acquired on the Web sites.

Ronald Ray was first attracted to the Internet by e-mail. It provided an extremely affordable and convenient way to communicate. At a time when other aspects of computer technology were not especially user-friendly, e-mail was relatively uncomplicated. As the number of people who embraced e-mail for communications increased, having an e-mail address was as important as having a telephone number. Today, Ray's e-mail address is promoted just as widely.

Once established with e-mail, the company got bolder and established its first Web site. After the first year it became readily apparent that the services of a Webmaster would be essential to gain maximum advantage and efficiency. Managing a Web site can take on a life of its own, requiring a considerable amount of time and expertise. Sites must attract visitors not only by their visual appeal and content but also by their accessibility. Registering with all the key search engines and establishing links with other sites is critical. Sites also must be constantly updated, including submissions to the search engines, generally three times per week. The goal is to provide current property listings along with new enticements to attract and retain visitors. Today, with the aid of faster technology and a young, savvy consultant, Mr. Ray has succeeded in efficiently managing effective Web sites for his company.

These Web sites connect people with an extensive network of resources to help prospective purchasers of the company's Florida waterfront listings. Yacht brokers, air-conditioning specialists as well as banks and title companies are on the sites. In addition, the sites provide a wide variety of information to help people relocate to Florida. Examples include procedures for obtaining a driver's license and changing Social Security registration, and details about Florida taxes, schools, parks and recreation facilities. In some cases, viewers are linked with other sites to obtain information; in other cases, information is compiled on the company's site. The company also offers free site space to local nonprofit organizations for their promotions.

As Ray's Real Estate has found, the Internet can play a significant role in a coordinated marketing program. Promoting e-mail addresses on for-sale signs and publishing e-mail and Web site addresses in every promotional medium, the company can establish a presence with today's contemporary consumers. By creatively networking other businesses on to its Web sites, a company can enhance both its alliances with these businesses and its services for prospective purchasers. Through one company's Web site, a wide world of consumers can be linked to not only real estate services but the services of other business as well.

Staffing and Directing

Regardless of how carefully you plan and organize the operation, your firm is unable to do anything without the people who work for you. Your human resources are the company's most valuable asset. Without them the company cannot provide any services, and without services there is nothing with which to produce revenue. This asset is entrusted to management to develop and nurture so that the goals of your organization can be achieved. Unit 3 is devoted to the staffing and directing functions of management—managing the company's human resources.

When you organized the structure of the company, you looked at the work that needs to be done and the human resources needed to do it. You determined the number of positions that need to be filled and from the job descriptions, the qualifications of the people you need to hire. But management's job doesn't end when people are hired. Just as you manage your financial resources to greatest advantage, you have to do likewise with your human resources. In the staffing function you are responsible not only for recruitment, selection and hiring but also for the professional development of your staff. As they develop, they contribute to the prosperity of the company.

A manager affects every aspect of people's lives on the job, which ultimately affects the company's ability to retain them. Their success or failure begins when you select the appropriate people for the jobs. You are responsible for providing supportive working conditions, helping people feel satisfied and accomplished and tending to their frustrations and concerns. The company needs them as much as (or more) than they need the company; therefore, a working environment that breeds resentment and discontent ultimately impacts productivity and can result in high turnover.

Managing the company's human resources involves

- recruiting, selecting and hiring the appropriate staff;
- creating opportunities for the staff to develop professional competency; and
- coaching people to accomplish the company's as well as their own goals.

The decisions managers make can be challenging. The directing function of management requires considerable interpersonal skill. Resolving conflicts, confronting unacceptable behavior and terminating a relationship with an employee are the less desirable aspects of your job.

They test your strength of character and management skill. But a good manager must be able to handle these situations with style and professionalism.

The chapters in this unit are devoted to the activities that are necessary to assemble, develop and retain your staff and create a working environment in which they can be productive for your organization.

10 Recruiting, Selecting and Hiring the Staff

Whom do you need to hire? What can you do to recruit salespeople? How do you select the best personnel for your company?

Recruiting salespeople is highly competitive. Your brokerage company is one of several in your area, all competing to recruit the top producers and newly licensed salespeople. And these people are out comparison shopping. One of the most pressing questions prospective salespeople ask is, "How do I select the right broker?" (And you may have noticed that brokers scramble over one another trying to get first crack at these people, even while they are still in classes and before taking their licensing exams.) Frequently prospective licensees are advised to

- interview with a variety of firms—several small, medium and large, some with franchise affiliation and others that are independent—and attend career nights;

- talk to friends in the business to get the practitioners' perspectives on various firms; and

- talk to people who recently have done business with real estate companies to find out what they have to say about various firms.

You're recruiting and they're selecting. In a similar fashion, experienced salespeople evaluate you and the competition when making their career moves. You should be pleased that they comparison shop. Salespeople who make informed decisions are more likely to feel good about their choice once they come to work for you. Salespeople look for companies with

- name recognition in the marketplace and a reputation for delivering quality services;

- secretarial and clerical support; and

- brokers and managers with high ethical standards.

You make a statement about your company as a place to work, beginning at the front door, when people enter your office and are greeted by a staff person. That echoes throughout the organization as people scrutinize your marketing tools, the working atmosphere in your office, the technology you use, the ethics in your firm, the way you treat the salespeople, whether you play favorites and how you enforce your policies.

People want a working environment where they can get maximum support so they can be most productive. Salespeople are also looking for an environment with the fewest barriers so they can work efficiently. Your ability to retain salespeople speaks volumes about the kind of organization where a prospective recruit would be working. Find out why people have left your employ to determine if changes are needed to attract the top producers. Think about this: if the commission split is the only thing that matters, salespeople would all be working in 100 percent commission firms. And they aren't. More than money matters when recruiting and retaining good salespeople (the later will be discussed in the next chapter).

STAFFING NEEDS

With your organization chart in hand, the assessment you did of the current work force and the calculations you performed to determine the number of salespeople you need

(Chapter 5), you can quickly determine who you are trying to recruit. You may need to fill positions to provide support services for your salespeople; you may need specific industry expertise, like an appraiser, a property manager or a mortgage loan representative; or you, like many other brokers, may be in the hunt for salespeople.

Staff Positions

We've frequently mentioned the importance of support services for the salespeople, particularly since demand for these services has increased. You have to decide the amount of staff support you can provide with full-time, part-time or temporary positions. For the most part, people who fill these positions are employees rather than independent contractors.

In Chapter 5 we discussed the development of job descriptions. Once you have determined the work that needs to be done and the responsibilities of a position, you can identify the qualifications people need to perform that job. This then tells you who you are trying to hire. With a job description in hand you can tell people exactly what they will be expected to do and to whom they will be accountable. Several staff positions for which you may need personnel are described below.

Receptionists and secretaries. Image makers know that the first impression is lasting. That first impression is typically made by the first person visitors see when they enter your office—the receptionist. While you may choose for the floor-duty salesperson to greet the public, you could find that a staff person specifically trained for this job is preferable. Salespeople get distracted by transaction business (their primary job), leaving the reception area unattended from time to time. Your company image plunges when people can't find a person to talk to when they walk into the office. Even if yours is a very small company, one person who can be receptionist as well as secretary is a valuable employee.

Secretaries and clerical employees are important for tending to the routine paperwork tasks that keep a business functioning. You have much greater control over the way this work is done when you hire staff personnel specifically trained for this activity. But you must be clear about whether the staff person is primarily responsible for providing clerical services for the company or for the salespeople. If they think the secretary works at their beck and call to type contracts, write letters or do mailings and you think the person is there to handle company correspondence and other business, you have a problem.

Transaction coordinators. Some companies hire transaction coordinators (or set up a separate company to coordinate transactions), who are responsible for orchestrating the flow of paper between the time a sales contract is signed and escrow or title closes. (Computer software programs are available to assist in this job.) This staff position provides support and convenience to the salespeople and offers you an advantage. Because the person is *your* employee, you have control over the coordinator's activities. This is an important distinction between a transaction coordinator and a personal assistant who is employed by a salesperson, which will be discussed shortly.

Department managers and employees. Depending on the internal structure you outlined for your organization, you may have designated work groups that are responsible for activities such as training, marketing and advertising, recruiting and accounting. These departments can be set up and staffed as they would be in any corporation, though a familiarity with real estate may be helpful in some of the positions. From the job descriptions you developed, you can determine the qualifications that are desirable for these managerial and staff positions.

Personal Assistants

As salespeople strive to free themselves from the administrative activities associated with their jobs and become more efficient, an important role for personal assistants has emerged. Surveys conducted by the National Association of REALTORS® have shown that the use of personal assistants to handle the non-sales-related aspects of the salespeople's business has boosted their productivity and increased the firm's profitability.

When a company decides to include personal assistants on its staff, a number of questions must be answered:

- What are the specific tasks an assistant will perform?
- Must the assistant be licensed to perform these tasks?
- Does the assistant work for the salesperson or the company?
- Is the assistant an employee or an independent contractor?
- Who pays the assistant?
- Who is responsible for paying benefits if the assistant is injured on the job or laid off?
- Who is responsible if the assistant violates the state's licensing laws?

While there are many good, practical reasons for using personal assistants, these questions indicate that a number of legal issues must be considered. One of the most critical involves your state's licensing law. This will determine whether personal assistants are required to be licensed, the activities licensed and unlicensed assistants are permitted to perform, the broker's accountability for their activities in either case and who is permitted to compensate an assistant. Even if a salesperson can hire a personal assistant, the broker must determine the liability the company has for the assistant's conduct.

Employment and tax laws also must be considered. Is the personal assistant an independent contractor or an employee? As will be discussed later in this chapter, this will affect the degree of control either the salesperson or the broker can exercise over the assistant's activities. This will also determine whether there is a requirement to withhold income tax and Social Security and pay statutory benefits, such as workers' compensation and unemployment compensation.

If the personal assistant is hired by the salesperson, you have to remember that you supervise the salesperson, and the salesperson supervises the assistant. Your company's policies and procedures should define the way salespersons' assistants are

TABLE 10.1   Personal Assistant Information

	All REALTORS®	Brokers/Broker Associates	Sales Agents
License Information			
Licensed	48%	55%	45%
Unlicensed	45	39	49
Both	7	6	6
Salary Expenses			
Paid By Respondent	65	59	69
Paid By Company	28	33	24
Both	7	8	7
Employment			
Full-Time	33	36	31
Part-Time	60	58	61
Both	7	6	8
Exclusively			
Exclusive Assistant	60	58	61
Shared With Others	37	38	35
Both	3	4	4
Employment Arrangement			
Independent Contractor	47	39	51
Employee	53	60	49
Leased Employee	*	1	*

*Less than one percent

SOURCE: *An Executive's Guide to* REALTORS®: *NAR Membership Profile,* 1996, National Association of REALTORS®.

accommodated in the organization, such as desk space and the use of the office equipment, the specific tasks they are permitted to perform and a specific code of conduct, including whether the assistant is permitted to represent only the salesperson or the company. Table 10.1 provides some insight about personal assistants from the 1996 NAR Membership Profile.

Salespeople

You have a basic, but very important, question to answer about the sales staff: "How many salespeople do I really want to hire?" Some brokers want to accumulate licensees while others want a small, highly talented group of people. The former group of brokers sees the size of the market share they can control being related to the number of salespeople they hire. Consequently, they plan for large sales staffs expecting that they will control a larger share of the market. The latter group of brokers sees a smaller sales staff as being more professional and more easily supervised. If that's a group of top producers, they will control a sizable share of the market, anyway.

When deciding which one of these strategies suits you, consider an important lesson other brokers have learned, which is reflected in a major shift in this industry—a trend to more streamlined sales staffs. Faced with increasing financial pressures to meet the demands of today's salespeople, organizations are learning to become more effective and cost-efficient with a smaller, highly skilled sales staff. Think about the following issues when forming your hiring strategy.

- *Financial implications*—Consider the cost you incur for each salesperson and the amount of added revenue you can expect. Remember the discussion of desk cost in Chapter 5.

- *Ability to manage the sales staff*—You need to be able to supervise and monitor the activities of the salespeople. In Chapter 6 we mentioned that as an office's sales force expands beyond 30 people, the job of supervising their activities becomes more difficult.

- *Profile of the salespeople*—Decide whether you want full-time or part-time salespeople and whether to concentrate on hiring newly licensed or experienced salespeople.

- *Size of the available pool of talent*—Consider the number of people you can reasonably expect to attract to your firm who match the profile you want to hire.

Full-time salespeople.   The definition of full-time can differ. Some companies define this to mean that salespeople devote 100 percent of their work time to real estate and have no other employment or profession. Yet there are salespeople who have other employment who can maintain the same level of production as those who work exclusively in real estate. And there are salespeople who consider themselves to be full-time but who really don't work intensely enough to warrant this title. If the company's policy is to hire full-time salespeople, define exactly what this means.

Frequently, the industry and the public perceive salespeople who have no other jobs or responsibilities to be more professional. While this perception is justified in some instances, it is not warranted in all cases. Depending on the skill and commitment of the individual, a salesperson may be quite effective handling another job while also providing competent and professional service to their customers and clients. Certainly, some jobs are easier to combine with a career in real estate than others.

As a practical matter, some salespeople need a period of transition to move successfully from their current jobs to a career exclusively in real estate, particularly if they are newly licensed. People have to survive financially, provide for their families and in many cases preserve benefits for a period of time. Some brokers and managers suggest that the best way to start a career is to jump in with both feet at once. But this is not realistic in all situations and could discourage an otherwise suitable hire. The company is wise to develop a policy to govern these situations.

One last point to consider is that you increase the level of commitment the company makes to the salespeople. Real estate companies tend to invest more time and money in the professional development of full-time rather than part-time salespeople. Training, education and the time managers devote to coaching a salesperson can be costly; the expectation is that the costs will be recovered over time with increased production and a commitment to the company. Full-time salespeople have come to expect this level of service from the company as well.

Part-time salespeople.   Are part-time salespeople ones who have other employment, or are they people who generally devote fewer hours to the real estate business? Some companies view part-time people as a unique asset to the firm. They feel they are hiring a network of contacts because of a person's involvement in the community with other business people or volunteer activities. Remember that if your salespeople are independent contractors, you cannot control the way they work, including the number of work hours per week. Typically, a part-time salesperson's production goals will be more conservative than a full-time person's. This is the best way to differentiate between the two.

Part-time salespeople are not precluded from being professional salespeople if you treat them as professionals. With today's technology they can be as connected to the information and resources other salespeople are. Because part-time salespeople could be less available to their customers and clients, they may rely more heavily on your support services. But you provide services for a reason—to help salespeople be productive. For a manager this may mean making time available to assist them on their schedules, which can play havoc with your personal life and the time you can devote to the full-time salespeople. This can be a balancing act so that you do not neglect the full-time people and create resentment.

Treat part-time salespeople as an important part of the team, rather than as outsiders, and they can make an important contribution to your company. Schedule events such as office meetings and educational sessions occasionally at times when part-time salespeople can attend as well. If you decide to hire part-time salespeople, you must be willing to take on the assignment to build an effective team.

License referral companies.   In some parts of the country real estate brokerage firms set up separate subsidiaries called *license referral companies.* These are licensed brokerage firms that hire licensed salespeople. But these people do not engage in sales activities. Instead, the firm is set up to be a conduit of referrals to the affiliated brokerage firm. We mention this because it is a way to attract or retain salespeople who do not meet a company's criteria for full-time salespeople, but who can contribute by referring business.

License referral companies normally exist where the licensing laws prohibit the payment of a referral fee to anyone who does not have a real estate license. The referral company is a legal conduit through which licensees receive fees for customer or client referrals. The fees are collected by the referral company from the conventional brokerage firm when the transactions close.

New licensees. Selecting the right newly licensed salesperson is critical. New licensees require considerable training, coaching and management supervision to get them started, which is a significant investment of time and financial resources. Most don't begin producing for several months, and even after that several more months will elapse before their transactions close. For at least six months the salesperson could be creating expenses while not generating any revenue in return. If that person turns out to be unsuccessful, the company will not recover its desk cost. It also will lose more time and incur more expense while bringing another new licensee up to speed. Protect your investment by picking suitable people at the outset.

There are advantages to building your sales staff with newly licensed people, however. The major one is that because they have not acquired any habits in the real estate business, they don't have any to overcome. It's relatively easy to train a newly licensed salesperson in your company's business philosophy, your company's techniques and your company's policies and procedures. Provided you retain the new people you've trained, as they gain experience and become solid producers, you will build a solid revenue base. This will keep you going as you bring more newly licensed salespeople on board.

Experienced salespeople. The obvious benefit of hiring experienced salespeople is that they have a customer following and the knowledge and skill to make a productive contribution to your company immediately. It's certainly easier to manage the company's finances when it has a more consistent stream of revenue than is typically the case when the sales staff is comprised primarily of newly licensed people.

Perhaps your company is looking for a top producer to provide a solid base for production. You pay a price to do this, however. A top producer generally earns top dollar, based on higher commission splits. Be assured, too, that top producers know the important role they play in a company's operation. So, they expect a working environment worthy of their stature in return. When a top producer feels that he or she is being used to support the company and is receiving little reward or recognition in return, that solid base of production will leave and go elsewhere to work. Top producers generally want to affiliate with top-producing companies.

Regardless of how attractive and competitive your services are, you're not likely to recruit a salesperson who's content with the current brokerage firm. You have to resist the temptation to "buy" talent. In Chapter 7 we discussed the importance of maintaining equity in your commission programs within the firm. Violating your company's commission plan to attract a salesperson can be very disruptive to the rest of the sales staff.

Often companies are really trading talent among themselves when they recruit experienced agents. And sometimes they are trading personnel problems. Not every experienced person will be suitable for your operation. A salesperson who blames the company rather than taking personal responsibility for his or her lack of success is not likely to do any better with you. On the other hand you may be giving talent an opportunity to flourish in ways that would not be possible with another company. Consider, too, that there are legitimate reasons, such as conflicts in business philosophy or personality conflicts, for a salesperson to do poorly with one company and then excel with your firm.

EMPLOYMENT LAWS

Mention discrimination to most brokers and the first thing that comes to mind is the fair housing laws. But there are many laws that address employment practices and protect against discrimination in the workplace. Among these are Title VII of the Civil Rights Act of 1964, the Civil Rights Act of 1866, the Age Discrimination in Employment Act and the Americans with Disabilities Act (ADA). Also be aware of laws that address pregnancy, family and medical leave, safety in the workplace, military service and overtime and wage laws. In addition, most states and some cities or municipalities have their own employment laws.

All of these laws are intended to prevent the employer from basing hiring and employment decisions on factors that are unrelated to the job an individual will be doing. They prohibit discrimination in employment activities such as job application procedures, hiring, firing, advancement, compensation, training and other privileges of employment. They also apply to employment-related activities such as recruitment, advertising, tenure, layoff, leave and fringe benefits. Each activity we discuss in this chapter is affected by the employment laws.

Equal Employment Practices

Don't start recruiting, selecting or hiring *anyone*, employees or salespeople, until you are familiar with all of the employment laws. Seek counsel from the agencies who enforce the laws and from a lawyer skilled in this area of law to be sure that the procedures you develop comply with applicable laws. You may find that some of your state's laws are more restrictive than the federal ones. As an example, you may not be required to comply with Title I of ADA (the employment provisions) because of the number of employees you have. But your state law may apply. (See Chapter 14 for further information about ADA.)

As a practical matter, it's somewhat hypocritical to support equal housing opportunities and then discriminate in your employment practices. The public relations fallout could tarnish the fine company image you work so hard to promote. Even if you would be technically exempt from a provision in an employment law, it could be in your best interest to take the extra step and enhance your reputation as an equal opportunity employer. As the industry today strives to serve a culturally diverse marketplace, brokers are recognizing the value of cultivating a culturally diverse workplace.

Your goal is to select those individuals who have the necessary job-related skills and credentials to perform the job for which they are being hired. Although you do not have to select everyone who expresses an interest in being hired, you do have to provide them with the equal opportunity to compete for and perform a job. You cannot discriminate in your selection and hiring decisions because of a person's race, color, religion, sex, age, familial status, handicap or national origin or evade other protections afforded by federal, state or local employment laws.

Shortly we will discuss several steps involved in selecting personnel. The purpose of the process is to gather information on which to base a hiring decision. But you have to be sure that the information you gather is relevant to the job. The job descriptions for each position are useful for keeping you focused on the activities and responsibilities of a job when you assemble applications, conduct interviews and finally decide to hire a person.

When developing application forms and conducting interviews, keep these questions in mind:

- Does the information have the effect of screening out people in the protected classes? (It should not.)

- Is the information necessary to judge a person's ability to perform the particular job for which he or she is applying? (It should be job-skill related.)

- Are there nondiscriminatory ways to find out the necessary information? (A legitimate query can be phrased to avoid discriminatory language.)

Guard against wandering into territory that could violate the laws by carefully planning a script to follow. Be sure to have your lawyer review applications you intend to use and the questions you plan to ask during interviews.

Avoid inquiries and discussions about:

- race, color, religion, sex, age, national origin (or origin of name), marital status (or marriage plans) and family status.

- education that is not a requirement for the job. (These cannot be arbitrary qualifications; you must be able to justify their relevance.)

- physical abilities or any handicap or disability.

- experience that is not a requirement for the job. (These, too, cannot be arbitrary qualifications; you must be able to justify their relevance.)

- date of birth or feelings about working for someone older or younger.

- availability for work on Saturday or Sunday.

- a spouse's employment.

- maiden names of females.

- number of children, their ages or availability of baby sitting.

For example, you should not assume that there is little in this business that a person with a disability can do. If an applicant can perform the duties of the job as outlined in a job description, with reasonable accommodations, that person should be considered along with all other qualified applicants.

RECRUITING SALESPEOPLE

Recruiting salespeople is like prospecting for customers–it's a constant, ongoing activity. Unfortunately, many managers and brokers see recruiting as something to do in their spare time (which never materializes). Or they embark on an aggressive campaign only after they lose a number of salespeople. Unless the company decides to scale back the size of its sales staff, you have to maintain a relatively constant number of salespeople with similar levels of experience to maintain a constant flow of revenue. Good managers are always recruiting *before* they have a critical need in their offices.

Track the turnover in your company for several years, and you'll have a good idea of the number of new hires you will need each year. Also investigate the reasons why people left your organization. These become very important when you are trying to replace salespeople. You may find that the attrition rates are typically higher among the least experienced salespeople. Did they leave the business or just leave your company? You have to anticipate hiring replacements for people lost due to attrition just to maintain a constant number of salespeople on staff (before you even think about expanding it). But you also must correct any problems that *accelerate* the rate of attrition in your company.

Just like prospecting for customers, you will make many contacts before a contract. That means you will talk to many people before you select the right person for your firm. Set a target for the number of new hires you need and then develop a plan. This will include the number of contacts you need to make and the number of interviews you need to conduct before you identify the right people.

There are many ways for you to network with potential salespeople. Some of them are more likely to reach unlicensed prospects; others will reach either newly licensed or experienced agents. The purpose of recruiting is to generate a pool of people from which you can then select the appropriate person to hire.

Recruiting Brochures

Just as a sales brochure is intended to make an impression on customers and clients, a recruiting brochure is intended to make an impression on people who contemplate working for you. A brochure is an important tool that can be used along with any of the other recruiting strategies that we discuss.

A recruiting brochure should be a high-quality, professionally designed and printed piece that reinforces the image of your firm. It gives people a tangible remembrance of you and your company (more so than your business card) and provides valuable information for them to study. Think about the questions you had before you got into the business or joined a brokerage company. Then provide the answers to those questions as well as information about your firm. Because this is a premier image builder for your company, use the assistance of a professional graphics or public relations person to develop a captivating brochure.

Recruiting Experienced Talent

If you're looking for experienced agents, the competition is the place to find them. In a previous chapter we mentioned that offices are often targets for recruiting when rumors about pending changes or discontent start to circulate. Brokers seem to follow a double standard where recruiting is concerned: "It's okay for me to recruit your salespeople, just you stay away from mine." Sending recruiting letters to another company's office, for example, can set up a chain of events for them to do likewise to you. Before going after the competition, think about how you would feel if other brokers did to you what you're about to do to them.

Recruit a manager. Sometimes brokers see hiring a manager from another company as a good way to recruit that firm's salespeople. Because good managers often develop a loyal following, it's common for salespeople to follow managers to another firm. However, recent litigation raises legal concerns about this practice. Often managers' employment contracts prohibit soliciting or recruiting salespeople from their previous firms for a period of time after their departure. Your company could be involved in a costly legal battle with the manager's previous broker over a dispute in the nonsolicitation clause of the manager's contract.

Network the industry. The most desirable way to get experienced salespeople on your team is to have them approach you. Therefore, you need to be approachable. Your company's image and reputation are important starting points. Salespeople are also attracted by the personal reputation of the broker or manager. Increase your visibility in the industry by getting involved with tours and with your salespeople's transactions—or anywhere you might make contact with other licensees. When demonstrating your knowledge of the business and management skills, you impress people, who will then seek you out.

When you get to know people in this business, you are in a better position to identify from those who contact you the ones you really want to recruit. They may contact you because they are definitely contemplating a change or because they are just curious about working for you. Remember that a person who's totally satisfied and secure in an office seldom will take the time for an interview. But any overture is an opportunity to tell your company's story and perhaps plant a seed that will benefit you later.

Respect people's allegiances. If you knock the competition or solicit at every closing or open house, people are likely to avoid you and may dismiss the idea of ever working for you.

Mobilize ambassadors. Current salespeople are also great ambassadors for the firm. Good salespeople prefer working with others who are just as dedicated and hard-working as themselves. We have a unique relationship in this business; we are fierce competitors, yet we frequently cooperate with one another on transactions. When salespeople see one another in action, they can identify those who would be an asset to your company. Some companies offer enticements such as bonuses or prizes for salespeople who recruit others to join the firm.

Recruiting Unlicensed Talent

Your potential pool of candidates extends beyond current licensees. Anyone you observe with the attitude, poise and intelligence to be successful in this business is a possible recruit, including previous customers and clients. You and your salespeople should always be on the lookout for prospective salespeople. The company could even establish a bonus or shared commission program to compensate the salespeople for these recruits. You may find a future leader of the industry.

Advertising

A variety of media can be used, including radio, TV, newspapers and even your Web site, to spread the word about a career in real estate with you. Traditionally, classified advertising in the help-wanted section of the newspaper has been a popular form of advertising. You may also find that it's easiest and most cost-effective to include a recruiting tag with other promotional messages.

Remember that any public advertising is seen by consumers as well as by potential new hires. Offers of overly attractive enticements—a luxury car, a trip, a promise of earning exorbitant amounts of money—can be harmful. After all, the consumers pay for your services. They may think twice about doing business with you, or look unfavorably on your fees, if they think you have large sums of money with which to pay salespeople.

Salespeople come from all walks of life, so your message should be targeted to a wide cross-section of the population.

Keep this in mind when you're selecting the media in which your ad will appear. Also be sure that the language in an ad is not discriminatory. The phrase "experienced salespeople only" could have a discriminatory effect if, for example, a woman has been home raising her children or a minority person has not had the opportunity to gain experience. Phrases such as "equal employment opportunity," "previous training not necessary" or "experienced or inexperienced invited" make a public statement that your company provides hiring opportunities to everyone.

The information in Chapter 9 about selecting advertising media and developing copy is also useful when promoting career opportunities. One ad placed on the same day of each week for a period of time will be more effective than one that appears sporadically every few weeks or months. Monitor what the competition does to see when and where they are advertising (you know they monitor you). Time an advertising campaign to coincide with peak times that real estate classes are scheduled if you are targeting newly licensed salespeople. Advertise consistently enough to be effective, but not so aggressively that people begin to wonder if something is wrong in the company. A sample recruiting ad appears in Figure 10.1.

Career Seminars

Career seminars are an opportunity for you to explain the real estate business and showcase your company in the process. People attend these programs for different reasons. Some are consumers who are curious about what we do. Of the people who have a specific interest in a career, some are just toying with the idea and others are actively searching for a broker. The program should appeal to the spectrum of motives, with the expectation that you will arouse sufficient interest from a number of attendees who will then follow up with a personal interview with you.

Just as people have various motives for attending, seminars are conducted for a variety of reasons as well.

FIGURE 10.1   Sample Recruiting Ad

☆☆☆A☆☆☆

SUCCESSFUL CAREER STARTS HERE!

Join a *winning* team of professional real estate salespeople. We support your success with

☆ Free career counseling
☆ Tuition assistance
☆ Sales training program
☆ Generous commission program
☆ Company paid advertising

Visit any of our offices or call our career counselor at 555-SELL (555-7355)

ABC REALTY

- Local educational institutions may sponsor seminars so that their students can explore career options and begin planning what they will do after completing their courses.

- Educational institutions may use seminars to stimulate interest in the industry as a way to get people enrolled in their classes. In this case you are providing a public service, along with other real estate companies, by showcasing career opportunities.

- Your franchise may conduct a career seminar to promote the advantages for salespeople to affiliate with the franchise's companies. Your role is to showcase your company among the other franchisees in the area.

- Your company may sponsor its own career seminar. In the previously mentioned formats your role is to contribute to the program agenda developed by the sponsoring entity. When you are the sponsor, you are in control and can prepare a program for your specific purpose.

Attendees sometimes see company-sponsored seminars as nothing more than glitzy commercials, masquerading as career seminars. There's nothing wrong with promoting your company. But if you promote the program as a *career* seminar, that's what you should deliver. Explain real estate careers, presenting a completely objective discussion of the options. Then explain how your company fits into the picture. Otherwise people can feel duped into attending an infomercial. If you intend to conduct a *recruiting* seminar, plan and promote exactly that—an opportunity for people to learn why *your company* is a superior place to work. Promote your advantages, but don't jeopardize your professional reputation by knocking the competition.

The goal of conducting career programs is to generate a pool of people for you to interview. Because the percentage of people attending a seminar who have the desire or ability to become real estate salespeople may be small, you need an audience that is large enough to justify the time and money involved. National companies and franchises provide guidance and support materials for planning these events, or you can use the following information to help you produce a profitable career seminar.

- Select a central location. Pick an area convenient to the people you want to attract. Your office may or may not be a suitable location. If the purpose of the program is to recruit for your company, the office showcases the actual work site. But you need a meeting room in which you can accommodate people appropriately for a seminar. An off-site facility is better for a true career program.

- Select a facility that is flexible enough to accommodate a range of group sizes. Hotels and conference centers are ideal for this purpose. They also offer a professional atmosphere for group meetings.

- Promote the career night. Prepare flyers that you and your salespeople can distribute. Coordinate press releases and advertising to announce the event at least seven days in advance. Request reservations and provide a telephone number. Designate a person who is briefed on handling these calls, and follow up reservations by sending tickets. Consider having the designated person make calls a day or two before the program to verify attendance.

- Confirm the room arrangements. Once you have reservations in hand, you know how many people to anticipate. Add 10 percent to accommodate people without reservations, but be prepared for no-shows as well. If the room is too large, people get the feeling that the event is not well attended.

- Make arrangements for equipment, such as projectors, screens, easels, sound systems, registration tables and a podium. Be prepared to cope with potential (which invariably turn out to be real) problems with malfunctioning equipment. Also be sure the atmosphere is comfortable; minimize distracting noise and erratic temperatures.

- Plan refreshments. A beverage and light snack are an icebreaker and create an opportunity to mingle with the attendees before and after the program and during a break. Name tags are also a nice touch.

- Prepare literature. A packet for each guest should include general information about careers in real estate and specific information about your firm, including your career brochure.

- Plan and conduct the program. The purpose of the program will affect the agenda you plan. If this is a recruiting seminar, showcase the services your company provides the public and the salespeople who work for you. Include people from your company to speak about their special areas of expertise and jobs within the company.

If this is a career seminar, the agenda should include a brief discussion of private ownership of real estate; its economic importance; statistics on current market conditions; and careers in real estate. When explaining the business, discuss realistic income possibilities as well as employment opportunities and specifics about your firm. It's important that people get a realistic picture about the amount of effort that is involved and income potential, particularly when they are just beginning a career. You may include several of your salespeople who will relate their experiences in the business.

The seminar should have a beginning (introductions of the participants and the purpose for the program), a middle (the information you want to impart, including visuals such as a video, slides, charts and handouts) and an end (question-and-answer period and an invitation for attendees to make an appointment for an interview).

- After the program, send thank-you letters to attendees and follow up with a phone call to extend a second invitation for an interview.

- Plan the next career seminar. When you conduct these events on a regular basis, you get more mileage out of your advertising and promotion dollar. If you have a regular schedule, people such as school directors and previous attendees know when to expect the event and will refer others to your program.

Licensing Courses

Brokerage firms and franchises often operate real estate schools as a way to recruit salespeople for their companies. But the students pay to be educated, not recruited. If your firm wants to operate a school, investigate the requirements in your state for a proprietary real estate school. You need to be clear about whether you want to be in the education business or just want a pool of potential recruits.

To protect the educational integrity of the classroom, some states' licensing authorities prohibit solicitation of students or the dissemination of class rosters. Even if the state's laws permit these activities, some educational institutions do not in order to protect the confidentiality of their enrollees. As a practical matter, if you recruit a prospective licensee and refer that person to an educational institution, you'd be upset if another broker or the instructor tried to scoop that recruit from you.

Managers may be instructors in real estate courses. When showcasing your expertise as an instructor, you also enhance your professional reputation. The point was made under "Recruiting Experienced Talent" that the more visible you are, the more approachable you are. But, if your purpose for teaching is to recruit students or gather student rosters, consider the earlier point about scooping other brokers' referrals to the institution. Even if the educational institution does not have a policy about its instructors recruiting students, remember that the entire class is expecting to learn from you. Any show of favoritism can disrupt the educational process.

Sponsorship

Some states require that a candidate for a salesperson's license be sponsored by a broker before taking the licensing exam. You may offer sponsorship "without strings" as a way of reviewing the talent pool. You can avoid making a commitment to employment at this point. Although paperwork is involved, it may be worth the effort if you identify a superstar.

Trial Training Sessions

Trial training sessions are an opportunity to showcase your company's sales training. You can promote a special training session via a newspaper ad or direct mail to the real estate schools. Your audience will include members of the public who are curious about the business, prelicense students and licensed salespeople who are already working or whose licenses are inactive. Training and education are very important to recruits. Let them see what you actually provide.

Scholarships

You can set up scholarship programs with local educational institutions to fund prelicense or degree courses in real estate. These programs benefit deserving students and provide considerable public relations benefit to the company. It's important, however, that the company not be directly involved in determining who the recipients will be. You can commit the funding and also set guidelines for the award, such as merit or financial need. Then the institution should screen applicants and determine the recipients. Any deeper involvement can tarnish your public relations, particularly with applicants who are not awarded a scholarship. You can reenter the process by participating in an award ceremony. In return for your generosity, the recipient may consider working for you.

Direct Mail

Direct mail can be a useful tool for a specific recruiting campaign. When planning a direct-mail program, investigate the costs for artwork, copywriting, paper and printing, first-class postage and the use of a mailing list. (Compare the costs and services of several mail houses.) Compare the costs with the number of anticipated responses. A rule of thumb is that for every 100 pieces mailed, you can expect to generate one response. You may conclude that this is a worthwhile expenditure, even if it produces only one qualified prospect to interview for every ten respondents. The benefit may be even greater if you target salespeople and middle-level executives in local industry.

SELECTING SALESPEOPLE

Selecting the right salespeople is the key to building a productive, stable work force. Don't hire people just to meet a quota. If someone is not suitable for your company or the business, do both yourself and the recruit a favor by not hiring the person. Otherwise you will invest a considerable amount of time and money in a person who does not succeed. Hiring right makes the rest of a manager's job much easier. It is also a key factor in your ability to retain a person, which will be discussed in a later chapter.

Many of the reasons people are attracted to the real estate business as independent contractors also contribute to their failure. People find the freedom to control their income and their daily work routine very appealing after having worked in structured environments as employees. But human beings by nature are not particularly disciplined. We either rely on others to create structure and discipline for us or we have to make a conscientious effort to create that for ourselves. Unless people can plan, prioritize and manage their time and activities well, they will not succeed in an unstructured environment as independent contractors.

Who are you looking for? We tend to assume that people are motivated by a desire to make money, but this is not always the case (remember our discussions in previous chapters about motivations and values). Successful salespeople have an affinity for selling as well as a natural interest in real estate. They must also be

- good communicators,
- disciplined,

- organized,

- self-directed, and

- well educated.

Salespeople must be able to withstand pressure while maintaining their composure, cope with rejection without feeling demoralized, and empathize with their customers and clients without losing their objectivity or letting their own interests interfere. If they are involved in commercial sales, a college education, strong verbal skills and experience in selling to corporations are also advisable.

Many people with different personalities may match this profile. Some successful people are outgoing and gregarious, whereas others are more laid back. Typically, we look for the traits that other successful people have. But, those may not be so important given differences in individual personalities. What *is* important is how well people can adapt their personal skills to the situation.

You have to make a judgment call based on the best information you can gather. None of us will always make perfect selections. We all get surprised that the least likely person turns out to be a superstar or the most likely person to succeed quickly falls by the wayside.

Although prerequisites for a real estate license vary from state to state, the majority require some amount of education before the licensing examination can be taken. The purpose of the prerequisites is to establish a level of proficiency necessary for licensees to provide real estate services to protect the public interest. These requirements are not designed to determine whether an individual has the personality traits or other skills to be successful in the business. The license a person is issued could be a license to fail. You can prevent this from happening, or at least minimize the possibility, by using a methodical process to select suitable people to become part of your sales force.

What is the selection process designed to do? This is an information-gathering process designed to help you make intelligent hiring decisions. *It is suitable for selecting employees or independent contractors, regardless of whether they are staff or salespeople.* The

FIGURE 10.2   Employment Process

Step	Activity	Purpose
Prescreening	Application and preliminary interview	Gather preliminary information to determine whether to pursue the next step
Formal Interview	Formally structured face-to-face job interview	Gather sufficient information with which to make a decision whether to hire an applicant
Selection	Review information gathered about an applicant	Determine whether applicant is suitable for the position
Hire	Make job offer and establish personnel file	Ensure new hire and company are properly prepared to begin a working relationship

process consists of a prescreening phase, which is normally an application and preliminary interview or conversation; a formal interview phase, which will consist of one and perhaps two formal interviews; and a selection phase, which is the time you make your final decision. Each step is a screening phase during which you decide whether you are interested in gathering more information to continue evaluating a person. Be sure to consider the points we made earlier about equal employment opportunity laws as you proceed through each step (see Figure 10.2).

Prescreening

We begin selecting candidates with the prescreening phase of the process. The purpose is to gather basic information and background about applicants so that you can decide whether to pursue them. Not every warm body is a candidate for a salesperson's position. Establish preliminary criteria for reviewing applicants at this stage so you can quickly weed out those who are not suitable candidates. This will help you make efficient use of your time in subsequent phases and also establish credibility for your selection process.

An application form and a preliminary interview are normally used to prescreen candidates. Use these tools in the order that suits either you or the situation. If a candidate stops by the office without an appointment, for example, you may choose to talk with the person and then hand out an application. Or you can ask the candidate to complete the application and then call later to schedule an interview (if you think that's appropriate).

Application.   An application gathers basic personal information such as name, telephone number, address, former employers, references and license status, education and sales experience, if any. Frequently there are also several questions that require brief written answers. These are useful for evaluating communication skills as much as, or more than, the content of a response.

Preliminary interview.   A preliminary interview is normally a brief meeting, lasting about 20 minutes, or a telephone conversation. This is an opportunity to tell a *short* story about your company and form some initial impressions about the applicant. To gather any meaningful information, though, you have to keep the company sales pitch brief and give the applicant a chance to respond to several open-ended questions.

If the person is seeking a position as a salesperson, find out why the person is interested in or likes the real estate business, why you should hire the person, what they know about the area, whether the person is seeking a full-time or part-time position and the financial implications of that choice. During this interview you can see how well a person expresses himself or herself, imagine how well the person would work with buyers and sellers and decide how well he or she would project the image of your firm. Make notes for yourself. This is also a preliminary interview conducted by the applicant, so expect to be asked questions. Remember, you are both narrowing the field.

This is the point at which you start eliminating people, so you need preliminary criteria by which to judge applicants. Compare what you've learned from the application and preliminary interview with the job description of the position for which you are hiring. If you're looking for a salesperson, define the characteristics of a salesperson that are most important to you and include them as criteria at this stage in the process. Be sure to apply the criteria uniformly for all applicants to avoid violating the equal employment opportunity laws.

Formal Interview

After the application and preliminary interview, you can identify the people you want to invite for a formal interview. The formal interview is the most important phase of the selection process. At the conclusion of this interview you need to have gathered sufficient information to make a decision whether to hire the applicant.

Conducting a good employment interview requires a lot of skill. You have to learn how to determine if an applicant has the necessary skills and attributes for the specific job. This involves asking the correct questions and phrasing them correctly to gather the information you need. This is not the time to try to convince applicants that they are suited for the job; rather, you are giving them an opportunity to convince *you*. For an interview to be productive, you need a plan to follow.

Prepare the interview. Review the application and any notes you took during the preliminary interview with the candidate. (You will impress the applicant with your "excellent memory" and establish your credibility with this preparation.) Prepare a script for yourself. By following a pattern for the interviews, you have a sequence of questions that are essentially the same for each applicant being interviewed. Because it is important to avoid claims of discrimination, have your interview questions reviewed by counsel, and then follow your script. The interview consists of

- *An introduction*—Greet the applicant, engage in improvised small talk and ask an opening question, which could be something like, "How did you become interested in our firm?" or "What do you know about our company?" Observe the candidate's appearance, ability to express himself or herself and the ease with which the person communicates.

You can set the stage for what follows by saying, "Certainly it's in your interest as well as ours to get to know one another before making a commitment to each other. So, let's start by exploring things like your experience, education, leisure activities and anything else you'd like to tell me about yourself."

- *A review of work experience*—You already have an application that details relevant work history, so there's no need to ask for a listing of job positions. This is the time to ask, "What have you done best? Less well? What are your major accomplishments? What are the most difficult problems you've encountered in your jobs? How did you handle them? In what ways are you most effective with people? Why have you changed jobs (if this is applicable)? What are you looking for in a career, and what are your goals and aspirations?"

You are looking for skill and competence that relate to the job, motivation, attitudes toward the job and employers, interpersonal skills, potential for growth and development and how well the applicant can adapt to situations.

- *A review of education*—Again, because you already have the education history from the application, you don't need to ask for the list. Rather, ask, "What were your special accomplishments? How did you choose the course of study? How has what you've learned related to your career? How do you feel about additional education? What would you like to study next? How do you normally get along with teachers?"

You are looking for motivation, reaction to authority, level of accomplishments and interests.

- *A review of present activities*—This is the time to find out about the applicant's leisure time activities and hobbies with questions like "What do you like to do in your spare time?" Also find out about any civic and community activities that are relevant to the job. This is personal information, so be careful not to intrude or get into discussions that could violate the equal employment laws.

You are looking for diversity of interest, social effectiveness and the applicant's ability to manage time, energy and money.

- *A summary*—This is the time to draw conclusions from what you've heard so you can identify the applicant's assets and areas for professional development. You can ask, "What do you think are your major assets or best qualities for the job? What strengths do others usually see in you? Why are you a good person for this company to hire? What are your shortcomings or areas that need improvement? What qualities do you want to develop further? What training or additional experience do you need or would you like for the job?"

At this point you are focusing on specific job-related and professional development issues that might not otherwise have been revealed during the conversation so far.

- *A closing*—The interview concludes with, "I've enjoyed talking to you and you've given me a lot of valuable information to help make a decision. Before you leave, are there any questions about the job, our company or anything else that you would like to ask me?"

You are keeping control of the conversation by indicating that you have learned what you need. Because applicants are still narrowing the field as well, you need to give them an opportunity to ask any questions that they have not yet explored. You may learn something more about them, depending on the nature of their questions, too.

Conduct the interview.   First, create an atmosphere in which you can learn about one another. By their nature, employment interviews are stressful for candidates. Create a low-threat environment to put people at ease and they can feel free to converse and be candid. Use first names; be informal. Don't sit behind your desk; this puts you in an authoritarian position and creates a communications barrier. Conduct the interview in private and without interruptions. You need be able to keep the interview focused and concentrate on what's being said. Conversations need to be spontaneous so that interviewees don't have time to reflect on a previous statement and retract it.

With a prepared script you can concentrate on listening rather than mentally planning what to do next. Work through your questions in a casual, conversational way. Don't talk too much (notice that there's no "company commercial" planned in the script) and listen beyond the words that are spoken. Play down any reaction to unfavorable information. Don't disagree; otherwise the applicant will try to retreat or tell you what the person thinks you want to hear. Don't telegraph the correct answer to a question with a statement such as "We are looking for highly motivated people. How would you describe yourself?" You've already told the candidate what to say. Watch, listen and take notes. You should be able to learn all you need to know within 45 minutes to an hour.

Bring the interview to a close by telling the applicant what happens next. "Thank you. We'll contact you in (a time period) with our decision" will suffice. Or you may state that you plan to invite several people for second interviews. If you're unsure about a candidate, suggest that both of you should think this over; suggest that the candidate interview with others in the meantime. Remember that candidates rely on you to determine whether they are suited for the job in your company. Although the formal interview is the last information-gathering step, it is not intended to conclude with a job offer. However, if you are inclined to hire the candidate, the conclusion of the interview is the time to discuss details about the position.

Selection

During the process you have been forming impressions and making tentative decisions. But you should carefully study the information you've gathered before making a final decision, especially if you have several candidates from which to choose. It is helpful to take notes from the interview and rate the candidate, perhaps on a scale of five to one (being least favorable), on the categories of the interview (general impression, work experience, education, activities, strengths and weaknesses). Envision the candidate working for you and the kind of training and supervision the person would need. Decide if you are willing or prepared to make this commitment. If you are, you have made a hiring decision. You may also decide that none of the applicants are suitable.

Before offering any candidate a position, there are still several things you should do. Check the person's references. Both personal and business references should be included on an application form. If the application does not include the most recent employer, question the candidate about this matter. In some states a criminal-background check is required for licensing purposes, or you can perform one. Some companies use tests as part of their selection process. But the testing instrument must be verified as a reliable predictor or indicator of performance on the job. Otherwise, it could be construed as an unfair way to eliminate job applicants and your company could be subject to litigation.

Remember that the person who hires is also the one who fires. You should be totally committed to the person you finally select to minimize the likelihood of having to do an about-face and show the person to the door. And your new hire also should be totally committed to your company. This means that before you offer employment to people, they need to know what your rules are. Be sure they see your policies and procedures manual before they make that commitment. If the applicant is a candidate for a sales position, be sure he or she is familiar with your compensation program, the expenses for which a salesperson is responsible, automobile liability and errors and omissions insurance, MLS procedures and franchise (if applicable) procedures.

HIRING

Now that you've made your decision and the offer of employment, there are several issues that need to be addressed.

Give the new hire a copy of your policy and procedures manual and obtain a signed receipt for it. If this individual is a salesperson, make the appropriate real estate license arrangements. You also need to begin a personnel file for the new hire. Obtain information such as Social Security number and W-4 forms (for employees) for tax withholding. Your lawyer may suggest other information that is appropriate as well.

One of the major reasons brokers hire independent contractors is that they are relieved of many of the costs and reporting requirements that are associated with employees. Under the federal tax laws, employers must file quarterly and annual payroll tax returns and employee information returns (W-2's). For independent contractors employers need to file only 1099-MISC for those who receive more than $600 per year. They are not required to withhold and pay social security, Medicare or federal income taxes. Depending on your state's laws, the requirements for withholding and payment as well as workers' compensation and unemployment for independent contractors may also differ from those for employees.

Independent contractor agreements.   To ensure that a real estate salesperson is an independent contractor, the federal tax laws require that the salesperson must be a properly licensed practitioner, that the gross income must be based on production rather than on the number of hours worked, and that the work must be done pursuant to a written agreement. This agreement must also state that the salesperson is not an employee for federal tax purposes. Because the IRS scrutinizes claims of independent contractor status, it is essential to meet at least these three requirements. Be sure to check your state's laws as well.

An independent contractor and the company should enter into a formal contract when the person is hired. A sample form that can be used for a salesperson as you prepare yours is provided in Figure 10.3. Have the contract reviewed by legal counsel to ensure that it complies with prevailing laws. In the following chapters pay close attention to the ways you manage an independent contractor versus an employee so that you do not violate the contract for either the company or the independent contractor.

CONCLUSION

The future of your company rests in the hands of the people you hire. Therefore, it's incumbent on you to make the right personnel choices, from identifying the skills and attributes that are needed for a position to developing a pool of talent from which to make the right selection. We can construct models and profiles from salespeople we know are successful in this business, but we have to rely most on what we can learn about a person through our selection process. A methodical process is designed to gather as much information as possible during the pre-screening phase and formal interview so that you can make an informed choice. And always follow a process that is sensitive to the equal employment opportunity laws.

As you can see, selecting a new salesperson involves more than just spending 20 minutes with anyone who is interested in selling real estate and then making a job offer. You should be concerned about the potential success of the salesperson for his or her sake as well as for your company's. Both the company and the salesperson are making a commitment to each other, so it's as important that the new hire know the rules under which she or he will be working as it is that you know about the person. With the right people on board, your job as a manager will be considerably easier, as you'll see in the following chapters of this unit.

DISCUSSION EXERCISES

From your point of view, discuss the pros and cons of hiring part-time versus full-time and newly licensed versus experienced salespeople.

* * *

What recruiting techniques do you think are most effective in your area?

* * *

If you've had experience conducting employment interviews, discuss ways to conduct a successful interview. As an interviewee, discuss your experiences during employment interviews.

FIGURE 10.3   Independent Contractor Agreement

NJAR 10/85

R
REALTOR®

BROKER-SALESPERSON
INDEPENDENT CONTRACTOR AGREEMENT

1   THIS AGREEMENT, is made and entered into this _____ day of _____, 19____, by and between
2
3   _____ (hereinafter referred to as the "Broker"),
4
5   having its principal office at _____
6
7   _____, and _____
8
9   (hereinafter referred to as the "Salesperson"), residing at _____
10
11   _____
12
13   **WITNESSETH:**
14   WHEREAS, Broker is engaged in business as a real estate broker trading as _____,
15   _____ with its principal office at
16   _____. and as such is duly licensed to
17   engage in activities including, but not limited to, selling, offering for sale, buying, offering to buy, listing and soliciting pro-
18   spective purchasers, and negotiating loans on real estate, leasing or offering to lease, and negotiating the sale, purchase or
19   exchange of leases, renting or placing for rent, or managing real estate or improvements thereon for another or others; and
20   WHEREAS, Broker has and does enjoy the goodwill of the public, and has a reputation for fair and honorable dealing
21   with the public; and
22   WHEREAS, Broker maintains an office in the State of New Jersey equipped with furnishings, listings, prospect lists
23   and other equipment necessary, helpful, and incidental to serving the public as a real estate broker; and
24   WHEREAS, Salesperson is duly licensed by the State of New Jersey as a real estate salesperson; and
25   WHEREAS, it is deemed to be to the mutual advantage of Broker and Salesperson to enter into this Agreement; and
26   WHEREAS, Salesperson acknowledges that he has not performed any acts on behalf of Broker nor has he been authorized
27   to act on behalf of Broker; and
28   WHEREAS, the parties acknowledge that they deem it desireable to enter into an agreement in compliance with the
29   provisions of N.J.A.C. 11:5-1.10;
30   NOW, THEREFORE, in consideration of the foregoing premises and the mutual convenants herein contained, it is mutually
31   convenanted and agreed by and between the parties hereto as follows:
32
33   1. **SERVICES.** Salesperson agrees to proceed diligently, faithfully, legally, and with his best efforts to sell, lease, or
34   rent any and all real estate listed with Broker, except for any listings which are placed with Broker exclusively with another
35   salesperson(s), and to solicit additional listings and customers for Broker, and otherwise to promote the business of serving
36   the public in real estate transactions, and for the mutual benefit of the parties hereto.
37
38   2. **OFFICE SPACE.** Broker agrees to provide Salesperson with work space and other facilities at its office presently
39   maintained at _____
40   or at such other location as determined by Broker at which Broker may maintain an office. The items furnished pursuant
41   to this Paragraph 2 shall be for the convenience of the Salesperson.
42
43   3. **RULES AND REGULATIONS.** Salesperson and Broker agree to conduct business and regulate habits and working
44   hours in a manner which will maintain and increase the goodwill, business, profits and reputation of Broker and Salesperson,
45   and the parties agree to conform to and abide by all laws, rules and regulations, and codes of ethics that are binding on,
46   or applicable to, real estate broker and real estate salespeople. Salesperson and Broker shall be governed by the Code of
47   Ethics of the NATIONAL ASSOCIATION OF REALTORS®, the real estate laws of the State of New Jersey, the Constitution
48   and By-Laws of the _____ Board of REALTORS®,
49   the rules and regulations of any Multiple Listing Service with which Broker now or in the future may be affiliated with,
50   and any further modifications or additions to any of the foregoing. Salesperson acknowledges that it is his responsibility
51   to familiarize himself with all current Code of Ethics, the Local Board By-Laws, the rules and regulations of any Multiple
52   Listing Service with which Broker is now affiliated, the Rules and Regulations of the Real Estate Commission and the License
53   Law of the State of New Jersey. Broker agrees to maintain copies of all of the foregoing and to make the same available
54   to Salesperson. Salesperson agrees also to abide by the rules, regulations, policies and standards promulgated by Broker.
55
56   4. **LICENSING AND ASSOCIATION MEMBERSHIP.** Salesperson represents that he is duly licensed by the State
57   of New Jersey as a real estate salesperson. Salesperson acknowledges that Broker is a member of the _____
58   _____ Board of REALTORS®, the New Jersey Association of REALTORS®
59   and the NATIONAL ASSOCIATION OF REALTORS®, and as a result thereof, Broker is subject to the rules and regulations
60   of those organizations. Salesperson agrees to be subject to and act in accordance with said rules and regulations. If Broker
61   requires Salesperson to become a member of any real estate organization, then Salesperson agrees that he shall become a
62   member thereof and shall pay all applicable fees and dues required to maintain said membership. As a result of Broker being
63   a member of the aforesaid groups, Broker and Salesperson agree to abide by all applicable rules, regulations and standards
64   of such organizations, including, but without limitation, those pertaining to ethics, conduct and procedure.
65
66   5. **COMPENSATION.** Salesperson's sole compensation from Broker shall be in the form of commissions. The
67   commissions for services rendered in the sale, rental, or leasing of any real estate and the method of payment, shall be
68   determined exclusively by Broker. Commissions, when earned and collected by Broker, shall be divided between Broker
69   and Salesperson after deduction of all expenses and co-brokerage commissions in accord with the Salesperson's Commission
70   Schedule attached to this Agreement as Schedule A which is an outline of compensation to be paid by Broker to Salesperson
71   during the Salesperson's affiliation with Broker.

FIGURE 10.3   Independent Contractor Agreement *(Continued)*

6. **MULTIPLE SALESPEOPLE.** In the event that two (2) or more salespeople under contract with Broker participate in a sale and claim a commission thereon, then and in that event the amount of commissions allocable to each salesperson shall be divided in accordance with a written agreement among said salespeople. In the event that the salespeople shall be unable to agree, the dispute shall be submitted to and be determined by Broker, in his sole discretion.

7. **RESPONSIBILITY OF BROKER FOR COMMISSIONS.** In no event shall Broker be liable to Salesperson for any commissions not collected, nor shall Salesperson be personally liable for any commissions not collected. It is agreed that commissions collected shall be deposited with the Broker and subsequently divided and distributed in accordance with the terms of this Agreement.

8. **DIVISION AND DISTRIBUTION OF COMMISSIONS.** The division and distribution of the earned commissions as provided for in this Agreement which may be paid to or collected by the Broker, but from which Salesperson shall take certain commissions, shall take place as soon as practicable after collection and receipt of such commissions, but in no event more than ten (10) business days after receipt by the Broker, or as soon thereafter as such funds have cleared the Broker's bank.

9. **RESPONSIBILITY FOR EXPENSES.** Unless otherwise agreed in writing, Broker shall not be liable to Salesperson for any expenses incurred by Salesperson or for any of his acts, nor shall Salesperson be liable to Broker for Broker's office help or expenses, or for any of Broker's acts other than as specifically provided for herein.

10. **ADVANCES.** Broker may from time to time and in his sole discretion make advances to Salesperson on account of future commissions; it being expressly agreed, however, that such advances are temporary loans by Broker for the accommodation of Salesperson which are due and payable on demand or as otherwise agreed to by the Broker, and are not compensation. Upon notice to Salesperson, Broker shall have the right to charge interest on any and all advances made to Salesperson, either at the time of making the advance or thereafter, at a rate chosen by Broker in his sole discretion, but not in excess of the maximum rate permitted by law. Upon receipt of payment of commissions, Broker shall credit the account of Salesperson (first toward interest, if any, and then toward principal) with the portion of such commissions due Salesperson. If at any time, the advances made to Salesperson together with interest thereon, if any, exceed the credits to his account for his share of commissions collected, then such excess shall be owing by Salesperson to Broker and shall be due and payable upon demand. After such demand, interest at the maximum rate permitted by law shall accrue upon the amount due Broker, notwithstanding the fact that any or all of the advances made to Salesperson have initially been interest free or at a reduced rate of interest.

11. **REAL ESTATE LICENSES, BONDS, DUES AND FEES.** Salesperson agrees to pay the cost of maintaining his real estate license, dues for membership in the NATIONAL ASSOCIATION OF REALTORS®, the New Jersey Association of REALTORS®, the local Board of REALTORS® and other dues and fees related to the rendering of services by Salesperson as a real estate salesperson.

12. **AUTHORITY TO CONTRACT.** Salesperson shall have no authority to bind, obligate or commit Broker by any promise or representation, either verbally or in writing, unless specifically authorized in writing by Broker in a particular transaction. However, Salesperson shall be and is hereby authorized to execute listing agreements for and on behalf of Broker as his agent subject to Broker's office policy.

13. **CONTROVERSIES WITH OTHERS.** In the event any transaction in which Salesperson is involved results in a dispute, litigation or legal expense, Salesperson shall cooperate fully with Broker. Broker and Salesperson shall share all expenses connected therewith, in the same proportion as they normally would share the commission resulting from such transaction if there were no dispute or litigation. It is the policy to avoid litigation wherever possible, and Broker, within his sole discretion may determine whether or not any litigation or dispute shall be prosecuted, defended, compromised or settled, and the terms and conditions of any compromise or settlement, or whether or not legal expense shall be incurred. Salesperson shall not have the right to directly or indirectly compel Broker to institute or prosecute litigation against any third party for collection of commissions, nor shall Salesperson have any cause of action against Broker for its failure to do so. In the event a commission is paid to Broker in which Salesperson is entitled to share, but another real estate broker disputes or may dispute the right of Broker to receive all or any portion of such commission, Salesperson agrees that Broker may hold said commission in trust until such dispute is resolved or sufficient time has passed to indicate to Broker in his sole and absolute judgment that no action or proceeding will be commenced by such other real estate broker regarding the subject commission. In the event Broker shall pay any commission to Salesperson and thereafter, either during or subsequent to termination of this Agreement, Broker shall become obligated, either by way of final judicial determination, arbitration award or good faith negotiation, to repay all or any part of such commission to others, Salesperson agrees to reimburse Broker his pro rata share thereof. In any such instance, Broker agrees to keep Salesperson reasonably informed of any proceeding.

14. **OWNERSHIP OF LISTINGS.** Salesperson agrees that any and all listings of property, and all actions taken in connection with the real estate business and in accordance with the terms of this Agreement shall be taken by Salesperson in the name of Broker. In the event Salesperson receives a listing, it shall be filed with Broker no later than twenty four (24) hours after receipt of same by Salesperson. Broker agrees, but is not obligated, to generally make available to Salesperson all current listings maintained by its office. However, all listings shall be and remain the separate and exclusive property of Broker unless otherwise agreed to in writing by the parties hereto.

15. **DOCUMENTS.** Broker and Salesperson agree that all documents generated by and relating to services performed by either of them in accordance with this Agreement, including, but without limitation, all correspondence received, copies of all correspondence written, plats, listing information, memoranda, files, photographs, reports, legal opinions, accounting information, any and all other instruments, documents or information of any nature whatsoever concerning transactions handled by Broker or by Salesperson or jointly are and shall remain the exclusive property of the Broker.

16. **COMMUNICATIONS.** Broker shall determine and approve all correspondence from the Broker's office pertaining to transactions being handled, in whole or in part, by the Salesperson.

17. **FORMS AND CONTRACTS.** Broker shall determine and approve the forms to be used and the contents of all completed contracts and other completed forms before they are presented to third parties for signature.

FIGURE 10.3 Independent Contractor Agreement *(Continued)*

150 18. **INDEPENDENT CONTRACTOR.** This Agreement does not constitute employment of Salesperson by Broker and
151 Broker and Salesperson acknowledge that Salesperson's duties under this Agreement shall be performed by him in his capacity
152 as an independent contractor. Nothing contained in this Agreement shall constitute Broker and Salesperson as joint ventures
153 or partners and neither shall be liable for any obligation incurred by the other party to this Agreement, except as provided
154 herein. The Salesperson shall not be treated as an employee for Federal, State or local tax purposes with respect to services
155 performed in accordance with the terms of this Agreement. Effective as of the date of this
156 Agreement, Broker will not (i) withhold any Federal, State, or local income or FICA taxes from Salesperson's commissions;
157 (ii) pay any FICA or Federal and State unemployment insurance on Salesperson's behalf; or (iii) include Salesperson in any
158 of its retirement, pension, or profit sharing plans. Salesperson shall be required to pay all Federal, State, and local income
159 and self-employment taxes on his income, as required by law, and to file all applicable estimated and final returns and forms
160 in connection therewith.
161
162 19. **NOTICE OF TERMINATION.** This Agreement, and the relationship created hereby may be terminated by either
163 party hereto with or without cause, at anytime upon three (3) days written notice. However, this Agreement shall immediate-
164 ly terminate upon Salesperson's death. Except as otherwise provided for herein, the rights of the parties hereto to any
165 commissions which were accrued and earned prior to the termination of this Agreement shall not be divested by the termina-
166 tion of this Agreement.
167
168 20. **SERVICES TO BE PERFORMED SUBSEQUENT TO TERMINATION.** Upon termination of this Agreement,
169 all negotiations commenced by Salesperson during the term of this Agreement shall continue to be handled through Broker
170 and with such assistance by Salesperson as is determined by Broker. The Salesperson agrees to be compensated for such
171 services in accordance with Schedule B attached hereto.
172
173 21. **LIST OF PROSPECTS.** Upon termination of this Agreement, Salesperson shall furnish Broker with a complete
174 list of all prospects, leads and foreseeable transactions developed by Salesperson, or upon which Salesperson shall have been
175 engaged with respect to any transaction completed subsequent to termination of this Agreement in which Salesperson has
176 rendered assistance in accordance with the terms of this Agreement. Except as expressly provided for in Paragraph 20 of
177 this Agreement, Salesperson shall not be compensated in respect of any transaction completed subsequent to
178 termination of this agreement unless agreed to in writing by the Broker.
179
180 22. **DUTY OF NON-DISCLOSURE.** Salesperson agrees that upon termination of this Agreement, he will not furnish
181 to any person, firm, company, corporation, partnership, joint venture, or any other entity engaged in the real estate business,
182 any information as to Broker or its business, including, but not limited to, Broker's clients, customers, properties, prices,
183 terms of negotiations, nor policies or relationships with prospects, clients and customers. Salesperson, shall not, after
184 termination of this Agreement, remove from the files or from the office of the Broker, any information pertaining to the
185 Broker's business, including, but not limited to, any maps, books, publications, card records, investor or prospect lists, or
186 any other material, files or data, and it is expressly agreed that the aforementioned records and information are the property
187 of Broker.
188
189 23. **COMPENSATION SUBSEQUENT TO TERMINATION.** Upon termination of this Agreement, Salesperson shall
190 be compensated only in accordance with the appended Schedule B.
191
192 24. **ESCROW DEPOSIT.** All contracts of sale shall be accompanied by an escrow deposit in an amount as determined
193 by Broker. Salesperson will, at all times, require purchaser or prospective purchasers, to put up such escrow deposit unless
194 a higher or lower sum shall be mutually agreed to by Broker and Salesperson. Salesperson is expressly prohibited from
195 accepting a smaller escrow deposit, a post-dated check, or agreeing not to deposit an escrow check, unless such action has
196 been expressly authorized by Broker.
197
198 25. **AUTOMOBILE.** Salesperson agrees to furnish his own automobile, pay all expenses in connection with the
199 operation and maintenance of said automobile, and that Broker shall have no responsibility therefor. Salesperson agrees to
200 carry throughout the terms of this Agreement public liability insurance upon his automobile with minimum limits not less than
201 _____ ($ _____) for each person and
202 _____ ($ _____) for each accident,
203 and property damage insurance with a minimum limit of not less than _____
204 ($ _____). Upon request, Salesperson agrees
205 to furnish to Broker certificates certifying as to such insurance prepared by the insurance company.
206
207 26. **ASSIGNABILITY AND BINDING EFFECT.** This Agreement is personal to the parties hereto and may not be
208 assigned, sold or otherwise conveyed by either of them.
209
210 27. **NOTICE.** Any and all notices, or any other communication provided for herein shall be in writing and shall be
211 personally delivered or mailed by registered or certified mail, return receipt requested prepaid postage, which shall be
212 addressed to the parties at the addresses indicated herein, or to such different address as such party may have fixed. Any
213 such notice shall be effective upon receipt, if personally delivered, or three (3) business days after mailing.
214
215 28. **GOVERNING LAW.** This Agreement shall be subject to and governed by the laws of the State of New Jersey,
216 including the conflicts of laws, irrespective of the fact that Salesperson may be or become a resident of a different state.
217
218 29. **WAIVER OF BREACH.** The waiver by the Broker of a breach of any provision of this Agreement by the
219 Salesperson shall not operate or be construed as a waiver of any subsequent breach by the Salesperson.
220
221 30. **ENTIRE AGREEMENT.** This Agreement constitutes the entire agreement between the parties and contains all
222 of the agreement between the parties with respect to the subject matter hereof; this Agreement supersedes any and all other
223 agreements, either oral or in writing between the parties hereto with respect to the subject matter hereof.
224
225 31. **GENDER.** When used in this Agreement, the masculine shall be deemed to include the feminine.
226
227 32. **SEPARABILITY.** If any provision of this Agreement is invalid or unenforceable in any jurisdiction, the other
228 provisions herein shall remain in full force and effect such jurisdiction and shall be liberally construed in order to effecuate
229 the purpose and intent of this Agreement, and the invalidity or unenforceability of any provision of this Agreement in any
230 jurisdiction shall not affect the durability or enforceability of any such provision in any other jurisdiction.

FIGURE 10.3   Independent Contractor Agreement (Continued)

231   33. **MODIFICATION.** This Agreement may not be modified or amended except by an instrument in writing signed
232 by the parties hereto. Any modification to this Agreement between the parties after the date of this Agreement shall be of
233 no effect unless such modification is in writing and is signed by both Broker and Salesperson.
234
235   34. **PARAGRAPH HEADINGS.** The paragraph headings contained in this Agreement are for reference purposes only
236 and shall not affect in any way the meaning or interpretation of this Agreement.
237
238   35. **SURVIVAL OF PROVISIONS.** The provisions of this Agreement shall survive the termination of the Salesperson's
239 services under this Agreement.
240
241   36. **COPY RECEIVED.** Salesperson acknowledges receipt of a fully executed copy of this Agreement, duly signed by
242 Broker and Salesperson.
243
244   IN WITNESS WHEREOF, the undersigned have set their hands and seals, or if a corporation, has caused this
245 Agreement to be signed and sealed by its duly authorized corporate officer, the day and year first above written.
246 WITNESS:
247
248 _____
249 WITNESS: (Broker)
250
251 _____
252   (Salesperson)

FIGURE 10.3 Independent Contractor Agreement *(Continued)*

SCHEDULE A

SALESPERSON'S COMMISSION SCHEDULE WHILE AFFILIATED WITH BROKER

Salesperson shall be entitled to receive the following percentage as his portion of the commission earned by Broker as a result of closed sales, listings, rentals, leases, after deducting all expenses and co-brokerage commissions:

SALES TRANSACTIONS

1. _____% for written listings produced by Salesperson.

2. _____% for written listings produced and sold by Salesperson.

3. _____% for selling property listed by co-operating broker.

RENTAL/LEASE TRANSACTIONS

1. _____% for written listings produced by Salesperson.

2. _____% for written listings resulting in a signed lease agreement.

3. _____% for signed lease agreement listed by a co-operating broker.

ADDITIONAL PROVISIONS (IF ANY):

FIGURE 10.3   Independent Contractor Agreement *(Continued)*

SCHEDULE B

SALESPERSON'S COMMISSION SCHEDULE AFTER TERMINATION OF AFFILIATION WITH BROKER

The rate of compensation to be paid by Broker to Salesperson pertaining to transactions which close and on renewals which occur subsequent to the termination of Salesperson's affiliation with Broker is as follows:

1. AS TO SALES TRANSACTIONS
   A. Listings
As to written listings which have been produced by Salesperson prior to the date of termination, Salesperson shall be entitled to receive the following percentage of his portion of the commission pursuant to Schedule A for each such transaction, upon collection by Broker.

   (I) _____% if a contract of sale has been executed by all parties and all contingencies contained therein have been satisfied as of such date;

   (II) _____% if a contract of sale has been executed by all parties but any contingencies contained therein have not been satisfied as of such date;

   (III) _____% if a contract of sale has not been executed by all parties as of such date.

   In the event a listing originally produced by Salesperson expires, and is renewed after such termination date, Salesperson shall be entitled to receive _____% of his portion of the commission for any such transaction upon collection in full by Broker.

   B. Sales
As to transaction in which a prospective purchaser has been produced by Salesperson prior to the date of termination, Salesperson shall be entitled to receive the following percentage of his portion of the commission pursuant to Schedule A for any such transaction, upon collection by Broker:

   (I) _____% if the title has closed, but the commission has not been collected as of such date;

   (II) _____% if a contract of sale has been executed by all parties and all contingencies contained therein have been satisfied as of such date;

   (III) _____% if a contract of sale has been executed by all parties but any contingencies contained therein have not been satisfied as of such date;

   (IV) _____% if a contract of sale has not been executed by all parties as of such date; but thereafter a contract is executed by all parties.

2. AS TO RENTAL TRANSACTIONS
   A. Listings
As to written listings which have been produced by Salesperson prior to the date of termination, Salesperson shall be entitled to receive the following percentage of his portion of the commission pursuant to Schedule A in any such transaction upon collection by Broker:

   (I) _____% if a lease agreement has been executed by all parties as of such date, but the commission has not yet been received;

   (II) _____% if a lease agreement has not been executed by all parties as of such date; but thereafter, a lease agreement is executed by all parties.

   B. Leases
As to rental transactions in which Salesperson has produced a prospective lessee prior to the date of termination, Salesperson shall be entitled to receive the following percentage of his portion of the commission pursuant to Schedule A upon collection by Broker:

   (I) _____% if a lease agreement has been executed by all parties as of such date, but the commission has not yet been received;

   (II) _____% if a lease agreement has not been executed by all parties as of such date, but thereafter, a lease agreement is executed by all parties.

3. ADDITIONAL PROVISIONS (IF ANY):

CHAPTER

11 Professional Development for Your Staff

What should a company do to orient new people to the organization? What can a company do to nurture the professional skills of people who work for it? How can you make your sales meetings worthwhile?

People are the lifeline to the company's success, the organization's most valuable resource. Invest in this resource, giving them the tools needed to enhance their business and creating an atmosphere in which they can thrive. As they develop professionally, your company becomes more productive. Your investment also pays dividends by making the manager's job easier and enhancing retention.

Each person on your staff has different needs to help them grow professionally. Just as there is no one property that suits all buyers, there is no one program or service that suits all of your salespeople. Newly licensed salespeople have different needs than experienced salespeople. People have chosen to work for you because they expect to be productive and successful in this affiliation. Don't disappoint them.

Mention professional development and the first thing that comes to mind for most people is education and training. Often these are seen as one and the same, but they are really two different exercises. Education builds knowledge; training develops skill by converting that knowledge into action. Education is needed before training. Consider this: the courses required for licensure are, for the most part, knowledge-based. They do not ordinarily take this knowledge to the next level, to help people develop the skill needed to use that information to its greatest advantage.

Unfortunately, brokers or managers sometimes say to their salespeople, "Forget what you learned in school. I'll teach you what you *really* need to know." However, this overlooks an important fact–salespeople need a wide range of both knowledge *and* skill to be successful.

Professional development will help your salespeople develop their skills as well as expand their knowledge. There are many forums in which you can accomplish this, such as orientation programs, training programs, sales meetings and retreats. The manager also works one-on-one with the salespeople. This not only helps salespeople develop but also enhances their quality of work life within your organization.

ORIENTATION PROGRAMS

Once people come to work for you, they are no longer outsiders; they now must become part of your team. Although you introduced people to your organization when they were hired, you provided only a brief overview. They need to know more about your organization to be productive team members. When you developed a plan for the company, defining its goals and objectives, you stated what the organization intends to do. But people can't make this happen unless they know how the organization functions and what it needs to accomplish.

The purpose of an orientation program is to present the organization to your new staff members. This is your company's "formal introduction," telling them where they're working, the background of the company and its administrative and operational policies and procedures. Orientation programs not only provide information but also create a sense of belonging. Welcoming new hires to the organization relieves much of the apprehension and strangeness they often feel and begins to integrate them into your team.

A standardized approach for introducing new staff to your firm is advisable. This way you can ensure people have been properly informed about how to work in your organization. Two general categories of information should be addressed in your orientation program.

1. *An introduction to the company.* Include the history of the firm, its general objectives, an organization chart and a general outline of the work that is done in the various departments or offices. The company's business philosophy and general policies, daily office procedures, benefit and compensation programs and opportunities for professional development also should be discussed. This part of the orientation program is meaningful to any new hire, regardless of whether he or she has a support staff or a sales position.

2. *The specific procedures that apply to the person's job.* For a salesperson this part of the program explains all of the firm's procedures for handling the various aspects of a real estate transaction and how salespeople are expected to service clients and customers. Internal procedures for handling paperwork and escrow funds, fiscal matters concerning negotiations of fees and cooperative transactions and the way the sales team works together and supports one another also should be discussed. For support staff, similar information relevant to the specific positions should be covered.

Orientation programs can be conducted in a group setting if a sufficient number of people are joining the company at the same time. Otherwise the broker and the immediate supervisor should do this one-on-one with the new hire. For a group program, senior management should introduce the company and explain its general objectives and business philosophy and policies. This is also an opportunity for new hires to meet the people who run the organization. Often in large organizations this is their only face-to-face contact with someone in upper management. An immediate supervisor can then discuss the specific details of the company's operations and its programs. If you're orientation is conducted one-on-one, include a "walkabout" the organization to introduce the new hire to other personnel.

Assessing new hires. Just as a new hire needs to be oriented to the company, you need to learn more about the new hire, the individual's abilities and personality. This helps identify education and training that would be beneficial and provides some insight into the personality with whom the manager will be working. In some organizations the training director or manager interviews new people to identify job-skill training needs.

Some companies administer tests to investigate intelligence, personality, sales aptitude or interests. Because of cultural or verbal bias or the lack of correlation between what is tested and a person's potential for success in the job, some testing instruments are more valid than others. Examinations may be useful for gaining insight about a person, but the supervisor should manage the person not the data that is gathered.

Business plans for salespeople. Orientation for salespeople, regardless of whether they are newly licensed or experienced, also should include the development of a personal business plan for their new affiliation. This includes their sales production as well as activities to promote their association with your company. Some companies provide announcements that can be mailed to each salesperson's network of contacts. These are then supported by a follow-up plan to reinforce the contacts with items such as the company's brochure, newsletter or giveaway novelty. Some salespeople develop their own self-promotion material as well.

TRAINING PROGRAMS

The purpose of training programs is to develop the skills the work force needs to do its jobs. In some cases this training addresses deficiencies in job skills, which could, for example, involve renewing a salesperson's proficiency in making listing presentations or qualifying buyers. In other cases training is proactive, that is, it addresses new techniques or strategies. This could involve skills related to a new company service, a new phone system or a new computer program. Today, technology training for staff as well as sales personnel is extremely important.

We've come a long way in this business from the days when we gave salespeople a desk and a phone and expected that by following their instincts they would be productive. Today we realize that this does them a disservice. We also realize that the firm's professional image is jeopardized and the risk and legal liability increase when the salespeople lack the technical competency needed to orchestrate transactions in today's complex world. Training has become important for organizations to function in a changing environment.

Before you design your in-house training programs, there are a number of decisions you have to make: whom to train, what you are going to teach and how you are going to deliver the training.

Whom to Train

The most obvious candidates for training are your salespeople. But all of your employees deserve the opportunity to develop professionally.

Managers. Some companies don't give much thought to management training because their primary focus is sales training. But managers, including brokers, should be able to develop the skills to enable them to be more effective in their jobs. Unless your company has a large enough management corps to warrant developing or conducting these programs, you can attend seminars, courses (which you may be attending now) and programs conducted by professional organizations. Because the job of a manager is to get work done through other people, a skilled manager plays a major role in the company's success in achieving its goals.

Sales mangers also should attend the sales training program. They are at a great disadvantage when they don't know what salespeople are being taught. Unless you are knowledgeable about the program, it's difficult to help implement and reinforce the techniques. And salespeople don't need to hear things from you that conflict with what they hear in the training sessions. Your critique of the program is also very helpful to whomever is responsible for developing the training, to ensure that it addresses the needs you identify from working with the salespeople.

Experienced salespeople.   Because the needs of experienced and newly licensed salespeople are different, there should be a program designed specifically for experienced people. This is an opportunity to dissuade them from using outdated or ineffective techniques, to help them integrate your company's sales practices into their methods and to bring them up to date with current laws and trends in the industry. When classes consist solely of experienced salespeople, they can build rapport with one another. You also are acknowledging their stature as experienced associates.

New associates.   You do the newly licensed person, your customers and your company's image a disservice if you send people into the field without the tools with which to work. It's not uncommon for new people to feel uncomfortable with or intimidated by situations they are about to encounter. They may even hesitate to pursue transactions to avoid situations they don't feel prepared to handle. Sales training accomplishes two things: it provides listing and selling techniques and it helps build confidence. Programs conducted exclusively for newly licensed salespeople enable them to develop the basic skills they need while also insulating them from the skeptical, even cynical, attitudes experienced salespeople may display when introduced to contemporary techniques.

Administrative staff.   Secretaries, clerks and other administrative personnel also should be involved in training programs. Any information about the inner workings of your organization, as well as tools to help them in their specific jobs, can be the subject of various training sessions.

What to Teach

When deciding what to teach, first you have to determine what people need. In some cases they may need education before they need training. Depending on the education required for licensure, you may need to concentrate on basic real estate principles and practices to be sure the new licensees have a good foundation of real estate knowledge. Or they may need education relating to listing and selling property.

Next, you have to determine the skills that people need to put their knowledge into use. An effective training program is based on a job-skills analysis, that is, you identify the skills people need to do their jobs. It's easy for someone to say, "This is what you need to know," but if the agenda isn't related to the job or people don't think that's what they need, then the training isn't effective. Some in-house training programs really are misnamed. They provide education and a lot of information, but fall short on helping participants sharpen their skills with what they've learned. This can happen because either the design of the subject matter or the methods use to deliver the training, or both, are faulty.

In the remainder of this section, we concentrate on sales training to give you an idea of how to proceed in developing your training programs. As we do, keep one very important point in mind about training. Regardless of how well designed a training program is, it won't fix every problem within an organization. *Training has one specific focus: to effect behavior in people so they perform their jobs more effectively.* Training will *not* correct such issues as defects in company policies or procedures or misaligned objectives or financial resources that inhibit a company's success.

Keys to effective sales training.   Have you noticed that sales training programs typically teach a script of what to say? "Just give them the words." This is commonly known as the "modeling approach." It presumes that the same strategies can effectively be used by all salespeople. Any who resist are accused of being timid or doomed to failure. This approach gives brand-new salespeople a starting point, a few "comebacks" to get them over the first hurdles. But then they're lost when they encounter a situation for which they didn't learn a response. You could arm them to handle every imaginable scenario, but the script would get too long to be manageable. Instead of building confidence, you would intimidate them.

A sales training program is far more effective when people develop skills to evaluate situations and learn to "think on their feet." Then they are prepared to respond to any situation in which they could find themselves. Salespeople also need to learn how to respond to customers or clients as individual people. When salespeople parrot other people's words, they can sound insincere, especially if the words are out of character with their own personalities. Furthermore, customers tire of hearing trite, rehearsed sales talk.

Training should bring people to the threshold of new opportunities and they then should be free to choose the strategies they want to adopt. We tend to assume that all salespeople must be good at all things, and that sales training will "fix" the salespeople who aren't. Sales training isn't intended to fix anyone. It's supposed to provide the tools to enhance their strengths and introduce them to new strategies they can use. Some salespeople are very effective at getting listings, for example, whereas others are more effective with buyers. We shouldn't lay a guilt trip on people by suggesting that unless they are superstars at everything, they are less valuable.

Without a supportive atmosphere in the workplace, the benefits a training program provides are only temporary. Have you noticed how long the effect of a motivational seminar lasts? About as long as the seminar. The purpose of these programs is to energize people but, unfortunately, that doesn't change people's behavior for the long haul. Consequently, they need another "fix" periodically. Motivation should be a "motive for action." People need to return to a work environment that reinforces what they've heard. Without support and encouragement for change, it's too easy to retreat to old habits and attitudes. The responsibility for providing this atmosphere rests with the manager.

Link the content of a training program to job skills, and most importantly, to what salespeople need to hear. These may sound like one and the same, but they're not. Certainly, the training has to be relevant to a job-skills analysis, which you can obtain from franchises, professional trainers and even testing services. But effective and cost-efficient training addresses those areas the salespeople need to develop. Don't waste people's time or your money. You can determine needs in a variety of ways: survey the salespeople, seek input from their managers and detect patterns of strengths and weaknesses from customer-satisfaction surveys. The content of sales training that you might consider falls into several general areas.

- Basic real estate information, including economic trends and changes in demographics and lifestyles, environmental issues, construction and development

- Sales and listing strategies, including sales techniques directly related to activities that enhance services and produce revenue

- Company policy issues, including new programs, services and sales tools, policy changes or issues that need to be clarified because of recurring problems or disputes

- Legal issues, including recent litigation that affects real estate transactions and ownership and changes in federal, state and local laws and ordinances

- Motivational subjects, including kickoff campaigns for new programs and the new year's objectives

- Personal development, including time management, personal business plans and goal setting and technology skills.

Develop objectives you want to accomplish with a specific program. Identify the specific behavior you expect the trainees to adopt at the conclusion of the program. This then tells the trainer and the trainee what you intend to achieve and forms the basis for other decisions needed to accomplish your objective: the type of forum in which the training will be conducted, the actual content or outline for the session(s) and any support materials that are appropriate, such as media that will be used, and handout or training materials for the participants. This design process is applicable to any training program, regardless of the audience or the forum for the program, including a short seminar or a sales meeting.

If you're not experienced in developing training curricula and learning objectives, seek the counsel of a professional trainer or educator to assist you. Or consider purchasing a ready-made training program that you can tailor to include your company's sales philosophy, sales tools and policies and procedures. Professional associations, franchises and outside consultants have a variety of programs you could consider.

Basic sales training program.   Basic sales training normally includes the skills a person needs to generate customers and clients and to handle all aspects of a sales transaction, from the time a property is listed to the time a buyer is introduced to the closing or settlement. The course of study must be tailored to reflect your firm's business philosophy and the services it provides. If you specialize exclusively in buyer-agency, for example, parts of this agenda are not applicable, such as methods for obtaining listings.

Unfortunately, many sales training programs focus on producing revenue for the company and shortchange the ethics and laws that pertain to these activities. (We're back to the results versus the process discussion in Chapter 8.) Attention-grabbing headlines that consumers are paying more for services than they are worth or that salespeople are paid more than is justified by what they do indicate, at the very least, a public relations problem. Perhaps consumers still see themselves as the "means to the end"—business for the licensee and the company; maybe the training program reinforces that notion in the minds of the salespeople as well.

A basic sales training program is a prime opportunity to foster a demeanor that will advance the professional image the industry desires. As we mentioned in Chapter 8, there's simply no right way to do the wrong thing. Demonstrate ways that salespeople can conduct business ethically and showcase the *benefits* of the service they provide to customers and clients.

If one of your company's major objectives is to serve owners who want to sell their properties, an objective for a program for newly licensed salespeople might be to enable them to get two listings within 60 days and accomplish this professionally and in accordance with your company's procedures. The outline of this program will incorporate information relating to

- the importance of listings to production;
- the sources of listings;
- prospecting techniques;
- listing presentations and a competitive market analysis;
- discussion of law of agency or the nature of services consistent with your state's law;
- ethical and legal issues relating to listings, including fair housing;
- handling objections;
- listing contract and disclosure procedures;
- internal paper, key and sign procedures; and
- listing follow-up programs, including advertising, open houses and periodic contacts with the seller to service the listing.

If you want to expand this agenda, depending on your company's general objectives, to include services to the buyer, an objective for a program for newly licensed salespeople might be to enable them to get two sales within 60 days, professionally and in accordance with your company's procedures. This program's outline will incorporate information relating to

- networking to find buyers;
- converting telephone inquiries to appointments;
- qualifying buyers (property requirements and financial ability);
- discussion of law of agency or the nature of your services consistent with your state's law;
- showing properties;

- obtaining and preparing an offer;

- financing the purchase;

- sales contracts, contingency clauses and disclosure procedures, including property conditions and agency;

- ethical and legal issues relating to the sale of a property,
including fair housing laws and procedures for handling
escrow money; and

- presenting an offer, negotiating a sale and handling objections.

The customs and MLS procedures in your area, the nature of
the legal relationship you have with buyers and sellers, the
nature of the services your firm provides and your company's
policies and procedures also should be addressed in the content
of the programs. Preparation for closing or settlement,
including satisfying contingencies, and the company's marketing
and sales tools are important topics as well.

Remedial program. These programs are designed with a
very narrow focus to concentrate on a specific skill. If your
company has a large number of overpriced listings that aren't
selling, for example, you may plan a session with the objective of
eliminating overpriced listings by convincing salespeople that

- the image of the firm suffers with stale listings;

- they mislead owners, which also increases the potential for
a lawsuit;

- they reduce the number of showings;

- they increase the probability of losing a listing or a sale or
the termination of a sale;

- they help other, reasonably priced listings sell;

- they frustrate everyone, including the listing and selling
agents, the brokers and managers and the buyers and
sellers; and

- they cost the firm advertising money.

How to Deliver Training

Are you going to tackle the training on your own? Bring in outside talent? Or send people to programs or classes outside your company? Your decision about how to deliver training will be influenced by the nature of the program's subject matter, the expertise required to design the program, the financial resources that are available, the number of people to be trained and the frequency with which a program should be offered.

When you use outside talent, providing training is relatively simple: schedule the classes, arrange the facilities and bring the talent to you. Or you can send your people to scheduled classes (some professional groups even will schedule classes exclusively for your associates). The curriculum is professionally designed, either as a preprepared program or one designed specifically for your purposes, and delivered by a professional trainer. Unless the course content is tailored for your organization, or the trainer is familiar with your state's laws and company's procedures, participants miss the benefit of learning to integrate your firm's sales tools, philosophy and procedures into their selling.

You have more control over the design, scheduling and delivery of training programs when you do them in-house. This, however, involves a major financial commitment to maintain a training department, even when staffed by only one person. Training directors with professional expertise, skills and credentials are prize employees, but they also can be expensive. Some people think that any broker, manager or experienced salesperson can be a trainer. But the skills required to design effective programs and deliver them effectively are quite specialized.

Even if the company has an in-house training department, you are likely to turn to outside resources on occasion. Specialized expertise may be required for certain subject matter. For a "tired" topic a fresh perspective can be stimulating. For programs that deserve extra punch or prominence, outside experts can make a greater impact or generate greater credibility than in-house staff people would. It's also effective to go outside your organization for inspirational speakers. With today's technology you can network the sales staff with outside resources through audio and video conferencing.

How to Conduct the Program

Training is intended to cause people to behave in certain ways. The trainer helps people

- become motivated to adopt the behavior;

- learn to process information and experiences;

- develop knowledge, skills, values and attitudes or creative ideas; and

- transfer learning into application.

Specialized skills are required to accomplish this. Even if you do not aspire to be the company's training director, learning how to be an effective trainer is important. Managers are involved in some aspect of training with their salespeople, even as they conduct sales meetings and one-on-one conferences.

Understanding how people learn is essential to creating an effective learning environment. Boredom, distraction, resentment and intimidation are immediate barriers to learning. We have to remember that we're teaching adults. Each of these people has many more life experiences, many more responsibilities and distractions in their lives and a greater sense of self and ego than they had as children. Consequently, we teach adults differently than we teach children.

The process by which adults learn, or **andragogy,** and adult education is a specialty of its own, which deserves a separate book. A useful publication on the subject is *How To Teach Adults,* by Dr. Donald R. Levi (see Bibliography). Regardless of whether you are leading classroom instruction or working one-on-one with people, there are several rules to remember.

- There are many demands on adults' time so they want their time to be respected. Sessions and meetings should begin and end as scheduled, and the content needs be substantive and worthwhile. Avoid disorganization and long-windedness.

- Most adults are unaccustomed to being in a classroom or subordinate to an instructor, especially if the instructor is younger than they are. Adults are more likely to be anxious over their performance and need to be respected. It's important to minimize intimidation and potential for embarrassment.

- It's possible to "teach an old dog new tricks," but the older we are, the slower we are to adjust to change. It takes patience and a little extra time to help adults adopt new behaviors. When working with a variety of age groups, this will be particularly evident.

- There are physical changes in adults that affect sight, hearing and motor skills. Depending on the person, these changes can begin as we approach our thirties. Changes in the size of type we can read easily, the colors we can see and the way we cope with glare, for example, are noticeable as we get older. Auditory distractions affect our ability to understand speech. These are things that should be considered in both the classroom and the office.

- Adults have learned to think and analyze. They are less likely to accept facts without explanation and rationale. "Just do it because I say so," may work with children (well, some children) because they are conditioned to follow authority. But adults are more inclined to question and screen information. They also respond to stimulating and thought-provoking exercises.

- Adults have many life experiences from which to draw. They integrate new information by relating it to their experiences and finding correlations. Stimulating them to recall experiences helps them as well as others in the group to learn.

Consider the fact that you are dealing with an adult audience when determine the setting in which you teach; the way you conduct the sessions; the pace at which you cover material; and the kinds of learning exercises that you use.

Classroom instruction.   People are geared to learning in the classroom because this is the environment in which they've been conditioned to learn since elementary school. Organized classroom instruction offers a number of advantages. There is a structured agenda and a leader who can keep the group focused and the discussions on track. Information is normally introduced in a lecture format, particularly for beginners. But once this is done, learning is facilitated by people thinking and doing. When trainees are gathered in a group, they can engage in many creative learning exercises together. Remember the earlier point about people learning to think, rather than learning to parrot.

Learning techniques such as skits, role-playing, brainstorming and problem-solving exercises enhance skill development. These techniques require considerable planning and preparation to be effective, however. Consider the personalities in your audience when selecting the techniques you are going to use. People need to succeed in these classroom exercises, particularly skits and role-playing, without being embarrassed. They must feel free to make mistakes without ridicule.

As desirable as classroom instruction is, it's only feasible when you have a sufficient number of people to gather together in a group. This may be more difficult with programs for new licensees, unless you have a large and consistent volume of new hires. Ideally they should attend the training program before they set foot in the field. But you don't want to dampen their enthusiasm by making them cool their heels until you can get a class together. A contingency plan in which you do some one-on-one training with the new licensee enables the person to perform certain activities until the next formal program is available.

Location. The facility you use contributes to the program's success or failure. The setting must be conducive to learning and the classroom techniques that will be used. Professional salespeople want to see professional programs conducted in professional settings. You want to showcase the importance of the program and give it credibility with the facility you choose. The worst place to conduct programs is at the salespeople's desks. There are too many distractions and interruptions, and this diminishes the perceived importance or value of the program.

If you are using a training or conference room in your office, establish very specific rules about interruptions for phone calls or other business. Otherwise it's too tempting for people to divide their attention between business and learning. For the person who's impressed with his or her own importance, this is an easy way to grandstand by leaving the session to attend to business. Regardless of where you conduct the program, prohibit pagers and cellular phones during the sessions.

A professional training facility provides desirable features for both the participants and the trainer: comfortable seating; adequate work surfaces; sufficient space to accommodate break-out groups or other learning techniques; and teaching aids— white boards, overhead projectors, VCRs, monitors and, perhaps, video-conferencing equipment. If you don't have sufficient need to justify such an in-house facility, take your programs off-site to a hotel or conference facility. It's worth the expense to produce a professional program. Regardless of where you conduct a program, be sure to consider any accommodations that your staff or guest speakers who have disabilities may need.

Some salespeople can find most any excuse to justify their not attending a training program. Of course, you'll have an uphill battle to encourage attendance if a previous program was shoddy or worthless. This is a persuasive reason for producing quality programs in the first place. No matter what part of town you choose to hold your program, you will not please everyone. So be prepared for some grousing.

Trainers.   The key to successful classroom training is the trainer. The trainer must be able to take command and establish credibility with the group, control discussions and keep them on track, and maximize the learning experience for each participant. The trainer should use examples effectively, without subjecting the audience to an endless stream of personal war stories, and facilitate discussions and exercises without allowing a few participants to monopolize the class. See Figure 11.1 for some practical rules for trainers to follow.

Even if they have many years of experience in the classroom or in the business, trainers must prepare for each session, rather than talking off the top of their heads. Simple things like orga-

FIGURE 11.1   Rules for Trainers

Do

Project a personal interest in each student as a unique person.

Respect the student. Be tactful, fair and objective.

Praise the students' accomplishments.

Set a good example by your appearance.

Demonstrate the competency students should achieve with quality examples and exhibits.

Relate the subject matter to real-life situations. The more relevant the subject appears to the students, the more interested and motivated they will be to learn.

Project a positive attitude and enthusiasm toward the subject to emphasize that it is important to the students' lives.

Display integrity: "We don't cut corners, lie, cheat or misrepresent at any time in any form."

Be modest and don't brag about yourself or your personal accomplishments.

Be prepared for each class. Follow a predetermined and logical outline.

Maintain student interest by planning a variety of learning activities.

Create a fast-paced and exciting rhythm with lectures, discussions, projects and case studies, videos, group sessions or other techniques.

Use tone and volume of voice and physical mannerisms to keep student interest, but don't distract the student from the subject.

Create opportunities for students to share their personal knowledge and experience, but don't let anyone monopolize the discussion.

Use lecture and dialogue rather than straight lecture in classroom presentations.

Reinforce key points by summarizing periodically during the class session.

Use humor occasionally, but be sure that it will not be offensive to anyone.

Use theatrical devices or drama occasionally if they make a point, but don't threaten your credibility by appearing unprofessional. People should remember the point, not the method.

Strive to improve yourself. Use classroom evaluations to analyze your effectiveness.

Avoid rambling, illogical or unproductive discussions.

Avoid telling the students, rather show them what you mean. Remember that you make a stronger impression when you appeal to several senses.

Avoid gossip and don't slander the competition.

Avoid making promises that can't be fulfilled or exaggerating potential earnings.

nizing notes, following an agenda that is focused on the program's objectives, and assembling exhibits are essential for a professional program. Reviewing topics to be sure that they are not disseminating information that is out-of-date or contrary to your company's policies and procedures will also solidify the trainer's credibility with the participants.

Handout materials should be included in the program. They are useful for the students to follow during the sessions, particularly when they include exercises for the attendees to complete. Handouts are also a blueprint or guideline for implementing the classroom subjects in their daily practice and a resource that can be used outside of the classroom.

Twenty-first century learning.   The discussion so far has focused on the traditional classroom, with learning facilitated by a live trainer using participative teaching methods between student and instructor and among students. Today, however, a wide range of learning methods are possible via technology. Students can engage in totally independent computer-based learning. A variety of training programs are available with which they can work at their own pace, on their own time. Programs also can be delivered on the Internet, via satellite and audio or video conferences. In the education field all of these methods are known as distance education. Don't overlook the wide range of opportunities that are available, not only the content but also the delivery methods, to enhance your training curriculum. Also become familiar with the appropriate ways these various methodologies should be used for maximum effectiveness.

One-on-one training.   Earlier we mentioned that many of a manager's activities with the salespeople involve training. One-on-one sessions may be the only feasible way to cover a training program agenda if there are only a few people, or perhaps only one person, at any given time. Make this a worthwhile experience by following a specific agenda, scheduling specific times dedicated to training and helping people develop skill with the information. A one-on-one training regime may be used to supplement an outside program to which you send your salespeople or to reinforce training your company does in a group program.

Many people think of on-the-job training when we mention one-on-one training. On-the-job training involves the salesperson and the manager working together in the field. While this is a useful exercise, it is rarely a satisfactory substitute for a formal training program for new licensees. Often the lessons they learn are disjointed. If broker or manager has limited expertise or is out of step with the times, the training is not particularly constructive. On the positive side, salespeople appreciate your support, rather than going it alone. Often they feel reassured when they see the manager encounter challenges in the field similar to theirs.

Use the opportunity to work in the field to enhance your managerial effectiveness. You can gain insight into what the salespeople are doing, including their daily frustrations, and what's going on in the marketplace. You can determine ways to help them and also foster a relationship with them.

Another form of one-on-one training involves partners or mentors. Team a newly licensed salesperson with an experienced one. The new associate benefits from the support of a mentor and the opportunity to learn from an experienced person. Sometimes it's easier for two salespeople to relate to one another than for a salesperson to relate to a superior. A long-term bond can form that can help you retain both salespeople (but may also cause you to lose both if one of them decides to leave).

The manager should select the individual who will be the mentor. In doing so, you can choose the quality of the work to which the new associate is exposed and minimize the formation of undesirable cliques. The mentor also must be willing to assume this role. Frequently there is a mentor agreement that clearly identifies the person's duties and obligations. You may consider a shared commission arrangement so that the mentor doesn't feel used. That's also an incentive for the mentor to be attentive to the assignment.

Evaluating Training

Companies invest a considerable amount of money in training, so they need to ensure that the expenditure is worthwhile. A variety of methods can be used to measure the effectiveness of training. Ask participants to complete surveys at the conclusion of a session or program. Or you can survey changes in their attitudes or administer formal examinations. The most obvious indicator of the effectiveness is reflected in changes in the company's operation, the volume of transactions or the bottom line.

The caveat in focusing on the bottom line, however, is that training intends to affect behavior. And behavior rarely changes immediately. You must be patient and give people the opportunity to try something new or different. The manager can be a tremendous asset by reinforcing the new skills that were introduced in training sessions and recognizing the efforts of people rather than focusing immediately on the results.

Reinforcing Training

One of the major failures of training is that, like a motivational program, training doesn't have a lasting effect unless it is reinforced. The responsibility for this aspect of training falls to the salespeople's manager, which is why it's important for the manager to be familiar with the training curriculum. By coaching the salespeople one-on-one, conducting follow-up sessions or devoting a sales meeting to a subject, the manager reinforces the training curriculum. This also showcases the company's commitment to the lessons being taught.

In the case of training programs for newly licensed salespeople, we tend to overload them with too much information too soon. We'd like to tell them everything they'll ever need to know so they are prepared to handle any situation. But this does them a disservice. Until a new salesperson has had some field experience, much of the information they're exposed to has no relevance. It's more effective to develop some very basic listing and selling skills and allow people to practice them for awhile. Then bring them back into the training room to develop more sophisticated skills and acquire more detailed, technical information.

SALES MEETINGS

Planning meetings with the sales staff is one of a manager's most common activities. Meetings can be an important part of the salespeople's professional development as well as a tool for enhancing the office's operation and the quality of life in the workplace. Meetings can be used to educate or inform, recognize accomplishments, problem solve and brainstorm, or announce important company decisions.

Salespeople often criticize sales meetings as being a waste of time. Once your meetings get this reputation, getting people to attend is increasingly difficult. The real value of the sales meeting is suspect unless people see how they will benefit from attending. They are concerned about what's on the agenda, what good it will do to hear it and how much time it will take away from other activities. Since your salespeople are probably independent contractors, you cannot *compel* them to participate.

Many of the frustrations managers have with sales meetings are a product of past events. When the agenda is devoted to information that can be circulated on a flyer, in a memo or by e-mail, is it any wonder people feel they've wasted their time? If salespeople are ridiculed or used as an example of unacceptable behavior in front of the group, is it any wonder that they want to stay away? When past meetings have not been planned or conducted properly, their reputation lives to haunt the manager, even if another manager was responsible for the meetings.

Meetings should be used when their purpose can be best served by assembling people in a group. Because your company relies on the collective accomplishments of the salespeople, meetings contribute to team building. However, there's still no need to call people together when a memo or e-mail would do or to address issues that should be handled one-on-one with a salesperson. If the agenda is most relevant for only a portion of the sales force, then invite only that group.

Unless you have a very clear objective for your meeting, *don't hold one!* Just because you routinely get together every Wednesday afternoon is no reason to do so if there's no agenda. On the other hand, if you really think about things you could accomplish you can seize a valuable opportunity.

Types of Meetings

Important meetings begin with good planning. But this isn't something you do Monday morning at 8:00 when the meeting starts at 8:30. For sales meetings to be truly worthwhile, they should be designed and delivered with the same degree of methodology as a formal training program. When the manager sees sales meetings as an meaningful opportunity, rather than an obligatory chore, salespeople will also.

Begin by deciding the purpose of the meeting and the topics that will be covered. Once that is determined, the rest falls into place, such as who conducts the meeting, who attends and the logistics for the meeting. Meetings fall into several general categories.

Education and information. Any information that affects the industry in your area, your firm's customers and clients or your salespeople falls into this category. There may be contemporary issues such as legal developments or litigation issues, financing techniques, development trends, environmental concerns, a sales technique or an in-house procedure or office system that deserve discussion or a formal presentation. The meeting could also be an extension of the company's training programs or address common weaknesses. Be careful about discussing the office's listings. Information that compromises the principals' positions could be divulged, which is especially dangerous if disclosed dual agency or designated agency is practiced.

When planning these meetings, ponder these points.

- Do the salespeople need this information to be more effective and efficient? If they do, then the meeting is a valuable use of their time.

- If you don't provide this forum, can you be sure the salespeople will get the information otherwise? Volumes of good tips and information are disseminated at seminars, in professional and business publications and on the Internet, but not all salespeople or managers see it.

- Are the meetings repetitious? If the agenda is the same old thing, the meetings grow stale after awhile. You can take some of the guesswork out of your planning by asking the salespeople for suggestions about useful topics.

Once you select the topic, select a suitable format. The manager doesn't always have to conduct the meeting. In fact, it's refreshing to hear a new voice from time to time and expose the staff to specialized expertise. The company's training or marketing director, the broker, a salesperson, a representative from the company that's installed a new phone or computer system, a representative from the local school district or municipality, a local builder to discuss a co-op plan, the company's attorney—the list of possible speakers is endless. If you're focusing on an in-house procedure or office system, invite other staff personnel as well as the salespeople.

Handout material is useful for informative and educational meetings. Unfortunately, we all gather an enormous amount of paper, most of which ends up in a useless pile on the desk. Establish a reference file in the office or scan it into your computer system so that a master set of the information can be accessed whenever it is needed.

Attitude and recognition.   A celebration can be planned around most any positive thing that happens to individuals or the company. Most companies have programs to award production. In addition, think about recognizing other professional accomplishments, such as obtaining a broker's license, a professional designation, a chairmanship or an office in a professional association or participation in a community service organization. Presenting individual awards in a public forum grants the recognition these achievements deserve. (The risk, however, is that people who are never recognized tire of being ignored, so while you're stroking the awardees you can be alienating others.)

If your company has had a banner year, honor all of your workers for their collective contribution to the company's success. Plan a rally to mobilize everyone around the company's objectives and financial goals for the new year. Or plan a social or athletic event just for fun.

When the company plans events that foster good feelings, you inspire people and help reaffirm commitment to the company. These also are opportunities to encourage camaraderie among the staff and enhance the quality of life in the workplace. (If you manage an office for a large company that doesn't have such an event, hold one just for your office.) Remember that all of the staff, management, support and administrative personnel, as well as salespeople, play on the same team and should be included in your celebrations.

Like any other meeting, these events must be carefully planned. Create an upbeat, nonthreatening environment. People should look forward to participating, rather than feel like they must attend a command performance. If the event is worthy of a grand celebration, hold the meeting off-site with great fanfare. If you're planning a formal program, schedule a keynote speaker and remarks by the broker or senior management. The informal social time before and after the program is an important part of the affair. In large organizations this is one of the few times the staff gets to rub elbows with upper management.

Be creative in planning icebreakers and activities that encourage socializing. Many of the people have nothing in common with one another except that they work together. Give people something to talk about or a fun project, unrelated to business, on which they can work together. Remember that the point is for people to relax and have fun. It also shows that management cares.

Problem identification. Any number of issues can cause consternation in your office. Problem identification meetings give people an opportunity to air their concerns in a relatively risk-free setting. These could be centered around situations in the company, the office or the business in general. Frequently people are hesitant to speak up for fear of retribution. Give people an opportunity several times during the year to share what's on their minds. This also demonstrates your concern for the quality of their work life.

The purpose of a problem-identification meeting is quite clear—to create a forum for people to voice their concerns. Announce the meeting by telling everyone its purpose and ask them to come prepared with issues they'd like to raise. You can set parameters if you like, such as office procedures, the company's advertising program, or a particular service the company offers. Or you can say that issues relating to any topic are welcome. Remember to include the support staff in some of these meetings as well.

Managers are sometimes intimidated by this type of a meeting, fearing that it will become an unruly gripe session or a shouting match. But these meetings can be very constructive when conducted properly. Set rules at the outset:

- everyone will be given an opportunity to speak;
- participants will be given a certain amount of time to speak;
- specify that no evaluations, solutions, long-winded examples or illustrations are permitted; and
- limit the length of the meeting.

Your role is to sit back, listen, take notes and nudge the group to stay focused. Maintain a nonjudgmental climate so that everyone feels free to express themselves. Any issue is worthy of consideration if a person feels it needs to be raised. If you're concerned about people being hesitant to publicly express themselves, gather written submissions. Then log them on a chart or blackboard for the group to see. You don't have to divulge the identity of the person submitting the problem.

The final step before you close the meeting is to prioritize the issues and gain consensus about which ones should be addressed first. You'll probably notice that many of the issues are related to one another, making it relatively easy to identify major problems.

Now that you have a fistful of issues, you have to decide what to do with them. Should they be referred to upper management or the broker, the training director or another department, or are they issues that should be handled within your office? You have taken on some responsibility for yourself by creating this forum. Unless the staff is going to participate in developing solutions and making decisions, you owe people feedback so they know that the company has heard their concerns. People welcome the opportunity to bring matters to your attention, but they also have to feel that their input is valued.

Brainstorming.   Your organization has a wealth of talent that can be utilized to help it confront the challenges of doing business in a changing environment. Brainstorming meetings give staff an opportunity to influence decisions the company makes. The purpose of these meetings is to generate ideas for solving a specific problem or addressing an issue. The focus could be a topic that was raised in a problem-identification meeting or it could be a matter the company offers to the staff for input. Be sure that the people who are affected by the problem are the ones who participate in the solution, including clerical or administrative staff if applicable.

Tell people what the subject is, then just let the creative energies flow. Everyone is entitled to speak. As one person makes a suggestion, others piggyback on it with refinements or variations. Because there are many heads in the room, a problem or issue gets evaluated from a variety of perspectives. These meetings can be quite enjoyable. You'll be impressed with the quality and creativity of the ideas that are generated and the enthusiasm people have for participating in the process.

Your job is to list the solutions on a flipchart or board and keep the group focused on the most important rule: *no criticism or evaluation of the solutions is permitted*. Keep the group moving at a fast pace. When they've exhausted all the possibilities, take a break or close the meeting.

Decision making.   After the staff has participated in a brainstorming meeting, the next task is to decide what to do with all of the suggestions. The logical step is to evaluate those suggestions and decide the best course of action. *The essential question, however, is who is entitled to make the decision?* Staff needs to be told what you intend to do with their suggestions. Can they proceed to the next level and either make a decision (decide their own fate) or make a recommendation that management will seriously consider?

An effective decision-making meeting involves no more than 15 participants; with a group any larger it's difficult to reach consensus. The group first discusses all of the alternatives that were generated during brainstorming. Some will be cast aside rather quickly, and others will get serious attention. Each of the serious contenders is evaluated on the basis of their

- pluses and minuses;

- feasibility; and

- perceived acceptance.

The manager can act as an impartial moderator. Or can participate in the discussions as an equal with the others in the group, according to the nature of the issue. Be aware that, depending on your management style, you may have difficulty sitting back and allowing the participants to work through the process by themselves. In any event the manager is responsible for keeping the group focused on the outcome–a decision or recommendation.

The meeting concludes when everyone in the room reaches a decision they can accept, even if everyone doesn't fully agree with it. Note that the goal is to arrive at consensus and not make decisions by majority vote. The minority loses the vote and anyone who doesn't favor the decision is unlikely to support its implementation. Often the course of action that has the fewest undesirable consequences is the one the group chooses.

In highly monolithic organizations, decision making, even about relatively insignificant matters, is rarely entrusted to anyone other than senior management or the broker/owner. Often senior management doesn't solicit input from anyone else, nor even invite suggestions from the staff. If this is the culture in your organization, you're not likely to be conducting brainstorming or decision-making meetings.

Announcing decisions. Finally, people hear that a decision has been reached and, hopefully, their problem has been solved. If the staff participated in the decision-making process, the focus of the meeting is the implementation of the decision.

You can feel relatively positive about the outcome of this meeting, knowing that the decision is a consensus of their efforts and they have positively affected their own quality of life at work.

When upper management or another department solves a problem or changes company policies and procedures, the outcome of this meeting is less certain. Often you have no idea whether the decision will be acceptable or unacceptable. A solution that makes sense to the marketing department, for example, may not appeal to the salespeople in the field. A new procedure implemented by the accounting department may seem cumbersome to the staff.

The way management announces decisions has a great bearing on the way they are received and the likelihood they will be implemented. People are far more willing to implement a decision they understand. The personnel involved in making the decision should explain their rationale. This is not intended to justify or defend the decision but rather to provide a company perspective, which often the entire staff does not see. Management must present a unified message, not bad-mouth the decision-makers or stonewall the implementation of a decision.

When major changes in the organization are contemplated, management must guard the confidentiality of a decision until it can be announced and explained properly. Otherwise the grapevine gets activated and people arrive at the meeting with preconceived notions, sometimes based on half-truths. Once a major company meeting is announced, people busy themselves trying to find out what's going on, anyway. Invariably the rumors are worse than the reality, which means that your announcement could be viewed rather favorably.

Major new company programs or policies should be announced with fanfare and a positive spin. Your public relations counsel is helpful in preparing a suitable announcement. To minimize apprehension, it's safest not to publicize a meeting to announce a major change more than two weeks in advance. You can help the company showcase a major announcement in a constructive manner by reassuring people that change isn't bad and encouraging patience until they get all of the facts.

Logistics

Meetings provide numerous opportunities, but their benefits are lost if the meetings are poorly executed. Decide how frequently you need to call people together and make wise decisions about when meetings are scheduled. Consider the needs of your salespeople and their work styles, including the number of people who work from home offices. You may find that using audio or video conferencing solves many of today's logistics problems.

A regularly scheduled meeting day, even if it's monthly rather than weekly, tells people how to plan. Avoid conflicts with other important events such as MLS tours, professional association functions and popular settlement or closing days. The best time of day (or evening) and day of the week will vary in different areas. Many people are geared to the Monday morning meeting to get everyone jump-started for the week and debriefed on the weekend's activities.

Plan the agenda around the purpose for which you called the meeting. A well-structured agenda keeps the meeting focused so that it does not ramble or stray off course. The meeting should have a beginning, a middle and an end. If you want to say something that doesn't fit into this format, plan another meeting with a different purpose.

- *The introduction*–Explain the purpose of the meeting. Although you've already included this in the meeting announcement, it's important to explain more fully what you intend to accomplish. This is also the time to get any important announcements out of the way or pat someone on the back for a job well done. However, don't waste people's time with things that they can read on the bulletin board, in a memo or on e-mail and thus distract their attention from the real purpose.

- *The substance*–As soon as you can, get people involved with the task at hand, whether it's an educational meeting with a speaker, a brainstorming exercise or a discussion of the marketing of a new subdivision. It's tempting when you have people gathered together to take advantage of the opportunity and cover a multitude of things. But this is when meetings can get out of control; they last too long and lose their punch.

- *The conclusion*–Summarize and reinforce the primary message of the meeting. People, including you, should leave the meeting knowing what has transpired and what to do next, if that's appropriate.

Once you've planned the agenda, decide how long the meeting should last, choose the location, using the same rationale we discussed earlier for training programs, arrange for any handout materials and media that you need and publicize the meeting. Give people sufficient advanced notice to plan their schedules, and publish the hours for the meeting and an agenda. Then, begin on time (even if you're talking to an empty room) and end on time, or earlier if you've accomplished your purpose.

Managing the Meeting

You've heard of Murphy's Law? Anything that could go wrong, probably will. Because you're the one in charge, it's up to you to manage the meeting and be prepared for any eventuality. The better you manage the meeting, the more likely people are to want to attend the next one.

Establish policies for your meetings to preserve the professional atmosphere and minimize disruption for everyone in attendance. How will you handle people who want to leave early? How will you handle late arrivals? If you get the reputation for starting meetings late, people know that there's no point in arriving on time. Once you begin the meeting, if you back up and repeat yourself for the benefit of late arrivals, there's no need for people to be present at the beginning. And no one needs to come to a meeting and hear you sermonize about attendance and punctuality!

You may not be the only one who has an agenda for the meeting. A disgruntled salesperson (or a clique of them), for example, may seize the opportunity to air a complaint or stir up trouble. A person could feel safer and supported when raising the issue in front of a group, especially if others share similar views. You should be aware of any undertow or discontent that could surface if you're being a vigilant observer in your office and are communicating with your staff (a good reason to schedule a problem-identification meeting). This is your meeting, so be prepared to control it.

Anytime you gather a group of people together the potential exists for the meeting to be disrupted. Certainly, the subject matter of some meetings is contentious, but every group has some disruptive personalities. Some are disgruntled and others are just seeking attention. Don't feed egos and don't antagonize. Take the person aside after the meeting and find out if there's a problem this person wants to address. If so, you can handle it individually. Salespeople, especially, are independent-minded and can be a cantankerous bunch, better suited to individual rather than group endeavors. Don't allow a meeting to be disrupted by a "showboater." Everyone has to work together after the meeting is over, so anticipate objections or problems that could arise and prepare to handle situations carefully.

RETREATS

Another forum for professional development is a retreat. While these require considerable planning, commitment and expense on the part of the company and commitment of time on the part of the people who attend, they offer benefits far beyond the program agenda.

Despite the fact that you're attempting to build a team, the reality is that salespeople rarely see one another aside from a periodic staff meeting. This isolation is increasingly more common because of home officing. A retreat is an opportunity to draw all of the full-time and part-time salespeople and support staff together. One of the reasons people enjoy professional meetings and education courses is the opportunity to brainstorm with other real estate professionals. When conducting a retreat, you're creating such an opportunity within your own company.

One of a meeting planner's greatest challenges is gathering a captive audience together with no distractions, telephones, appointments or office business. Take people to a conference facility and perhaps an overnight stay. Once people are totally immersed in the subject of the meeting, you'll be surprised how much can be accomplished, especially if you want brainstorming and decision making. Give people a problem today and by tomorrow they'll have a solution, including a plan for implementation.

There are a variety of purposes you can accomplish with a retreat. You can reflect on the past year and plan for the next; hold a strategic planning meeting; strategize the design of a new system, service or department in the organization; focus on the production and financial management of the company or do management or sales training.

The purpose of the retreat will determine who attends and the length of the time for the program. You may bring the entire organization together in an educational forum or motivational rally (a miniconvention for your firm) or assemble only management or certain department personnel. Planning the facilities, the program, food service and other accommodations for a retreat is a major undertaking. But it's worth the effort because results can be achieved in a shorter period of time than with other forums you can create.

PERSONAL INTERACTION

Although group forums offer many advantages, they are not a substitute for personal contact between the manager and an individual salesperson or other staff member. Each person is an individual, with his or her own needs, problems and aspirations. A manager's one-on-one interaction with each person is a critical part of his or her professional development. You do not need to hover or micromanage (oversee every detail of every task). But you do need to be accessible and attentive when called upon. Seek out your staff members periodically for personal consultation. We discuss techniques in greater detail in the next chapter.

ADDITIONAL OPPORTUNITIES

The primary focus in this chapter has been on ways the company contributes to the professional development of its human resources. We should not overlook the range of opportunities that exist for people outside your organization as well. In fact, a company that is committed to professional development encourages people to seek out these opportunities. People can benefit from associating with other professionals with similar interests, as well as from the education and training that are available. There are many forums for these opportunities, including colleges, universities, real estate schools and professional organizations. People can also further their education with correspondence courses.

Professional organizations conduct seminars, training programs and more intense courses related to the activities in which their members are engaged. There are also designations that people can pursue, involving fairly comprehensive courses of study. People who earn these designations enjoy professional stature in the industry. The National Association of REALTORS® research group reports that people who have designations from its institutes, societies and councils also earn more money. Most every real estate activity has related designations or organizations, including residential sales, buyer-agency, appraising, property management, nonresidential brokerage and management, counseling and investment and international brokerage.

Don't overlook the professional development of the management and support and administrative staff. There are organizations and councils for brokers and managers, educators and trainers, marketing and advertising specialists, accountants, secretaries and professional women and business owners. People should be encouraged to explore opportunities beyond forums that focus on real estate. Exposing the company's personnel to a broad range of business education and professional associations adds a dimension to the organization as well as the individual jobs people do. They are able to provide insight and vision as your company manages its operations in a changing climate.

CONCLUSION

When people feel satisfied with their jobs, the place in which they work and the progress they are making toward their career goals, they can be more productive for your company. Professional development is about creating opportunities for people both to gain proficiency in the skills they need for their jobs and to influence their quality of life at work.

The company can create many structured forums for this to occur, including the orientation and training programs, sales meetings and retreats. But the one-on-one interaction that people have with their managers and the educational opportunities and relationships with similar professionals outside your organization are just as important. As people grow professionally, they grow as human beings. Your company benefits in the process.

DISCUSSION EXERCISES

What are the most important things a new hire should know about your company that should be included in an orientation program?

* * *

From your experiences in training programs, what would you like to see your company do the same or differently in the programs it conducts for the salespeople?

* * *

Select one of the types of sales meetings and develop an agenda and a plan for promoting the meeting. Discuss your rationale for your selection and the purpose you intend to accomplish.

* * *

From your experiences with sales meetings, either as a participant in a sales meeting or the manager in charge of one, discuss some of the successes you would emulate or solutions for problems you have observed.

12 Coaching Your Staff

What can you as the manager do to contribute to the productivity of salespeople? How do you evaluate their performance? How does the way you handle situations in the office affect the retention of your salespeople?

We made the point in the first unit that the goal of planning is to ensure that the *right* things happen in the organization. Glance around the office, and you see that things are happening. Everyone is busy—doing *something* (even nothing is something). Some people feel that they have to be seen in the office for you to think they're working. (And that's the way some brokers feel, too.) But they may not necessarily be engaged in activities that contribute to the company's goals.

In the POSDC (Planning, Organizing, Staffing, Directing, Controlling) model we're following, we've reached the next dimension of a manager's job as we explore *D*—the *directing* function. This is essentially the management of the organization's human resources. Unfortunately, too many managers focus on statistics, transactions and systems rather than on people. The fact is that without these people the company has no bottom line. The manager's job is to direct their activities to achieve the organization's goals and make a profit.

The contemporary view of a manager's job is to energize and empower people, rather than dominate them. (See Chapter 16 for a discussion of management styles.) Look at this job from the perspective of a coach. The coach helps players reach their goals, which means the coach must be a leader, a teacher, a counselor, a negotiator and an arbitrator. You need to be an astute observer of human behavior to determine which role suits the occasion. Managing personnel is not a simple task. You are managing a complex environment of human beings, with dynamics that increase exponentially with the number of people you are supervising. One of your tasks is to create an environment in which they can be productive. If you are a sales manager, this is the function in which you are most directly involved.

Remember that the organization *and* its workers have needs. Unless both are satisfied, you'll be in a win-lose rather than a win-win situation. Coaching your staff involves activities that help people feel satisfied and keep them productive. This is an important part of their professional development as well as the company's success.

MANAGING EMPLOYEES AND INDEPENDENT CONTRACTORS

In today's office you are likely to be supervising people who are employees as well as others who are independent contractors. It's important to understand the difference between the two and adjust your supervisory methods accordingly to preserve the relationship that is intended. The essential difference, from a management perspective, is the degree of control that you can exercise over a person's activities, as dictated by the Internal Revenue Code.

Step out of the real estate brokerage business for a moment and think about the working relationship that exists between employers and a large portion of this country's work force. The company dictates the hours people are expected to work, meal times, allotments for vacation and personal days, meetings they are required to attend and just about every other activity employees are expected to perform. This is a very structured work environment, giving the company maximum control over the methods employees use to perform their jobs.

For many people being an employee is far more familiar and instinctive than being an independent contractor. People who are used to working as employees expect, even rely, on the structure the company imposes on their work life. Managers feel a strong sense of control over every aspect of the employees' day.

Independent contractors, on the other hand, work in a much less structured environment. As the name implies, they are independent. They contract with the company to achieve certain outcomes or performance objectives. The independent contractor rather than the company determines and controls the methods used to accomplish these objectives. A written contract, similar to the one that appears in Chapter 10, is used to define the responsibilities of both parties. Even though responsibilities are defined, the contract cannot unduly restrict the independent contractor's methods.

It is totally appropriate to control the work environment in the way we described when you are supervising employees. But you cannot attempt to *control* independent contractors the same way. You cannot, for example, *require* attendance in the office at prescribed times (i.e., floor time, office hours) or at certain meetings or training programs. Nor can you set vacation or conference schedules; specify daily activities, such as the number of sales calls, listing presentations or open houses; restrict the properties and buyers the independent contractor services; or specify dress codes. You can only *recommend, suggest* or *encourage* certain behavior for independent contractors.

The company can't have life "both ways"; that is, it can't enjoy the financial benefits of hiring independent contractors while controlling them as if they were employees. One of the major reasons salespeople have customarily been independent contractors is, as discussed in Chapter 10, the company is relieved of many of the costs and reporting requirements associated with employees. Independent contractors also enjoy benefits, including tax breaks and larger deductions for nonreimbursed business expenses and self-directed pension funds. But you defeat the benefits for both the company and the independent contractor if the Internal Revenue Service determines that the person is really an employee. Your actions must be consistent with the provisions of the independent contractor agreement to preserve this relationship.

It *is* possible to manage independent contractors. Some managers relinquish their responsibilities entirely, feeling that because they can't control the independent contractors' work life, there's little point in trying to supervise them at all. But this defeats the purpose of being a manager. You can expect only scattered or sporadic attempts by the salespeople to produce when they receive little direction, motivation or guidance. Instead, demonstrate how their careers will benefit from doing the things you are encouraging them to do, much like we sell benefits to our customers. Helping independent contractors achieve their objectives creates a "win-win" situation for them and the company.

COACHING PERFORMANCE

A manager who coaches performance empowers salespeople to direct their activities in constructive ways to satisfy the company's goals. This process begins by first identifying what needs to be done. Once this is established, the manager's role is to encourage and support the performance so that it doesn't stray off course.

Each person is in charge of his or her own behavior, and everyone else is a bystander. A manager may find it difficult to be a bystander when there are certain things the salespeople need to do for your office or company to achieve its goals. The truth of the matter is that no one really motivates another person to do anything. Yes, you can recognize or reward performance with the expectation that it then will be repeated. But regardless of whether a person is an employee or an independent contractor, you can't *make* another person do anything. Once you recognize what you can't do, it's easier to understand what you can do.

From a production standpoint you can identify what needs to be done based on the planning and budgeting the company does. In the example in Figure 12.1 the total amount of com-

FIGURE 12.1   Annual Company Production Goals, 1999–2000

Name	1st Quarter 1999 Actual	1st Quarter 2000 Goal	2nd Quarter 1999 Actual	2nd Quarter 2000 Goal	Total Year 1999 Actual	Total Year 2000 Goal
FORD	5,000		5,800		24,000	
		7,500		9,000		30,000
SMITH	8,000		4,700		29,000	
		8,000		5,500		35,000
ADAIN	5,000		6,000		30,000	
		8,000		8,000		37,500
DINKEL	7,500		8,000		34,000	
		11,000		10,000		40,000
FRANKS	5,500		4,200		26,900	
		6,000		6,000		30,000
RIGGS	9,500		9,500		48,000	
		10,000		10,000		50,000
KEAST	13,000		0		39,800	
		12,000		10,000		60,000
JONES	2,100		4,000		8,100	
		2,000		4,000		18,000
COSTA	5,500		3,300		25,600	
		6,000		6,120		24,000
BOWERS	0		3,000		13,000	
		6,000		6,000		24,000
COMPANY	10,766	130,500		127,500	278,300	350,500

mission revenue the company expects for the year is $350,500. Notice that for two quarters of the year, the example shows actual production in the previous year and the goals that ten salespeople are expected to reach in the new year. Using previous production, you can identify fairly realistic goals for the salespeople as you distribute the responsibility for the $350,500 among them. You have an idea of how to accomplish the goal for your office. Now you need the support of your salespeople.

Personal Success Plans

One way to define what a salesperson is going to accomplish is with a personal success plan. This is the salesperson's business plan. Salespeople benefit from having plans for the same reasons the company does. A plan converts aspirations into action by defining specific, measurable goals and strategies to guide them along the way. Plans are a tool that empowers salespeople to direct their own activities and satisfy their needs while at the same time they are working toward the company's goals.

A personal success plan is a holistic approach to defining what a person intends to accomplish as a professional salesperson. For the person who's aimless, disorganized or complacent, a plan provides the direction he or she needs to get on track. Personal success plans, in addition to including a production quota, give you a basis for guiding their professional growth and evaluating progress periodically throughout the year.

Because salespeople have their own motives for working, their individual views of success and what you need for the company may be different. One person may feel successful if he can provide food and shelter for the family. Another may feel successful if she is still selling next year. These are basic survival needs. Unless their goals for survival are sufficiently productive to achieve the company's goals, your job is to help each salesperson strive beyond this point. Sometimes people are hesitant to set their sights high (or at any level for that matter) for fear of failure. But with your support and encouragement, a person can commit to a plan that is attainable. Also, you demonstrate that you believe in that person.

Developing a plan.   Once the company's plan and budget are established for the coming year, the manager should meet with each salesperson to help him or her develop a personal plan. Your role in this meeting is to provide guidance. (*Professional Real Estate Development* by Patrick Keigher and Joyce Emory, listed in the bibliography, is useful for this purpose.)

While you discover what the salesperson wants to accomplish, you also can be sure that the goals are aligned with those of the company. The *process* is as important as the product. You build relationships by giving people your undivided attention in a one-on-one meeting, an opportunity to learn about one another.

The rules for a personal plan are similar to those for a company's business plan. Measurable goals must be defined along with strategies for accomplishing them. For example, a salesperson's goal may be to have a broker's license three years from now. Strategies would include a plan for obtaining the necessary education and experience per the licensing laws. Now the salesperson is turning the elusive *success* into a definite accomplishment.

Top producers are geared to planning their business this way. They are very goal-oriented people, so a plan crystallizes their focus and gives them a road map to follow. Plans help them prioritize their activities and be efficient time managers. They can focus on activities that are directly related to achieving their goals and delegate other tasks so they can make better use of their time.

Developing a plan forces people to make specific commitments, which can be intimidating for some. Because the plan is written and someone else (you) knows what it says, they are accountable for it. They have to face facts when it's time to review their progress. The truth, whether they're on track or not, will be quite evident. Because you are coaching the development of the plan, you can provide some reassurance to minimize a person's trepidation.

Achievable plans.   A plan can be a great motivator, but only as long as the goals are attainable. Unrealistic goals discourage, rather than inspire, and set people up to fail. Goals should be tailored to a person's level of experience and expertise and capitalize on strengths. A less experienced salesperson, for example, will be energized by achieving in one year what a more experienced person may accomplish in several months. While the manager can rally support for the salespeople's accomplishments, the individual salespeople must believe that they are capable of achieving their goals. And it's far more rewarding to exceed a goal than never to reach one.

Unfortunately, brokers and managers sometimes are responsible for a person's lack of success. Arbitrary expectations about what people should be accomplishing set up unrealistic expectations and produce little more than frustration. For example, setting unrealistic goals for listings for a salesperson who excels at working with buyers distracts the person from what he or she does best. Not only have you discouraged and alienated the salesperson, but your office will lose in the long run.

Goals and quotas.   While you are helping a salesperson develop a personal plan, you also can help determine annual production goals that are part of the plan. Identify benchmarks during the year, as was done in Figure 12.1 with quarterly goals, to help monitor progress and adjust for the seasonal nature of the business.

If your salespeople are independent contractors, you must be careful how you use quotas and personal success plans. You cannot *control* the way your salespeople conduct their business. It is totally appropriate for you to *mutually agree* to certain general performance objectives. In fact, this may be part of your independent contractor agreement. Beyond that point, these plans and quotas are used to *monitor* a salesperson's progress and *encourage* performance throughout the year.

Incentives to Perform

Incentives are a tool for encouraging people and rewarding performance. They are intended to appeal to their various motivations for working. Motivations differ with each individual, but we're not psychologists, so we can't be sure what those motives are. Consequently, managers typically make assumptions about which incentives will produce the desired outcome. Incentives such as money, bonuses or luxury trips spark production for some people. For others the main reward is the respect they gain from the supervisor and fellow staff members. As people feel more competent in their jobs they develop aspirations for advancement. Although it appears that people are becoming increasingly materialistic (a motivation that money will satisfy), you can't overlook the importance of other rewards that inspire people in the workplace.

Praise. Praise can be powerful because it not only affects performance on the job, but also enhances a person's sense of self-worth. Encouragement such as a simple "thank you," "well done" or "congratulations" from the manager is often sufficient recognition to spark continuing and possibly increased performance. The manager can be the company's most valuable incentive program. Look for praiseworthy accomplishments in each of your staff. (This is your day-to-day coaching.) These might include conquering the tenacious hurdles in daily business, like getting an obstinate seller or a cantankerous buyer to finally sign a contract, as well as reaching a production quota. Note that you are praising *performance*, not making judgments about a person's character.

Status. Some people glow with internal pride in their accomplishments, while others are not content until they feel recognized by the organization. In either case, people's efforts and talents deserve to be recognized by the organization. One way to do this is to give a person an assignment on behalf of the organization, which gives status in the company that others don't have.

There are numerous ways to enhance a person's status. For example,

- assign a salesperson with exceptional skills to be a mentor or partner for a newly licensed salesperson, such as we mentioned in Chapter 11;

- ask a salesperson with good writing skills or a background in publishing to be the editor of the company's newsletter;

- assign someone to be a counselor to sales staff in your absence; or

- invite a salesperson to make a presentation at a sales meeting.

Some special assignments deserve compensation. Unless people are compensated properly, they can feel used rather than elevated. Also think about this—while you are creating ways for people to shine, you also can identify talent that could be valuable elsewhere in the organization.

Use this incentive carefully; otherwise you could create problems. A person whose status has been elevated may have difficulty relinquishing the position. Don't let someone (who may be just waiting for the opportunity) be sales manager for a day if that person might try to undermine your authority, for example. Consider the personality of the individual and the nature of the assignment so that you don't fuel politics or create power plays that could disrupt the harmony in the office. Be very clear about the details of the task and the limits of authority.

Contests.   Not all brokers agree on the value of sales contests. One problem may be the nature of the prizes that are offered. You might find an inexpensive or a unique prize. But if the salespeople aren't interested in it, the prize is not an incentive and you might as well forgo the contest. In fact the salespeople might be insulted. The pressure cooker you found on sale won't appeal to too many thirty-something salespeople. You could use it for its humorous value, making fun more stimulating than the reward. Fun is good for reducing tension (real estate sales is one of the most stressful jobs) and building camaraderie, but that's a different goal than is intended for a true sales contest.

Another issue to consider about contests is whether everyone has a chance to win. People must be able to compete on an equal basis, especially if the contest is based on production. Otherwise you are favoring only the top producers, frequently the same people who win all the time. This sends a message to the others that their contributions aren't valuable. People won't bother participating in the program unless they feel there's a chance to win, regardless of how attractive the prize is.

When you do venture onto the sales floor with a contest, be prepared to monitor the salespeople very carefully. If people are really motivated to win, they could be inclined to try winning at any cost. Suddenly you can have more conflict over the ownership of leads, an increase in disgruntled sellers or buyers or more overpriced listings than you want to advertise. Remember the comment in Chapter 8 about the company's philosophy about process versus results.

Awards. Awards are common ways to recognize past and encourage future performance. Awards to the listing leader of the month or year or to the sales leader of the month or year are typical. The recognition might be a name plate added to a plaque in the reception area or a trophy that moves from desk to desk each month.

Award programs must be structured carefully. They are useful in recognizing people's accomplishments but they may not be effective in encouraging the people who consistently lag behind. These programs can polarize the sales force into two groups: the "outstandings" and the "also-rans." The "outstandings" compete with one another, trading a trophy back and forth. The "also-rans" don't even bother trying. Eventually awards can become meaningless, or even embarrassing to the person who constantly wins. The point about giving everyone an opportunity to compete on an equal basis is applicable to award programs as well. This is not to suggest that you eliminate the leader for the month award, but you should consider other programs as well.

Refer to the discussion in Chapter 11 about meetings and events conducted for attitude and recognition. This makes some valuable points about ways to increase the value of awards programs and also create opportunities to recognize everyone's contribution and a sense of belonging in the company.

Graduated commissions. Graduated commission programs are the most common, tangible incentives. Salespeople, however, often view commissions as only just compensation for their efforts rather than as incentives. As was mentioned in a previous chapter, these programs operate on the theory that salespeople will be motivated to produce more if they can earn more. For example, after one year of production in which the salesperson has split 55/45 with the broker, the salesperson can advance to a 60/40 split in the following year. Each year's commission split is determined by the previous year's production, with the expectation that the salesperson will strive to equal or exceed previous earnings. Of course, this only works if money is the motivation. Furthermore any split that is too low insults and drives people to a company where they feel their efforts will be appreciated.

Bonuses. We'd be remiss if we didn't at least mention bonuses as a possible incentive. But we'll go no further than to suggest that you consult your lawyer and accountant before structuring a bonus plan for independent contractors. There can be serious implications for both the company and the salespeople that could threaten the independent contractor status.

Negative incentives. Parental- or dictatorial-style managers may see fear, embarrassment, punishment, reprimand and criticism as incentives for people to change their behavior. They believe that if an experience is sufficiently unpleasant, people will strive to avoid similar experiences in the future. Yelling at a salesperson who hasn't had a listing in three months and doing so in front of the entire staff certainly lets everyone know what you think. But it is not only embarrassing to be the subject of ridicule, especially in front of the other people, it is also insulting–as if the salesperson isn't already aware of the listing deficiency.

Negative incentives can do more harm than good. At best, they work only momentarily. The embarrassed salesperson may get out of the office in a hurry, *perhaps* to find a listing. But the person is more likely to run away until the feelings of the moment wear off. The confrontation is normally felt as an attack on the person rather than on performance, so you damage self-esteem. The failure in this scenario is that no constructive plan exists for changing behavior. You also have created an antagonistic atmosphere in the office.

PERFORMANCE REVIEWS

Performance reviews are used to evaluate people's accomplishments. Often people see these reviews as report cards employers use to criticize, and possibly reprimand, personnel.

While performance reviews do reveal weaknesses, they are also positive and constructive exercises. They are opportunities to acknowledge achievements and help people grow professionally as well as to uncover issues, especially within the organization, that negatively affect people's ability to perform. One of the most valuable features is that they provide another opportunity for managers to converse one-on-one with people. Look at the information you can gather while doing performance evaluations.

- Identify areas in which salespeople can benefit from individual counseling and professional development based on their strengths and weaknesses

- Identify people for promotion to other positions in the company, such as manager, sales trainer or relocation director

- Identify people who are better suited for non-selling positions, such as appraiser, transaction coordinator or settlement officer

- Determine if your expectations of the entire sales force are unrealistic, which will be obvious if *everyone* is performing poorly in certain areas

- Determine if you need to revise any of the job descriptions within the company based on changes in the marketplace, in your company's policies and in the jobs of other staff members

- Determine if the training program, recruiting or hiring procedures or company policies and procedures should be revised

- Identify information that may lead you to terminate a person

Performance reviews not only help people know where they stand, but they also tell management what it needs to be doing. The manager is ultimately responsible for company goals, so the manager has to take some responsibility for creating a supportive environment. By uncovering people's concerns or frustrations, managers can then identify ways to assist them and perhaps changes within the company that are necessary. The reviews are also important for keeping the broker informed about the activities of the licensees because he or she is ultimately responsible under the licensing laws.

Performance reviews are used for all personnel, not just salespeople, based on individual criteria that is determined with each person in the organization. For salespeople their personal business plans, including goals and quotas, will be a good starting point. Don't wait until the end of the year to talk to people about what they should have been doing. The manager should be coaching performance and reviewing progress throughout the year. Typically, a formal performance review is done about midway through the year (six months into the plan) and after year's end. During the first and third quarters of the year, you can schedule shorter, less comprehensive meetings to "touch base."

Performance Criteria

Before you can conduct a review you need to identify the criteria by which each person will be evaluated. People need to know the rules for the game. Otherwise, they'll feel like they've been penalized for breaking a rule they didn't know existed. People need to know ahead of time exactly what you plan to evaluate and a sufficient opportunity to move forward in constructive directions. Ideally performance criteria is developed at year-end for the coming year. (For salespeople this would be after the personal business plan has been formulated.) People should also participate in the process of developing criteria. The likelihood of achieving "buy in" is greater and often they have useful suggestions.

For salespeople, begin with their personal success plans. These contain measurable objectives and emphasize accomplishments in addition to production quotas. Also you may develop criteria related to other issues. These could include the quality of services the salesperson provides (see the section on Quality Service Standards in Chapter 13), the number of transactions that didn't go to settlement, specific company policies that are critically important or ones that have been compromised, or other activities that are related to the job description for a salesperson.

Now you can develop a list of performance-based issues for each person. Typically the list is comprised of two sections: one that is designed for the individual person; and another that relates to all personnel in the same job category. This gives you the "script" with which to rate a person's performance on each issue, perhaps on a scale of five to one or ten to one.

Remember that these are performance reviews; that is, the issues you are evaluating must be related to job performance. They are *not* an assessment of an individual's personality or character. When developing criteria, consider how you will use them to review people's performance objectively. These reviews must be fair and equitable, and you must be even-handed with each person you review. Once you have developed your performance evaluation, have your lawyer review it to be sure you're not violating the equal employment laws.

Self-Evaluations

One of the most interesting ways to conduct performance reviews is to ask people to do *self-evaluations*. These are forms developed from the performance criteria as we've just discussed. The salesperson or staff member completes these forms, rating themselves independently before meeting with the manager or supervisor. Sometimes people are far more critical of their performance than you might be. It also gives them an opportunity to tell you what matters most to them about their performance. Sometimes they see things you don't see. They can also express things they want you to know that they may hesitate to share otherwise.

A self-evaluation form can include questions in addition to the performance criteria. For example, ask people to rate what they think about the amount of money they're making, the potential for advancement in the company, opportunities for professional development, their level of satisfaction with their careers or the company, or the amount of time devoted to work or outside activities. They could describe their proudest accomplishments, their greatest weaknesses or frustrations and the assistance they would like from you and the company.

Performance Interviews

The purpose of a performance interview is for you and the salesperson to *discuss* the person's progress. The interview should be a forum to objectively appraise a person's accomplishments, not to interrogate. These are times to praise as well as to help a person develop strategies to improve in areas where she or he is faltering.

Performance interviews are one of the rare meetings set aside solely for the purpose of addressing general concerns of the salesperson without some other business at hand. You and the salesperson deserve to know where you stand with one another. As you gather information, you also get an idea about how your office is going to fare at the end of the year. The following points will help you conduct a successful interview for staff as well as salespeople.

- People should know the purpose of the meeting ahead of time and the evaluation criteria. If you want them to do a self-evaluation, they need time to prepare it.

- Follow your "script." These are the performance criteria you developed. It is essential to keep these interviews on track to make efficient use of time and keep the discussion focused.

- As you address each of the performance issues, you and the interviewee can compare your respective assessments.

- Don't dominate the meeting. It's the salesperson's forum to tell you about how she or he is doing as much as it is yours.

- Don't criticize! If the meeting is perceived as the manager's opportunity to beat up on a salesperson, there will not be any constructive two-way dialogue. The salesperson will just bluff his or her way through the meeting until it's over.

- Don't dwell on faults. This is the time to praise sales-people's accomplishments and develop solutions when they seem to be straying off track. Remember as a coach and mentor you can be a valuable resource.

- Take notes and stay focused on information that is relevant to the person's job description. Otherwise you could stray into areas that cause legal problems.

Your lawyer can advise you about legal and ethical requirements when conducting performance evaluations, documenting written and oral statements and retaining records of the interview.

Evaluating Performance

In order to evaluate performance you have to determine acceptable standards, that is, the level of performance that you think is satisfactory for each criterion. Earlier in the chapter we mentioned a rating scale, which requires that you determine numerical values for various levels of performance. These quantitative measures are then used to rate each criterion. For example, a score of 6 on a scale of 1 to 10 (10 being the highest) on a performance criterion, says that the person is performing at a satisfactory level. Using this method you can then tally the scores of all criteria for an overall assessment of a person's performance.

An alternative is to evaluate performance of each criterion as "meeting expectations," "exceeding expectations," "outstanding" and "below expectations." This technique is easy for people to understand and for managers to use. (It eliminates arguments over a rating of 6 instead of 7.) After each criterion is evaluated, overall performance can be evaluated similarly. This assessment method focuses clearly on the criterion rather than venturing into the more subjective "outstanding," "good," "fair," "needs improvement" or "poor" assessments. What does "good" mean, for example. A person did what they were supposed to, which is a good thing. Or the person did slightly better than OK but not earthshaking.

A person's performance must be evaluated objectively, but there are subjective factors that can enter the evaluation process if you're not careful. Even if you use a quantitative evaluation system, you can't be more critical of some people while being more lenient with others. Look at what can happen.

- Your star producer may have had a lousy year. The tendency is to overlook this year's performance because of past production. Unless you are going to overlook this year's performance for everyone, you're not being even-handed. However, the people who did improve will resent your lack of acknowledgment.

- You may have better relationships with some salespeople than others. Some never complain or criticize; others are constantly challenging you. Don't let a lousy relationship influence your evaluation of a person.

- Some salespeople are not perfect (an understatement!) But there's a tendency to overlook flaws that are similar to your own to criticize flaws that you don't have. There is also a tendency to be overly critical of everyone if you're a perfectionist.

- Some personalities are easier to appreciate than others. Some are likable; others abrasive. Some people are members of cliques, such as the one that's trying to undermine you or the clique of the poor performers, that may color your perceptions. However, everyone's performance should be evaluated fairly and objectively.

There are other situations that you need to consider when you are evaluating each salesperson's performance. You have to distinguish between legitimate problems the salespeople face and excuses for lagging performance.

- The most significant situation that affects performance is the economy. Economic conditions are reflected in changes in interest rates and shifts in employment and consumer confidence, all of which affect supply and demand of your product and, consequently, the demand for your services.

- A competitor may launch a major new program or service (which affects market share as well as recruiting for salespeople) or make significant changes in its operation with new ownership, an infusion of money from an investor or a merger with another company. Situations like this can have an effect on all of the competition, even if only temporarily.

- Your organization may have made significant internal changes in the past year. The ownership or affiliation may have changed, the size of the sales force may have changed dramatically or there may have been other changes in personnel that affect either morale or the amount of staff support the salespeople have.

You could be hard-headed and say that true professionals can rise above these situations and won't let them affect production. But the truth is that legitimate factors that affect the company's bottom line also affect the salespeople's production. Salespeople grow impatient when the company's attitude is that they are superhuman. They want support, not criticism, from the company.

The evaluation of performance is only the *beginning*. The process doesn't end with the assessment. The point was made earlier that performance reviews are an opportunity to gather information for both the salesperson's and the manager's benefit. Both should leave the interview with an action plan. In your role as counselor, help the salesperson develop a plan for improvement where it is needed. If there are things that you need to be doing differently, make a commitment to the salesperson to change. While you are documenting performance, you can also gauge professional progress from year to year.

TURNOVER

The work culture or environment that you create to recruit salespeople is the same environment you expect will retain them. People resent your waving attractive bait just to lure them into your camp, only to find out later they've been deceived. Although no one can fully anticipate what the working relationship will be like, you need to be honest and realistic when hiring people. Then be supportive while they make the transition into your organization. It takes time for even the most experienced person to get established with a new company.

When a salesperson walks into your office and announces that she or he is leaving, it's usually too late to convince that person to do otherwise. You have to resign yourself to the fact that everyone will leave your company eventually, and some leave for their own good reasons. But you should hear a wake-up call anytime a salesperson wants to go. This is a signal to review what's happening in your office and determine if you should be doing some things differently. There may have been signs of discontent or frustration that you should have seen but didn't.

Salespeople are more likely to leave you because they are dissatisfied with you or other salespeople rather than because of your company's commission split. According to a study conducted by Abelson & Co., 55 percent of the top producers were dissatisfied because low producers were not asked to leave, 35 percent cited conflicts with others in the office and 18 percent cited conflicts with the manager. This suggests that you have a big job to do in managing the performance of your salespeople and solving problems in your office to keep your sales force intact.

To determine if an agent is producing a profit, establish the *minimum average production* (MAP) needed from each agent. That means you take your desk cost and add a percentage that represents the minimum profit you expect from the operation. Divide that figure by the number of agents. The result is the MAP. You can determine if your agents are making a profit by comparing the MAP with their actual production. You'll find that some agents consistently fall below the MAP, some are average and others exceed the MAP by a wide margin. These are the super-stars.

In the beginning of the chapter we mentioned that as the coach you also are a teacher, a counselor, a negotiator and an arbitrator. These roles are critically important in retaining the people you hire. For example, you are the teacher and counselor to help people meet or exceed the MAP. You are the negotiator and arbitrator to identify and resolve the conflicts that ultimately affect the retention of your salespeople. The manager is the key to minimizing turnover.

PROBLEM SOLVING

Ask managers in any real estate office how they spend most of their time and they'll say solving problems. Coaching the performance of your salespeople and resolving problems or conflicts are two of a manager's most important human resource activities. For the moment we will focus on issues that need to be addressed with the people who work for you. We'll deal with handling customers, clients and other brokers in Chapter 13.

You can divide problems into two categories: (1) problems that you have with a salesperson's behavior that is unacceptable to you and (2) issues that are problems for a salesperson. In either case you are the counselor whose job is to be the catalyst to bring about a solution. Some people think that problem solving or managing any conflict means there must be a winner and a loser. Because neither you nor the salespeople can afford to lose, your objective is to resolve the situation in a manner that is satisfactory to both of you.

Your Problem with a Salesperson

Salespeople can be a high-strung, competitive group of human beings, which means there's bound to be conflict. Petty jealousy, commission disputes, personality conflicts and charges of pirating prospects brew, and cliques among salespeople form. In addition to morale issues, specific problems with transactions and company policies and procedures arise. You also have to protect the company from problems like employee discrimination and sexual harassment. Unless you identify and correct situations, little problems become big ones. Soon the office is in disarray or the company is involved in litigation.

Case in Point.   The morning you discover that a salesperson has lost an earnest money check begins when you haul the person into your office. You slam the door and wave the company's policy and procedures manual under the person's nose. You scream, *"Don't you know any better than to be so careless? See what the manual says you're supposed to do with the check. Don't you know how much trouble we can all be in? What if the buyer backs out and we don't have the deposit in our account? I'll take that money out of your next commission check! Now, get out of my office and don't ever let that happen again!"* Okay! Problem identified; problem solved.

In this scenario, you identified what happened (the check got lost) and some of the difficulties that could result. But, did you identify the problem? Maybe the check wasn't lost but was filed incorrectly by the secretary. There was no discussion between the salesperson and you about what really happened. Chances are the problem is not resolved. The poor salesperson didn't get in a word (which may have been better than getting into a shouting match). Then you presented a solution (well, as a leader you're supposed to be decisive), but it certainly was an ill-conceived one. This encounter missed the mark in a number of ways.

First of all, identifying problematic behavior is a necessary part of a manager's job. But managers need to approach this task with a purposeful, constructive plan. Serving notice to a person that he or she has conducted himself or herself in an unacceptable manner is only part of the process. Next, you need a solution or a course of action acceptable to both of you, that corrects the situation and prevents it from occurring again. These meetings don't have to be combative or confrontational. *Never* address problems in a group, only one-on-one. Even if several salespeople are offenders, you need to develop a solution with each one and obtain each individual's commitment to the resolution.

These are commonly known as disciplinary meetings. In reality what you're trying to do is problem-solving. The following guide will help you conduct effective ones.

- *Identify the problem* before you schedule a meeting. You know that something happened, but first you must determine whether you have misread a situation. You also need to be sure that you are addressing the issue with the appropriate person.

- *Study the problem* before you confront the salesperson. This slows you down long enough so that you can gather your facts and describe the situation correctly.

- *Describe the problem* for the salesperson from your point of view. When you present the problem in a descriptive fashion, the person knows exactly the behavior you are observing. Avoid being judgmental or accusatory; don't attack the person; don't speculate why or try to evaluate the situation. Keep the description factual.

- *Gather information from the salesperson.* There may be information that you don't know. The meeting may end here if you learn that you interpreted the behavior incorrectly. Be fair and give the salesperson a chance to make some observations, but not excuses.

- *Keep the meeting objective.* This sounds difficult, but the purpose of the meeting is not to prove who's right or wrong, to pass judgment on a person's character or to clobber a person's self-esteem. You want to minimize tension and defensiveness. "Yes, you did" and "No, I didn't" won't get you to a solution.

- *Don't sugarcoat the problem.* This is not a meeting to praise and then sneak the problem into the agenda. The person needs to know precisely the point you are making.

- *Agree that a problem exists.* You may be the only one who thinks there's a problem. Because you have policies and procedures in your firm, it's up to you to see that they're followed. You can't allow one person to break the rules. Everyone has to live up to the same standards. But your standards may mean more to you than they do to the salesperson. Before you can expect the salesperson to change, she or he must agree that this issue needs attention.

- *Develop mutually acceptable alternatives* as possible solutions. It is important that the salesperson participates in generating a solution. You can't change another person's behavior. You are asking the salesperson to change behavior. Because this is the person who has to implement the final decision, a solution that is acceptable to the salesperson is more likely to work. However, you have the right to veto alternatives that are unacceptable from the company's point of view. You also must be ready to do your part if there's something you can contribute to the solution.

- *Agree on a course of action* and the time frame within which the correction will occur. Both of you must select the same course of action from the list of alternative solutions.

- *Agree on a follow-up meeting* at the end of the time frame to be sure that the problem is resolved.

- *Conclude the meeting* once you have agreement. Don't drag it out and cloud the issue.

- *Focus on one problem at a time.* It's tempting to unload on a salesperson and find fault with everything he or she does. But this is not a gripe session. It's a problem-solving meeting.

- *Acknowledge the change.* Remember your job is to praise as much as it is to correct problems. You brought the problem to the salesperson's attention, so don't ignore the steps the salesperson takes to correct the problem.

Using this as a guide, how would you handle the scenario of the lost earnest money check?

The Salesperson's Problem

You may be gliding through your day, satisfied that everything is under control and everyone is content and working well.

You may not realize that trouble is brewing on the sales floor or that a salesperson is quite disgruntled. It's important for you to be approachable so that people feel free to bring their concerns to you and *the sooner the better*. They may need a little encouragement like, "I notice that you seem to be. . . . Would you like to talk?" or "How can I help?" Keep your eyes and ears open. Watch the group dynamics.

- Do people hush as you stroll through the office?

- Is there a clique that huddles together over lunch, particularly after you announce a new office procedure?

- Are you playing favorites?

- Do you ignore enforcing the company's ethics or policies and procedures?

- Are you unavailable when the salespeople need you?

You have to be willing to accept that you may be the cause of a problem.

When a salesperson approaches you, or after you nudge a little, your first role is to be a counselor and *listen*. Give the person an opportunity to tell you the problem without interfering or getting defensive. This can be a very emotional or delicate conversation for the salesperson. If the problem is you, don't argue; be willing to accept responsibility. If the problem is someone else in the office, don't take sides, make excuses or defend the other person. If the problem is outside the office, with someone in another office, a customer or the person's private life, listen.

If you're the source of the problem, you're responsible for the solution. Define precisely what you intend to do or how you intend to handle the situation. You only make matters worse if the person feels that frustrations have fallen on deaf ears or that you're using appeasement just to get the person out of your office. Just as in the disciplinary meeting, you have to end this conversation with a commitment to a course of action.

If the problem is someone other than you, you can either intervene (this means you're taking responsibility for the problem) or you can help the salesperson find ways to deal with the situation.

Case in Point. Your dilemma is similar to that of a parent confronted with two children picking on one another. One child comes to you with a long tale about what his brother did to him. Now what do you do? Maybe all the child wanted to do was air his frustrations. He's totally content to run off and forget the matter or handle the situation himself. Maybe he wants you to go tell his brother off. Doing this, though, means taking sides. You alienate one person to satisfy the other. What does this accomplish in the long run? Another point to consider: Do you have all the facts? Maybe the reason his brother lashed out is totally justified. If you intervene, you may be condoning unacceptable behavior.

Take this analogy back to the office, and you see that handling conflicts is a delicate task. The first thing you should do is get more information. What does the salesperson want you to do? The purpose of this conversation may be simply to inform you of something that's bothersome; you're not expected to take any action. If the salesperson asks for help, find out what kind of help is being requested. Maybe all the salesperson wants is for you to be a sounding board while the person thinks through the situation and finds a solution.

If salesperson *A* asks you to intervene in a problem with salesperson *B*, remember that there probably are two sides to the story. Rather than risk your relationship with two people, it's best to help *A* find a solution first. Depending on the nature of the problem, you may decide on your own to have a conversation with salesperson *B* to investigate whether there are also other problems that need to be addressed. You have to approach *B* objectively so that *B* doesn't feel that she or he has been targeted by *A*. And don't betray confidences. Then, if it's appropriate for you to be the negotiator and arbitrator, you need to get yourself out of the middle and help *A* and *B* find a solution that is acceptable to both of them.

RESIGNATION AND TERMINATION

After you invest considerable time and effort in a salesperson, it's difficult to face the time when that person leaves. Sometimes people do so on their own initiative, and sometimes it's appropriate to relieve both the company and a salesperson of a relationship that's no longer beneficial for either one.

Resignation

If the salesperson has decided to leave, it's probably too late to convince him or her to stay. But that doesn't mean you shouldn't investigate why the person is leaving and where he or she is going.

- If the person wants to change specialties or positions, consider finding a new role for the person in your organization.

- If the person wants to change companies as a salesperson, determine whether you have an internal problem or whether your company is losing its competitive edge to other real estate companies.

Be careful. Don't let yourself get set up in a bargaining position to retain a salesperson. If you feel that there are legitimate changes you can make to retain a top producer, that's fine. But remember that playing favorites to keep salespeople is as bad as playing favorites while they're working for you.

Sometimes a salesperson does you a favor by volunteering to leave. If this is the office malcontent or poorest producer, you're off the hook for not doing something about that problem sooner. If this is a relatively new salesperson who's decided real estate was a poor career choice, you probably have a miserable salesperson. Even though you may think the person has great potential, let him or her go do something more rewarding or enjoyable.

Maybe a salesperson is just discouraged for the day. (How many times do salespeople quit when the business gets frustrating?) Rather than accepting a hasty decision, help the person over the hurdle or encourage the person to rethink the decision before taking action.

Termination

Now we get to the personnel decisions that are really difficult—asking someone to leave. *Termination represents failure*—on the part of the salesperson, the manager or the company. Even if the salesperson failed, the company—or the manager—is still responsible to some degree for errors in selection, training, coaching and/or counseling. Some managers look at human resources as expendable commodities, especially when they see the number of potential licensees floating around. They would rather sweep people out of the office instead of investing time in their professional development. Terminating a person because of the company's failure won't fix the problem. So look internally before you take out your frustrations on the salesperson.

Some salespeople are fast learners and become highly productive in a relatively short time. They also may get on a very fast track and burn out quickly, drop out of the business or move on to open their own offices. Other salespeople may be much slower to catch on. But they can be productive and loyal to your firm for many years. The slowest learner should not be allowed to wallow in misery and frustration for more than a year. It's unfair to that person and costly to you both in time and financial resources. If a person is unable to carry his or her share of the load, there's no reason to continue an unprofitable relationship. Undue delay also increases the resentment of the people who are carrying the major burden for the office's production.

You have two issues to consider when terminating a salesperson: the grounds for termination and the legal implications and procedures that are involved. First, you have to review the independent contractor agreement to see what you and the salesperson agreed to with respect to terminating the contract.

- Can either of you terminate the agreement *at will* without cause? Or does the contract specify the causes for which you can terminate the salesperson's affiliation?

- What does your policy and procedures manual say about termination? Are certain grounds specified?

- Are the policy and procedures manual and the independent contractor agreement in harmony with one another?

- Was your salesperson informed when he or she was hired about the grounds for dismissal?

Before you do anything, contact your lawyer to find out the company's as well as the salesperson's legal standing.

Common reasons for showing people to the door include lack of productivity, violation of laws, violation of the company's ethics and policies and procedures or a personnel problem. Once you reach a decision to terminate, this should not come as a great surprise to the salesperson. Because all of the grounds are problem-oriented, you already should have had problem-solving and performance interviews with the worker.

Never fire in a huff! You create enormous legal problems. In addition, no human being deserves that kind of treatment. In the case of a flagrant transgression, it may be safer to suspend a person from the office temporarily until you get direction from legal counsel.

There are several procedures that your lawyer can help you follow when terminating a worker.

- Document evidence of the behavior that necessitates the termination. If you documented the performance review, you have a start. You also have to remember that you can misinterpret a person's behavior. As you gather evidence for your documentation, you can verify whether your accusations are justified.

- Communicate your concerns or observations to the salesperson. Also inform the salesperson that the situation is serious enough to warrant termination.

- Develop a plan for corrective action, document the plan and provide the support and assistance that is necessary to help the salesperson correct the situation.

- Communicate the final decision to terminate to the salesperson. This should be done privately and confidentially with a clear description of the reason for termination. You need to remain calm, firm and professional. Chances are the salesperson won't, but that's to be expected.

- Resolve the details for departure, including the date of departure and the way pending business is to be handled. Your policy and procedures manual should already address how pending listings and closings, mail, phone calls and commissions are to be handled as well as the return of company belongings, keys, signs and the like. You must also make arrangements for handling the salesperson's license according to your state's law.

- Protect your firm against sabotage. This is not easy because of the nature of this business. There are pending issues, such as those discussed above, that preclude severing all contact with the person. This should be addressed with your lawyer before you give notice of termination so that you know what procedures to implement when the time comes.

Exit Interviews

Regardless of whether people leave voluntarily or involuntarily, there should be one final opportunity for conversation. People who leave your company can be either your greatest advocates or your greatest adversaries. You can promote the former or defuse the latter by conducting an exit interview. The purpose of this meeting is to debrief the worker and gather information. It also gives the person one final opportunity to voice opinions directly to you. While you can't prevent someone from discussing your business behind your back, at least you get some idea about what will be said.

Some exit interviews will go better than others. But do your best to create an informal, relaxed, compassionate atmosphere. Once the fire-storm from the notice has passed, this will be easier. Find out what the person has to say about you, your company and the way the resignation or termination has been handled.

Listen and don't argue or be defensive. You're not likely to change anyone's opinion at this point. Remember you may have to work with this person again in the industry. Even if people have been asked to leave, you may be surprised to learn that both of you just want to end the relationship as professionally as possible. Make sure all of the transition details have been addressed. Then send the person off with your best wishes.

Sit back and learn from this experience. Is there information you should take to heart?

CONCLUSION

The manager affects the professional development of the salespeople, the morale in the workplace and ultimately, the retention of the sales force. As you perform these functions you are constantly learning about your individual salespeople and better ways to help them. You are also learning about your organization, the way it's perceived by the people who work for you and changes that can be made to enhance their support. Your interpersonal skills are essential to your success as the manager of the company's human resources. You either can be effective or can create more problems than you solve, depending on how you address situations. Your personal development as a manager, discussed in Unit 5, will be a great asset in managing the company's human resources.

DISCUSSION EXERCISES

What things can you as the manager do to help energize and empower your salespeople to be productive and develop professionally?

* * *

Discuss your experiences either with conducting performance reviews or with being reviewed.

* * *

Select a problem that you are currently dealing with in your office and discuss how you plan to handle it.

In Conclusion of This Unit

This unit has been devoted to discussing the human aspect of the organization. The organization is prepared to conduct business by recruiting, selecting and hiring not only the people who are necessary to provide the company's services and conduct the sales transactions but also the personnel who have support and administrative responsibilities. Once hired, people need to be supported by the organization if they are to do their jobs. The support the company provides includes education and training to help people develop professionally. The manager plays a major role in coaching the staff, primarily through one-on-one interaction, encouraging their performance and removing barriers in the workplace that inhibit the efficient and effective conduct of business.

Depending on whether you are the broker/owner, a senior manager in a large organization, a sales manager or a department manager, your involvement in the various human resources activities will differ. As a guide for understanding your role(s), the following summary is provided.

➤ Recruiting, selecting and hiring the appropriate staff:

- The broker/owner(s) and possibly senior management have previously determined the overall manpower requirements for the organization in the organizing function.

- The broker/owner is normally responsible for selecting and hiring senior management. The broker may also prefer to be an active recruiter for salespeople, depending on the size of the organization and the amount of other responsibilities that have been assigned to the sales manager.

- Either senior management or the broker/owner selects and hires office or sales managers.

- Sales and department managers are normally responsible for recruiting and selecting the staff whom they supervise. The procedures in the organization will dictate whether the manager or someone higher in the organization has the ultimate authority to hire.

➤ Creating opportunities for the staff to develop professional competency:

- The broker/owner(s) and possibly senior management are normally responsible for making decisions about the nature of the professional development the company provides and committing the necessary financial resources.

- The department manager, specifically the training director, and the sales managers are actively involved in assessing training needs and developing the orientation and training programs.

- The sales manager is responsible for supporting training and the professional development of the staff in group functions such as sales meetings and in one-on-one involvement with the salespeople. In small organizations the sales manager also may be the trainer.

➤ Coaching people to accomplish the company's as well as their goals:

- Anyone who directly supervises people is responsible for coaching their performance, conducting performance reviews and handling problems, conflicts or other issues that directly affect the performance of the people who work for them. In small organizations, the broker/owner may also be the sales manager.

- Depending on the procedures in the organization, the person who supervises an individual may have the authority to terminate a worker. In some organizations this person may need the approval of an individual at a higher level in the organization to do so.

THE
BUSINESS, FIRST HAND

An important ingredient in professional development today is technology training. Companies can invest substantial financial resources in the latest technology, but they will not realize a significant return on that investment unless their human resources are skilled at using it. Sales associates can invest in their own laptops and software programs, but they will be disappointed with their investment if they are unable to utilize it to maximum advantage. While many resources are available to help people develop the necessary skills, one way this can be done is through a company's training department. The following example demonstrates the way one real estate company has integrated technology training into its operations.

Early in the 1990s, when technology was just emerging in the real estate industry, Iowa Realty Company and First Realty Better Homes and Gardens sought ways to prepare the company and its sales staff to function in a contemporary environment. People would have to be mobilized to incorporate new methods into their daily work life as well as to develop the skills needed to become effective users of these tools. To accomplish this the company created a new position within its training department—a technology trainer.

The technology trainer provides not only skill-based training for the sales staff and administrative personnel, but also is an in-house technology resource for the company's staff. Jay Hytone, who has held this position since it was created, observes that his experience in the real estate business is one of his most valuable assets for this job. Having been a sales associate and then an office manager, he is familiar with both the needs of licensees and an organization, which is invaluable when deciphering the maze of technology for real estate users.

During the time that Mr. Hytone has served in this capacity, the number of sales associates who own their own computers increased from less than

17 percent to over 55 percent today. In fact, usage increased from 40 percent to 50 percent during a month-and-a-half-long period. He attributes the increased acceptance of technology to the company's concerted effort to offer a wide range of programs, seminars and workshops in real estate task-oriented training. In addition, the company has provided a resource to help guide in the selection of appropriate hardware and software, thus decreasing the mystery that often intimidates new computer owners.

Interestingly, the age of the users does not seem to have been a factor among those who have chosen to buy into technology. Nor does geography seem to be a factor. Iowa Realty and First Realty Better Homes and Gardens is based in Des Moines; however, as the organization has forged alliances with real estate companies throughout the midwest, its markets encompass small-town communities as well as large metropolitan areas. The use of technology has been incorporated in some fashion throughout these operations.

In the company's training programs for sales personnel, technology has been integrated in several ways. Sessions that are devoted to typical sales activities include technology-based tools. A typical example includes the demonstration of computer-generated portfolios for listing presentations. Some training sessions are devoted to ways general purpose software can be used in specific real estate applications. Other sessions concentrate on real estate-specific software such as contact and transaction management programs. One of the latest additions to the curriculum includes the use of digital photography. By maximizing the use of technology in the delivery of training, the company further demonstrates its value.

The challenge for any trainer is to develop programs that people want to attend. Mr. Hytone suggests that the content and the schedule are two key ingredients. One is to focus on what technology can do, that is, task-oriented skills people need to use the elements of a software program in their business. This is the virtue of providing real estate-based training in-house. The second is to conduct sessions at convenient times and not burden people's schedules. Short programs, one hour to one-and-a-half hours in length, and lunch-and-learn formats have been very appealing.

Companies can succeed, as this one has demonstrated, in institutionalizing technology. The goal is not just to provision the organization with hardware, software and networked systems, but most importantly, to provide the supportive services that are essential for the company's sales and administrative personnel to gain maximum benefits.

UNIT
4

Controlling the Organization

Together we have planned, organized, staffed and directed the organization's activities. Now the last management function we study is controlling the organization. There are many things happening in the company at one time, regardless of its size. You're on for the ride, but you have to hold onto the reins and steer the organization so that it doesn't stray off course. There are many reins to hold, and each guides different aspects of the company. You have services and transactions, contracts and documents, money and people to monitor, all of which affect your income and expenses and create risk for the organization.

It's easy to get caught up in the day-to-day activities of running the business and not to pay attention to whether any of the activities are helping you get where you want to be. Most organizations won't stray so far that they will run aground in one year. But it's easier to nudge a company in the right direction than it is to shift it onto a new course in a short period of time.

In the control function of management, you are protecting, preserving and promoting the growth of the company. In the previous management functions, you assembled the infrastructure for the organization to run. Now you make sure it is running on course as you

- monitor its operations and
- manage its risk.

Corrective steps may be necessary to improve its operations. You also need to be sure that you are providing quality services to the customers and clients. If you rely on the accountant to keep you posted on the financial status and the lawyer to bail you out of trouble, their intervention may be too little and too late. One of management's responsibilities is to monitor what the organization is doing. It's important to detect problems early and take action long before you have a negative balance on the income statement or are involved in litigation.

13 Monitoring Your Operations

Do you know how many newspaper ads you've run so far this year? Were they effective? Are you over or under budget? Is your income ahead or behind budget so far this year? How many transactions do you have pending settlement? Are your customers and clients satisfied with your service? How many sales contracts fail to go to settlement or closing? Why?

You can answer these questions if you have information and take time to scrutinize it. To do an effective job of monitoring the company, you need a process to collect information and review it systematically. Just as you track and review the performance of individual salespeople, you do the same for the company—except that you're evaluating all facets of its operation.

The organization has charted a course to follow with its business and financial plans. The next task is to compare the company's current status with these plans. This can be done by monitoring the transaction and service activities, which produce the income, and the internal operations, which create the expenses. On the income side, you need to be sure that you're taking all the steps necessary to maximize income. On the expense side, you need to be sure that all of the expenditures are as effective and productive as possible. With a methodical routine for monitoring, you can readily identify whether corrective action is necessary. You can also detect trends that need to be considered when planning for the coming year.

But it's important to track more than your income and expenses. The life of the organization depends on your customers and clients, and the future of the company depends on the reputation it develops with them. Just because the organization generates income does not ensure that the services are being delivered at their highest quality or warn you that future income could be in jeopardy. Manufacturers strive for quality control to produce quality products. A brokerage company also should have quality control to ensure that it's delivering quality services.

MANAGEMENT OF INFORMATION

With today's computer systems you can generate reports about almost any aspect of your operation and do so with much less effort than when these reports are compiled manually. In Chapter 6, when we set up the company's information systems, we indicated that a wide variety of brokerage management software is currently available (see the Appendix). It's relatively easy to track individual transactions and monitor total sales production, the production of individual salespeople and various expenditures. But the value of the information is only as good as the data that are assembled in the system. Data-collection procedures must be established to generate the information needed to manage your operations.

This discussion focuses on the management and maintenance of information and records. As you establish procedures to do this, consider that the information that is assembled must be accurate, complete, and timely.

Missing or inaccurate information can skew the picture of your operations. You won't have a true picture of the listing inventory unless you have current statistics about the number of listings, the length of time properties have been listed and their current listed prices. If you want an accurate picture of the sales transactions, you need complete information about the status of contingencies and preparation for settlement, anticipated closing or settlement dates and details about cooperating brokers who may be involved in the transactions. If you are monitoring the effectiveness of your advertising, you need accurate records of the sources of the listings and sales and the sources of phone calls.

Don't bog down your operations with cumbersome data-collection procedures that make work more tedious. Provide forms to gather only the essential information, and establish time frames for the completion of forms and the maintenance of records. When a transaction is closed, for example, the file should be closed and removed from the pending file. Do you expect this to happen within 24 hours after the settlement? Within what time period do you expect a new listing to be logged into your company's files? Because some salespeople are more attentive to these details than others, stress the importance of everyone's complying with your procedures. Utilize support staff whenever possible.

A number of people, including salespeople and support staff, are likely to be handling documents, money, files and computer input. An *office procedures manual* that charts the flow of information and paper in your company should be developed. Because there are legal issues that affect the maintenance and retention of your records, the procedures manual should address these as well.

Transaction Files

The information in transaction files should help you monitor a number of aspects of your operation. One is to ensure that you are complying with the laws that affect the transactions. Most states' licensing laws have specific requirements for the ways documents are to be handled. These include the use of certain forms, disclosures, closing cost statements and escrow documents; the delivery of documents to the signatories; and the retention of these documents by the broker for a certain period of time. There should be evidence in the transaction files that these requirements are being satisfied.

After you read Chapter 14 you may decide that other documents, reports or correspondence should be incorporated in your transaction files to protect the company's legal liability.

One of the benefits of having good transaction records is that you have supporting documentation if you ever need it.

We mentioned in Chapter 7 that state licensing laws are quite specific about the way escrow funds are to be handled. It's safest to use transmittal forms so that the funds can be traced from the time they are turned in by the salesperson through each step along the way until they are deposited (either by you or a cooperating broker) and then released. Include copies of these forms in the transaction file so that you can follow the money trail associated with the transaction.

In addition to the legal issues, the transaction file provides useful information for monitoring the effectiveness of the organization's listing and sales activities. If you are using transaction management software, you can easily access what you need to know, provided the necessary data are assembled by the salespeople or support staff.

Listing activities. You can monitor the effectiveness of listing activities by looking at the listing dates and prices in comparison with the results of the contracts.

- How long are listings on the market?
- What's the difference between the listing and the actual selling price?
- How many listings terminated or expired?
- What is the source of the listing contacts?

You can learn about the effectiveness of your salespeople's techniques and your marketing efforts and identify ways you can help the salespeople improve their skills.

Sales activities. When you compare the pending sales files with the closed transaction files, you can learn how well your company services buyers and sellers. The most significant piece of information is the cause of transactions that fall through. In many cases you know the stories intimately because these are problem transactions that you had to help nurture and defuse along the way. You'll learn about the conditions in the marketplace, as well as the technical proficiency of your sales-people.

- Were buyers improperly qualified?

- Are appraisals coming in low?

- Are certain types of mortgage loans or lenders a problem?

- Did buyers feel deceived, or were there misrepresentations?

- Are contracts being lost because contingencies aren't being satisfied?

- Were there defects in the way contracts were prepared?

- How well were transactions prepared for settlement?

A seemingly smooth transaction can suddenly explode at settlement only because a minute but important detail was overlooked. Is it any wonder that salespeople appreciate the value of transaction coordinators to tend to the details needed to get transactions to the settlement table? Unless you have such a person on staff, you must depend on the salespeople to do this. (Transactions management software is useful for prompting the steps that must be taken.) Management should be monitoring settlements to identify tasks that might be overlooked or additional procedures needed to correct any problems. This is the final step in the transaction when your public relations are on the line.

Once transactions close, you can gather valuable marketing information, such as the sources of buyers; the productivity of a referral or relocation network affiliation; the number of properties that were sold in-house versus those involving a cooperating broker; the number of transactions in which a buyer was a client rather than a customer (depending on your company's service policies and state laws); and trends in market values, financing and the pace of the market.

An unpleasant but realistic fact of life is that some of your transactions may end up in litigation. Or your company may end up in a dispute with another brokerage firm. Although we discuss risk management in the next chapter, we should not over-look the value of transaction documentation in these circumstances. In the event you do get involved in these situations, you can learn valuable lessons about your procedures for future reference.

License Records

Because the company's ability to provide real estate services depends on its being properly licensed, you need good license management procedures. No one should be permitted to perform activities for which a real estate license is required until that license is properly issued. There are procedures for license applications, renewals, transfers and departing licensees, as well as license requirements for the company's real estate offices. While a staff person could be assigned the responsibility for tending to the paperwork, the broker is ultimately responsible for seeing that all requirements are satisfied. The broker also should periodically review the license records to ensure that the company is in compliance with all of the requirements.

Personnel Records

The company should maintain personnel files for each of its workers. These become a history of a person's affiliation with you. Personal data; employment applications; independent contractor agreements (if applicable); wage, salary or commission records; notes and reports from interviews with the person's manager; performance reviews; and any other information your lawyer recommends should be in the files. Because this is personal data, there should be procedures to limit access to and maintain the confidentiality of these records.

Closely related to this subject are your referral rotation procedures. One of the greatest sources of controversy in a real estate office is the distribution of referrals and leads. You should have clear procedures that not only are publicized and followed but also track the distribution of referrals. Keep a master ledger as these assignments are made, and also record them in each salesperson's file so that you have accessible and authoritative documentation.

Financial Records

Accounting and bookkeeping functions can be automated, as was discussed in Chapter 7, making it possible to translate accounting information into meaningful management information. Using the company's general ledgers, accounts payable, accounts receivable, payroll records and commission records, plus the various budgets that were developed, you can monitor the way the company is using its financial resources.

Document Retention

As you get ready for a new year, it's tempting to clean house and rid your office of excess paper, particularly because most offices don't have unlimited storage space. The more you rely on computerization, the less of a problem this will be because a sizable amount of information can be stored on disk and tape. But we've not completely eliminated paper in our business.

State licensing laws normally require the retention of escrow account records and documents relating to the real estate transactions for a period of time. Perhaps there are requirements to retain reconciliations of bank statements as well. In addition businesses need to retain wage, salary and salesperson compensation records, legal correspondence, tax returns and depreciation schedules. Follow the guidance of your lawyer and your accountant regarding the kinds of documents that should be retained and the period of time that is advisable.

MANAGING WITH INFORMATION

With the volume of information that is assembled, it's relatively easy to analyze the company's status. Typically the broker and senior management conduct monthly reviews of the budget and income and expense reports. Office managers, division managers and other staff people review budgets and reports that track various aspects of income-producing activities and expense items related to their areas of responsibility.

Trends develop as money flows in and out of the organization. People develop habits that may affect the effectiveness or efficiency of the operation. The purpose of monitoring the organization monthly is to watch these trends and habits so that corrective actions can be taken during the year, rather than wait until the company is in serious trouble. If there is a major deviation from income or expense projections, these may be occurrences you anticipated and for which you already have a contingency plan. Otherwise, the discussions later in this chapter that relate to maximizing income and minimizing expenses will be particularly useful.

Involve the people who work for you, especially the salespeople. They can suggest ways the company can work more efficiently or cost-effectively. As you review the company's financial status and the transaction files, you may identify areas in which problems exist. In the previous discussion about transactions, we identified a great deal of information that a manager can use to assess the technical proficiency of the salespeople. These may be subjects for training programs or brainstorming meetings, as discussed in Chapter 11, or they may be issues to be addressed in problem-solving meetings, as discussed in Chapter 12.

As you monitor the company's operations, don't forget your business plan. Even though it's a three-year or five-year plan, don't wait until the end of the term to see how you did. The business plan is a road map that should be reviewed periodically. There are likely to be goals that you intend to accomplish in one or two years. As you get halfway through the first year, these are the goals you need to look at closely to see how the company is doing. You have to accomplish the short-range goals if you're going to achieve the long-range plan.

MAXIMIZING INCOME

It's prudent management to strive to maximize income, regardless of whether the company is meeting its projections or needs to take corrective steps to get back on track. You're building a future for the company that can certainly be enhanced by exceeding projections as well. In Chapter 12 we looked at ways of coaching and monitoring the performance of individual salespeople. But helping them reach their goals and meet their production quotas is only one way to maximize the company's income.

The quality of the services the company provides has a significant bearing on income. Both the salesperson and the manager can be more productive when they direct their efforts to new endeavors instead of spending time unraveling problems that could have been avoided in the first place. People are more effective and feel more satisfied with their jobs when transactions run smoothly.

But the real beneficiaries are the customers and clients. When details fall through the cracks, at the very least you end up with disgruntled customers and clients. The worst-case scenario is that a transaction ends up in litigation. The costs to your public relations, and ultimately to your bank account can be great. Customer satisfaction goes a long way towards maximizing your income because you want their repeat business and their referrals for new customers.

Quality Service Standards

Just as you consider a bakery to be "your" bakery or a tailor to be "your" tailor, you want a person to consider your company as "their" real estate firm. This is increasingly important today as the industry strives to protect its role in the real estate transaction. This won't happen unless people feel satisfied with the services that the company and, most importantly, the salespeople provide.

In Chapter 3 we analyzed the market to plan the way the company could best serve its consumers. Today's consumer-driven business demands that you listen to them, even exceed their expectations, so that they will embrace your company as their real estate firm. To ensure that you are delivering quality services, you need to establish standards for the services you deliver. As a practical matter, these standards will help the salespeople as well, because they have as much at stake in the transactions as the company does.

Develop quality service standards that correspond to the nature of the services your firm delivers. Then incorporate these standards in the policy and procedures manual. As with any company policy or procedure these quality service standards must be institutionalized. This means that they must become an integral part of the company's operation. A commitment to delivering quality services can become part of your company's signature. Remember that consumers expect companies to serve their needs, not be a means to the company's end–your revenue.

Servicing sellers.   If your company lists property you should develop standards for the services associated with this activity. As you do this, consider the sellers' most common complaints. Addressing these issues ahead of time will help prevent them from arising within your firm.

- Salespeople don't return phone calls.
- Salespeople don't contact sellers frequently enough.
- Sellers don't know what the salespeople are doing to get the property sold.
- Salespeople make promises when the properties are listed that aren't fulfilled.
- The property took too long to sell.
- The settlement didn't go smoothly.

In many cases these problems can be avoided at the time a property is listed simply by fully explaining the listing-to-sales process and exactly what the company and the salesperson intend to do throughout this process. Certainly, requiring that salespeople provide a comparative market analysis and a discussion about contemporary market conditions goes a long way to avoid unrealistic expectations about prices and the time within which a property should sell. Your service standards also can incorporate such items as home warranty programs, referral or relocation services or discount or cross-marketing programs that your company uses. For risk management purposes, be sure to include contract and consumer protection issues, including agency, property and lead-based paint disclosures.

Servicing buyers.   You can develop service standards for buyers as well. As you do this consider the factors that influence buyers' choices of homes to give you an idea about the kinds of services that are meaningful.

According to the NAR 1998 Home Buying and Selling Survey, homebuyers indicated the factors that influence their choice of a home as follows:

- 79 percent indicated the neighborhood. This suggests that guiding people to comprehensive information about the area is essential.

- 73 percent indicated price. This suggests that financial matters as well as an analysis of the investment are important.

- 40 percent indicated work. This suggests that a variety of services associated with relocation may be in order.

- 34 percent indicated schools. This suggests that, similar to the neighborhood concerns, comprehensive school data is in order.

Interestingly, the survey indicated that 23 percent reported friends and family; 20 percent indicated parks/recreational facilities; 17 percent indicated shopping centers and 13 percent indicated that the real estate salesperson influenced their choice of home.

Quality service standards for buyers would also address agency (if appropriate) contract and disclosure procedures, standards for preparing and negotiating sales agreements and assisting the buyer seamlessly through the transaction to settlement. These could include mortgage financing, home inspections or warranties, insurance, title and settlement services. Also, you would include services such as referral and relocation and cross-marketing programs that are offered by your company. Consider consumer protection and risk-management procedures as well, including procedures for documenting the showings, conversations and negotiations with a buyer.

Tracking business.   Quality service standards intend to ensure that current customers and clients receive the utmost professional consideration from the company and its sales staff. In addition to the procedures the company adopts, the sales staff has an invaluable resource in today's transaction management software. These computer programs guide virtually every step needed to serve sellers and buyers. In addition, they help salespeople capitalize on current business by suggesting steps to develop future relationships. After all, one of the benefits of delivering quality service today is the repeat and referral business you will derive in the future.

Quality Control

Once you've established the standards, the next task is to monitor the services. There are several *internal quality control* measures you can use. One is to review the transaction files, which we mentioned earlier, to monitor the salespeople's activities. Another way is to incorporate quality service standards in the salespeople's performance criteria used for performance reviews. In Chapter 8 we made the point that the process should be as important as the result. The company can demonstrate its commitment to quality by emphasizing the importance of its service standards at review time.

Customer feedback.   Your perception of the company and the public's perception can differ, so you should also go outside the organization to evaluate the quality of your services. This can be done using suggestion boxes, 800 phone numbers, comments on your Web site or **customer service surveys.** Find out what customers and clients think about how well you've performed. No one should conclude business with the company without an opportunity to bring closure to the relationship. After a closing or settlement, have both the buyer and seller complete a survey about the experience.

Keep several things in mind when conducting surveys:

- Gather only important information. Keep the questionnaire short and easy to complete to maximize response. Several yes/no queries, several scaled queries (ranked excellent, good, satisfactory or poor) and one or two open-ended questions should be adequate.

- Gather only information on which you plan to act. Don't waste people's time if you have no intention of remedying a situation.

- Develop a plan for reviewing the surveys and acting on the information. Customers appreciate the opportunity to tell you what they think, but they become dissatisfied when the company doesn't act on what they say.

In addition to information for monitoring your services, you also can gather suggestions about new ways to enhance your services and ideas to consider in future planning.

Don't overlook surveying people who have terminated their relationship with your company. The seller who terminates a listing or whose listing expires before the property sells, for example, should be given an opportunity to critique the experience. Not only can you take corrective steps that might be necessary, but you also can learn what the seller is broadcasting about the experience. The fact that you solicit the person's opinions may also help defuse negative feelings a person may have.

Personnel competency. One final comment about quality control—at some point you have to look closely at the competency of the salespeople and the broker. Earlier we mentioned the valuable information that can be gathered from transaction files with which you can monitor a variety of aspects of the company's services. Now we add information gathered from customer feedback. None of a company's monitoring activities are meaningful unless management acts on what it learns. These lessons can be factored into the coaching management does with the salespeople, the company's professional development programs and the training department's activities. Perhaps the quality of the services can be improved by enhancing the competency of the company's personnel. Table 13.1 provides an example of a study that reveals competencies associated with tasks today's licensees perform.

Problem Solving

In Chapter 12 we discussed the role of the manager as a negotiator and problem solver in dealing with issues that arise within the firm. But for many managers a considerable amount of time is spent tending to problems that arise with people outside the company—buyers, sellers and cooperating brokers. Although injured parties can pursue formal courses of action, many issues can be handled informally. Frequently problems arise because of miscommunication or misunderstandings that a third person, the broker or manager, can resolve. As we indicated earlier, the number of these cases can be minimized at the outset if the company is committed to providing quality services.

A disgruntled customer, client or another licensee often feels that the way to get satisfaction is through the salesperson's manager or broker. You may be the one who gets the irate phone call from a seller who's disturbed because his house hasn't sold or from the buyer who's upset because her settlement is delayed, for example. Or you may get a call from another broker claiming part of the commission on a transaction. In some of these cases you may find yourself squarely in the middle between the salesperson and the disgruntled caller. The way you handle these situations will be either a winning solution for you, the company and the customer, or someone will be the loser.

The first goal is to satisfy the customer or resolve the issue with the competitor. Begin by getting all of the facts straight. You should be able to do this by reviewing the information in the transaction files and talking with the salesperson involved. Then, telephone calls to all of the parties may be all that's necessary to resolve the matter. Perhaps a meeting with the parties will be needed to rectify a situation.

The company, management and the salesperson are all on the same team. It's essential to present a united front to the public and your competitors. Internal matters must be handled inter-

TABLE 13.1　Broker/Agency Competency Study*

Agent Competencies			Broker Competencies		
Order of Importance	Item	Comparable Broker Item	Order of Importance	Item	Comparable Broker Item
1	Working with customers and clients		1	Ethical conduct in real estate	
2	Negotiation skills	9	2	The real estate contract	8
3	Process from sale to close	6	3	Effective verbal communication	5 and 13
4	Offers and counteroffers	9	4	Escrow account management	
5	Listening skills	3	5	Effective written communication	
6	Disclosures	8	6	Process from contract to closing	
7	Closing costs, fees and taxes	7 and 14	7	Closing transaction	7
8	Obligations of parties to contract	2	8	Disclosing defects	6 and 14
9	Assessing buyer needs		9	Negotiation skills and knowledge	4
10	Concept of agency	10 and 13	10	Agency license law	10
11	Marketing self, service and property		11	Required documents for closing	7
12	Understanding and completing forms		12	Knowledge of business management	
13	Sales and communication skills	3 and 5	13	Concept of agency	10
14	Required disclosures		14	Basic closing statements and costs	7
15	Working with agents and brokers		15	Agency disclosure form and timing	

*Performed by Abelson & Company and the Institute for Community Research at the University of Tampa, 1996. Funded by the Florida Real Estate Commission.

Reprinted with permission from *Real Estate Confronts Reality*, by Dooley, Swanepoel and Abelson, Real Estate Education Co.®, Chicago. For more information, contact Dr. Michael Abelson, 888-223-5766.

nally so don't disparage one another in front of outsiders. However, you must be forthright and acknowledge mistakes. If you detect an egregious error on the part of the salesperson or the company involving a legal matter, refrain from making any comments. Seek advice from the company's counsel about how to proceed.

Once the matter is resolved you can delve into the internal or company issues. Digressions from company policy should be handled one-on-one with the individual salesperson. Solutions should be developed, following the guidelines suggested in Chapter 12, to prevent problems from arising again.

MINIMIZING EXPENSES

Minimizing expenses does not mean you have to cut or eliminate valuable services to your customers or your sales staff. There are a number of ways that you can make more efficient use of your money by monitoring expenses and instituting certain cost-containment measures. If you are monitoring frequently, you can identify places where the company is over budget and take corrective action before the company hemorrhages from overspending. The following are cost-efficiencies that you can consider.

Telephone

The cost of communicating can be significant. One of the best places to look for hidden expenditures is in your phone bill. Billing errors are difficult to spot unless someone takes the time to scrutinize the monthly bill. Duplicate charges and charges for uncompleted calls often are hidden among legitimate charges. But you'll not know which ones are legitimate unless you know what calls people make. Use a phone log or call slips on which each person details long-distance calls, including the number, the name of the person called and the purpose of the call. Discourage personal long-distance calls, even if you are to be reimbursed. (You may or may not get the reimbursement.) And caution people about the length of their calls! They may not realize how windy they are.

Local telephone/fax calls from a business telephone line can add up quickly. Although we don't hesitate to make local calls from our home phones, a company is charged message units. One way to control communication costs is to minimize local outgoing calls and encourage incoming calls. Voice mail and call-forwarding systems can relay calls for salespeople, which saves both the cost of returning the call and the time of the person who takes a message.

Take advantage of cheaper calling times and other cost-saving programs offered by communications companies. Encourage evening and weekend calling, and fax after 11 P.M. whenever possible. Because of the current competition among carriers, numerous discount programs and incentives also are available. In the case of long-distance service, carefully compare costs in addition to per-minute rates to be sure the carrier you select is your best deal. Also warn staff that only an authorized person from the company is permitted to change long-distance carriers.

Computers

Use your computer to communicate. Flyers, letters or messages can be sent via computer modems at a much lower cost than that of duplicating and mailing. Don't forget the option of communicating via e-mail and commercial online services.

Use the computer for some of your printing needs. Instead of printing and storing large supplies of these materials, you can design (or your software may include) business forms, flyers, letters or even real estate contracts that can be printed as needed. When it's time to revise these items, it's cheaper to revise a computer document than it is to discard and replace a stock of printed material. There is also less wasted paper when a document or form can be completed, proofread and revised on the computer before it is printed. Using quality paper and a laser printer gives your documents a professional appearance, making the computer a satisfactory substitute for professional printing in many cases.

Marketing and Advertising

Cost-containment in advertising is a major challenge, particularly as you get close to the end of the year. If you embarked on a major marketing program in January or were very generous in your classified advertising to capture the spring market, you might be coasting on fumes by September. If you are, you'll have to put the remaining dollars where they will do the most good.

Use logs to track the number of inquiries and the sources of calls. As the volume of calls fluctuates, you can gauge the potential for income during the year as well as determine which marketing and advertising activities generate inquiries. Before you make major changes in your advertising strategy, watch for trends to gauge which activities have been most effective. The effectiveness of some may correlate with the seasonal nature of the business.

Once you have a feel for the effectiveness of the marketing program, you can redistribute dollars to vehicles that have shown the best return during the year. And this year's data are useful when developing the marketing plan for next year. As the use of Internet Web sites increases, your entire marketing strategy may need to be revamped and some of the traditional tools eliminated.

Two other issues to consider when evaluating your advertising expenditures are:

- the quality of the inquiries that are generated and

- the conversion of the inquiries to closed transactions.

Before you jump to conclusions about why the phone is ringing off the hook but there are no transactions on the board, or why the phone has stopped ringing entirely, determine the nature of the problem. The fault may be the salespeople's telephone technique. Or it could be that the company's advertising is not reaching the target audience. There also could be internal problems: salespeople may not be getting their messages or not following up on the inquiries. Perhaps the amount of phone activity is an indicator of a changing market and you'll need to adjust your income expectations for the rest of the year.

There are ways to minimize costs in classified advertising if you're astute. Proofread each of the ads for typographical errors. Newspapers will usually give credit for these mistakes. Count the number of lines and compare the line charges on your bills. If you check the length of your ads, you may find that one or two fewer words can save you an entire line charge. Also check with the publisher to be sure that you're getting the best deal. A package plan may be cheaper than running an ad for only two days.

Consider the size of your display ads. A half page may be just as effective as a full page, or a quarter page may do instead of a half page. The savings can be substantial as long as the quality or purpose of the ad is not compromised.

It may be time to retool the way you distribute the responsibility for advertising and promotional costs. Consider sharing advertising with the salespeople, provided this does not negatively impact your equity with the competition. The salespeople may be happy to participate in the costs of classified advertising, giveaways or self-promotion if this means preserving or adding exposure. This is preferable to suddenly burdening them with all of the advertising costs. You win by promoting the company's signature and services and the salespeople win, especially if they can direct expenditures where they feel they will benefit the most.

Postage

As we've previously discussed, faxes and modems are frequently cheaper than communicating via the mail. E-mail has replaced mailing short notes and confirmations of a meeting or appointment. But you can't escape using the mail for certain things. However, there are ways to economize. Put a scale in your office! Make the most of first-class postage. If the mailing is lighter than the maximum weight for one stamp, include a flyer or other promotional piece. For letters that need extra postage, keep the correct stamps on hand to avoid using two first-class stamps. Or rent a postage meter if you have a large volume of mail. The rental is not cheap, but it may be less expensive than the cost of time spent stamping by hand.

Use second-day delivery rather than overnight delivery if possible, and compare prices and services of carriers. Some delivery services are very helpful in planning the most cost-effective way to send a parcel. Encourage people to choose packaging wisely, because a fraction of an ounce can push delivery cost into the next price category. And remember, it's cheaper to fax the message someone forgot to include in the overnight letter than to send another one.

Don't scrimp on details that could cost you money later. If you need a return receipt or proof that notice was served on a certain date, get it. These are legal issues that could come back to haunt you.

Mass mailings can be expensive, but they are an important part of the sales business. (Though the Internet can be more economical and will eventually reach as broad an audience.) For mass coverage, consider bulk mailing. The price of a bulk permit each year and the extra attention needed to prepare the mailings properly are considerably less expensive than using first class postage. The services of a mail house may be more cost-effective than the cost of using a staff person to prepare a large mailing. It's important to plan bulk mailings in advance to ensure receipt in a timely fashion, especially if they contain time-sensitive information. Otherwise, they are less effective and may even be embarrassing.

Economies in the Office

The little things add up! Have the utility company do an energy audit if you're paying for your own utilities. Consider energy-efficient lighting. Insist that the person responsible for stocking the office supplies does some comparison shopping. It's easy to pick up the phone and place an order, but there may be economies available from other vendors. It also could be worth the time and effort for a staff person to do the pickup and delivery.

Buying in bulk can be cost-effective, provided you use stock such as pens or rubber bands before they must be discarded or spoil. Be attentive to shelf-life, particularly of brochures that contain time-sensitive or dated material. And don't make all of the stock readily available. Set some aside to discourage waste.

Use paper wisely. Don't skimp on the quality of the paper stock and graphics on your letterhead and envelopes, but don't use them for interoffice communiqués or scratch paper. Buy cheaper paper for this purpose, and scatter scratch pads generously around the office. Test using recycled paper in the computer printer or duplicating machine. It is cheaper stock, provided you don't compromise the quality of the printed project.

Waste management offers significant savings. Malfunctioning equipment is a major culprit. It used to be a typewriter that skipped spaces or blurred characters that was the offender (or perhaps it was the typist). Today it's the copy machine or the computer printer. Keep the equipment maintained to eliminate filling the trash can or recycling container with many light, dark or smudged sheets of paper. Consider remanufactured cartridges for laser printers (purchase one at first for a trial).

The cost of duplicating keys for listings and rental units can add up. The cost in inconvenience and emergency locksmith services because of misplaced or lost keys can be even greater. If you have a large volume of keys to duplicate, it may be feasible to purchase key-cutting equipment or even have someone in the office certified as a locksmith. If you handle property management as well as sales, this could be a big plus.

Keep track of yard signs and lockboxes. Use a log to identify locations where these items are being used and the persons who checked them out. Missing tools are as aggravating as they are expensive to replace.

Salaries and Benefits

It's tempting to cut support staff when the year and the money don't seem to be coming out even. But remember all the reasons for creating these positions in the first place. Consider ways to economize by out-sourcing some tasks or activities. A contractor's service might be cheaper than salary and benefits for a staff person. Ask employees to participate in the costs of benefits such as health care. Before you start manipulating hours and wages, though, be sure you're familiar with the labor laws.

Costs of Sales

The cost-of-sales line on the income statement, as you may recall from Chapter 7, includes all of the costs for commissions, referral and franchise fees that are associated with the sales transactions. Before cutting commissions to control costs, remember the rationale for setting the commission schedules in the first place. Track referral and franchise fees over the long run to determine if there is sufficient added benefit to warrant the expenditure. Add in to this evaluation "after the fact" fees charged by your referral company in transactions when its client's employee began working with your company without the benefit of the referral.

While you monitor the costs of sales during the year, pay attention to the number of in-house versus cooperating sales. Depending on your commission arrangements with the salespeople and other brokers, one way brokers minimize costs is to encourage the salespeople to sell their company's listings. This strategy is only feasible as long as it does not conflict with agency laws or compromise the quality of service provided to customers and clients.

LOOKING INTO THE FUTURE

The information you gather about the organization when monitoring this year's activities is critical when charting its course for the future. As you saw in Chapter 3, when we analyzed the current organization in the planning process, new plans and budgets are forecasts based on past experiences. As we've already indicated, planning is an ongoing activity. You are now prepared to develop a new three-year or five-year plan and specific goals. Sometimes the new plan is a reaffirmation of the existing one or requires only a bit of tinkering; other times it may send the company in a dramatic new direction.

We set the stage in the first chapter by making the point that we are surrounded by change. The secret to coping is to be smart enough to stay the course when necessary and visionary enough to become a leader in a new industry of services or business methods. The structure of your organization is bound to change. If certain services are not as profitable as you would like, this may mean that you should close a division and concentrate on other activities. Or you may decide to expand the organization, either vertically or horizontally. You may plan to increase your capacity for providing current services (vertical growth) or increase the number of services or target markets that you serve (horizontal growth) (see Figure 13.1).

CONCLUSION

Monitoring the operations involves keeping in touch with all aspects of the business and controlling activities or making adjustments where necessary. Ultimately, the goal is to ensure that you have a business to manage next year. There's nothing quite so exhilarating as seeing the company exceed your expectations. And there's nothing quite so unnerving as discovering that the company is struggling, especially if this is the firm's first year in business and reserves are dwindling.

Planning can be viewed as the proactive function that sets the organization on a course to prosperity. *Controlling* is the reactive function that nudges activities so that the organization can fulfill that plan. Managers need certain information to do this, however, whether it's income or expense information, transaction documentation and customer service reports or license or personnel information. Once the successes or pitfalls are identified, managers need to act by either praising the progress or remedying the faults. Controlling should not restrict the organization, but rather should inspire the company to grow by directing its resources to the most productive activities.

FIGURE 13.1 Growth of an Organization

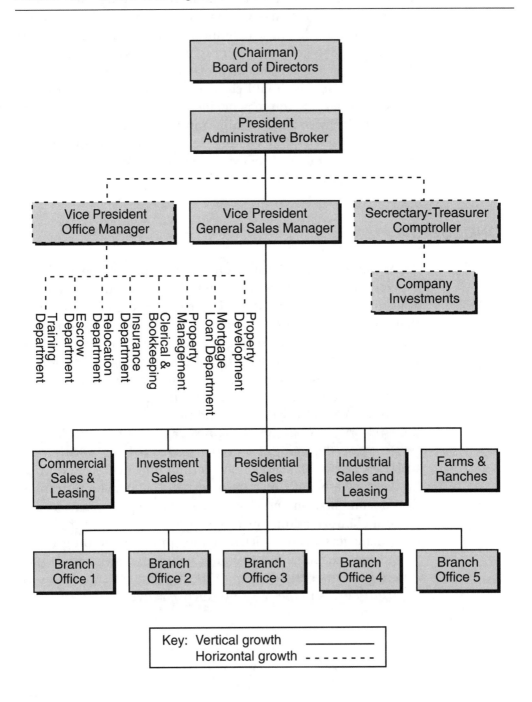

DISCUSSION EXERCISES

Discuss transaction management software that you use; share transaction tracking forms that you use or design a tracking system for your office.

* * *

Discuss ways you have found to economize on expenditures in your company, office or department.

* * *

What are your experiences with customer service surveys?

14 Managing Risk

What issues pose the greatest risk for doing business in your area? What procedures can you use to build a good offense to avoid these risks?

Risk begins at the time you make up your mind to go into business and sign the partnership, corporation and/or loan papers. It sits on the slippery doorstep to the office, in the seat of the first employment interview you conduct and at your feet with the first employee you terminate. As soon as you step into the field with your first listing presentation, show the first buyer a house, negotiate a sales contract or meet with your fellow brokers for lunch, you are in the riskiest arenas of the real estate business. Add more salespeople, several employees and a lot more buyers and sellers to the mix—well, you'd better read on.

Despite how well you perform all of the management functions we've discussed in this book, the company cannot survive for the long term (or maybe even the short term) without a solid plan to confront the legal risks of doing business. Risk management has been one of the hottest topics of conversation in meetings and seminars in recent years, and with good reason. We have become a nation whose court dockets are choked with lawsuits. Today's "sue mentality" is not likely to fade any time soon, especially as the number of areas in which risk lurks continues to increase.

Risk management means different things to different people. To some it means preparing themselves financially and mentally for the inevitable: they will eventually get sued. Some brokers do this by resigning themselves to that fact and chalk up the cost of litigation to the cost of doing business. Some brokers are a bit better prepared, setting aside reserves for a litigation fund. Many more brokers consider the purchase of insurance as the most cost-effective way to manage risk. All of these are reactive measures in which the brokers may be managing on hope—hope that the costs won't exceed their financial resources.

But there are proactive steps that can be taken to minimize your risk. Also you can protect the company's financial resources so they can be directed to more constructive or productive endeavors. Risk management involves preventive measures that can minimize the potential for litigation; it also helps to prepare financially for the day it happens.

BUILDING YOUR OFFENSE

Building a good offense is the *proactive* approach to managing risk. This means assessing vulnerabilities and preparing policies and procedures to avoid problematic situations. Confronting risk from a positive point of view takes some of the fear out of doing business, knowing that the organization is managing its risks rather than allowing it to be intimidated or paralyzed by them. The procedures that evolve also benefit customers and clients by enhancing the quality of services and increasing customer satisfaction. There are a number of ways to build a good offense.

Use Lawyers and Accountants

At the risk (pardon the pun) of sounding redundant, we can't emphasize strongly enough the importance of your lawyer and accountant in your business. You need these people not only to get you started in business but also on most every step along the way. One of the most valuable lines in the budget is their monthly retainer fees.

Because you are paying for legal and tax advice, you have to decide what to do with it. Lest this sound like a peculiar observation, consider that you pay these people to keep you out of trouble. Will you take their advice, even if they don't tell you what you want to hear? Are you going to search until you find someone to give you the answer you want? Or are you going to ignore the professionals' advice entirely? Second opinions can be useful, but ducking the facts can be dangerous. Lawyers and accountants can't defend indefensible actions.

While we're discussing lawyers and accountants, it is appropriate to mention the negotiation of their retainer fees. Define which services will be performed for the retainer and those, beyond the retainer, that will be billable hours. Also clarify who in your organization is permitted to contact these advisers and for what purposes. Otherwise, you could exceed the services covered by a retainer and could be very surprised by the amount of the legal and accounting bills.

Use Enforcement Agencies

While a number of laws impact the business, your state's licensing laws and the federal, state and local fair housing laws are several of the most important. The licensing authorities and fair housing agencies are invaluable resources for clarifying and interpreting their laws and answering specific questions. Unfortunately some people see them as adversaries that should be avoided. However, these agencies can help you stay out of trouble, which lightens their workload too.

Everyone on the management team should have the phone numbers of these agencies and the most recent versions of their laws for reference. Also include them in your sales training program.

Your Training Programs

Sales training programs typically emphasize sales techniques and teaching salespeople how to sell. But the most important thing we should be doing is training them how to sell legally and ethically. License laws, consumer and agency laws, fair housing laws, environmental issues, antitrust and disclosure laws, and ethics should be incorporated into the training programs. When salespeople develop sales skills that are consistent with these laws, they are not only more professional but also they can be one of your most powerful risk management assets.

Your Policies and Procedures

We've already mentioned that it's useful to anticipate events that could arise when developing the company's policies and procedures. Issues that create risk either in the internal operating procedures or in consumer services should be addressed in the policy and procedures manual.

In Chapter 8 we provided a relatively comprehensive checklist to follow when developing policies and procedures, including personnel policies, and writing a manual. This document is a powerful tool for incorporating risk management procedures into the company's operations. Often the industry's professional organizations have legal hot lines that are helpful for developing these procedures.

However, don't sit back, content that once you have written these procedures, you are thoroughly protected. When the day comes that you have to defend yourself, your opponent can wave this document in a courtroom as evidence of your company's procedures. You will be defenseless if the contents are erroneous (a powerful argument for having legal counsel periodically review the manual), you do not enforce your policies or you purposely engage in activities that contradict the ideals you set for the company. Actions speak louder than words. Use the document to protect you rather than create liability.

Areas that can pose significant risk which should be addressed include agency, antitrust, disclosures, fair housing, equal employment opportunity, RESPA and licensing laws. In addition we call to your attention two issues that are emerging as the latest hot topics.

Anti-harassment policies. Recent Supreme Court decisions have expanded the rights of workers, both male and female, in the workplace. Because of these developments and a generally heightened awareness in society, sexual harassment in the workplace has risen as an important issue. Real estate offices are no exception. In fact the National Association of REALTORS® has included this in its risk management manual. It also has developed guidelines for creating anti-harassment policies.

Title VII of the Civil Rights Act of 1964 bars sexual discrimination. In the context of this law, the Supreme Court has ruled that sexual harassment is a form of illegal discrimination and that employees are entitled to work in an environment that is free from sexual harassment. The Equal Employment Opportunity Commission (EEOC) defines sexual harassment as unwelcome sexual advances, requests for sexual favors and other verbal or physical conduct of a sexual nature.

Two kinds of harassment have been defined. *Quid pro quo* harassment involves requiring an employee to submit to sexual activity in return for a raise or promotion or to retain a job. However, no tangible job benefit has to be lost in order to file a claim of sexual harassment. A *hostile environment* is one in which a worker does such things as making unwelcome sexual requests, gestures, remarks, jokes and the like directed towards another worker in the environment where the individual must work. While the offensive conduct was deemed at one time to occur between workers of the opposite sex, the Supreme Court has determined that the conduct can be equally offensive between workers of the same sex. Consequently, the rights to legal remedies have been expanded.

The Supreme Court has further determined that employers must have policies and procedures in place so that an aggrieved person knows what to do in the event of sexual harassment. The policies should define sexual harassment and explain reporting, investigation and disciplinary procedures. Brokers should seek legal advice about the intricacies of the regulations of the EEOC, court interpretations and any state laws when drafting these policies. Also consider devoting a meeting to the subject of sexual harassment for all workers in the company, especially management and supervisory personnel.

Internet policies. The Internet has created a wide new arena for risk. In Chapter 9 we mentioned the challenges of protecting your intellectual property or assets when the company posts information on the Internet; but the problems don't end there. Because your salespeople are using the Internet, you need to protect the company from problems they may be creating for you.

Companies today need to incorporate Internet policies into their policy and procedures manuals. It's likely that over time we'll discover problems that haven't even occurred to us yet, but some of the important issues that have surfaced so far include:

- *Ownership of listings*—The broker owns the listings, which means that the broker must authorize the posting of the company's property, which in many cases has been addressed through MLS membership. Furthermore, the broker is liable for the information being disseminated by the salespeople about their listings.

- *Confidentiality*—Simply providing a seller's name or address along with a property listing can launch a number of linkages to personal data that could harm the seller. Furthermore, the broker is liable for the dissemination of information about the transaction that breaches the fiduciary duty of confidentiality.

- *License law*—Advertising, and perhaps Internet procedures, are commonly included in the states' license laws. While salespeople have a duty to adhere to these laws, brokers are liable for any of their violations as well.

- *Civil and criminal offenses*—A variety of other laws get networked into areas of risk when salespeople have their own Web sites. When they establish domain names, communicate via e-mail and develop content for their Web pages, are they infringing on copyright or intellectual property rights? Could their messages prompt defamation, sexual harassment or racial discrimination suits? Are they using the Internet to commit wire fraud or engage in child pornography?

- *Computer security*—The company must protect its database, including company or transaction files, from being accessed and linked on the Internet. Conversely, the company must protect against virus-infected files being downloaded into its system. The company's operation could be paralyzed, to say nothing about the costs associated with unraveling the problems.

Any of the issues we've mentioned can not only tarnish the company's good name but most importantly, cause you significant legal problems.

Your Transactions

Establishing quality service standards should contribute greatly to minimizing risk in your transaction. Hopefully, those standards include educating buyers and sellers about the "rules of the game" when they start working with you. Minimizing violated expectations and educating them about certain laws, like fair housing, agency, environmental and property disclosures, will avoid problems later.

Many states require that the owner of the property complete property disclosure forms, disclosing what he or she knows about its condition. Owners, not your salespeople, should complete these forms. Otherwise, they have created another problem for you. These disclosures also should be part of the company's service standards. They are good business even if their use is not required by law.

Misrepresentations can be one of the areas that create the greatest risk. (We discuss this in detail later in the chapter.) You know your market best and where the liability flashpoints are. Each area has its own, such as wetlands, flood plains, water rights or restrictive covenants, septic systems or sand mounds.

Managing risk also involves knowing the limits of your expertise. The caveats are that real estate licensees are not authorized to practice law or give tax advice. Nor are they authorities on environmental or health issues, building construction and insect infestation. We need partnerships with people who are, which is why you need the proper resources for authoritative information. Another caveat, however, is that salespeople should *not* recommend a specific person or inspector to a customer or client. In doing so, they could incur liability for themselves and the company for the quality and accuracy of the services these people provide.

Your Contracts

Some of us may remember the day when a sales agreement amounted to words that fit on one side of a single sheet of paper. These agreements are no longer adequate. In fact, they have grown to multiple pages and commonly include disclosures regarding agency, property and environmental conditions and various addenda. Agency agreements (listing contracts or buyer agency) or facilitator documents, leases, property management or other contracts must meet certain standards.

The preparation of contracts is frequently governed by state licensing laws. Salespeople must understand the limits of their authority when they prepare contracts and draft addenda. In some states they are limited to negotiating binders, which are followed by sales contracts drafted by lawyers. In others, salespeople are permitted to "fill in the blanks" on preprinted forms. The broker is responsible for reviewing the contracts assembled by the salespeople in some states. The parties to the contract also have the right to have the documents reviewed by counsel before they sign them. In fact, some states have specific laws regarding attorney review. All of these procedures protect the parties involved as well as the company.

Your Files

In the event of a problem, you are defenseless without records. In fact your lawyer may recommend that you prepare every transaction and document it as if it were certain to end up in litigation. In Chapter 13 we discussed records and the retention of documents. In addition to fulfilling the license law requirements, there are several other things you should consider doing.

There should be copious notes, beginning from the time of the first conversation with a potential client or customer throughout the transaction to closing or settlement. This is not necessarily a monumental task for the salespeople or anyone else who has contact with a customer, client and cooperating broker. A telephone log and transaction files are good for tracking the trail of events. Several words or key phrases on a transaction sheet or in an appointment book that will help reconstruct what happened is normally satisfactory. Pay particular attention to conversations relating to property conditions and fair housing.

PREPARE FOR DEFENSE

Litigation can be financially debilitating and time-consuming, diverting both financial and human resources from productive endeavors to the preparation and defense of legal cases. While you can minimize the occurrence of litigation with a proactive posture, you must also minimize the burden to the organization from certain events that could arise. There are a number of ways to do this.

Insurance

Insurance can be viewed as an investment of financial resources to pay for events that you hope never occur. The company is often seen having deep pockets. While the cost of insurance can be a considerable expense, it will return great benefits if it is ever needed. The company normally insures for a number of events.

The first is workers' compensation. The purpose of workers' compensation is to protect people against loss of income due to injuries sustained on the job. Workers' compensation insurance is a statutory requirement for employees and, depending on your state's laws, may also be required for independent contractors. In addition, you may consider offering disability insurance to employees to cover loss due to any illness or injury, regardless of whether it is job related or not.

Another is liability insurance. This comes in many forms, but automobile liability is the most common. Insist that each salesperson carry an adequate amount, which in today's economy should be at least $300,000 per person, $500,000 per accident and $100,000 for property damage. In addition, the company can get an umbrella policy to cover its liability over and above that of each salesperson in the event of an accident while on company business.

Other types of insurance include liability insurance to cover injuries to clients or customers on the company's premises, fire and comprehensive coverage for equipment, replacement of records and business interruption insurance.

Given today's business climate, errors and omissions (E & O) insurance is a must. In fact some states *require* that licensees carry this insurance. The company's E & O insurance covers certain claims against *the company* because of the actions of the salespeople. In addition, licensees should have their own coverage or the company could offer a group policy in which the salespeople can participate. E & O insurance includes the legal defense against a claim as well as damage awards for insurable events. Check your policy to determine what events are insurable. (Violations of the law are normally excluded.)

Dispute Resolution

The legal system in this country is designed to ensure that justice is served, to give everyone his or her day in court and an opportunity to be heard. Nevertheless, the system is stressed to its limits, particularly with civil matters. Often people must cool their heels for years before they are heard. Both the plaintiff and the defendant incur sizable legal bills in the process.

Mediation and arbitration are alternatives for resolving disputes in a speedy, affordable manner, in lieu of going to court. These methods are being used in many types of disputes, and real estate is no exception. Mediation is a forum in which the parties sit with an impartial mediator and negotiate a resolution to their dispute. Arbitration involves an arbitrator, or panel of arbitrators, who hears the two sides present their cases (as would be done in court). Then the arbitrator renders a decision. In most jurisdictions this decision is as binding as any court decision would be.

Consider recommending these alternatives to your buyers and sellers. These are advantageous for the company as well, because brokers and the companies are frequently implicated as parties in disputes. There are services throughout the country that are sanctioned by the legal community to provide mediation and arbitration. Some are sponsored by real estate organizations. The services may provide only mediation, only arbitration or perhaps both resolution systems. Some sales agreements include language that requires the parties to resolve disputes over specific matters in this manner.

Arbitration Between Brokers

Buyers and sellers are not the only ones who find themselves in disputes. Controversies between brokerage companies arise, particularly over commissions. Professional real estate organizations frequently offer their members an arbitration forum in which these matters can be settled. Again, the advantage is a speedier, less costly way to resolve these controversies. (Note, too, that these organizations provide forums for ethics complaints as well.)

POWER OF INFORMATION

Information empowers us to manage risk. The balance of this chapter is devoted to several of the current issues that pose the greatest liability in the industry from a national perspective. Inasmuch as there are also state laws, some of which are more restrictive or apply in more numerous situations than the federal laws, it is incumbent on you to be familiar with them and be prepared to practice accordingly. The legal environment is constantly changing with each new law that is adopted, each amendment that is passed and each decision that is rendered by the courts. It's imperative that you monitor these developments.

You are encouraged to acquire the complete text of the laws governing the issues that are discussed to use as authoritative legal reference. (Selected references are provided in the Bibliography.) It is helpful to assemble a library of federal, state and local laws to which managers and salespeople can refer. Many of these valuable resources can also be accessed on the Internet. This information also is useful for sales meetings and training programs.

ANTITRUST

Real estate is an aggressively competitive business, particularly in the quest for listings. When properties are in high demand, competition is even more keen. Once the quest for the listing is over, a unique relationship develops between brokers who, once competitors, now cooperate with one another. The manner in which brokers compete is subject to antitrust scrutiny.

Although the antitrust laws do not mention the real estate industry specifically, three have been applied to the industry. We begin with the **Sherman Act,** which is intended to curtail large trusts, cartels or monopolies that are perceived to threaten healthy competition and the growth of businesses. The theory is that competitive forces must be allowed to function, with the ultimate result being the lowest prices, highest quality and greatest progress in the marketplace.

Any conspiracy, that is, joining in a secret agreement to perform some unlawful act, is illegal regardless of how the conspiracy is created. There may be *direct evidence*, such as a document, contract or personal witness, that shows that two or more businesses actually agreed on some conduct to restrain trade. Or there may be *circumstantial evidence*, conduct that is perceived to constitute a conspiracy to restrain trade. A conspiracy itself is not illegal. Rather it is the *effect* of the conspiracy—the *unreasonable* restraint of trade that suppresses or destroys competition. An action is deemed to be unreasonable if its anticompetitive effect outweighs its procompetitive effect.

The U.S. Supreme Court has determined that certain restraints are so destructive to competition that their anticompetitive effect is automatically presumed. These include activities such as price fixing, boycotts, territorial assignments and tying agreements. They are illegal under the *per se rule,* which means that they cannot be defended as being reasonable under any circumstances. Because the court has already concluded that these are anticompetitive activities, the only determination that remains is whether an individual or business participated in the conspiracy.

Another antitrust law is the **Clayton Act,** which prohibits certain practices that arise from a number of activities, brokerage being one of them. This act differs from the Sherman Act by identifying anticompetitive practices before they occur, rather than focusing on the effect of the restraints as the Sherman Act does.

The third is Section 5 of the **Federal Trade Commission Act,** which prohibits "unfair methods of competition" and "unfair or deceptive acts or practices." The Sherman Act applies the test of unreasonableness, whereas the Federal Trade Commission Act inquires into the *unfairness* of an action. It extends beyond the Sherman Act by covering injury to consumers as well as competitors.

Price Fixing

Pricing practices are the most scrutinized and potentially dangerous activities in the industry. Brokerage firms and real estate industry groups must establish "zero tolerance" policies for any price-fixing activities. There are two prices that are the subject of potential violations. One is the fee, rate, price or terms for brokerage services and other real estate activity. The second is the price or fee that is offered in cobrokerage arrangements, that is, the commission split.

Fees for services.   Any agreement between two or more brokers in competition with one another to fix, control, regulate, increase, decrease or stabilize fees, rates, commissions or other prices is illegal. These are *per se* violations, which means that they are not defensible on any grounds. Price fixing relates to any economic terms. Therefore, agreements between competitors that fix, control, regulate or limit the terms and conditions or the form of listing or other agreements between the brokers and the public or the form of compensation, such as payment by flat fee or percentage, are also illegal.

The courts have determined that price-fixing agreements effectively eliminate a major form of competition because of their power to control the market and to fix arbitrary prices. They have been declared illegal regardless of the intent, purpose or effect of the agreement. An agreement between a few competitors in a given marketplace is just as illegal as an agreement that involves all competitors.

Any economic terms must be established by a broker unilaterally, independently and without any discussion or conversation with competitors. They must be defensible as being procompetitive. This is an important consideration when the broker determines the fee policies for the company, as discussed in Chapter 7.

The fact that fees or commissions are uniform is not, by itself, illegal. But uniform fees that are the product of an agreement are. Uniformity does, however, raise the question of whether there is an underlying or covert agreement. It may be used as circumstantial evidence unless the individual brokers can independently justify the business rationale for the fees and prices each charges. The question arises as to how independently each broker acted in making these decisions, especially since the natural tendency is to discuss general business conditions with competitors. Because price fixing can occur without a formal agreement, simply a conversation between two competitors may be all that is necessary to effect a conspiracy.

The broker must analyze economic and market conditions, transaction costs and income to determine policies and procedures for the firm, particularly the fees or prices that are charged. The broker who can justify the price charged for a service as being fair and reasonable based on this analysis, even if it happens to be the same as the competition's, should be able to defend inferences of conspiracy arising from uniform commissions.

Commission splits. An agreement between two or more brokers regarding the amount of commission that they will offer other cooperating brokers is illegal. It is permissible for two brokers to agree to fee-splitting arrangements between themselves (or between salespeople and employing brokers). They should not, however, discuss the matter in the presence of a third competitor. The illegal activity is an agreement among competitors to fix the price at which they will cooperate with *other* brokers. This agreement may also be viewed as a boycott that either excludes other brokers from the market or creates a price advantage that would not otherwise be possible.

Varying commission splits are permissible; that is, the broker can have different arrangements with each competitor. The splits are questioned only when the same firm is offered less by all of the competitors.

Group Boycotts

Group boycotts involve two or more competitors banding together to exert pressure on another competitor for the purpose of eliminating competition. It may involve withholding goods, services or patronage that are essential to the competitor's economic survival or dealing only on unfavorable terms with the competitor. Group boycotting is a *per se* offense if it is done for the express purpose of reducing or eliminating competition. The fact that the boycotted competitor is a small business whose demise would not decrease competition does not excuse the action.

Typical group boycotting cases involve practices affecting competitors who are "discount" brokers and those who offer limited service programs for a flat fee. Recently concerns have also arisen about boycotts directed toward brokers who are exclusively buyers' agents. Conduct that has an adverse effect on a competitor is an antitrust violation if it is engaged in as a conspiracy. Evidence of such schemes include certain policies governing subagency agreements, discussions at meetings of industry practitioners and sanctions of industry-group members who have cooperated with flat fee or discount brokers. One result of these schemes has been punitive or discriminatory splits imposed on a broker whose practices deviate from the local industry norm.

Case in point.   Where the policy was for brokers to pay 50 percent of the commission to cooperating brokers, they agreed to pay the discount, or flat fee, broker only 50 percent of what that discount broker would pay them. In one case, these brokers also made derogatory statements about the discount broker's practices to his sellers, which illegally interfered with the discount broker's contractual arrangement with his principals (a civil rather than an antitrust matter).

Boycotts also may be imposed on other entities besides direct competitors. For example, if brokers were to agree to withhold advertising in a newspaper until or unless the newspaper refused to accept advertisements from another broker, that could be viewed as a boycott. Because of the conspiracy this would be a *per se* violation.

Membership practices and benefits or services within industry organizations can also be problematic.

- *Membership requirements*—Organizations cannot arbitrarily or intentionally exclude people who directly compete with their members or whose views or business practices are unpopular. Restrictive membership requirements may deprive people of the ability to compete equally with the members in the marketplace.

- *Business practices*—Organizations cannot restrict members' business practices such as hours of operation, expansion of member firms or the adoption of new business strategies.

- *Benefits and services*—Those that offer a significant competitive advantage must be available to all industry practitioners in a *reasonable and nondiscriminatory manner.* Services that offer a *significant competitive or economic advantage* cannot be denied to nonmembers who request them. (This is the issue that opened multiple listing services to nonmembers of the professional associations who owned the services.)

Territorial Assignments

Agreements between competitors to divide the market geographically or by some other market segregation are *per se* violations. These destroy competition as severely as price fixing, because the purpose of segregating the market is to establish power in that marketplace.

A *per se* violation in real estate would be an agreement between competitors that defines areas in which each broker agrees to take listings or exclude cooperation on listings by the other brokers. The theory of such activity is that the broker in a specific territory becomes the power in that market area, thereby increasing the number of listings, the number of in-house sales and overall revenue for the firm. In reality, however, despite the fact that such agreements are illegal, it is unlikely that such agreements would have the desired effect unless the broker already has a significant power presence anyway. Competitors who are not parties to such agreements are not prevented from practicing in the market area, thus diluting the effect of the agreements.

Other attempts at market segregation involve agreements to separate markets on the basis of price range or types of property. Again the purpose is to establish a powerful presence by eliminating competition. This should not be confused with the practice of specializing in certain properties, such as historic properties, one-family to four-family rentals, custom-built exclusive housing and the like. Rather, the conspiracy between competitors who divide the market by assigning segments to each for the purpose of creating a powerful position is the illegal activity.

Tying Agreements

The U.S. Supreme Court defines a tying arrangement as one in which a party agrees to sell one product only on the condition that the buyer also purchases a second, different (*tied*) product. Frequently the tied product is less unique or desirable than the *tying* product. The courts have declared these agreements to be *per se* illegal, having concluded that the only purpose of a tying arrangement is to extend the market power of the tying product. Both buyers and sellers are injured by such practices. The buyer relinquishes his or her choice of tied products to gain access to the tying product.

A *per se* tying agreement must involve two distinct and separate products or services that are tied together. The seller of the tying product must have sufficient power in the market to effectively restrain trade in the tied-product market. Several practices in the real estate industry could be vulnerable to scrutiny for this kind of activity.

"List back" clauses.   "List back" clauses involve a sale that is conditioned on the buyer's relisting the property with the broker who sold the property in the first place. For example, a developer who is also a broker sells a lot in a subdivision to a builder with the condition that the builder agrees to list the improved lot with the developer's brokerage firm. The courts will examine if the developer has power in the market by considering the size of the subdivision and the number of other lots in the community to determine if this is an illegal activity.

Third-party contracts.   Third-party relocation companies may require as a condition of their purchasing a property that the seller agree to buy a property through a firm owned by the relocation company. For example, a corporate relocation firm agrees to purchase the transferee's home. The transferee must agree to purchase the home in the new location through a brokerage firm owned by the relocation company. The courts would look at the power the relocation company has over the third-party homebuying market to determine if this is an illegal activity.

Another practice that is vulnerable to antitrust scrutiny involves services provided by affiliated corporations. Today's corporate structures often include real estate brokerage, title insurance, mortgage banking and other businesses providing transaction and nontransaction-related services. Each of these is a separate corporation owned by a single holding corporation. Although the antitrust laws do not prohibit such ownership arrangements, any *requirement* for the purchase of services from one firm as a condition of the sale of goods from another could be scrutinized for antitrust violations.

Antitrust Procedures

Brokers and salespeople must learn how to conduct their affairs to ensure compliance with the antitrust laws. It is equally important to guard against any hint of inference of anticompetitive activities to ensure that activities cannot be misinterpreted if they are scrutinized. An allegation is time-consuming and costly to defend and causes adverse publicity for the industry. Affirmative compliance efforts are necessary to achieve these objectives. They may involve a commitment of time and financial resources, but the benefits far outweigh the consequences.

Sales presentations. Salespeople must learn to promote the firm and justify its fees in relationship to the services the company provides. A working knowledge of what to say and how to make a sales presentation that positively promotes these services without comparisons with the competition is essential. Disparaging the competition is not only unprofessional but also invites discussions about competitors that can be perceived to violate the antitrust laws, even if that was not intended.

Relationships with other salespeople. Salespeople have numerous occasions to associate with salespeople from other firms. The natural tendency is to discuss the real estate business, so it's important to be cautious in these conversations. Even casual remarks about fees or commissions or comments about the practices of other companies can be perceived as, or develop into, price fixing or boycotting. Any such overtures made to a salesperson by a person from another firm should be reported to management and the broker.

Broker responsibilities. Antitrust education should be an ongoing part of a company's training. Each newly recruited salesperson should participate in antitrust training, which also includes the company's antitrust policies and procedures. Follow-up training should be conducted periodically to keep the sales force and staff focused on antitrust concerns. The reputation of the company depends on the activities of those affiliated with it.

Written antitrust compliance policies should be included in the company's policy and procedures manual. These should clearly state that you will not tolerate any form of anticompetitive conduct and stipulate procedures for termination in such an event. The company also should have procedures to identify incidents that could be construed as antitrust behavior initiated by salespeople from other firms. Include steps the broker or senior management will take to intervene in those cases. The company's procedures for retention and destruction of documents should be scrutinized by legal counsel for antitrust implications.

The use of standardized listing and buyer brokerage agreements is permissible. However, they should not contain preprinted specifications as to the form of compensation (percentage or dollars), the amounts of fees or rates or predetermined listing or protection periods. Your state's licensing law may require certain disclosures in these contracts regarding negotiability of the amount of commission and term of the agency agreement.

As mentioned earlier, the broker must independently and unilaterally determine the prices and listing terms for the company. Competition in the marketplace will determine if the policies are viable. The broker must be able to defend the rationale used to determine these policies, including the length and type of listing and the formula on which compensation is based. The broker should *inform the salespeople of the rationale* used to make these decisions, so they can properly handle these discussions with consumers.

Brokers should seek the advice of legal counsel well versed in antitrust law. Counsel can assist in the preparation of policies and procedures to ensure they are in compliance with the law. It is also important that counsel periodically review the firm's practices and be involved immediately if any allegations are filed.

DISCLOSURES

The purpose of this discussion is to focus on disclosure of property conditions. In Chapter 3 we discussed agency services and the range of issues, including agency disclosures, that are currently swirling through the industry. The most advisable risk-management practice is to be a vigilant observer of developments in agency or nonagency laws and construct company policies and procedures accordingly. Now we turn our attention to property conditions, the source of an increasing amount of litigation in real estate transactions.

Increasing concerns about health and safety as well as the structural and mechanical conditions of properties have added a complex dimension to real estate transactions. Consumers are demanding complete and accurate representations of the condition of properties. Licensees and property owners are being held liable if a buyer is financially or physically harmed. Lenders are concerned about the condition of the properties they accept as collateral. Appraisers are challenged to identify a broader range of conditions that affect the value of real estate.

The modern judicial trend is to cast aside the doctrine of caveat emptor under which sellers and licensees were required only to respond truthfully to any questions posed by a buyer. They had no obligation to disclose any other adverse factors about a property. The trend today requires the *disclosure of any known defects* in the property, even if a buyer does not inquire about them. Silence creates liability. The courts continue to redefine obligations by holding the sellers and licensees *accountable for erroneous representations*, even if they are unintentional. Licensees are responsible for *diligently searching for any additional information that is pertinent to the transaction.* The solution? Be aware of the liability, make proper disclosures and guide consumers to specialists who can provide the technical information they need.

Fraud is an *intentional* deceptive act or statement with which one person attempts to gain an unfair advantage over another. It may be either a *misstatement* or *silence* about a defect. A fraudulent statement is made with the intention to deceive or is made without knowledge of whether it is truthful. A statement such as, "The house is in perfect condition," could be fraudulent if there is no knowledge to support or justify this comment. A person who relies on a fraudulent act or statement is subsequently injured.

Misrepresentations are false statements or concealment of a *material fact*, that is, information deemed to be pertinent to a decision. Misrepresentations may be motivated by an attempt to deceive, though unlike fraud, they are limited to facts that are material to a transaction. If it is determined that the misrepresentation is not material, there is no consequence of the act and therefore, no injury. State laws and court decisions continue to define the information that is considered to be material in a transaction.

A misrepresentation may be negligent, such as when a person fails to exercise reasonable care and diligence in obtaining or communicating accurate information. Although a licensee may rely on representations by a seller, if there is *reason to know or suspect* that the information is not true, the licensee could be guilty of negligent misrepresentation for failing to verify such information.

Charges of negligence also can arise out of the way a licensee *should* have acted to prevent a party from being injured, even though there were no specific representations about the property condition. Most states have consumer protection laws that regulate unfair and deceptive practices. Negligence is established by comparing the conduct with a standard commensurate with the level of service that should be provided by a competent professional. This is the area that can create the greatest liability.

A source of debate involves whether a statement is a fact or an opinion. A statement by a person who is licensed and hired to give advice could be construed as a fact rather than an opinion. A salesperson's statement such as "I believe the zoning ordinance permits your proposed use" may be claimed to be only an opinion. But because it is made by a licensee, who is expected to have superior knowledge, a buyer could interpret this statement to be factual, even though the salesperson may not have any knowledge of its truth or accuracy. Statements of opinion are not generally the basis for findings of fraud or misrepresentation. However, a licensee cannot anticipate whether the customer or client will rely on the statement to be opinion or fact. Every effort must be made to ensure that the comment is properly interpreted.

Property Defects

Any portion of a building or other improvement on the land is likely to have some defects. "Perfect" doesn't exist, even if a building is newly constructed. In addition to leaky roofs and wet basements, any structural, mechanical or sanitary system as well as the land itself may be the object of an investigation and disclosure.

The best way to respond to a consumer's quest for accurate information and the property owners' and your desire to minimize liability is to use disclosure forms. In fact, your state law probably requires the seller to complete such a form. Some people may argue that these requirements make properties more difficult to market or create additional liability for sellers. Consider though that they are more likely to protect consumers from false or incomplete information. By completing these disclosure forms, sellers are protected from accusations that they failed to disclose or be forthright about information they know about the property. Sellers must be cautioned to be accurate, however, so that they do not create additional liability for themselves. The honesty and openness of the seller and licensee also create a positive atmosphere in which a sale can proceed to closing.

A licensee who makes representations about a property's condition should make it very clear that they are based on the seller's disclosures. Otherwise, the *licensee* could be liable if they are inaccurate. Remember that a licensee can rely only on the seller's representations, *provided there are no indications* that a defect might exist that the licensee could have detected.

Case in point.   The failure to disclose can pose greater risk than just financial loss. For example, a Burlington, Vermont, businessman was convicted on October 10, 1992, of involuntary manslaughter as a result of the death of three people who inhaled carbon monoxide fumes from a gas-fired heater used to de-ice a driveway. According to testimony, the seller knew but did not disclose that the heater was faulty when he sold the house in 1988, nor was it listed as a repair that had been made to the property. The court determined that the seller had an obligation to disclose that the heater was faulty and also stated that this case sends a clear message that this type of behavior can result in criminal prosecution.

Professional Inspections

Another way to satisfy the buyer's quest for accurate information and protect the company and the licensees is by using professional inspectors. Outside experts are useful at several points in a transaction. If a seller is unsure about a representation that should be made in a disclosure form, a report from a roofer or contractor, for example, can help the seller make an informed disclosure. It is customary in some markets to conduct inspections before preparing an offer to purchase. In other areas these may be included as a condition or contingency in the sales contract.

In any case, it is important that buyers at least be informed about the various kinds of professional inspections that are available. It is common to conduct inspections of the structural integrity of the building, of the mechanical and sewage systems and water supplies and for wood-boring insects and environmental hazards. A procedure to document that the consumer was informed about these opportunities insulates you from allegations that "nobody told me." Then it is the buyer's choice whether to take advantage of the inspections. In some parts of the country brokerage companies make home warranty programs available to further protect the consumer.

Earlier we mentioned the practice of recommending a particular individual to conduct an inspection and the liability that could arise from this practice. Although there are conflicting interpretations as the courts scrutinize the circumstances of individual cases, there are cases in which a licensee has been held liable for the accuracy or competency of an inspector. It's safest to provide a list of resources from which a buyer can select an inspector. Be sure that the salesperson does not influence the inspection in any way. The advantage of using professional inspectors, in addition to their expertise, is that they are impartial third parties who should have no interest in the transaction or the property.

Stigmatized Properties

Stigmatized properties are those that people consider to be "psychologically impacted." For the most part, these are properties in which certain events have occurred that individuals may find offensive or that provoke emotional reactions. These include such events as a suicide, a murder or other felony, paranormal activities (ghosts), a lingering illness or death. Fear of contracting diseases could stimulate psychological reactions to properties.

In some parts of the country there are statutory or case laws that define certain events as material to a purchaser's decision and that therefore must be disclosed. In other states there is no such guidance for dealing with stigmatized properties. These can be difficult properties to handle because there's little way to know in advance what a buyer may claim to be a material fact that should have been disclosed. Unless there is guidance in your state's laws about stigmatized properties, the best advice is to consult a lawyer for guidance about how to handle these situations.

Do not allow public misunderstanding and fears to violate the rights of individuals with AIDS. These people are protected by the federal fair housing laws.

ENVIRONMENTAL CONDITIONS

Environmental issues have become an important factor in real estate transactions. Consumers are becoming more health- and safety-conscious and therefore, demanding that their surroundings be free of hazardous substances. An increasing number of environmental hazards are identified each year, adding to the number of property conditions that affect our transactions. The government has responded by implementing additional laws and regulations that affect the use of real property. The presence of hazardous substances has a significant impact on a property's value and often requires extensive expenditures for removal or abatement.

Although it's important to ensure the health and safety of the user of a property, the burden for disclosure and/or elimination of hazards seems to arise at the time the ownership transfers. Health issues have become real estate issues. It is extremely important not only to make proper disclosures but also to see that prospective purchasers get authoritative information to make informed decisions. The following are some of the environmental issues that may affect your transactions.

Asbestos

Asbestos is a mineral that was widely used in building materials prior to the 1970s because of its insulating and fire-retardant properties. According to some estimates, asbestos is found in one of every five public buildings in the country today. In the majority of cases, it is harmless. Only when the asbestos-containing material ages and begins to deteriorate or is disturbed by remodeling are fibers likely to become airborne. They can cause a variety of respiratory diseases when they are inhaled. As the level of contamination reaches dangerous levels, the buildings can become difficult to sell, lease, finance or insure.

Asbestos contamination is most prevalent in public and commercial buildings, including schools. But it also can be found in older single-family homes. Asbestos was used to cover pipes, ducts and heating and hot water units; in floor tile and exterior siding; and in roofing products. Though it may be easy to identify asbestos wrap around heating and water pipes, it may be more difficult to identify elsewhere.

Procedures.   Anyone who is involved with public, commercial and apartment buildings should be familiar with the Asbestos Hazard Emergency Response Act and should consult the Occupational Safety and Health Administration (OSHA) and local ordinances for guidance. Asbestos is costly to remove, and frequently the structure is further contaminated in the process. Encapsulation of disintegrating asbestos may be a preferable remedy. Tests can determine the level of airborne asbestos to provide accurate disclosure in a sales transaction. A more thorough analysis of a building can be performed by an environmental engineer.

Lead

For many years lead was used as a pigment and drying agent in alkyd oil-based paint. The Department of Housing and Urban Development (HUD) estimates that lead is present in about 75 percent of all private housing built before 1978. It may be on any interior or exterior surface, particularly doors, windows and other woodwork. Lead is estimated to be present in 57 million homes, ranging from low-income apartments to million-dollar mansions.

Elevated levels of lead in the body can damage the brain, kidneys, nervous system and red blood cells. Poisoning occurs when the body is exposed to high amounts of lead that it is not capable of eliminating. The degree of harm is related to the amount of exposure and the age at which a person is exposed. In 1991 the Centers for Disease Control and Prevention lowered the threshold at which children are considered to have lead poisoning. One estimate is that as many as one in six children may have dangerously high amounts of lead in their blood.

There is a common misconception that a person must ingest paint chips to incur lead poisoning. Though infants and toddlers will eat most anything that looks attractive, lead can be ingested from a variety of other sources. The water supply can be contaminated from lead in pipes and solder that were permitted in old building codes. Lead particles from paint and varnishes and even gasoline emissions can become airborne, contaminating the air the occupants breathe.

Procedures. Anyone involved in the sale, management, financing or appraisal of properties constructed before 1978, which is the time before lead-based paint was banned, or with any properties where lead contamination is present must be aware of this problem. There is considerable controversy about practical approaches for handling the presence of lead paint. Some suggest that it should be removed. Others suggest that it should be encapsulated rather than increasing the contamination or exposure that could result during removal. Still others advocate testing to determine the amount of lead to which occupants are exposed and then disclosing the results of these tests to prospective owners or residents.

Congress enacted the Residential Lead-Based Paint Hazard Reduction Act in 1992. Section 1018 of Title X sets forth procedures for disclosing to buyers and tenants the presence of lead-based paint in residential properties built before 1978. The general provisions of the law require that the seller/landlord or the seller/landlord agent

- distribute a federal lead hazard pamphlet;

- disclose any information known to the seller or agent concerning lead-based paint and/or lead-based paint hazards in the housing; and

- provide a 10-day, or mutually agreeable, period of time for a lead paint assessment or inspection to be conducted before the purchaser is obligated to perform on the sales contract. This is not a mandatory testing or abatement requirement, but rather gives the prospective purchaser the option to have a test.

Sales contracts on covered properties must contain a standard lead warning statement, in large type and on a separate sheet of paper, that purchasers must sign. The statement indicates that they have been given the pamphlet, have read and understood the warning statement and have been given the opportunity to have the property tested for lead hazards. Violations can subject the seller or the agent to federal criminal and civil penalties and treble damages in civil lawsuits. You may also have state laws or local ordinances that govern lead-based paint in the sale or lease of properties.

Enforcement.   Brokers should be aware that a program to enforce the provisions of the lead-based paint disclosure law is underway in some parts of the country, especially in large urban areas where lead-based paint hazards are most likely to be present. Federal inspectors are visiting real estate companies, unannounced, to review their records to determine that firms are following the requirements of the law. Brokers should be sure they have good record-keeping procedures so that they can readily document their compliance.

The Environmental Protection Agency has determined that inspections are an effective and important enforcement tool. Although neither the federal regulations nor the lead-based paint statute compel compliance with these inspections, the agency is expecting voluntary cooperation. Refusal, however, can be followed by a written request or even a subpoena. The agency is also monitoring complaints about certain activities of property owners and real estate companies. In addition HUD has the authority to enforce the disclosure regulations, though it is concentrating on rentals rather than sales.

PCBs

Polychlorinated biphenyls (PCBs) were used in the manufacture of electrical products (such as transformers, switches and voltage regulators), paints, adhesives, caulking materials and hydraulic fluids. PCBs can cause birth defects, cancer and other diseases. Although they have not been used since 1977, PCBs pose a risk because many of the products are still in use. Although commercial and industrial sites are most vulnerable to PCB contamination, many homeowners are becoming increasingly concerned about PCBs in electrical transformers and transmission towers in their neighborhoods.

Procedures. An environmental engineer or consultant can assess the property and recommend cleanup procedures if necessary. It may be advisable to replace old electrical equipment. Unfortunately, contamination, particularly after electrical equipment fires, is very costly to remedy.

Radon

Radon is a radioactive gas that is produced by the natural decay of other radioactive substances. Although it can occur anywhere, some areas are known to have abnormally high amounts of radon. If it dissipates into the atmosphere, it is not likely to cause harm. However, when it infiltrates buildings and is trapped in high concentrations, it can cause health problems. Radon can enter a structure through the basement, foundation or crawl spaces and has also been found in natural gas and water supplies. There are differences of opinion as to minimum safe levels of exposure. But there is evidence that radon may contribute to lung cancer, particularly in children, individuals who smoke and people who spend a considerable amount of time in buildings that are not well ventilated.

Procedures.   Because radon is odorless and tasteless, it is impossible to detect without testing. Tests should be conducted carefully to ensure that the results are accurate. Radon levels will vary, depending on the amount of fresh air that circulates through a house, the weather conditions and the time of year. It is relatively easy to reduce radon levels by installing ventilation systems or exhaust fans.

Urea Formaldehyde

Urea formaldehyde was first used in building materials in the 1970s, particularly in insulation. Urea formaldehyde foam insulation (UFFI) has received a considerable amount of adverse publicity, prompting buyers to be concerned when purchasing properties in which it was installed. Gases leach out of the insulation as it hardens and become trapped in the interior of a building. In 1982 the Consumer Product Safety Commission banned its use for insulation in housing. The ban was reduced to a warning after the courts determined that there was not sufficient evidence to support the extreme action of banning its use. There is scientific evidence that it causes cancer in animals, though the evidence of its effect on humans is inconclusive.

Formaldehyde is a common environmental allergen, causing respiratory problems and eye and skin irritations in some people. Because it is prevalent in a number of other building products and fixtures, consumers are becoming increasingly wary of its presence, particularly if they are sensitive to formaldehyde.

Procedures.   Tests can be conducted to determine the level of formaldehyde gas in a house. However, again, care should be exercised to ensure that the results of the tests are accurate and that the source of the gas is properly identified. It could emanate from carpeting, wall coverings, wood products (including furniture) and upholstery or insulation. If a sales contract is conditioned on a test for formaldehyde, it should be properly worded to identify the purpose of the test, such as to determine the presence of the insulation or other source of formaldehyde.

Underground Storage Tanks

There are approximately 3 million to 5 million underground storage tanks in the United States today. No one knows how many are leaking hazardous substances into the environment. They can contaminate not only the soil where they are located but also adjacent parcels of land and groundwater. Underground storage tanks are commonly found on sites where petroleum products are used or where gas stations and auto repair shops were located. There are a number of other commercial and industrial establishments where they could be found, including printing and chemical plants, wood treatment plants, paper mills, paint manufacturers, dry cleaners and food-processing plants. In residential areas, they were used to store heating oil. Underground tanks can sometimes be detected by fill pipes, vent lines, stained soil and fumes or odors.

The removal of leaking tanks and the surrounding contaminated soil, which must be disposed of in a hazardous waste facility, is quite costly. Recent federal laws impose very strict requirements on the owners of land where underground storage tanks are located to detect and correct leaks in an effort to protect the groundwater. The 1984 amendment to the Resource Conservation and Recovery Act (RCRA) established a program called Leaking Underground Storage Tanks. This program established regulations for installation, maintenance, monitoring for leaks and record-keeping procedures. It also requires that landowners have sufficient financial resources to cover damages resulting from leaks.

Procedures. Buyers and lenders are concerned about any undue financial burden for complying with federal cleanup requirements, which affect not only the property that is the source of the contamination, but also any affected adjacent property. Chemical tests can be obtained to determine the presence of contaminated soil before a purchase or as a condition for a mortgage loan.

Other Hazardous Conditions

Industrial sites, landfills and toxic waste sites, and even vacant land, can pose significant problems in real estate transactions. The Comprehensive Environmental Response Compensation and Liability Act (CERCLA) imposes responsibilities on owners, lenders, occupants and operators for correcting environmental problems on a property. The Superfund Amendments and Reauthorization Act of 1986 (SARA) establishes funds to clean hazardous waste sites and respond to spills and releases on a property. The Superfund statutes establish a means for identifying parties who are liable for cleanup as well as provide for reimbursement by the parties who are ultimately responsible for the cleanup costs.

The sweeping approach under the Superfund creates potential liability for current and past owners and operators of a hazardous substance facility and persons who transport or arrange for treatment or disposal of hazardous substances. The statutes define strict liability without regard for who is at fault for any spills, leaks, discharges or dumping into the environment. Numerous regulations and licensing and notification requirements also are enforced by the Environmental Protection Agency, which is responsible for enforcing CERCLA and SARA as well as RCRA. Compliance with the numerous regulations as well as the financial responsibility for cleanup can be quite burdensome.

Procedures.   Because of the broad liability under these laws, anyone who considers selling, buying, leasing, managing or lending money on a property that could contain hazardous substances is affected by these laws. Environmental screenings should be done to identify potential problems. Experts are used to conduct a Phase I audit of the property to investigate the site, public records and surrounding properties and, if necessary, identify corrective or remediation efforts that are necessary.

FAIR HOUSING LAWS

The purpose of the fair housing laws is to ensure that people in the protected classes as defined by these laws have the same rights as all other persons to access property of their choice within their ability to pay. The federal Fair Housing Act as it stands today defines the protected classes to include *race, color, religion, sex, handicap, familial status and national origin*. In addition, state and local laws may define protections and practices that are more comprehensive than the federal laws.

Real estate practitioners must do their part in fostering an open housing market in accordance with the fair housing laws. Meeting this challenge means being meticulous in complying with the laws and ensuring that no action can be construed as being discriminatory. Illegal discrimination is more than racial discrimination—it affects all people in the protected classes. Society has become increasingly intolerant of discrimination as demonstrated by an increase in legislative activity and enforcement efforts. Real estate practitioners are conspicuous in the community which means that any activity that creates the appearance of illegal discrimination jeopardizes the reputation of the industry as well as rights of the people the laws intend to protect.

Customers and clients need to be educated. They must understand that salespeople cannot select or guide them to properties or neighborhoods based on the racial, ethnic or religious composition of a neighborhood. They also must understand that the fair housing laws do not apply only to licensees. Remember that no one is exempt from the laws, including the owner of a property, when a licensee is involved in the transaction.

Prohibited Practices

The federal laws define a number of practices that are discriminatory and are therefore prohibited. The following explains those activities.

Refusal to sell, rent, lease, finance or negotiate.   The purpose of the laws is to enable people to acquire real estate they desire; therefore, it is *their* right to choose the property they rent or purchase. Any action by which others, including the owner, the landlord or the real estate salesperson, limit their choices is discriminatory. This is otherwise known as **steering.** Some activities are more subtle than merely refusing to sell or lease a property to a person. Discriminatory tactics that have the effect of restricting the availability include

- imposing burdensome conditions on a purchase or lease;

- using delaying tactics;

- manipulating waiting lists;

- reluctantly providing assistance;

- refusing to accept or consider an offer;

- coding applications and qualifying forms by protected class; or

- identifying voice and speech characteristics of a prospective purchaser or tenant for the purpose of restricting access to a property or services.

Differentiation in terms or conditions or provision of services.   These should be equal for all people in similar circumstances or under similar conditions, regardless of whether they are or are not in the protected classes. While the practices do not have to be the same for everyone, they must be the same in similar situations. The services that are provided for a first-time home buyer, for example, may be different from those rendered to a more experienced purchaser. These are not similar situations, so it is appropriate to handle them differently.

However, the services cannot be different for the first-time home buyer in a protected class versus another first-time home buyer.

Offering a unit in only a selected building or on only selected floors of a building to a family with children or a person with a handicap, when units are available elsewhere, are also examples of discrimination.

Any of the following could have the effect of being discriminatory:

- Differences in the quality or timeliness of service, sale or rental price, date of availability, amount of security deposit or qualification criteria for purchase, lease or financing

- Selective or inconsistent use of applications or qualifying forms

- Failing to provide or delaying maintenance or repairs

- Limiting privileges or use of facilities on a property

Printing, publishing or circulating discriminatory statements or advertisements.   Statements or advertisements may not indicate any preference, limitation or discrimination. Promotion of property or services through any print or electronic media must be done in such a manner as to ensure that they are equally available to everyone.

Targeting certain populations by advertising in selected media, such as an ethnic newspaper or a radio or TV station targeted to a minority audience, is discriminatory unless promotion is also made to the general population through general circulation. Otherwise the effect could be to limit the choices of prospective property seekers or to restrict services to certain populations.

Pictorial representations of customers or residents through the use of human models in print or electronic media must include a cross section of the population to indicate that the real estate and services are available to everyone.

Language that makes reference to the protected classes or indicates a preference or limitation is discriminatory. There are certain words, as we indicated in Chapter 9, that should not be used in advertising.

Representing that a property is unavailable.   Reprsenting that a property is not available when in fact it is effectively limits people's choices or discourages them by "chilling their interest." Discriminatory activity that would have this effect includes

- assigning a person to a floor or a building to the exclusion of other property that is available;

- representing that a property is sold or rented or refusing to accept an offer; and

- suggesting that a person would not be comfortable in an area or compatible with existing residents.

Inducing or attempting to induce for profit.   These activities are commonly known as *blockbusting* or *panic selling* and were described in Chapter 9.

Discrimination in financing.   Financing must be available to all people under the same terms and conditions. Financial information must be provided with the same diligence for everyone, and application procedures and standards must be uniformly applied. There is nothing illegal about establishing procedures that are justified by business necessity relating to the financial security of the transaction or protecting against default. But establishing different down payment requirements or credit qualifications for people in the protected classes, for example, is illegal. Secondary mortgage market activities that involve residential loans also cannot be discriminatory.

Interference, coercion or intimidation.   Enjoyment   of the rights granted under the fair housing laws is protected against interference, coercion or intimidation. As an example, a group of African American tenants was threatened with eviction because of loud noise and raucous behavior. In fact, they were not home at the times the activity is supposed to have occurred. These charges were alleged to be a way to force the minority tenants out of the property. The tenants prevailed and were awarded a settlement.

Intent and Effect

Notice that there were references above to activity that could have the effect of being discriminatory. An individual may *intend* to discriminate by such overt activities as refusing to show a property or inflating the amount of rent to a person in a protected class. But some activities can have the *effect* of discriminating even though no discrimination is intended.

Certain actions may not have any apparent relationship to a protected class, but the effect of the action may. The effect is known under legal doctrine as **disparate impact**. The fact that an action has a significant impact on people in a protected class determines that the action is discriminatory. Certain occupancy requirements, zoning ordinances or answers to questions about the composition of the neighborhood are examples of activities that could have this effect. Actions, practices and policies should be scrutinized for effect to ensure that they do not discriminate.

Fair Housing Compliance

As indicated earlier, the real estate industry is conspicuous in the arena of fair housing by virtue of the services it provides to buyers and sellers. It is not uncommon for advocacy groups in the community to scrutinize the activities of brokerage companies in an attempt to ferret out sources of discrimination. In Chapter 8, we mentioned the importance of establishing a fair housing policy for the company, illustrating the commitment of the organization to furthering equal opportunity in housing. But there should also be procedures to convert the policy into action.

Using the discriminatory activities that are listed above, the text of the federal law and any state and local laws that affect your practices, design your office procedures to help ensure equal professional service. They should address

- listings and methods for handling situations that commonly arise with sellers;

- the use of lists of properties for sale or rent and ways to ensure that accurate and uniform information is provided to the public;

- qualifying procedures to ensure uniform treatment of prospective purchasers and tenants;

- procedures for showing properties and holding open houses, including situations that commonly arise in these activities;

- presentation and negotiation of offers and methods for handling questions and other situations that commonly arise;

- marketing and advertising guidelines;

- procedures for handling compromising situations and suspected discrimination; and

- record-keeping procedures.

As with any procedures the company establishes, fair housing procedures are of little value unless they are followed and periodically reinforced. Fair housing training and the company's policies and procedures should be included in orientation programs, as well as in ongoing sales training programs. Some firms designate a person in the company to act as its fair housing officer. This person could be responsible for training and monitoring the company's compliance with its fair housing policy and procedures and be a resource for the organization and the salespeople. Tracking recent cases and developments in the law would be included in this person's responsibilities. The goal of the company's fair housing compliance program should be to ensure that equal opportunity is a routine part of the quality services the company provides.

AMERICANS WITH DISABILITIES ACT

The federal government estimates that more than 43 million people in this country have a handicap or disability. Because this segment of our population historically has been isolated and segregated from the rest of society, laws at the federal, state and local levels have been adopted to protect people with disabilities from discrimination.

The Americans with Disabilities Act (ADA), which was adopted in 1990, intends to enable people with disabilities to become part of the economic and social mainstream of society. This law seeks to "open doors" both literally and figuratively to eliminate the isolation and restricted access that people with disabilities encounter, by addressing a wide variety of conditions that have prevented this from happening in the past. Employment practices (Title I) and access to goods, services, facilities and accommodations (Title III) are two provisions of the law that are most likely to affect real estate companies.

People who are covered by this law are defined as one *who has* or *has a record of* a physical or mental impairment that substantially limits one or more major life activities. Review the law (see the Bibliography for legislative reference) for a complete definition of a disability in all of its various applications.

Providing Real Estate Services

According to ADA anyone who provides goods and services to the public must do so in ways that enable people with disabilities to access them. Because real estate companies provide services, they must be sure that people with disabilities not only can access those services, but also are accommodated throughout the transaction.

As was mentioned in Chapter 6, regardless of whether the company owns or leases, the office must be accessible to people with disabilities. Or there must be accommodations to enable these people to access the broker's services. Structural barriers pose the greatest challenge. Accessibility can be accomplished by either modifying the existing premises or providing other accommodations to ensure equal enjoyment of the services. The laws provide that if it is an undue hardship to make certain structural alterations, acceptable alternatives exist.

Open houses and new construction sites are also places from which a broker conducts business and offers services. It would be ideal if all of these sites were readily accessible. None of the laws, however, requires that all single-family houses be readily accessible and usable. If a model home, for example, is not readily accessible, videotapes or slide presentations may be a reasonable alternative for a person whose mobility precludes viewing an entire property.

Brokers and salespeople must be prepared to accommodate the needs of people with disabilities in a number of other situations as well. Consider the following as you plan ways to deliver your services and develop your company's policies and procedures.

Communications with people who are deaf or hearing-impaired.   In Chapter 6 we discussed communications systems and the way these systems can be designed to accommodate people who are deaf or hearing-impaired or who have speech disabilities. We cannot initiate an inquiry about a person's disability or be selective in our offers of assistance. Salespeople must be instructed about the proper ways to encourage requests for accommodations a person may need. Then they need resources available with which to respond to those requests.

Face-to-face communications with people who are deaf or hearing-impaired can be facilitated in several ways. These normally involve an interpreter skilled in a sign language or finger spelling. Because not all people who are deaf, hearing-impaired or without speech use the same kind of interpreter to communicate, determine what accommodations are necessary. Salespeople should be advised that a professional interpreter, rather than a family member or other individual who may be biased, is best to ensure accurate communication.

Communicating with people who are blind or have vision loss.   As was mentioned in Chapter 6, these people need to be able to not only evaluate the property, but also to understand the written documents we use. They rely on auditory and tactile communications. There are numerous options available, particularly because of electronic technology. Large-print or raised-print publications can be easily provided with today's computer and copier technology. Translation of documents into Braille is also easier and quicker because of computers. Because many people with vision loss rely on auditory assistance, audiocassettes provide a convenient way for people to review contracts and other materials before signing them.

People with mental disabilities. Real estate practitioners must be careful not to make assumptions about whether a person is able to comprehend or be attentive to his or her business decisions. Normally a person with a mental disability will specify what accommodations are preferred. It may be a request to provide explanations in simple terms or a request to review documents independently and in privacy at his or her own home.

Public functions. Real estate companies frequently conduct seminars and other types of programs for the public. Licensees, organizations and educational providers who conduct these meetings, conventions, conferences or classes must ensure that people with disabilities can not only access but also be accommodated in these programs, including programs that are conducted for real estate practitioners.

When selecting the facility for these gatherings, be sure that it is accessible. The person or group that is sponsoring the function can be held liable even if a public facility, such as a hotel, convention or conference center, is not in compliance with all applicable laws.

People with disabilities should be able to participate in the program to the fullest possible extent in an integrated setting rather than being segregated from other participants. All participants should be able to interact with one another and take advantage of the scheduled events and exhibits. Be sure that restroom facilities and sleeping facilities are accessible and that seating for people in wheelchairs is available. Any use of separate facilities or programs should be at the option of the person with a disability.

Providing accommodations for people with disabilities includes providing auxiliary aids that they request. These may include listening devices, interpreters or signers and large-print or Braille material. The aids must be available at no additional cost to the person with the disability unless doing so poses an undue financial burden or a fundamental alteration in the nature of the goods or services. The person with the disability should request the kind of auxiliary aid that is suitable. The laws do not require that we provide personal items such as wheelchairs or individually prescribed hearing aids or eyeglasses.

Registration procedures should offer a person with a disability the opportunity to request any aids or other accommodations that are needed. This can be done simply with a printed request on the registration form. If you plan to accept walk-in registrations, there should be a notice on the registration form that every effort will be made to accommodate a need, although this cannot be guaranteed without prior notice. It is impossible to anticipate what a person may need, and it is a financial burden to have all kinds of aids available at all times.

The more sensitive you become to the needs of people with disabilities, the easier it will be to identify ways to incorporate accommodations into a program. When choosing videotaped programs or training materials, for example, investigate whether a closed caption version is available.

People First

One of the most helpful guides about ways to serve people with disabilities, that can be incorporated in a policy and procedures manual, is provided in this "people first" discussion. Put people first, not their disabilities by learning to see them as individuals with dignity and capabilities, rather than as physical or mental conditions. Positive or negative attitudes are frequently revealed in language. Well-chosen words can communicate powerful messages about a company's services.

- *Avoid referring to or focusing on a disability.* There are very few circumstances in which it is necessary to refer to a disability. The term *disability* is not used as an adjective before—but always after—person, such as a "person with a disability," not "a disabled person." Use of the terms *able-bodied, normal* or *healthy* to refer to people without disabilities is just as offensive as referring to a blind, crippled or handicapped person.

- *Do not sensationalize a disability.* A person is not a "victim of," "afflicted with" or "suffering from" a disability. Nor is the person a "patient," a "case" or an "invalid." In fact, the majority of people with disabilities are not sick, nor are they necessarily remarkable. This implies that it is unusual for people with disabilities to have talents or skills.

- *Avoid using the word* special. This serves only to segregate rather than integrate people with disabilities. Refer to an "accessible" entrance or lift-equipped buses, rather than a "special" entrance or "special" transportation.

- *Do not patronize.* People with disabilities should be addressed personally in conversation rather than through a third party. A real estate salesperson, for example, should ask the person in a wheelchair what kind of housing would be suitable, rather than ask the individual who may be accompanying this person.

- *Avoid overfamiliarity.* A person with a disability deserves the same courtesy of reference as a person without a disability. If a salesperson, for example, normally addresses parties as Mr. or Mrs., the salesperson should address a person with a disability in the same manner.

Architectural Barriers

Title III of ADA provides comprehensive rules about architectural barriers and accessible design features that should be reviewed when selecting an office and planning the way the company will provide services. Because a number of accessibility guidelines are published by various government entities, there is no one standard for architectural design. The Americans with Disabilities Act Accessibility Guidelines for buildings and facilities (ADAAG) are the guidelines most applicable for commercial property, unless a stricter standard for a specific property is required by a separate law. Although the laws intend to eliminate existing barriers, accessible design features will become the norm rather than the exception.

ADAAG includes specifications for

- parking and passenger loading zones;
- curb ramps;
- stairs, elevators and doors;
- drinking fountains and water coolers;
- alarms and detectable warnings;
- water closets, toilet stalls and urinals;
- signage and telephones;
- medical care facilities;
- business and retail establishments, including grocery checkout aisles;
- libraries; and
- transient lodgings (hotels, motels).

Existing facilities. The laws require that barriers be removed to maximize accessibility if it is *readily achievable* to do so. Readily achievable means that the removal of architectural or communications barriers can be accomplished *with little difficulty or expense.* Although the specific alterations that are readily achievable are determined on a case-by-case basis, the *nature of the alteration, available financial resources* and the *impact of the alteration on the overall operation* of the facility are considered. Retrofitting a building to install an elevator, for example, may not be readily achievable in many cases.

Typical *readily achievable* items that are cited in ADAAG, in addition to those already mentioned, include

- repositioning telephones;
- adding raised markings on elevator control buttons;
- installing offset hinges to widen doors;
- eliminating turnstiles or providing an alternative accessible path;

- installing accessible hardware. (Inappropriate hardware can be identified by the "closed fist test." Can you operate the door or mechanism with a closed fist?);

- insulating lavatory pipes under sinks to prevent burns;

- installing a full-length mirror in a rest room;

- repositioning the paper-towel dispenser in a rest room;

- installing an accessible paper-cup dispenser at an existing inaccessible water fountain; and

- removing high-pile, low-density carpeting.

Noncompliance with ADA creates liability for the owner of the building as well as for the agent of the owner, particularly the property manager. A manager who is authorized by the owner to make decisions affecting the accessibility of a building is independently bound. It is important to have a building assessed to determine if it complies with ADA. This normally is done by having someone who is knowledgeable about the requirements conduct an audit of the property. Although there are no certified ADA auditors, there are a number of resources from which to obtain technical assistance, including architects who specialize in ADA and organizations representing people with disabilities.

Once the audit is completed, a plan can be developed to bring a building into compliance. The removal of barriers does not need to be done all at once. Adopting a long-range plan demonstrates a good-faith effort to comply with the law. ADA recommends certain priorities that should be addressed first, however.

Providing *reasonable accommodations* is an alternative to the removal of a barrier that may be too costly. Providing personal assistance for removing items from inaccessible shelves, installing a call button at a door and providing at-home services (at no extra charge) are examples. Previously we mentioned other reasonable accommodations, such as providing videotapes of model homes.

New construction.   The requirements for accessibility are more strict for new construction than for existing properties.

New commercial property must be designed to be *readily accessible and usable* as defined in ADAAG, to the extent that this is not structurally impractical. It is estimated that the cost of incorporating accessibility features in new construction normally amounts to less than one percent of the overall construction cost. It is preferable to ensure that a building and its site meet the legal requirements for accessibility before starting construction. Any adjustments that may be necessary are less costly at this stage.

ADAAG acknowledges certain reasonable considerations for accessibility in new construction. For example, elevators are generally not required in facilities of less than 3 stories or with fewer than 3,000 square feet per floor, unless the building is a shopping mall, a professional office for a health care provider or a transit station or terminal. It would be structurally impractical to make a building in a marshy area that has to be constructed on stilts readily accessible. In this case providing other reasonable accommodations would be satisfactory.

ADAAG contains general design standards for both the building and the site. Elements such as parking, accessible routes, ramps, stairs, elevators, doors, entrances, drinking fountains, bathrooms, controls and operating mechanisms, storage areas, alarms, signage, telephones, fixed seating areas, assembly areas, automated teller machines and dressing rooms are addressed.

Employment

In Chapter 10 when we discussed employment practices we mentioned a number of laws (including ADA) that must be considered. Use the following discussion as a guide when developing those practices. ADA does not expect preferential treatment or preference for people with disabilities over other applicants or employees, but it does intend to protect against discrimination. Title I requires employers with 15 or more employees to adopt nondiscriminatory employment practices. Be sure to consult your state's laws; they may be more restrictive and may also clarify protections for *independent contractors*.

Covered employees are people with disabilities who meet the legitimate skill, experience, education or other requirements of an employment position. The job applicant or employee may be able to perform the essential functions of the job with or without any accommodations by the employer. The law requires that if an employee needs accommodations to perform these functions, the employer is obligated to make these provisions as long as doing so does not impose an undue hardship on the operation of the business. An individual who has a minor, nonchronic condition of short duration, such as a sprain, infection or broken limb, would not be covered.

Employees who are associated with a person with a disability also are protected from discrimination. This intends to protect against actions based on bias or misinformation about a disability and unfounded assumptions that the relationship would affect the employees' performance. For example, an employee with a spouse who has a disability cannot be denied employment because of an assumption that the employee would need excessive leave to care for the spouse. Likewise, an employee who is involved in community service activities, such as volunteering to help people with AIDS, is protected from discrimination.

The laws intend to prevent employers from basing hiring and employment decisions on assumptions about the effects of a disability. They prohibit discrimination in all employment practices, including job application procedures, hiring, firing, advancement, compensation, training and other privileges of employment. They also apply to employment-related activities such as recruitment, advertising, tenure, layoff, leave and fringe benefits. Be sure that anyone who is responsible for employment decisions is familiar with the following procedures.

- By identifying the functions of a job and distinguishing between essential and nonessential functions, the employer and the prospective employee can determine whether the qualifications of the employee suit the requirements of the job.

- An employer must institute application and screening procedures that are related solely to the ability of the person to perform according to the job description.

Employers are permitted to establish qualification procedures that exclude people who pose a direct threat to the health and safety of others. But these determinations must be based on objective and supportable evidence that there is a genuine risk that substantial harm could occur in the workplace.

- The employer cannot ask if a job applicant has a disability, but is permitted to ask if the applicant can perform the duties of the job as they have been described. The person with the disability is responsible for informing the employer of the disability and requesting any accommodations that would be necessary.

- A specific job description that a prospective employee and broker can review will keep the interview on track, focusing on the job rather than on issues that can violate the law.

- Application forms should not contain questions relating to disabilities. Aptitude tests and other screening procedures should relate to the essential functions of the job.

- Medical exams can be required only after an offer of employment is made and if they are customary for all new hires in the same job category. Drug tests are not considered medical examinations. Because the laws do not consider people who currently use illegal drugs to be qualified individuals with a disability, employers can make decisions based on the results of the tests.

Reasonable Accommodations

Reasonable accommodations must be provided in the workplace to enable a person with a disability to perform job-related functions for which he or she is qualified. These must be provided in all services, programs and activities related to employment, including the nonwork facilities such as cafeterias, lounges, transportation services, recreation facilities and auditoriums. Employees with disabilities cannot be segregated from other employees in workstations or lines of advancement and must be provided equal access to health insurance coverage.

Although the preferences of the employee should be considered, ultimately the decision regarding which reasonable alternative accommodation to select rests with the employer. The accommodation may not necessarily be the best or most expensive as long as it provides what is required for the employee to perform the job. The employer is not required to provide an accommodation that imposes an undue financial hardship on the operation of the business. *Hardship* is defined as an action involving significant difficulty or expense, considering the nature of the accommodation and its net cost, the overall financial resources of the employer, the type of business operation and the impact of the accommodation on the operation and other employees.

Examples of reasonable accommodations include

- modifying employment tests to enable an employee to take them;

- providing large-print materials (such as photocopier enlargement);

- eliminating the use of drivers' licenses as identification (unless a license is necessary for the job);

- rearranging furniture to widen aisles;

- lowering a shelf to enable an employee to reach it;

- allowing flexible work hours or telecommuting from home; and

- raising a desk with blocks or books to provide clearance for an employee in a wheelchair.

Compliance with the laws not only avoids potentially expensive and time-consuming litigation but is also good business. Employers can benefit from the talents and skills of people who may have previously been overlooked or underutilized. Opening doors to consumers whose access has been restricted expands the pool of potential customers.

Tax Breaks

The Internal Revenue Code provides some tax relief to businesses making expenditures to comply with ADA. This provides an incentive for making the expenditures and also mitigates the financial burden that could arise from complying with the law.

Tax deduction.   Up to $15,000 of the expenses associated with the removal of architectural barriers can be deducted each year. Consult your tax adviser for specific details.

Tax credit.   Small businesses, that is, ones with a workforce of no more than 30 full-time employees or gross receipts of no more than $1 million per year, qualify for a credit of 50 percent of the expenditures that exceed $250 but total no more than $10,250. Allowable expenditures include the necessary and reasonable cost of removing barriers, providing auxiliary aids and acquiring or modifying equipment or devices for employees. Again, consult your tax adviser for specific details.

RESPA

The Real Estate Settlement Procedures Act (RESPA) was enacted by Congress in 1974 to further the national goal of encouraging home ownership. It intends to protect consumers from practices that are considered abusive as well as to see that consumers are provided with more complete information about certain lending practices and closing and settlement procedures.

Since the time when RESPA was first enacted, numerous amendments, regulatory initiatives and administrative interpretations have been issued to clarify the procedures that RESPA seeks to regulate. A continuing source of frustration in the real estate industry is the inability to get authoritative clarifications that accommodate contemporary developments in the business. Today's practices involving technology and attempts to provide the seamless service consumers desire further necessitate revisions and clarifications in RESPA. Adding to the confusion are state laws governing real estate settlement procedures that may be inconsistent with RESPA.

Several activities that fall under RESPA's control arise from our ability to utilize today's technology and offer a variety of services relating to the real estate transaction. The most obvious is the acquisition of a mortgage loan, but they also may include title and settlement services and property inspections. The caveat in providing integrated real estate services is that arrangements with affiliate companies can violate not only RESPA but also antitrust laws, unless they are properly structured. With each recent amendment to RESPA, there has been an attempt to clarify the way these affiliations can best protect the consumer and to give much-needed guidance to the real estate and mortgage industries when they offer these services.

Consumers have grown accustomed to one-stop shopping and the ease with which they can access the services they want. **Controlled Business Arrangements (CBAs)** are networks of interrelated companies that offer real estate services. By bundling services, CBAs offer convenience to these time-conscious consumers and enhance the services the broker provides by being able to control all phases of the transaction.

As attractive as these arrangements are, their critics suggest that when consumers are steered to a package of services, they may be discouraged from shopping the market and could end up paying more than they would if they purchased the services separately. The referring employee who recommends a service could also be motivated by a referral fee rather than the interest of the consumer. RESPA intends to preserve this valuable consumer service while also safeguarding the consumers' interests.

Because of technology, **computerized loan originations (CLOs)** are possible. Consumers are accustomed to real estate salespeople providing assistance in figuring their mortgage payments and assembling information about the financing that best suits their needs. CLOs are automated systems that go several steps farther by enabling a purchaser/borrower to locate a lender, submit a mortgage application and obtain a conditional loan commitment right in the real estate office. The consumer can comparison shop the various mortgage lenders and all of their loan products and can make multiple loan applications, if they desire, to see which program is most suitable and where they can obtain a commitment in the shortest time.

Disclosure Obligations

Congress intended that consumers be provided "with greater and more timely information on the nature and costs of the settlement process." Consequently, there are a number of disclosures that are required at the time of loan application and settlement. RESPA also requires certain procedures to disclose the relationships between real estate companies and their affiliates and regulates the way employers can compensate employees for referrals to the affiliates. As of this writing amendments to RESPA and clarification of procedures are still pending.

When a consumer is referred for service by a company affiliated with the real estate brokerage firm, the affiliation must be disclosed at the time the referral is made. The nature of the relationship, including the ownership and financial interest, between the affiliate and the referring party as well as an estimate of the charges for the service must be included. (There is a suggested form that should be used.) The consumer must be permitted to obtain the service elsewhere if so desired.

Most of us are familiar with disclosures at the time a loan application is made, which include the special information booklet prepared by HUD and the good-faith estimate of closing costs that a prospective borrower receives. But there are additional disclosures that result from the use of CLOs. The concern is the amount of information that is provided to the borrower about the loan products available in the marketplace. The question arises of how many lenders must be tied into the computerized network so that the borrower will have sufficient competitive information to make an informed choice before making a loan application. Pending regulations are attempting to find a balance between the amount of information that best serves consumers and the amount that will boggle their minds. The borrower must, however, be informed that other competitive loan products exist that are not part of the system.

At the time of closing, the HUD-1 form is used to itemize all settlement-related charges imposed on the borrower, regardless of whether the borrower is directly or indirectly funding them, and those for which the seller is responsible. After closing, if the mortgage loan is to be assigned, sold or transferred to a servicer, the borrower must be notified. The lenders and servicers also are obligated under RESPA to adhere to certain procedures to account for monies held in escrow or impound accounts for taxes and insurance.

Kickbacks and Unearned Fees

Congress concluded that payments for the referral of a customer to a settlement business tend to increase the cost of settlement services without providing any benefit to the home buyer. Consequently, Congress intended to eliminate both the payment and receipt of kickbacks or referral fees. Payments from title underwriters to attorneys who merely placed orders for insurance, attorneys splitting fees with other attorneys or real estate brokers for referrals of customers, or payments by a title underwriter to a subsidiary of a lender when the subsidiary has performed no substantial services are among the practices that were cited.

Fees or goods may be paid and received, however, *as long as there are services that are actually performed.* The fee must be disclosed and agreed to in writing by the buyer. The *prohibition* is against fees and payments only for *referring* when no other service is provided. Because fees for services to affiliate companies in CBAs and loan application fees may be charged for the services of CLOs, it is important that the consumer be informed of these fees. The real estate industry continues to seek clarifications about permissible ways in which these fees may be charged and paid.

Before any broker embarks on controlled business arrangements, a lawyer should be consulted not only to assist in structuring the arrangement properly but also to help establish procedures that comply with the disclosure and compensation provisions of RESPA. It is important that salespeople, too, know what referral fees may be accepted or paid under RESPA. Note that commission splits and referral fees paid between real estate brokers are not prohibited.

FOREIGN INVESTMENT IN REAL PROPERTY TAX ACT

The Foreign Investment in Real Property Tax Act (FIRPTA) is a federal law that subjects nonresident aliens and foreign corporations to U.S. income tax on their gain from the disposition of an interest in real property. The tax laws are complicated, as is the calculation of the tax liability. There also is a requirement that purchasers of properties owned by nonresident aliens may have to withhold 10 percent of the gross sales price to cover the tax liability. The amount of the tax and the withholding requirement will depend on circumstances, including whether the property is to be used as a residence by the purchaser and the amount of the selling price.

It is important for the brokerage company to establish procedures for handling listings and sales from foreign investors. It may be prudent to have a foreign seller sign an affidavit if the seller is a resident alien. Otherwise the broker may be liable if the owner is a nonresident alien and the buyer is not advised to withhold the required 10 percent.

CONCLUSION

We've taken a positive, proactive approach to managing risk by building an offense empowered by information and procedures to minimize litigation and violations of the law. Antitrust laws; disclosures and environmental issues; fair housing laws; and ADA, RESPA and FIRPTA are selected issues that deserve attention. There may be specific laws in your state that also should be addressed in your company's procedures and training programs.

We have not approached risk from a punitive perspective, assuming that it is sufficient to suggest that civil or criminal penalties or damage awards are onerous enough to persuade prudent businesspeople to avoid them at all cost. Consult the various laws in your jurisdiction for specific information. They may overlap or supersede the federal laws that were reviewed. Inasmuch as the circumstances of individual cases will dictate the jurisdiction of specific legal proceedings, legal counsel should guide you in the compliance of and the rights and remedies under the various laws.

DISCUSSION EXERCISES

What procedures has your company adopted to manage the risks that are prevalent in your practice?

* * *

Discuss the general circumstances of legal cases of which you are aware, and the final rulings and ways that the litigation could have been avoided.

* * *

What issues do you anticipate will pose the greatest liability within the next five years?

In Conclusion of This Unit

In the beginning of this unit we said that the control function of management should protect, preserve and promote the growth of the company. This should empower the organization to pursue its goals and not restrict or burden the operations. Because certain events can inhibit the company's progress, especially risks that could divert the firm's resources into litigation, it's important to be proactive in establishing procedures and monitoring activities to facilitate the way business is conducted. The things you learn about the company in the process are useful as you revisit the management functions and begin planning for the future.

Depending on whether you are the broker/owner, a senior manager in a large organization, a sales manager or a department manager, your involvement in the various activities that are associated with the control function of management may be different. As a guide for understanding your roles, the following summary is provided.

➤ Monitoring the operations

- The broker/owner and senior management are normally involved in evaluating all aspects of the organization's activities.

- Lower levels of management are most involved in monitoring the activities for which they are directly responsible, though they also may have access to reports of other aspects of the company to see how their areas of responsibility affect the "big picture."

➤ Managing risk

- Although the broker/owner and senior management are normally responsible for establishing policies, a proactive risk management program must involve everyone who works for the company.

THE
BUSINESS, FIRST HAND

The real estate industry has been thrust into the forefront of civil rights issues through the fair housing laws and laws that protect people with disabilities. Often the industry, advocacy groups and enforcement agencies are at odds with one another over the best ways to achieve compliance with the laws. As our country's population grows increasingly diverse and society becomes increasingly less tolerant of discriminatory attitudes and behaviors, enforcement of the laws could be intensified. The proactive approach to managing this situation is for the industry to become increasingly vigilant about the way it conducts business. With the following example we offer a simple constructive way to reach out to perhaps an unserved or underserved population in your area and also to demonstrate commitment to protecting the rights of one group of people in the protected classes.

People who are blind or who have limited vision have housing needs just like any other person. Typically, we rely on people's ability to be visually engaged in our real estate transactions. Real estate companies promote their services in visual media; properties are demonstrated through visual inspection; and transactions are negotiated and financed using written contracts. For people with visual impairments, each of these is a barrier to their ability to access services and acquire rentals or housing purchases.

Although the fair housing laws and the Americans with Disabilities Act intend to protect people with print handicaps, the prescriptions in the laws have to be converted into action. The housing industry and other transaction-related industries must become aware of the barriers that people with print handicaps encounter and be mobilized to provide suitable accommodations to service this population. Radio Information Services (RIS), a nonprofit organization whose mission is to promote independence of people who are blind or who have print handicaps, embarked on just such a project to provide education and outreach. Representatives from various sectors of the housing industry who participated in the project found that accommodating this population is really quite easy and, most importantly, extremely rewarding.

Radio programming is an integral "companion" in the lives of people with print handicaps. Commercial radio stations link this population with real estate services through commercials, public service announcements and interview programs. Public (nonprofit) stations are an invaluable resource for information as well. Some also provide broadcast hours during which printed material is read expressly for the benefit of people with print handicaps. In the case of RIS and similar stations that are members of the National Association of Radio Reading Services, programming is dedicated to broadcasting printed news, magazines and contemporary books for the benefit of people with print handicaps. One of the most popular programs at RIS is "The Buyers Guide", during which weekly advertising circulars are read to help people assemble their shopping lists. In the case of the real estate education and outreach project, 26 hours of programming were dedicated to educating consumers about a wide variety of issues related to a real estate transaction and people's rights under the fair housing laws.

With today's technology and a resource such as RIS, real estate practitioners can provide virtually every print material they commonly use in an accessible format. Brochures and contracts can be converted to large print (18 points or larger). Using readers, audiotaped versions can easily be created. With computer equipment and translation software, any document on disk can be converted to Braille. Once a master set of these materials is created, additional copies can be created easily to provide the resource that real estate licensees need to assist people who request these accommodations. Interestingly, RIS has a broad-reaching project in which restaurant menus, concert programs, textbook materials, bus schedules and computer manuals are also converted to Braille.

For individuals with print handicaps who have the appropriate technology, computers provide an additional source. Translation software converts the contents of the printed screen as well as user directives to an audio format. A computer disk on which any real estate brochure or document is created can be provided to an individual with this technological capability.

The point of this example is to offer some insight to the kinds of things that can be done to open doors for people with print handicaps. Think about the vast amount of information that we gather and the activities in which we routinely engage because of our ability to read. Think about the barriers that exist for those without that ability. It's simply good business to expand our horizons and serve the needs of this population in the market-place.

Your Personal Growth

Each of us brings to the workplace all of the dimensions of our lives and the stresses of modern living. We are trying to balance demands in our personal and professional lives. We are challenged to define our roles in a society and a management culture that are undergoing considerable change. Being successful in all of these efforts begins with introspection. It continues with our growth as human beings so that we can command a leadership position and manage the interdependent relationships of the people within an organization.

Many contemporary publications on management and leadership emphasize the role of people in the company. Perhaps one of the most persuasive reasons for that is the evolution of management philosophies since the 1930s. The evolution began with theorists studying human relations, the psychology of work and motivation, participative management styles and job enrichment. The participation of people at all levels of the organization is one common characteristic that has been identified as organizations strive for order, structure and solutions to their problems. People are the organization's most valuable resource, not just because of the products or services they produce but because of the contributions they can make to the operation of the organization.

Few of us have seriously contemplated our role in the organization, particularly since as salespeople we were probably more focused on producing listings and sales. Our professional development was focused on acquiring the selling skills, the one-two-three-step formulas, to be successful. Managers who grew up with this orientation seek formulas for running their businesses. In the previous units of the book we attempted to provide the technical guidance for those activities. But an important part of your personal growth as a manager is not based on formulas or specific skills. It involves understanding yourself and how you affect the human dynamics in the organization.

In this unit we intend to encourage you to reflect on yourself and on ways you can meet the personal challenges of management. We explore

- leadership and the characteristics in leaders that inspire people to follow;

- management of the company's human resources and the impact of human behavior; and

- communications and ways to communicate effectively using verbal (oral and written) and nonverbal messages.

Self-knowledge is most valuable when you profit from what you learn and use the lessons for personal growth. There are also entire publications (see the Bibliography) by notable authors that will enhance your personal growth and effectiveness in the organization. This is important, regardless of whether you're the broker/owner of the company or in another level of management. In any of these roles you affect the lives of the people who work for the organization.

15 Becoming a Leader

Who have you admired as a leader? Why? What do you know about yourself that will help—or hinder—your ability to be an effective leader?

The essence of leadership is the ability to inspire other people. People are inspired to be supportive and cooperative when the leader commands their respect, when it is obvious that the leader has a clearly defined purpose or mission. Leaders have a keen sense of self-awareness and are passionate about what they believe. Because of the strength of their convictions and their determination to pursue certain principles or ideals, it is clear where they are headed. This strength engenders faith in others that following such a person is the best thing to do.

We spend much of our lives as members of groups—at work, in the community, in the family or in the classroom. A hierarchy forms in which someone becomes the leader either by formal appointment, such as the boss, chairman or teacher, or informally, by taking charge. Most all of us find ourselves in a leadership role at sometime in our lives. This can be a rewarding experience or a nightmare, depending on the level of acceptance or hostility we encounter when we assume the position.

Leading implies that someone is following. Are you striding down a path, thinking you're doing wise and wonderful things, yet no one is following? *Just because you've assumed the role or have been given a title doesn't make you a successful leader.* Have you noticed that sometimes a person commands the respect of the group but is not the one formally designated as its leader? People embrace the person because of his or her qualities, not because of the title.

For the purpose of this discussion we need to distinguish between a boss or superior and a leader. In the military, for example, there are highly structured ranks. The organizational culture requires that people in subordinate ranks must acquiesce to those in superior ranks, and there are serious consequences for doing otherwise. Sometimes the superiors in highly structured cultures really do possess leadership qualities that inspire the cooperation of subordinates. But this is different from controlling them.

In organizations today management does not control or dominate as in the previous example, but rather intends to inspire. The ability of managers to do this depends on their leadership. The title of manager presumes that you will lead and persuade people to follow. Because one person doesn't force another person to do anything, demonstrating a strong sense of self and purpose will convince people that you are a worthy leader. You can't succeed at this by relying solely on competency in real estate and management functions. By exploring the essence of leadership and developing the qualities that cause people to view you as a leader, you will be able to command a following.

UNDERSTANDING YOURSELF

Contemporary writers on leadership, such as Warren Bennis and Stephen Covey (see the Bibliography), stress the importance of self-awareness as a crucial part of leadership development. This involves evaluating your personal strengths, weaknesses and values. Development does not end with introspection; it is a process in which a person uses the knowledge that is gained to grow. While there are many things to learn about yourself, several characteristics seem to be particularly valuable for a leader.

Are you willing to learn? Earlier we mentioned that leaders have a clear mission and are passionate about what they believe. This evolves from personal reflection and an internal conviction that is developed from what they learn. This is not limited to scholarly learning, such as reading or taking courses and training classes. It is the continual process of evaluating past experiences, probing, asking questions, listening and observing.

Leaders are thinkers who use information to form new ideas rather than accepting the status quo. In Chapter 1 we talked about meeting the challenges of change and the importance of vision to confront these challenges in the future. Vision evolves from intellectual and emotional curiosity, which is utilized to liberate a person from the past. When organizations are guided by leaders with vision, they can be bold and innovative.

Are you willing to take care of others? None of us lives in absolute seclusion. We can't escape contact with others— spouses, fellow workers, neighbors or family. Each of us has an innate ability to nurture that we must be willing to use to benefit others, to contribute to their lives and rejoice in their successes. This is the difference between being *selfless* and selfish. As we reach out and care for others, we continually learn and improve ourselves as well.

Do you have a positive attitude? Leaders are able to capitalize on their strengths and rejoice in the positive aspects of their lives. They do not allow weaknesses or negativity to hinder their personal growth. Some people tend to take positive experiences for granted; they may not even recognize the good and pleasurable aspects of life. Maybe they don't slow down long enough to enjoy them. Or because negative experiences are unpleasant, they allow them to make a stronger impression. Focusing on faults and failings restricts the ability to see opportunities for one's self and for others. This can manifest itself in a harsh or cynical view of the world.

A positive attitude is exhibited by a spirit of optimism and strength of resolve, evidenced by a willingness to persevere. Doing things that others refuse to do, being able to withstand rejection and avoiding the "if only" mentality has a positive effect on you as well as on those around you. If even in your darkest hour you "Think SNIGTH"— Something Nice Is Going To Happen—it will be difficult for people around you to do otherwise.

How compassionate are you? Because none of us is perfect, we must expect weaknesses in everyone. What's most revealing about you is the way in which you respond to these human conditions. Do you use the weaknesses in others to build yourself up? Or can you look beyond yourself to create a climate in which others can grow and develop? We have to believe in other people, allowing them to reach their untapped potential while forgiving their weaknesses. If we are tolerant of human behavior and compassionate, we free others to grow.

How open-minded are you? There is little in life that is black or white or either/or. But there are people who insist on dividing everything into two parts, viewing the world by absolutes. These are the obsessive/compulsive, workaholic, zealot or fanatic personalities. They are not only unable to see all dimensions of a situation but also invariably offend someone with their absolute or extremist views. From a leadership perspective, this one-dimensional approach to life appeals to like-minded people. Just as this is a very narrow view of the world, it appeals to only a narrow segment of the population. Hence it is a characteristic that is not admired by many.

By evaluating each situation, decision or viewpoint with an open mind, we can see advantages and disadvantages and form opinions, make decisions or plan a course of action on a case-by-case basis. People who can do this are more moderate and temperate in their views and are easier to get along with. Invariably they are better listeners because they have an open mind and, being able to see multiple aspects of an issue, are more likely to be tolerant of others.

What about ego and empathy? Webster characterizes *self-esteem* as being synonymous with *ego,* that is, our confidence and self-respect. In other words, these are attitudes about ourselves. *Empathy* is our ability to be sensitive to the feelings, thoughts and experiences of others. In pondering the previous questions, you can see a correlation between those issues and the elements of ego and empathy. Confidence and self-respect contribute to the ability to be compassionate and tolerant and to nurture others. Greater confidence is gained as you learn more and grow from experiences.

CHARACTER OF A LEADER

Learning about ourselves as leaders includes assessing the values and the moral and ethical traits that are inherent in our character and guide who we are. A person's character is revealed by such things as integrity, honesty and trustworthiness, or the lack thereof. One of the ways people judge the worthiness of a leader is based on what they see in a person's character and the congruity between that person's value and their own.

An essential element of leadership is inspiring others to cooperate. Therefore, people must have faith that their personal desires will be satisfied and faith in the integrity of the leader. This faith is rooted in their ability to trust the leader.

Integrity

Webster defines *integrity* as a firm adherence to a code of especially moral or artistic values, implying trustworthiness and incorruptibility. Integrity comes from a person's intrinsic sense of values or moral order. One of the dilemmas in leadership is that no one universal value system exists. Societies and organizations form their own values and moral codes. Flaws in character according to one system may be acceptable in another. All of us evaluate the integrity of others according to our own values or our perception of those that are generally accepted in society.

When the values of a leader are inconsistent with those of the people she or he expects to influence and vice versa, a moral dilemma ensues. This threatens the effectiveness of the leader and causes people to question the person's character. People must be confident that the leader is incorruptible and will not succumb to the temptations of the position. Consequently, it is incumbent on the leader to strive for the highest degree of integrity, which guides the values and moral code of the group he or she leads.

Consider how your attitude toward money is reflected in the way you and your organization do business. Do you value money regardless of how you get it? Or do you sleep well at night, knowing that the way you get money is honorable? Yes, you want the organization to be profitable. But at any cost? One decision that is inconsistent with ethical values sets the stage for more, which eventually erodes a person's fundamental integrity and that of the organization.

The notion that "business is business" and ethical values or principles are useful only when they do not prevent the company from gaining profit or competitive advantage undermines the integrity of the institution. In the discussion of ethics in Chapter 8 it was suggested that one value system should prevail in all aspects of one's life, rather than separate systems for business and private life. The integrity of an organization is a reflection of the integrity of its leaders.

Honesty. Honesty and integrity are frequently associated with one another. According to Webster, *honesty* implies a refusal to lie, steal or deceive in any way. Honesty is unswerving fidelity to the truth. Knowledge is powerful, but knowledge possessed by a dishonest or deceitful person can be equally powerful. The character of a person is revealed by whether that person uses knowledge for truthful and honorable purposes or to manipulate people or situations for self-serving gain. People lose faith when they feel that they have been deceived, which erodes their perception of a person as a worthy leader.

Trust

We are willing to risk putting our lives in another person's hands when we feel that he or she is worthy of this responsibility. "When I give you my trust, I expect that you will be trustworthy in return." Trusting one another is risky, but it is a risk we are willing to take when we feel that we will not be harmed. Once harm occurs we are no longer inclined to take that risk. People trust leaders to use their positions responsibly, to be compassionate and respect those they lead. People put themselves on the line for their leaders and expect the same in return. But when people feel used, abused or deceived, this undermines their trust.

Because of the nature of the position, there are many opportunities for a leader to violate a person's trust. The true test of a leader's character is the ability to use trust wisely and demonstrate that he or she is trustworthy. Some leaders are so successful at engendering people's trust that they are able to persuade people to believe in them despite their gross failings— consider Adolf Hitler, for example. This certainly is not to suggest that he is a model to emulate, but it does make the point that leaders have an enormous responsibility to use their positions wisely so as not to abuse the trust that people have in them.

Loyalty.   People will be loyal and pledge their unswerving allegiance to a person or a cause when they feel that their needs are being met in the process. Because managers are responsible for seeing that the goals of their organizations are accomplished, they depend on the people they supervise to perform. But people work to satisfy their own needs first. They have to believe that through the leader they can grow and develop. When they trust that the leader will honor their needs, they will be loyal. But once their trust is violated, they feel betrayed and loyalty is jeopardized.

Respect.   A leader gains respect by consistently demonstrating a thoughtful regard for the welfare and rights of others. People will have a high regard for you if they feel you regard them highly; in other words, there will be mutual respect. We may not like or feel any particular kinship with certain people, but we still can respect them. *Don't expect to be loved!* Your job will require that you make tough and unpopular decisions from time to time. But these decisions do not have to jeopardize people's loyalty and respect. If you treat others fairly and justly, as evidence of your regard for their worth, they will respect you.

Power

The nature of their positions gives leaders the authority to make decisions. Their positions give leaders power to affect other people's lives. The use of this power is a reflection of a leader's character. The way others react to a leader's use of power is a reflection of their perception of his or her trustworthiness and integrity. The leader's responsible or irresponsible use of power is judged by the people who are expected to follow.

Power is sometimes used to coerce people to do things. Obedience in this case is the result of fear rather than respect. This can breed resentment. Coercion no longer works once people feel that they've surrendered too much control to the leader or suspect her or his motives. We often hear that power corrupts. If power is vested in the hands of a corruptible person, it will. Power in the hands of an untrustworthy person can be abused.

The power of the position will endure when people feel that the leader is honorable and is not using that power for self-serving purposes. The leader is constantly being scrutinized and will have influence only as long as people feel that power is being used fairly and justly. For example, if a salesperson feels that the manager does not respect the needs of the salesperson, is willing to compromise the principles or ethics of the company or expects the salesperson to compromise his or her own ethics, the manager can be judged unworthy of the power associated with the position. The most enduring influence the leader has is when both a leader and the followers share a commitment to similar goals.

LEADERSHIP SKILLS

As you can see from the preceding discussion, people are persuasive because of who they are as individuals. While the perceptions people have of the leader are important, there are also skills a leader must have to command a following.

Accountability and Personal Responsibility

Leaders are willing to confront challenges and find solutions without regard to the personal consequences instead of surrendering the responsibilities of the position. They are accountable for the decisions they make and the direction in which they persuade others to follow. If mistakes are made, they are up front in acknowledging an error in judgment; they take the necessary steps to correct their mistakes. Leaders aren't perfect or infallible, but they have courage to acknowledge both their weaknesses and their strengths.

Children learn that there are fewer undesirable consequences if they let the other kid take the blame for breaking the window. Or they fault a rule as being unreasonable to give them an excuse to disobey it. Likewise, a manager may say, "It's the fault of the inept sales staff that I inherited; that's why production is down." "It's the broker's fault for establishing an unrealistic policy; that's why no one complies with it." "It's the lenders (or the appraisers or the lawyers) whose procedures are to blame for my office's not meeting income projections." These are cop-outs, excuses for the manager to cease to manage.

Leaders don't duck responsibility, and brokers *cannot afford to* cop out on their responsibilities. The real estate license laws hold brokers accountable for the activities of the licensees who work for them. The regulators will not accept the excuse that a salesperson is inept or that it's impossible for a broker to know everything that the salespeople are doing. The broker's failure to supervise the salespeople not only jeopardizes his or her license but also creates enormous liability, particularly because litigation is so prevalent.

Decisiveness

You've heard of rudderless ships? This has become a synonym for "lacking in direction." People expect direction from the leader, but they'll be on a rudderless ship if you can't choose a course of action or make a decision and stay the course, that is, follow through with the decision.

Most people don't function well with ambiguity, especially when its source is the person on whom they rely for direction. People need to know what to do. If the organization is to succeed in its goals, someone has to see that the appropriate steps are being taken to reach them. Lacking direction from elsewhere, people will make decisions for themselves. There are risks in this, however. Their decisions may be unacceptable or undesirable from your point of view. But they should not be subjected to you telling them so after the fact if you failed to provide direction in the first place.

Being decisive means putting yourself on the line and taking a risk. It takes courage to be decisive and to be a risk-taker, both of which are characteristics of a good leader. It's far better to make a decision and risk being wrong than to do nothing. There is a difference, however, between being decisive and making snap judgments. Wise decisions require evaluation and consultation. Knowing at what point a decision needs to be made and when not to interfere in a situation is critical. Decisions must be communicated with conviction so that there will be no doubt or ambiguity about what you mean. Once you make a decision, you're accountable because of your position. Rarely will you be chastised for making the wrong decision, provided you've been thoughtful and responsible in the process.

Some people approach situations deliberately, analyzing options before deciding a course of action; others size up situations quickly and take immediate action (which is different from making snap judgments). Some people are focused on the long-range implications as they make short-range decisions; others are geared to making decisions for today with less concern for the long-range implications. Organizations benefit from different approaches at different times. There is merit to keeping the organization moving as well as keeping it from being diverted from its long-range pursuits.

It's important to know what kind of decision-maker you are. There are studies and publications devoted to decision-making processes that can give you some insight. The point here is not to pass judgment on various approaches. Rather it is to suggest that the processes people use to make decisions will affect whether they're in concert with one another. If you are a quick decision-maker, you may be put off by another person who devotes a considerable amount of time to analyzing before acting. Or if you're the methodical type, a person who's looking for the quick response could be frustrated waiting for you. There are times when managers must make immediate decisions so as not to appear indecisive, which can be difficult for people who are more deliberate and analytical.

Team Building

To succeed, companies depend on the collective efforts of everyone without regard to the reasons individual people have for working for them. The contemporary view in management is that people are valuable for their individual talents and are not "things" the company uses for production. Taking these two observations together, the leader's challenge is to energize everyone in a unified force for the company and to draw individuals into participative roles in the organization.

If the leader does nothing, people will do their own thing, working to satisfy whatever their personal reasons are for working. Each person may be striving to accomplish something different.

- Some may just want to be busy and will spend a lot of time doing "busywork." They'll be perfectly happy eking out whatever living they can.

- Some may be building their resumes and consider working for you as only a pause in their travels.

- Others may be using you as a means to an end, to satisfy their financial needs.

- Some may seek the satisfaction of contributing to the lives of their customers and clients.

The failure in this approach is that the organization is not making the best use of its human resources.

The essence of team building is to mobilize people to work toward the goals of the organization while at the same time satisfying themselves. Even if the goals of the individuals and the organization are different, it does not mean that they are adversaries. But this is the message people get when they think the company doesn't respect them. The common thread is that there are needs to be satisfied. It is the leader's job to see that this is accomplished.

There are a number of ways collective efforts, or teams, are evident in a company. One is the partnership between the manager and the person being supervised. The manager coaches individual salespeople, as discussed in Chapter 12, helping them develop their personal success plans, coaching their performance and facilitating solutions to problems. This is the first step toward helping both the salesperson and the organization benefit from what the salesperson does. But the job doesn't end there.

Another way people are involved in collective efforts is in group endeavors to aid the company, such as brainstorming, problem solving or quality control. One of the best ways to elicit the cooperation of independent people, which is what salespeople usually are, is to involve them in rather than isolate them from the organization. As they are drawn into these activities, they are inspired to get further involved in their business as well as yours.

It's tempting to say that a sales force of independent contractors, who often are highly independent personalities, cannot realistically be expected to work together in collective efforts. The fact that they may be classified as independent contractors for tax purposes does not change the fact that they work for the company. They are an integral part of the organization, along with the support staff and management.

When people use their talents, their sense of self-worth increases and their creativity is nurtured. When people work together ideas are stimulated; this also encourages them to work together on their own initiative. They gain an appreciation for the increased efficiencies and higher rewards that are possible in collective efforts. Some salespeople have already discovered this as they form sales teams.

Delegation

In Chapter 1 we said one of the adjustments a manager has to make after being a "doer" is to learn how to delegate. Delegation is an essential skill for a good leader. Aside from the obvious fact that one person can't do everything, this is an opportunity to demonstrate the trust and respect you have for other people. You also show that you are neither insecure in nor all-consumed by the position.

Delegation stimulates the initiative of people, enables them to grow and develop and enhances their self-confidence. In delegating you demonstrate your willingness to care for others. The tasks that you delegate have to be meaningful, though. Otherwise you risk insulting people rather than demonstrating your confidence in them. Delegating is not always easy.

- You have to identify the best people for the specific tasks. They must have the experience, knowledge and skill to carry out the assigned task. They also must be willing to accept the responsibility and be accountable for performance.

- You must be willing to let go. People must be given the authority to perform a task without interference from you. Because you are accountable for seeing that the work gets done, there is a tendency to micromanage or interject yourself into every detail. Don't interfere! Once you've delegated a task, let the person to whom it was delegated decide how to do it and get it done.

If you delegate the task of writing the ads for the week or the job of supervising the office for a week during your vacation, back away and let that person do the job. If you feel that he or she needs your prodding every step of the way, you may not have chosen the right person for the job. Each person may approach a job differently, but that doesn't mean that one way is right and another is wrong. You have the right to expect the assignment to be accomplished, but don't second-guess every decision that's made.

Delegation means taking chances. Perhaps you fear that others can do the job better or that your importance in the organization could be diminished by their performance. Perhaps you fear not knowing every detail that is going on or that you'll lose some prestige with your boss by sharing credit for accomplishments with others. These are barriers to delegation and signal to others that your confidence is threatened. Everyone in the organization has talent and capabilities. In fact, *good* leaders or managers are grooming their replacements. This is good for the organization, which depends on continuity and stability, and it is also a sign of progress. Each of us can grow beyond the point where we are now.

SOCIAL AWARENESS

Our discussion so far has focused on the leader within the group or organization. But these institutions don't function in a vacuum. We need to step out into the rest of the world and seek places where our initiatives as leaders can be beneficial. Leaders are concerned not only about the good of their own institutions but about the community at large as well. As your social awareness increases, you become a role model for others to follow.

A good example is to look at the impact of government on the real estate business and the rights of private property owners. We see aggressive regulations affecting all aspects of land use, from planning and zoning requirements to environmental issues. Leaders become part of the solution rather than standing by as problems develop. If we consider ourselves to be the real estate experts, it is incumbent on us to share our expertise for the benefit of municipal and state governing bodies, zoning and planning commissions and community development committees.

Businesses are an integral part of the community; both are dependent on one another for survival. A business can solidify its commitment to the community by getting involved in community activities and social service projects. The image and reputation of the company are often measured by the organization's willingness to reach out for the public good. This is particularly important if the public perceives that an industry as a whole is self-serving. Your involvement in the community can inspire other people in your organization to step forward as well.

LEADERSHIP VERSUS MANAGEMENT

By introducing the discussion of leadership and the personality and character traits that cause people to regard a person as a leader, we've attempted to inspire personal growth in this direction. Certainly you will be more effective at energizing or mobilizing the people you manage if you are a leader. But the point needs to be made that there is a distinction between the way leaders and managers influence the direction of the organization to meet the challenge of change.

Not all managers are leaders. The difference is that managers are caretakers, whereas leaders are innovators. Managers focus on the bottom line and solutions to problems so that the organization can stay on course. Leaders look beyond the status quo and are the long-range thinkers. For them, problems are opportunities to explore new venues and be creative; the organization's people are more important than its procedures. In a sense, managers are good at functioning within established systems and seek orderly formulas, whereas leaders are independent thinkers and are willing to risk new approaches. With leaders, organizations will thrive in the future.

CONCLUSION

Leaders have a powerful influence over the culture and character of a group or organization and its individual members. The ability to use that influence wisely and cause others to follow is affected by who we are and the way we conduct ourselves. By the nature of the position, our integrity and trustworthiness is constantly being scrutinized, particularly the fairness and justice that is demonstrated in the way we use power. Leaders succeed in commanding a following because of their willingness to take charge and their willingness to be accountable, their ability to be decisive, their ability to draw people into collective endeavors and their willingness to delegate.

Leaders bring the best of themselves to a position and are constantly striving to improve. As leaders inspire other people, they become a model for them to emulate. From this, new leaders emerge.

DISCUSSION EXERCISES

What have you learned about yourself as a potential leader? What do you think your greatest challenges will be?

* * *

Discuss from past experiences situations in which you felt that the trust you put in another person was violated, in which you questioned another person's integrity.

* * *

How do you assess your ability to build a team? To delegate responsibility? To be decisive?

CHAPTER

16 Developing as a Manager

Think about people you've worked for. What do you admire the most about the way they handled the job? What do you admire the least? How do you feel about the way they treated you?

Managing a company's human resources is really an exercise in managing the complexities of human behavior. Real estate salespeople tend to be independent and free-spirited. They work under stressful conditions, dealing with irregular work hours, repeated rejection and other people's problems. Add the manager's personality and daily challenges and we have an intricate mix of individuals, all of whom must work together.

In Chapter 15 we looked at the personality and character of leaders—people who influence other people. The next step is to look more closely at the human behavior within the group the manager intends to lead. Understanding yourself and the role you play in the group dynamics is an essential part of developing as a manager. There are various ways, that is various management styles, that managers can effect certain behavior in the group. Obviously, the goal is to affect that behavior in constructive and productive ways.

Mentors or models have a powerful influence over the style of management we adopt. They may be parents, teachers or previous managers. We tend to embrace their styles because we know no other way, even if we don't like the way these models treated us. This is one of the reasons why abused children often become abusive parents; stifled workers become dominating and controlling managers. Not only do these models influence our management style, they also affect the way we learn to respond as workers. Our past experiences mold our future behavior.

Can we adjust to new styles and cultures? It's possible. But if old habits are deeply ingrained in us, it may take a conscious effort. This means gathering new knowledge, learning new ways and perhaps finding new mentors or models. At one time managers were very dictatorial: "I say, you do." No questions were asked, no suggestions were requested, no latitude for creativity or initiative was given. If this is the only model you know, this is the model you're likely to emulate. Although there are still some managers who think their job is to control and dominate, as we've indicated several times, the trend in management philosophy today views workers differently. They are a resource that should be supported, energized, and encouraged to be creative and participate in the affairs of the organization.

STYLES OF MANAGEMENT

Management styles, or approaches to managing, are essentially ways managers use their authority. That is their right to make decisions, give orders and require the actions of others. Authority includes the right to make certain commitments, use resources and take other steps that are necessary to accomplish the work for which they are responsible. Not all managers have the same scope of authority. Their responsibilities differ according to their job descriptions and the policies and procedures of the company. While using authority is an essential function of the manager, it can be approached in different ways, depending on the style of management.

Dictatorial Style

The dictatorial manager has absolute and total control over the entire scene and all decisions. Nothing is delegated, only orders are issued. There is little interaction with the people being supervised and little concern for them as human beings or their capabilities. Most communications are one-sided—the manager speaks and people are expected to respond promptly, enthusiastically and without questioning the directives. No explanations or rationale are provided for the directives.

This is an oppressive atmosphere in which to work. People are not permitted to exercise initiative or creative thinking; no suggestions or opinions are requested, nor are any permitted to be offered. The dictatorial manager tends to view such actions as a threat to his or her authority or a challenge to his or her judgment. Obedience is compelled by fear, punishment and other negative incentives.

While this style of management may still exist in some workplaces, it is inconsistent with current management philosophy and the discussion of leadership in Chapter 15. We said that the leader is self-confident, does not feel threatened, respects other people and enables them to grow and develop. There is no similarity between these traits and those of the dictatorial manager, who creates a very stifling and intimidating environment. It's inconceivable that your independent real estate salespeople will respond to this style of management. They'll decide, "Who needs this?" and go elsewhere to work.

Autocratic Style

Autocratic managers are authoritarian but not in the same way as the dictatorial manager. The autocratic manager dominates the scene and makes all decisions, but the style is more humanistic or benevolent than that of the dictatorial manager. Greater concern is demonstrated toward people, which enables them to feel more secure and comfortable. The atmosphere is more relaxed.

The autocratic manager is a caretaker, structuring all of the activities and relieving people of any need to be self-directed. Little initiative is expected from people because all of their thinking is done for them. The manager makes the decisions; other people do not participate in or influence the decision-making. The autocratic manager usually assigns tasks with an eye toward individuals' capabilities, whereas the dictatorial manager does so without regard for people's strengths or limitations.

Many people respond to the autocratic style of management because it is familiar, reflecting what they've known from parents, teachers and previous work situations. For most managers, the autocratic style is the model that is most familiar because this is the style under which they themselves have worked.

This style offers some advantages. Because the manager makes the decisions, they can be made quickly. Clearly, accountability rests solely with the manager. It is assumed that the decisions will be high quality because of the manager's expertise. There are some potential drawbacks, however. Without the additional information or expertise that others may have to contribute, decisions may not be as high quality as they could be. People may question or even sabotage a decision, which affects its implementation, if they feel the decision is flawed.

The autocratic style of management doesn't foster the degree of self-development and growth that is possible in the participative style discussed below. However, it does foster a more constructive and compassionate environment than the dictatorial style. The manager has more respect for people, even though this is not a participative environment.

Participative Style

The participative style fosters a more democratic environment than any of the previous styles. Participative management is a humanistic approach that promotes initiative and recognizes the value of the human resources. Participative managers enable the organization to thrive by utilizing the talents and insights of people to a greater extent than is common in the other styles. This style also enhances the sense of belonging and productivity because people feel greater kinship with the organization.

Participative managers encourage individual or group participation in decision-making rather than making decisions unilaterally or without input from others. The problem-solving or brainstorming exercises discussed in Chapter 11 are examples of the ways this is done. Often better quality decisions are made because a number of people are involved in generating a variety of creative ideas. By participating in decision making, people have an opportunity to influence the outcome as well as to satisfy their personal needs during the process. Participation tends to achieve greater acceptance and willingness to implement the final decision.

Varying degrees of participation may be invited, and the final responsibility for decisions may differ, depending on how this style is used. The manager may

- solicit input one-on-one or in a group;

- pose only selected issues or all issues for consideration;

- gather input and then make a decision alone; or

- require the group to arrive at consensus and make a decision that the manager can accept.

This style is not without risk to the organization or the manager, however. The manager must maintain leadership so as not to appear indecisive, weak or fearful of taking responsibility. Work also can get bogged down. The manager must keep people focused on the issues at hand to reach an outcome in a timely manner. Because the amount of time needed to address issues or make decisions increases when more people are involved, many managers are selective about the issues that are funneled through this process.

The human dynamics and morale in the office can affect the process as well as the outcome in this type of decision making. Some people are more dominant than others, which inhibits the meek. Conflict can arise as ideas are evaluated and conclusions are sought. And if the final decision is contrary to a position or point of view that a person advocated during the discussions, this person may resist or boycott its implementation. "Why did you ask if you aren't going to listen to me?"

Laissez-Faire Style

Laissez-faire management is really a contradiction because it is essentially *non*management. It's a hands-off, do-nothing approach, characterized by nonintervention and indifference. This creates a chaotic environment because the manager really doesn't exercise any of the position's authority. The manager doesn't seem to care what does or doesn't happen, so why should anyone else? "Manager" is only the title, not a description, of the position because the person is not providing the necessary leadership.

New managers can fall victim to this style, fearing that their popularity or acceptance will suffer if they take charge. (Remember we said in the first chapter that being a manager is not a popularity contest.) They may be intimidated by the responsibilities of the position or fear making a wrong decision. So they don't make any decisions. Even experienced managers can succumb to a laissez-faire style once they've lost control and there's little hope of reestablishing themselves as leaders. Some managers feel that real estate salespeople are so independent that there's no way to take charge. But unless you harness all of that independent energy, you've surrendered your job as manager.

So what style manager will you be? If you're starting a new organization, you can adopt a management style for yourself, which will then determine the management culture for the company. If you're managing in an existing culture, you'll be influenced by the style that is predominant. In practice, most organizations today develop their own style, using different styles in different situations. One style predominates, perhaps the autocratic style; another is used in certain situations, such as bringing people into participative problem solving for selected issues. The quality of the decision, the level of acceptance of the decision and the time available for a participative exercise normally determine which issues will be addressed this way.

HUMAN BEHAVIOR

The style of management prescribes the way the organization views the formal roles of managers and the people they supervise. But human behavior is another aspect of the work environment that affects the way people conduct themselves in these roles. People interact daily, even if not face to face. Managers must be astute observers of human behavior. If it adversely affects the harmony in the workplace or your relationship with the people who work for you, your job as manager is far more difficult.

Do you know why people behave the way they do? There are those who suggest that a manager needs to understand what makes people tick. Once this is known, they say, then we're supposed to be able to appeal to people's inner psyches so that we can elicit the desired behavior from them. But you can't be sure why they do the things they do. Because people come loaded with all kinds of "programs," you'd need to get inside each person's head to learn about each one's motivations, attitudes, perceptions and experiences. There are professionals whose careers are devoted to such exercises, but it is unrealistic to expect that most managers are equipped to do this.

We do not intend to discount the work of the behavioral scientists, many of whom you've probably heard about. Abraham Maslow theorized that human beings do things to satisfy their needs, which are grouped in a hierarchy beginning with basic human necessities and progressing to the most selfless. Douglas MacGregor classified management approaches as Theory X and Theory Y, making certain assumptions about human nature and human motivation in the workplace. Fredrick Herzberg studied the relationship between aspects of the workplace that satisfy and dissatisfy workers and the effect on motivation. These are all attempts to identify why or how we work. By knowing what motivates people, we should know how to manage them.

Although there is a great deal of merit in these studies, they are difficult for anyone other than scientists, psychiatrists, psychologists or far more expert managers than most of us are to use with any degree of certainty or validity. The most logical, or less dangerous, approach is presented by Ferdinand Fournies in his book *Coaching for Improved Work Performance.* He contends that a manager really needs to be a psychoanalyst to do a creditable job of identifying a person's real motivations. Because we're not likely to be trained in psychoanalysis, it's far easier to observe and address someone's behavior than it is to figure out *why* he or she behaves in certain ways.

Consider this: behavior is a function of the alternatives one sees at the time. This sounds like a rather profound notion because most of us never thought about behavior this way. But it is really a very simple concept. Think about it. A person assesses a situation, makes a choice and responds to the situation. The entire process could take only a second or two or it could take several minutes, hours, days or weeks.

A number of variables affect the way a person sizes up a situation before responding. These variables include past experiences, intellectual ability, emotions, the amount of time devoted to the assessment, the amount of information that is gathered and the way it is evaluated. Sometimes this is a conscious and deliberate exercise; other times it's a reflex response or is clouded by a lot of emotion. All of these variables affect the number and quality of alternatives from which a person selects a course of action. A bystander may see other alternatives that would have been a better course of action. Even the person may have second thoughts about the choice after the heat of the moment has passed.

"Confronting" Behavior

Perhaps *confronting* is not the preferable term because it suggests a judgmental or critical view of our fellow human beings. In reality, though, this is the instinctive way that most managers and parents see their positions—that they have the right, even the obligation, to criticize and correct people. But we should really be *evaluating behavior* as being desirable or undesirable, acceptable or unacceptable, *not judging people.* The following will help you understand some of the points that were discussed in Chapter 12 regarding the behavior of salespeople and the way it is addressed in problem-solving and disciplinary interviews.

Think about this: people don't purposely decide to behave badly or do stupid things. "I want to look stupid today, so I'll do something stupid" is a very rare mind-set, if it exists at all. Many things can affect behavior. Some behavior is not conscious, and often it is guided subconsciously by motivations. People may select a course of action because it was the only one that occurred to them at the time. Or they may make a rational choice but not see an alternative that someone else might see. We're back to our quandary, wondering why people behave the way they do.

Praise acceptable behavior. A manager's job is to address behavior. Unfortunately, too often we take desirable or acceptable behavior for granted, because it's what people are expected to do anyway, and address only unacceptable or undesirable behavior. Hence we're long on criticism and short on praise.

At the risk of venturing too close to the motivational theories, we do need to make a very strong case for *praise!* Behavior that is reinforced is likely to be repeated. People thrive on attention or recognition and seek to please. Unfortunately, what normally gets our attention is their mistakes or most irritating actions. Children learn the reward of negative attention. They will repeat the most obnoxious behavior because they know that someone will notice them. Being noticed is better than being ignored. It's easy for the people who work for you to feel taken for granted when you ignore their accomplishments. Eventually they think you don't care about them and give up. What's happened to the compassionate and caring leader?

Regardless of your management style, genuine praise and recognition are in order. In fact, this is one of the best ways to give people positive feedback and encouragement. (See the section Incentives to Perform in Chapter 12.) It's usually easy to heap praise and recognition on the top producers. But that's not many of the salespeople. The production gap is great if you acknowledge the 80-20 theory—80 percent of the business is conducted by 20 percent of the people. And the gap seems to be widening—perhaps as much as 95 percent of the business is conducted by 5 percent of the people. So reward and recognition programs usually single out the same people most of the time.

Everyone must do something good that merits your attention. We put a lot of emphasis on production (sales and listings) outcomes. But there are other efforts involved in fostering a sales transaction or contributing to the company good that are worthy of recognition. By observing the salespeople, the problems they're trying to overcome or the behaviors they've corrected, you'll get clues for actions that you can praise.

Before you say this sounds like you're coddling, consider that we all deserve to feel good. Perhaps this is overlooked in the workplace because many people expect that work is not supposed to be a pleasurable experience. Consequently, some people merely *tolerate* work so that they can enjoy other pleasures in their lives. It takes very little effort on your part to share a kind word or a pat on the back to keep a salesperson from feeling taken for granted or worthless. And you'll feel good, too, when you see a stressed face light with a smile or a bowed head lift with pride.

Praise must be genuine. Don't read this book and, like a little automaton, walk into the office tomorrow and start praising every move your salespeople make. If you sound insincere or like you're following a programmed ritual, you'll do more harm than good. People spot a phony. You must *believe* that the actions are praiseworthy. Don't overuse praise. The element of surprise will make someone feel even more special.

Acknowledging things people do must be done with care. *Praise the performance, not the performer.* You're judging the performance rather than the person. People don't like to feel like they are constantly being evaluated and judged, although they do appreciate positive feedback about what they do. Also remember that some people are very uncomfortable about being recognized, so be careful not to embarrass them.

Address unacceptable behavior. Here's the part many managers, and again, parents, do best—spot undesirable or unacceptable behavior. That's not to say we address it very well, however. In the heat of the moment, any of us can fly off the handle and confront people. But depending on the nature of the transgression or the basic nature of the person being confronted, the behavior may change for only the length of time it takes to lash out, if it changes at all.

Most of us don't have the patience, nor is it necessarily appropriate, to ignore behavior that we consider unacceptable. But not every missed step deserves attention. Eventually people can feel that it's futile trying to please you when they get criticized for everything they do. Pick your battles. *Decide whether the consequences of an undesirable behavior are serious enough to warrant your action.*

- How jeopardized is the company—its mission, goals and objectives or legal position?

- How jeopardized is the salesperson—his or her professional growth and development or achievements?

- How jeopardized are the company's policies and procedures or the jobs or morale of other workers?

- How jeopardized are your public relations—your reputation with consumers, competitors or the community-at-large?

- Are you just annoyed or frustrated—is it a bad day?

Once you decide a behavior warrants your attention, chose a method for addressing the behavior that is likely to cause it to change. Yelling and screaming, even threatening, is one approach. But this rarely does much for the long term except anger or frustrate people. Remember the basic rule: your job is to address the behavior, not to attack the person. You want to preserve self-esteem while at the same time help the person change the conduct that you find unacceptable. As you saw in Chapter 12, this is done by first clearly identifying the behavior and the reasons why it is unacceptable, then agreeing on solutions for change.

This is probably a more deliberate and insightful approach to human behavior than is instinctive to most of us. We are usually more focused on the outcome—new behavior—rather than on the process that causes the change. But it is an unrealistic view of your power to expect people to "do as I say just because I say so." The person whose behavior must change is the one who has to buy into the process of changing.

A Manager's Behavior

Because we're discussing human behavior, it's appropriate to be introspective again. Consider the manager's human tendencies and behavior and how they affect the dynamics in the office and the relationships with the people being supervised.

Labeling.   It's natural to assign labels to people. In fact, some people pride themselves on being able to "size people up." But one fact about labels—people tend to behave in ways that are consistent with the labels they've been assigned or the way others perceive them. This does not necessarily mean that a label accurately reflects a person's ability or character. Nonetheless, it is the "handle" that person has been given, though it does little to help us manage effectively.

Look at the "successful" salesperson, for example. This label has a positive connotation. The person gains a positive attitude about himself or herself; the manager views the salesperson positively. The label may genuinely reflect the salesperson's ability and accomplishments and can even be a great motivator as he or she strives to live up to the reputation. *The tendency is, however, to manage the label rather than the person.* We could surrender the responsibility for supervising successful salespeople because we think they don't need us. Or we may overlook their mistakes or failings because these are inconsistent with the connotations of the label. The result is inconsistent management, even favoritism, because the manager is lenient with some salespeople and more critical of others.

How about "the loser"? We can label this poor soul into failure. As the so-called loser becomes increasingly less confident, the behavior deteriorates to match the label. The manager expects little or is more critical of the "loser," thinking that this person can't do better. Again, we're responding to the label rather than the person. There must be some redeeming value in this person's abilities that can be nurtured. Relinquish the label before you give up on the person.

Managers cannot afford to allow their perceptions of or attitudes toward people to affect the way they manage. All workers deserve to be viewed as individuals. When we label or stereotype people, we can't do this. We have an obligation to them and to the organization to keep an open mind and manage people as individuals, each with their own strengths and weaknesses. The manager's job is to help them reach their full potential. And when you do, they may surprise you!

Good days and bad days.   Everyone has good and bad days. Often we carry the effect of things that happen to us in one sector of our life into other sectors. The family gets the residual effect of a bad day at work, and vice versa. Before we're too quick to dismiss this behavior, consider how it affects our effectiveness as managers (and as partners or parents, for that matter).

People tend to associate your behavior toward them with something *they've* done rather than with something that's going on in your life. Everyone wants to know where they stand with one another. Consequently, they seek indications of approval or disapproval or acceptance or rejection. They monitor your words and actions toward them, expecting that these will provide the indicator they're looking for. However, your behavior may be unrelated to their behavior. Consequently, they can draw the wrong conclusions.

For example, a manager walks into the office one morning, grumbles a quick "hello" and heads directly to his desk. Normally, this manager delivers a cheery good morning and stops to chat with the salespeople before starting work. This uncharacteristic behavior can spark numerous reactions. The salesperson who's in a production slump reads this as displeasure with her. The salesperson who forgot to get the seller's signature on a disclosure form fears that the manager has discovered the oversight as well. Or the sales staff knows that the manager was hastily called to a meeting with the broker last night and feels threatened by the meaning of this. Yet what really happened that morning was that the manager had a flat tire on the way to work.

Must managers always have good days? Of course not. But they do need to think about how people can react to them on their bad days. We know that people can draw erroneous conclusions, so we owe it both to ourselves and others to clarify our behavior. In the above example it would have been appropriate for the manager to explain his or her actions. Before you say, "I don't owe anyone explanations," consider the consequences when you don't provide them. Misunderstandings and conflicts that result can do considerable damage to relationships and morale in the workplace. This only makes your job as a manager more difficult.

Prejudice.   All of us have different personalities, talents, styles and physical and cultural characteristics. Some people are even more likable than others. One of the most sensitive things managers have to do is scrutinize the prejudices or stereotypes they may have developed about others. Just as we must refrain from labeling people, we must refrain from allowing any of our preconceived notions about particular characteristics or traits to affect our view of people as individuals.

We deal with diversity in the people who work for the organization, as well as in our customers and clients. Whether a person is short, tall, fat, skinny, male, female, white, black or Hispanic has nothing to do with the ability of that person to do a job for the company. Not only it is clearly *unfair* to treat people differently but, depending on the nature of the characteristic, may also be clearly *illegal*. Such things as the degree of criticism, possibility for promotion or the evaluation of performance reviews should not be influenced by anything other than the job performance of an individual. Managing in multicultural environments requires the same kind of awareness and sensitivity that is required in providing equal opportunity in housing.

PREPARING TO COPE

Many of the situations that have been discussed arise because of stress in people's lives. Managers experience stress in their professional and personal lives. Enter the stress in the salespeople's lives and you can have a highly charged atmosphere. Then the manager aggravates the situation, creating additional stress, and you have a vicious cycle. In order to foster a constructive, productive working environment, managers must defuse the atmosphere rather than perpetuate the cycle.

Real estate sales is cited in a number of studies as one of the most stressful occupations. You can minimize the salespeople's stress by helping them feel worthwhile and appreciated and by being sensitive to their stresses outside the workplace. To be good to others, however, managers must first learn to be good to themselves. This means learning to cope with the physical and emotional demands of our lives. Today's fast-paced life styles only exacerbate the problem.

Stress Management

For many people, though, the harder or faster they run, the more their bodies long to slow down. Then when they do, they feel like they're wasting time or neglecting their responsibilities—more stress. According to the American Academy of Family Physicians, 67 percent of visits to family doctors are prompted by stress-related symptoms, ranging from asthma, allergies, headaches and excessive fatigue to indigestion, insomnia, anger, anxiety and depression.

Stress, either at home or work, often is not caused by external forces, but rather by the way people react physically or emotionally to situations. Major life experiences such as job changes, unemployment, divorce, death, serious illness and financial crises are likely to cause all of us stress. But other situations are stressful or not, depending on the person. Understanding how people's varied perceptions of situations contribute to their levels of stress is key to understanding how to cope.

Because stress is not likely to go away, we need to learn to deal with it, which means making changes. One of the reasons major life experiences are stressful is that change itself can create stress. Many times people in these situations find that support groups comprised of people in similar situations provide valuable coping skills. Often simply the experience of talking about and processing what is happening to them is very therapeutic.

In many cases you can change situations to manage or eliminate the source of the stress. Frequently we have to rethink how our work and personal lives fit together so that one is not tugging at the other. Titles such as "Superhuman" or "Super-Mom" create expectations that can be unrealistic and increase stress. Outside resources to assist with child or elderly care or flex work hours (which you were accustomed to as a salesperson) make it easier to cope with family responsibilities. Other irritants can be moderated or eliminated with a change in attitude. You can either do something about the unkempt yard by hiring a gardener or decide that you're not going to let it bother you until you can tend to it.

If stress is taking a toll on your health, changes in diet and exercise may be in order. Many people selling real estate never learned particularly healthy habits. We skipped meals; resorted to fast-food diets; and abandoned any routine for rest, exercise or relaxation, especially when business was good. Over the long haul, these abuses deplete the body's reserves. We need to reprogram our living patterns to break some of these habits so that our bodies are better prepared to cope with the demands of daily life.

Time Management

Living from crisis to crisis, being driven by problems that need solutions, is a major source of stress for many people. It's easy to feel that life is out of control when events or circumstances control us rather than us controlling them. One way we can calm the situation is to take charge by being effective time managers. In doing so, many of the situations that might otherwise develop into problems are tended to before they reach that level. Planning ahead also minimizes the stress of living from deadline to deadline.

Time management involves setting priorities and organizing things that need to be done around them. This begins with thinking about what you really value in life and doing things to protect what's most important. Taking a proactive approach puts you in control before situations flare into problems on either the home or the job front. Use a strategic approach to set long-range goals, short-range goals and arrange tasks accordingly. These tasks are then categorized by "have to's," "should do's" and "would like to's" for each day.

Another source of stress is feeling dissatisfied with what's been accomplished at the end of the day. This can be minimized by being realistic about how much can be done, concentrating on the "have to's" before the other tasks and anticipating that detours are bound to occur. Most of us have periods during the day in which we are most productive; these are the times to use to maximum advantage. The "down times" can be set aside to pause and regroup or to do routine tasks. Time management should help us be more efficient rather than overscheduled.

One way to set a realistic, constructive schedule is first to keep track of what you do each day for a week. Once you see how you use your time, you can identify how to be more efficient. (But don't lament the past; this can create more stress, and there's nothing constructive in that exercise.) Now you know what steals time from the things that are really important to you and can plan ways to improve. Learn to work smarter, not longer. And plan to have fun!

PROFESSIONAL GROWTH

Developing as a manager includes taking stock of your professional credentials. It's difficult to feel confident without the tools to the job, and it's difficult to establish credibility when people are unsure of your competency.

Most of us who start our own real estate brokerage companies or become sales or office managers have a background in real estate sales. As a result, many of us rise to these positions knowing more about selling real estate than about managing a real estate business. The experience we acquire as salespeople is an asset because it is certainly easier to run a business when we are knowledgeable about the industry. But as salespeople, we were not trained to manage the operations of the company or supervise people.

It is fairly common in the corporate world to promote effective workers to management positions. In doing so, we frequently take our most productive workers out of the jobs in which they are most successful and make them managers. In the real estate industry, many states' license laws also support this progression by requiring that brokers be experienced as licensed salespeople. And in some states the sales manager of an office must have a broker's license before assuming this role. It is possible to be successful in these new endeavors, but you'll enhance that possibility by learning how to be a supervisor, manager or business owner.

Education

Three areas of study will help you develop the knowledge and skills to enhance your professional credentials:

- real estate;

- business management; and

- leadership and personal development.

It is important for anyone in management to be current in the technical and legal aspects of the real estate business. These affect both the operation of the company and the daily activities of the salespeople. Being in touch with the latest trends and developments in the industry is also essential to guide the organization into the future.

As you've seen in this book, learning how to run the business affairs of the company and manage people is also crucial. Many valuable management and leadership courses and seminars are available, such as credit and noncredit courses, professional designation programs, seminars and training programs. Even those that do not focus exclusively on the real estate industry include many strategies that are universally applicable and others that are adaptable. There also are many fine publications, including those listed in the Bibliography, in which you can explore the ideas of visionaries in the business and real estate arenas.

Licensing Requirements

Each state has enacted laws governing certain education, experience and examination requirements for broker licensure, ranging from minimal to highly sophisticated procedures. In addition, there are continuing education requirements to retain a license in many states. The Association of Real Estate License Law Officials (ARELLO) publishes the *Digest of Real Estate License Laws–United States and Canada,* that provides information on prelicensing and continuing education requirements for the various states and territories. It is a useful resource for general information. For specific requirements and procedures, contact the regulatory body in your state's capital.

CONCLUSION

Developing as a manager involves learning how to manage the company's human resources and the human dynamics in the workplace. The way you do this is uniquely personal because it is a reflection of your own personality. Even though there are certain styles that define the way managers use their authority, such as dictatorial, autocratic or participative, the central issue is that everything a manager does affects human behavior.

Human resource management is a "people business." The goal is to learn about human beings so that what you do facilitates rather than inhibits constructive behavior and thus benefits the organization. Because you have a tremendous impact on both the atmosphere in the workplace and the quality of life of other people in this setting, much of your success as a manager depends on how well you understand and manage your own behavior and the stress in your life.

DISCUSSION EXERCISES

Discuss the management style that most closely approximates your instinctive style. What is most constructive about your approach? What is most destructive? How would you revise your style based on what you've learned?

* * *

What human tendencies do you have that work for or against you as a manager or in your personal life?

* * *

What have you learned about approaching the behavior of your salespeople? Consider typical scenarios or problems in an office and ways to handle them.

CHAPTER

17 Being a Communicator

Think about a conversation you've had with a buyer. What style house did the buyer say he or she wanted? What did you hear the buyer say? Were both of you thinking about the same thing?

Think about the last disagreement you had. What was the issue? Did the issue change before the argument was over? Did either of you hear one another? What changed after the argument?

Talking doesn't necessarily mean that people are communicating or exchanging information. What you say rarely causes people to react unless it's, "Don't sit there, it's wet!" And even then the message may not have any effect. The person sits down on the wet seat anyway. You see a very surprised look on the person's face, to which you reply, "I told you the seat was wet!" At least you didn't say "Dummy, I told you . . . "

The way we communicate with one another affects whether there is an exchange of messages or information between two people. What happened in the scenario above? Maybe you didn't have the person's attention when you delivered the warning. Or perhaps the person heard but chose to ignore your message. Several variables affect this scenario. One of them is you. Either your credibility is suspect or your reputation for being controlling or an alarmist negated your message. Another variable is the other person. The individual may be the type of person who has to find out for himself or herself. Perhaps the person thinks she or he has information you don't have (the seat didn't *look* wet).

Take this scenario further and you could say, "It's not my problem the person has to walk around in damp clothes—I tried," and walk away from the situation. But as a manager, you can't afford to walk away. If the message is really important (and you shouldn't be wasting people's time if it isn't), you have to take responsibility for seeing that it makes an impression or causes a reaction. When the tables are turned and people have a message for you, it's your responsibility to listen and react so people know they've been heard.

The fitting final step in this unit, as well as this book, is a discussion about ways to be an effective communicator. Communications is central in *everything* you do in management. You communicate with people as you plan, organize, staff, direct and control the company's operations. Your effectiveness as a leader, a team-builder, a coach, a decision-maker and a manager in a complex human environment depends on your ability to transmit and receive messages accurately. You also must be able to communicate effectively with the public, the customers and the clients you serve.

ESSENTIALS OF COMMUNICATION

We communicate because we have something we want someone else to know. It may be a fact a person can use; it may be a feeling we want to express; it may be an idea we want to explore; or it may be a request for an action or reaction. Regardless of the nature of the message, we want to make an impression so that the person receiving the message is changed in some respect because of the information we impart.

We deliver information or messages by what we write and say and with our mannerisms or our bodies. We receive information with all of our senses; everything that registers with our senses sends a message. The challenge is to send and receive messages accurately and effectively. There need to be ready and willing participants, and information must be transmitted and received in ways that ensure that the correct message is exchanged. As a manager, you must communicate exactly what you want people to do in ways that ensure you are understood. You also need to hear precisely the message people are trying to communicate to you.

It may take "two to tango," but in communications there are four "players" to consider: (1)the sender, (2)the receiver, (3)the atmosphere and (4)the message. More than just two human beings influence communications—the situation in which the communication occurs and the nature of the message are equally important. The four elements exist, regardless of whether communication is nonverbal, oral or written.

The Sender

The sender is the speaker or writer, the person with the message to impart. Messages are more than just the words we use. They are loaded with personal attitudes and meanings that are influenced by knowledge, education, culture and experience. Messages are codes of the sender.

The way the sender imparts a message in the first place affects whether it's heard. The sender's attitude and tone immediately affect whether the receiver tunes in or tunes out.

- "You" messages typically order, admonish, judge or ridicule the receiver and are very likely to get tuned out. When the receiver feels assaulted or attacked by the sender's tone or attitude, the reaction is likely to be, "Who needs this?" The sender won't hear the rest of the message even if it's not offensive.

- "Why" messages can also seem like an affront. "Why did you do . . . ?" sounds like a demand for justification, which also can turn off the rest of the message. "I would like to know about . . ." is far more constructive, less intimidating.

To capture and hold a person's attention and ensure that the message makes the desired impression, the sender must approach the receiver appropriately. Then the sender must take an active role in ensuring that the message is understood correctly. Don't rely on the receiver to do this. Provide sufficient information or explanation about your meaning. But there's a balance between providing sufficient information to clarify a message and overloading the receiver or clouding your point. We've all heard people kill a message either with extraneous detail or with so much repetition that we tune out until they get to the end.

In oral communications messages are being sent in addition to spoken words. Your body "tells a tale," which we'll discuss shortly, giving the receiver additional information. When the verbal and nonverbal messages appear to contradict one another, the sender is communicating mixed messages, which can interfere with or cloud the intended message.

The Receiver

The receiver is the person (or group of people) for whom the message is intended. The receiver must take responsibility for decoding the sender's message. The sender's and the receiver's codes are not likely to be the same because the receiver's is the product of that person's attitudes, perceptions, experiences and the like. These affect the receiver's ability to interpret the message the way the sender intended or even to listen to the message in the first place.

Most of us spend more time receiving or assimilating messages than we do sending, especially because everything that registers with our senses is a message. Consequently, learning how to receive accurately or listen actively is extremely important. The receiver can minimize miscommunications, such as mistakes, misunderstandings or misinterpretations, by taking responsibility for getting the message straight. What kind of listener are you?

- Do you interrupt or try to finish a person's sentence?

- Do you "tune out" until the person finishes talking?

- Do you think before you respond?

- Do you have a response before you're sure you've heard what the person is saying?

If your answer to any of these questions is "yes," you could be distorting the sender's message. Before we interject ourselves into the communications, we have to be sure we're on the same wavelength. The listener needs to take an active role in learning to see the things as the sender sees them. This requires listening with objectivity, empathy and patience and then reaffirming what we *thought* we heard before accepting the message or storing the impression.

We need to listen with open minds and not be judgmental of or threatened by either the sender or the message. Active listening skills, such as restating in your own words what you thought you heard or asking questions, help to receive and decode messages accurately. Miscommunications arise because people don't take time to do this. Instead they jump to conclusions, which can be erroneous. This sets up a cycle of miscommunications or shuts down communications entirely.

Active listening stimulates thinking. When problem solving was discussed in Chapter 12, for example, the manager was advised to facilitate a solution by asking questions. This guides people as they think through a situation, which is far more constructive than telling someone what to do. This way managers energize people to utilize talent, skill and intellect in self-directed ways.

The Atmosphere

The atmosphere is the condition under which a message is sent and received. Both the sender and the receiver need the undivided attention of the other, free from distractions. Communicating occurs accurately when it is done in the right place, at the right time and under the right conditions.

We've all had the experience of approaching a person with an important issue we wanted to discuss, only to be disappointed with the outcome of the conversation. The message got lost or misinterpreted; perhaps it was only partially heard. Static in the atmosphere, which may be a mental distraction, noise or an interruption, distracted the receiver. Written communications get lost in the atmosphere as well. Look at the pile of correspondence on your desk, the number of memos hanging on the office bulletin board or volume of postings in your e-mail file. How many of these get read? Attention to your message can be diverted by other messages.

If the atmosphere is emotionally charged for either the sender or receiver, it's difficult for people to communicate in an objective or nonjudgmental manner. One of the reasons arguments or disagreements rarely reach a satisfactory conclusion is that there's a lot of sending and no receiving. People rarely listen effectively during the heat of emotion. Someone has to take responsibility for defusing the atmosphere and cooling emotion. Otherwise people unload more messages and stray from the original point. They end up attacking each other rather than focusing on the issue.

The Message

As stated earlier, information is the message that is being communicated. *Information* in this context is anything the sender needs to say. Regardless of the form of the message, be it nonverbal, verbal or print, they still are messages sent in codes that need to be decoded.

The receiver is the one who controls whether to listen to a message, even though it may be very important to the sender. We can easily suffer from information overload when we are bombarded with many messages. The protective mechanism is to tune out messages. There may be just too much information to process; or the message itself provokes too many emotions. As we've seen, oral messages can easily be tuned out, and written messages can easily get tossed. If the message is important enough to warrant being communicated, the sender has to be sure it's transmitted in ways that enhance its reception.

The Response

The communication cycle closes when the receiver of the message responds. The same four elements of communication are involved, except that the roles are reversed. Now the receiver becomes the sender. The response, which can be either verbal or nonverbal, is a new message, sent in a new code, that must be decoded. Possibly the atmosphere is also new, depending on what transpired when the first message was sent.

The timing of the response is critical. The receiver must be sure that he or she has really heard the message before responding. But receivers get impatient and short-circuit the cycle. Interrupting the sender or anticipating the complete message before the sender is through won't help either the sender or the receiver to understand one another. In order to respond in a meaningful way the receiver must give the sender adequate opportunity to express the message and seek clarification.

Depending on how the senders and receivers are interacting with one another and the nature or purpose of the communication, the cycle either ends with the response or it continues. If people are communicating effectively, the dialogue will conclude when both the sender and receiver are satisfied that all the messages that are appropriate for the time being have been exchanged.

One person can always shut down the cycle before the other one feels the communication has reached a satisfactory conclusion. Sometimes a person has to take one more turn—one last shot at getting a point across—even if the atmosphere has started to deteriorate. Or a memo may get tossed in the round file before it's read. As the manager it's incumbent on you to see that the cycle doesn't shut down prematurely.

COMMUNICATIONS BREAKDOWNS

In earlier chapters we talked about our human tendencies and their effect on other people. People pick up messages, some that we don't intend, because of our behavior. When we discussed addressing people's behavior and solving problems, we saw how the way a situation is approached affects the outcome. Look at some of the other things that happen when we're trying to communicate.

Consider the source.   A person's credibility, trustworthiness and integrity affect the listener's level of attention. If we don't perceive that the person with whom we are communicating is worthy of our attention, we just turn off. If we have reason to believe that the person is deceptive, we listen with only half an ear. There may be nothing objectionable about the message; we simply don't hear it because of its source.

Need to be right.   Some messages intend to confront behavior that the sender considers undesirable or unacceptable. These messages can be interpreted as judgmental. If you're right, that must mean that someone else must be wrong. Pit two strong-willed people against one another and typically neither one wants to give in to the other. The longer this battle of wills continues, the more determined each one becomes that he or she is right. The point of the communications now is not the original purpose of the message but rather the need for one to be declared victor as the one who is right.

Parallel talk.   We hear about very small children being engaged in parallel play. That means they are each "doing their own thing" but doing it in proximity to one another. Parallel talk is essentially the same. Two people are talking in proximity to one another, but they are not exchanging messages. The missing ingredient is *listening*. They're doing what could be called listening with their mouths open; both are talking and neither is hearing what the other is saying. This frequently happens when people are very emotional.

Power of perceptions.   We may be speaking the same language but that doesn't mean we speak from the same frame of reference. Words mean different things to different people. We're back to differences in perceptions, like right or wrong, ethical or unethical, even hot or cold. In a management context, consider what happens when you tell people they're conscientious. You may mean that you see them as being capable and attentive to detail so they can take the necessary action to correct a problem. However, they may *hear* that there's no need for them to take any further action because being conscientious means that they've already done all that is necessary. Unless meanings are clarified messages get distorted.

Selective hearing. Could adults possibly hear only what they want to hear? We know that children do, particularly if the message seems unimportant ("Clean up your room") or is something they don't want to hear ("You didn't clean up your room"). Adults have selective hearing as well. Messages that seem like criticism or seem irrelevant or trivial are discounted. Sometimes information just doesn't register.

Perhaps you've seen an exercise with a wristwatch to prove this point. Without looking at the watch you are wearing, do you know the color of the wristband, the style of numbering used to indicate the hours, or whether the watch has a sweep hand or displays the date? Perhaps you never noticed these details, because you habitually focus on the time each time you look at the watch.

Our attention is often drawn to only that information we think we need. However, we may discount other information that is truly relevant. When we do this, communications break down because we don't hear everything that is being said.

Reading between the lines. We don't always tell people exactly what we think. Instead we send codes and expect people to read between the lines to get the message. People sometimes do this to sugarcoat or take the sting out of a message they are afraid to share. For example, telling a person that you weren't too impressed with the way he or she handled a situation can be cast aside as a passing comment. But you really intended to communicate your displeasure with the violation of a company policy. Don't cloud important messages in mystery or assume that because a person is reasonably intelligent, he or she will get your point.

Games people play. Some people like to play communications games. Sometimes they're jousting just for fun, being humorous; other times they have a hidden agenda. They may be testing the waters to see how you'll react. Sit in a meeting and listen to someone say, "Let's just raise the price!" Is this comment intended simply to break the ice around the conference table and to be taken seriously? Does this person like to play devil's advocate (Some people just like to be contrary or nonconformist.) Or is the person a serious proponent of this solution who is trying one more time to gain support for an idea? In any case, the comment is likely to provoke a reaction. But the reaction may be inappropriate or unwarranted because no one has a clue as to what game the person is playing.

COMMUNICATING EFFECTIVELY

Relationships with people are built or fractured by the way we communicate. For managers this is a critical lesson because it affects their ability to energize, support and inspire people in the organization. Communicating is as much a sensory experience, through sight, hearing and touch, as it is the words we read and write. Building on the discussion about the essentials of communication and ways communications break down, let's look at ways to become more effective communicators.

Nonverbal Communications

Many of us don't realize how much we communicate without saying a word. Our posture, facial expressions, tilt of the head or an arm or hand movement can tell anyone who is watching what we are thinking. People can read acceptance, rejection, openness or defensiveness just by observing our nonverbal behavior. Some of the most powerful messages we send are not spoken.

We can use nonverbal communications as purposely as we use words. Nothing needs to be said; we speak volumes with only a body or a facial movement. We all know people of few words, yet we rarely wonder what they are thinking or feeling. Nonverbal communications can send positive messages like agreement, pleasure or encouragement. They also can be used to minimize a verbal confrontation. Displeasure or aggravation, for example, can be communicated without using words that might spark a confrontation or inhibit a constructive exchange.

Our body language also can send messages that we don't plan or intend to communicate. A gesture or facial expression may give away a thought or feeling unconsciously. (This is how people pick up signals that you didn't know you sent.) Or your body may reveal thoughts you are processing that have nothing to do with the current conversation or the people around you. Remember the discussion in the previous chapter about conclusions the salespeople could make from the manager's behavior. A manager or supervisor is "on stage" all the time. To prevent communications from going astray, a manager must be vigilantly conscious of the messages being sent.

What message do you get from a smile, a frown, eye contact, a raised eyebrow, a scowl, for example? What message do you send when you drum your fingers on the table, lean forward in your chair, roll your eyes, reach out and place a hand on a person's arm, look away from the speaker? The messages can range from acceptance and attentiveness to impatience and dissatisfaction. Remember that not everyone will interpret actions the same way. What messages do *you* get from these acts?

- How do you feel when someone makes eye contact with you, especially when the person doesn't look away? Does this eventually become so uncomfortable that you need to break the spell? Locking eyes can be intimidating. People can conclude that you're disagreeing or trying to stop them from pursuing a line of thinking. This is different from the acceptance or attentiveness that is normally associated with more casual eye contact.

- How do you feel about people touching you? Some people are naturally very "touchy-feely;" people who are not are sometimes put off when others touch them. Placing a hand on a person's arm during a conversation could communicate openness, acceptance or compassion. But the gesture could be offensive. The point to be made is that any action a person considers to be an inappropriate advance is *never* suitable.

- How do you feel about people getting close to you? People define their space as that reserved for themselves and only selected others. When anyone else gets too close, they feel uncomfortable or violated. Going nose to nose with a person during an animated conversation can disrupt the message if a person feels attacked. Have you noticed the silence and lack of eye contact that is common in elevators? People are too close to strangers for comfort.

- How do you feel about people grinning at you? Do you wonder what's going on in their heads? Perhaps they're grinning with you, but perhaps they're laughing at you. We appreciate what appears to be warm acceptance, but a smile could be misinterpreted unless it is timed well.

- How do you read people who fold their arms across their bodies, slump down in their chairs or shuffle their feet? Normally these actions communicate that they are no longer willing participants in an exchange; they have become defensive or impatient or have "turned you off." However, for some people these actions may be related to nothing more than physical comfort.

Just as oral communications require active listening to clarify the messages, nonverbal communications require clarification as well. As you have seen, nonverbal behavior is subject to interpretation. When you pick up a clue, verify it. This is important when addressing a group as well as in one-on-one communications. Look at the messages people are sending with their eyes and bodies. Verify your position with them or gauge the effectiveness of your message by asking questions.

The power of silence.   Silence sends a powerful message. It is both impressive and persuasive. Observe the way good public speakers use well-timed pauses or silence for emphasis. They make an important point and then are quiet, allowing people time to contemplate the message. In sales we learn to do the same thing: make your point and then be quiet. Silence is powerful because it gives people time to process the information or message; silence that follows certain points also can signal their importance.

Some people feel that the way to keep control or keep someone's attention is by talking. Perhaps a few more words will be convincing, especially if the speaker is unsure how a message is being received. The speaker may fear what's really going on in the listener's head when the speaker's not talking. But listeners can't assimilate information when attention is diverted by more words. During silence you can hold people's attention with your eyes and facial expression, even create anticipation so they will want to hear more. Silence also slows the speaker down long enough to gauge reactions before unloading information that could be irrelevant or inappropriate.

Oral Communications

Being heard and being understood are the primary concerns of any two people engaged in a conversation, a discussion or a meeting. As a manager, you initiate some of these events; other times these events are initiated by someone you supervise. In either case your position requires that you take responsibility for seeing that both of you communicate effectively.

When you are the speaker, don't rely on the listener to decode what you say. Encourage feedback. Check for understanding; then you can clarify or expand upon what you said. This is safer than assuming you are understood. Encourage feedback by using *open-ended questions*. These are questions that require explanations, that begin with *How, What, Who, When or Where*. Messages also can be clarified simply by stating in your own words what you thought you heard.

Using open-ended questions to clarify messages.   For example, after describing a new office procedure, conclude with, "How do you think this will work for you?" This creates an opportunity for the person to react to the procedure and keeps the dialogue flowing. Also you can gauge how well the person understands what you've explained. Using open-ended questions to stimulate feedback is better than closed-ended questions, those which are answered with only "Yes" or "No." These tend to shut down dialogue. If you ask, "Do you understand the procedure?" you have no verification of *what* the person understands if the response is affirmative. If you ask, "Do you like the procedure?" you create an opportunity for someone to say "No." Now you have a negative reaction to overcome.

As the listener, give the speaker your undivided attention and respect. Resist the temptation to talk until it's your turn. Otherwise you'll have two senders, as with parallel talk. Even when someone asks, "Did you hear me?" this may not be intended to clarify communications. Instead it expresses frustration or is a plea to listen some more because the speaker feels a loss of attention. When you confirm what you thought you heard, you not only clarify the message but demonstrate that you're interested in what the person is saying.

Suppose someone says, "I think the new office procedure will make more work for me." You can shut down communications by responding, "That's not the way I see it." You can encourage dialogue by saying, "Do you think there's too much paperwork involved?" If the person says "Yes," you've identified the issue that must be pursued. If the person says "No," ask, "What aspect do you think will make more work for you?" The purpose is to identify the problematic issue. You might find that the person didn't really mean "more work" but instead sees something else as the potential problem.

Using statements to clarify messages. In the previous example, the comment about the new procedure making more work could be restated by saying, "It sounds to me like you anticipate that there will be more paperwork. Is that right?" Then the dialogue would continue with the person responding "Yes" or "No. I was thinking about how much more time it will take to explain what the buyer will have to do." Continue the process by restating and clarifying until both parties are speaking the same language. Restatement is very useful when people offer opinions and feelings. These messages are often loaded with attitudes and perceptions that you need to understand.

As you saw in earlier chapters, some of the meetings or conversations you have can be very upbeat and casual and others can be more intimidating or uncomfortable. The way you handle these situations can either facilitate or inhibit communications. The following ideas will help you.

- *When people express feelings—acknowledge them.* Each of us is entitled to feel the way we do. No one wants to be told a feeling is not legitimate or be required to justify a feeling. Sometimes all a person wants is someone to listen. When a salesperson says, "I'm really frustrated with . . . " or "I'm really disappointed about . . . ," the best response is "Tell me about it," rather than "Don't feel that way" or "Why?"

Feelings are highly personal. It can be very frustrating, even aggravating, for someone to hear, "I know exactly how you feel," because the logical response is "You can't possibly know what I'm feeling inside." We all want respect and support for our feelings. Provide understanding. Help a person cope by offering some information or a different perspective. Recognize that ultimately each of us is responsible for feeling the way we do.

- *When people express anger—don't argue with them.* Confrontation only heightens the tension, and soon no one is listening. Some people don't want to be angry alone. They're not satisfied until they get someone else as riled as they are. You can really frustrate them during a tirade by calmly interjecting, "Are you finished?" Clarify the cause of the anger and then find out what the person expects you to do. Otherwise you can fall into the trap of intervening in a problem that really isn't yours to solve just to quiet the storm. Or you may prescribe a solution you'll later regret. Maybe all the person wanted to do was vent.

- *When people share thoughts and ideas—thank them.* They're taking a risk by sharing with you because you could ridicule or laugh at them. One of the reasons suggestion boxes are popular is that they solicit comments or ideas in a non-threatening manner. People don't have to witness your reaction face-to-face. If you use a suggestion, give credit where it is due. You want people to play on your team and take an interest in where they work, so acknowledge their contributions.

- *When people express a problem—decide who is responsible for the solution.* Don't play hero and intervene where you don't belong. In Chapter 12 we discussed problem-solving and the process a manager uses to identify who *owns* the problem. That is the person who's responsible for implementing a solution. If it's your problem, you fix it. But if the problem belongs to someone else, help that person find a solution.

If the problem is office grousing, remember that a little grousing is normal. It's a healthy safety valve that frequently doesn't require intervention. Leave it alone, unless it could be really destructive.

- *Avoid asking for justification.* The natural inclination is to ask people *why* they did something. Earlier we mentioned that people bristle at the sound of a "Why?" question. They feel like they're being accused or backed into a corner that they have to justify their way out. You may want to know why a person chose a course of action. But it's more constructive to inquire how someone chose a course of action or what the person was thinking about. We're not playing games with semantics, just staying away from emotionally charged words that can inhibit communications.

- *Avoid telling people what to think.* This puts people on the defensive: "I'm an adult and quite capable of forming my own opinions. Stay out of my life." If you are asked for advice or are trying to help someone find a solution, provide suggestions rather than directives. This gives people the opportunity to exhibit initiative and take ownership of an idea. They are more likely to act on an idea that is theirs rather than someone else's.

- *Avoid setting people up for a "fall."* These are the " . . . but . . ." messages. "You're really a good producer, but . . . " While attempting to cushion a blow, it's tempting to slide a negative under cover of a positive. This doesn't mean you should hit a person between the eyes, or be cruel and insensitive. If you have to discipline someone, say, for example, "There is a situation I want to discuss," and describe the issue so that the person understands exactly the behavior that is problematic. Save the praise for another time so that you don't send mixed messages.

Conversely, if you have outstanding news or something very flattering to say, don't reduce its importance with

"You did a good job solving the mortgage problem, now make sure the sale closes." This is another "but" message in which one comment diminishes the meaning of the other. Remember, too, that people deserve to be praised. Don't refrain out of fear that you'll inflate an ego or cool production.

While these techniques are presented in the context of work situations, they are equally applicable in any interpersonal communications. Try them in your personal life, too. They become habit-forming with use.

Public Speaking

Sometime during our careers, perhaps each week in sales meetings, all of us will be addressing a group of people. Public speaking is different than one-on-one communications in several respects. The obvious differences are that messages are prepared to meet the needs of a group rather than individual listeners, and there's no immediate feedback or response from the receivers, in this case the audience. When the speaker is uncomfortable in front of an audience, the effectiveness or impact of the message is compromised. Learn to be an effective public speaker and you can be an effective communicator in this forum.

Look at the way the same essentials of communications we've been discussing work in group settings.

Sender. This is the speaker. Capture and then hold people's attention while you clearly communicate your message. Sometime during or after the presentation get feedback to ensure that your message has been heard correctly. Remember that senders use codes in public speaking the same way they do in one-on-one communications. Because there's rarely immediate dialogue between the sender and receivers, it's important to provide sufficient explanation to minimize misinterpretation.

Preparation is the key to any successful public speaking engagement. This includes preparing both the message (which we'll discuss shortly) and yourself. It's not uncommon to feel a bit of anticipation as the adrenaline begins to pump. After all, being invited to make a presentation is very flattering and you want to do a good job. Most butterflies flutter over concerns about the delivery of the presentation and its reception by the audience.

One of the best ways to build confidence is to become thoroughly familiar with the topic, which includes preparing your message carefully. It's easier to command the group when you have command of the information. Enhance that confidence by preparing to deliver the presentation. The strength of your voice, your posture in front of the group or behind a podium, your eye contact with the audience and your mannerisms during the presentation will reveal your confidence level. Some speakers are very captivating, not just because of what they say, but because of the way they say it.

Rehearse. Plan exactly what you will do to take command of the group, especially during the first minute after you're introduced and before minds start to wander. Practice your entire presentation in front of a mirror with a tape recorder so you know how you'll look and sound. Rehearse with your notes so that your delivery looks natural while using them. Be sure you can make eye contact with the audience. Even experienced speakers run through their presentations to determine where to pause or raise their voices for emphasis and to gauge the pace or length of the presentation. A bit too short is better than too long. Extra time can be used for questions and answers. Don't read a speech! That's deadly for the audience and can shut down communications.

Plan your delivery to suit the occasion. A classroom or training session is different from a luncheon speech or a keynote address. The former can be less formal than the latter, making it easier to interact with the group, especially when you're not confined to a stage, and behind a podium. Anything that creates a mental or physical barrier, such as a podium, a microphone cord or an overhead projector, can inhibit communications. These may provide a sense of security for the speaker (a place to hide). But good public speakers learn to communicate over and around these barriers with their personality and eye contact.

Don't take yourself too seriously—have fun! If you make a mistake, you're likely to be the only one who knows. So keep going. If it's obvious to the group, acknowledge that you misstepped and get back on track. Just because you're the speaker doesn't mean you have to be perfect. Every speaker has an "off day" once in awhile. If you're using humor, think twice about what you're going to say. Jokes are fine as long as you select them carefully and can tell them well. Think about whether a joke could be offensive! Humor is easily misinterpreted. If jokes aren't your style, light-hearted tales or examples can be used. The more opportunities you have to be a speaker, the more you will find that being on stage is a very enjoyable place to be.

Receiver. This is the audience. People have a variety of reasons for attending, so the motivations of receivers can be different. This affects their attentiveness and their receptiveness to your message. Also remember that each individual in the group decodes what you are saying with his or her own codes. There are as many opportunities for your message to be distorted as there are people in the group.

Read the audience and respond to their cues. Do people appear to be restless, puzzled or defensive? Learn to think on your feet and tailor your presentation to the signals you're receiving. Pick up the pace, interject an anecdote, add another example or emphasize the benefits of the message. It's rare that everyone in the audience will be totally captivated by you or what you are saying. Play to the group as a whole, and don't be intimidated by a few participants who stray from you on occasion.

Rarely will everyone hear the precise message you intend to communicate. Just as in one-on-one communications, you need feedback to clarify the message. Encourage feedback by fielding questions or comments. This can be done during or at the end of the presentation. Communications are enhanced by addressing questions or inviting comments at appropriate intervals during the presentation, but you have to keep control of the topic, time and crowd while doing this. Even if you handle questions and comments at the conclusion of the presentation, you can enhance your rapport with the participants as well as the communications by being available after the program to address individual inquiries.

Atmosphere. This is the physical environment of the forum. The arrangement of the room and seating, lighting, audio system, heating/cooling and visual aids affect the message. When people are comfortable and there are minimum distractions such as whispering within the group, the message is more likely to be heard.

The speaker's job is to manage the atmosphere as well as the message. Although you may not always have control over the physical environment, you can take steps to avoid problems. Test the audio and video equipment and evaluate the room for the comfort of the participants before the program. During the presentation don't allow distractions to interfere. Assign someone the responsibility for being your "gofer," to look after lighting, heating/cooling and audiovisual problems and other distractions. Don't be surprised if you encounter technical difficulties; be prepared to adjust the presentation accordingly.

Message.   This is the presentation. Tailor the message to suit the audience. Otherwise, it won't be meaningful and you'll lose people's attention (which also discourages them from attending any of your future presentations). If you're in charge of selecting the topic, learn about the audience before picking it. If you've been told the general nature of the topic, you still have to learn about the audience to select the proper approach. It's as dangerous to make assumptions about people in groups as it is to make them about individuals.

Because the group is comprised of varied interests and levels of understanding or familiarity with the topic, the choice of message and the development of its presentation is critical. Before preparing the presentation, crystallize in your mind the major points you want to make and the reason they are important to people. Then develop the supporting detail. Do some research to prepare yourself and to assemble interesting facts or figures that prove your points. Now prepare your notes.

The presentation should include an introduction, the substantive content and a conclusion.

- Tell people what you're going to say;
- tell them your tale; and

- tell them what you told them.

Use the introduction to capture people's attention with the objective of and rationale for your message. The substantive content, which is about 80 percent of the program, should be supported with examples and tools such as handouts and visual aids. The conclusion should be a summary of the major points you made. Anticipate the kinds of questions that people might raise and assemble resource information or exhibits to take with you in case you need them.

Now you should have your act together. As you can see, good productions take preparation. You'll be less rattled and ready for the show if you get your act together ahead of time. Then arrive early, get the stage set and enjoy the crowd before it's curtain time.

WRITING EFFECTIVELY

There are times when written communications are preferable to oral ones. Our minds can absorb more detail in print than they can follow via oral delivery. Written communications are effective for disseminating information and provide a printed document for future reference if necessary. They are an expedient way to communicate because communicating face-to-face can take more time.

Some people, however, use written communications to do the wrong things. They generate a memo rather than addressing an important issue face-to-face, or they hide behind a piece of paper or an e-mail rather than risk confronting a situation personally. These are situations in which oral communication is most suitable. Important issues should not be trivialized in a memo. Problems need feedback and resolution, which can't be accomplished as satisfactorily in writing. Communicate announcements, updates and impersonal things in print; handle the really important and personal issues face-to-face.

Capture Readers

The receiver of the written word is in control rather than the writer. People may not (and many just plain don't) take time to read. Communicating is becoming increasingly difficult as people try to insulate themselves from information overload, especially because of the volume that is currently available electronically and in print. People are becoming very discriminating about the information they choose to access. Have you sat through a meeting or a conversation when people behaved as though they never heard about the subject of a discussion? Just because you sent the agenda ahead of time or forwarded a valuable article doesn't ensure that you imparted your message.

After we've said all this, be aware that you still need to communicate in writing. The challenge is to do it effectively, regardless of whether the written word is delivered on paper or electronically. First you have to get people's attention. Written communications must catch the eye. If it looks attractive or has an attention grabbing title or header so that people will at least pursue it, you're part way home. Then you have to hook their minds. Ask yourself, "If someone only skims my writing, what's the essence of my message?" Most people today won't bother wading through a lot of background or history. Letters and memos, the most common forms of written communications in business, must be compelling and to the point.

There are six steps involved in preparing a written communiqué:

1. Draft the document (this is the creative step).

2. Write the introduction.

3. Walk away from the document and let some time pass.

4. Edit the document (this is the analytical step).

5. Prepare the final copy.

6. Proofread the final document.

Two of the most critical steps are steps 3 and 4. A written message can strike you much differently after some time passes than it did during the drafting stage. You may decide to rethink or clarify what you wrote. All documents, even the shortest memo, should be scrutinized for grammar, spelling and punctuation. As good as computers and word-processing programs are, human beings see things the computer can't. Ask someone else to proofread for you. This is useful to clarify communications as well as to catch typographical errors that the author is not likely to see.

Business Letters

Business letters normally intend to inspire the reader to respond to an inquiry or a request for information or to attend a meeting. Or they convey information, explanations or expressions of appreciation or regret to the reader. Before you put pencil to paper or fingers to the keyboard, clearly define what you want to accomplish. Otherwise you'll have a collection of words that won't accomplish much more than to waste the reader's time.

Next plan the letter. Jot down several major points that you want to make and the significant details. This helps avoid the "nice-to-know" kind of information that can distract from your message. As you assemble the details, research the facts to avoid making mistakes. Remember that you're preparing a tangible document, which means you are also recording your errors. Now you are ready to draft the letter.

Write the body of the letter, using the major points and details you compiled. Arrange the points in a logical sequence rather than rambling. There are two approaches you can use.

1. Build to a climax by beginning with the least important point and ending with the most important. Or reverse the sequence.

2. Begin with the most important point and follow with the less important or supportive points. If you are tracing events, present the information chronologically.

The objective of the letter and the nature of the information will affect the arrangement.

Be natural as you write. You have an advantage if you are writing to someone you know because you can personalize the message. In fact friends and acquaintances may be offended if the tone of the letter sounds like you're writing to a stranger. Even if the letter is written to a group, such as your customers or clients, use a friendly, personal tone.

Be specific about what you want the reader to do. (If you don't know, how will the reader?) If the reader's supposed to confirm attendance at a meeting, specify how and when this should occur. If you want a response, specify what you want to know and when and how to contact you.

Now write the opening or introduction and the closing. (It's easier to introduce the message after you know its content.) The opening should capture the reader's attention and explain why you are writing. Readers are unlikely to pursue the rest of a letter if you don't get to the point immediately. If the opening is wordy, convoluted or dull, this suggests that the letter will be too. Say, "Thank you," instead of, "I want to thank you." Say, "The next meeting of the executive committee is Monday, April xx," instead of "This is to inform you that the next meeting of the executive committee has been scheduled." Close with a summary of the major points, an expression of good will or something to motivate the action you've requested. Finally, end with "sincerely," "best regards" or other similarly friendly closure.

The product you have at this point is a draft of the letter you plan to send. Follow the steps listed earlier to convert this to its final form. Because the appearance of the letter makes an impact on the reader, use a current stylebook or follow a template in your word-processing program to format a readable, professional-looking letter.

Memos

Many more memos than letters circulate in business today, particularly in interoffice communications. They are useful for short directives or disseminating information that does not require a great deal of explanation. Especially with e-mail, memos circulate quickly and efficiently. Unfortunately, many memos are little more than clutter. It's not uncommon for recipients to wonder whether some people have nothing else to do except generate memos. Consider why you're writing a memo and whether it's worth a person's time to read it. Are there other, better ways to send the same message?

Memos generally are shorter (preferably a single page), more concise and less formal than letters. The image and format of the memo are critical. Readers should feel compelled to read it; they should be able to grab its essence by scanning it. Memos begin simply with the name of the recipient and the sender, the date of the memo and a statement of its subject. The opening or first several lines (and that's as long as the paragraph should be) should capture the essence of the message. Additional information or supporting detail can be outlined, bullet-pointed or listed in simple sentences rather than in lengthy paragraphs. This way readers can easily pick out important points. Be sure the content is only that which can be seen by anyone because memos are commonly seen by more people than the intended recipients.

Draft a memo using the same process that was discussed for letters. Define the objective of the memo and the major points that you want to make, then write a draft. Memos often do not contain a closing unless there's one last important point, such as, "Please call me by noon on Friday to confirm the arrangements." Memos get cluttered with summaries or cliché endings. Review and edit the memo to ensure that it's professional before committing it to final form.

E-mail and the Internet.   Memos can be easily and efficiently be circulated via e-mail or internal computer networks. However, they are less private than you probably imagine. Anyone with sufficient computer expertise, including someone outside the company, can read another person's e-mail. Furthermore, people can easily forward any message or memo to anyone. Take great care to avoid comments that could be misinterpreted or discussion of information that should not be widely circulated. As in any written communication, review it for clarity and make it look professional, using correct grammar and spelling. E-mail or the Internet is suitable for short memos when only the essence of the message and little other detail is necessary. Before sending the communication, make a copy for yourself in case you need a record.

Effective Editing

The way you share your message is as important as what you say to the reader. Because we stressed the importance of being concise and precise in your writing, there are some rules to follow that make written communications effective.

- *Avoid wordiness.* Don't use two or three words when one will do. Messages are more powerful when fewer words are used. Use "analyze" instead of "perform an analysis of . . ." or "because" instead of "due to the fact." Some words are simply redundant, such as "circle around" instead of "circle" or "cooperate together" instead of "cooperate."

- *Avoid pretentiousness.* Stilted writing is less personal and can create a barrier with the reader. Refer to the "previous" paragraph instead of the "aforementioned" one; ask the reader to "get the facts" instead of to "ascertain the data."

- *Avoid awkwardness.* It's more direct to say, "You have a problem for which there's only one solution," instead of, "There's a problem you have only one solution for." (Try not to end a sentence with a preposition anyway, unless the alternative is unbearably awkward.)

- *Avoid jargon.* Insider words and phrases commonly used in specific industries and professions have little meaning to other people. Even people in an industry tire of hearing the same jargon repeatedly. Keep it to a minimum. If you must use jargon with outsiders, explain the meaning the first time it's used.

- *Avoid sexism.* Pronouns and designations are the most common forms of sexist language. *Salesperson* can be used instead of *salesman.* Pronouns such as him, her, he and she can often be avoided by changing the noun (and therefore the pronoun) to the plural form or by rewriting a sentence to avoid the pronoun entirely. Say, "Writers can edit their work," instead of "A writer can edit his or her work." The "his/her" construction is awkward for the reader and should be avoided wherever possible.

- *Avoid condescension.* Address readers directly rather than "talking down" to them. This is more a matter of tone than specific language. "As you are aware . . ." could be interpreted as, "I told you so."

- *Avoid overly long sentences and paragraphs.* Frequently the "punch" of the message gets lost in too many words or digressions. Make concise points in focused sentences. Avoid long trails of thoughts that are patched together with numerous commas. Single sentences containing related thoughts, however, must flow smoothly into one another. Often you'll see more effective or efficient ways to express your thoughts after the writing sits awhile before you edit.

Written communications have the same essential elements as other communications. However, each functions slightly differently. Written communications can seem one-sided because the sender, in this case the writer, is solely responsible for

- capturing the receiver's attention;

- delivering the message accurately;

- ensuring that the message will be interpreted correctly; and

- preventing the message from getting lost in the atmosphere.

Once the message is sent, the writer has lost control of what happens next. Consequently, the sender must anticipate the receiver's reaction, the atmosphere in which the message will be heard and the meaning of the message itself when preparing a written communiqué. Although there's no guarantee that you'll avoid all of the ways communications can go astray, a well-presented, organized and well-written message is far more likely to be effective than one that is carelessly or hastily produced.

CONCLUSION

Effective communication requires that people tune in to one another so that there's an exchange of information. Otherwise, communicating is like playing a radio that's not tuned quite properly. There's just too much static. Static in communications includes attitudes, perceptions and emotions of people and other distractions that inhibit the exchange of information. The goal is to communicate for understanding. This can be achieved by managing the elements of the communication cycle to ensure that both the sender and receiver are all on the same wave length, especially when their relationship is adversarial or emotionally charged.

Oral, nonverbal and written messages are a manager's most powerful tools. Consider, too, the influence people as leaders achieve when they learn to use these tools effectively. Certainly, our private lives can be enhanced as we gain greater awareness of the way we communicate in our interpersonal relationships. We trust that our messages throughout this book will have a positive impact on the professional growth of you, our readers. Perhaps our messages will enhance your personal life as well.

DISCUSSION EXERCISES

How effective are you in oral communications? What is the most difficult aspect for you when you are engaged in conversations or discussions with other people? Are you impatient or inclined to jump to conclusions? Do you ask questions or ask for feedback?

* * *

How comfortable are you with public speaking? What do you enjoy the most about it? What do you enjoy the least? Discuss your experiences.

* * *

What is easiest for you about writing letters or memos? What is most difficult? How confident do you feel about your writing ability, composition and grammar, punctuation and so forth?

In Conclusion of This Unit

Management involves more than developing a business plan, conducting a recruiting seminar or monitoring advertising expenditures. These are important activities, but they are no more important than managing the human dynamics in the workplace. Organizations are groups of human beings. Therefore, the ability of the manager to command a position of leadership and inspire other people involves understanding human behavior. This begins with understanding one's self, which is important, regardless of your level of management in the organization. As you contemplate the issues we discussed in your development as a leader, a manager and an effective communicator, you will grow—not by magic formulas but by becoming a student of human nature.

THE
BUSINESS, FIRST HAND

Organizations adopt cultures that reflect the business philosophies and management styles of their leaders. Often the time comes when the culture that has been deeply ingrained inhibits the organization. It no longer fosters the effective or efficient environment that is needed for a contemporary organization. Philosophies, rules, procedures and expectations of human behavior are challenging to change. But change can occur, as we demonstrate by the way one organization shifted from an autocratic to participative culture.

A company that was started more than 40 years ago functioned for many years with a staff of 12 people, including the principal and one clerical/bookkeeper staff person. Today it has a staff of about 80, including two senior managers; a second tier of managers, each of whom is responsible for one of the company's business units; and an accounting and clerical department. As this organization grew, it outgrew the management methods that were deeply ingrained since its beginning.

The management style in the organization was fairly autocratic. The sole principal was the sole decision-maker. The staff was a highly talented group of professional experts whose efforts were focused on providing the organization's services. Because the scope of work at the time was not exceptionally complex, the principal could be relatively effective at monitoring all of their activities. The person in this position was a competent administrator and felt passionately about the organization's success. Often staff members were invited to counsel as the individual contemplated decisions, but clearly the principal controlled virtually every move that was made in the organization.

Although the organization functioned well with this culture, several situations began to inhibit the organization over time. As its agenda grew more ambitious, the organization had to find ways to administer a larger array of services. Considerable technical expertise was needed to make quality decisions; the manner in which decisions were made had to be expedited. Staff members began reacting to the autocratic culture, feeling somewhat stifled by their inability to influence their quality of life at work and to grow professionally. Because the organization was highly dependent on one person, its continuity was vulnerable in the event of this individual's departure.

The solution was to begin shifting the culture toward a more participative style. The process began by introducing the most senior principal to the philosophy, organizational structure and procedures involved in participative management. A focus group of people in the field was impaneled to gather perspectives about their daily challenges in the business as well as observations about the company. Then a second tier of management and a process for engaging the people in the field in the operation of the organization was created. Periodic meetings to do planning, problem-solving and brainstorming on both the management and staff levels were instituted. Training in both technical and organizational skills was enhanced. Personnel procedures were strengthened to enhance goal setting, performance evaluations and feedback between supervisors and workers.

As could be expected, this cultural shift hasn't happened overnight. Organizations can create new structures and procedures on paper, but changing attitudes and behavior takes time. Senior management has begun to delegate decision-making authority, lightening its burden and enhancing the organization's efficiency. The ongoing challenge has been learning to let go, to trust people to make meaningful decisions, then hold them accountable without interference. Staff has begun to feel like stakeholders in the organization and to develop as a team. Hidden and untapped talents have been unleashed, benefiting both the organization and the individuals. But staff also has been challenged as it wrestles with uncertainty about the legitimacy of management's new, more constructive attitude toward them.

The cultural shift is still evolving, but the horse is out of the barn, so to speak. Systems are now in place to mobilize the organization from the bottom to the top as well as from the top down. This will enhance the cultural shift and the institutionalization of the new philosophy. In many respects it's easier to move from an autocratic to participative culture rather than vice versa. People respond far more favorably to being given new opportunities to influence their work than they do when those opportunities are taken away. However, none of these opportunities would have existed in this organization without the vision and leadership of senior management.

Appendix: Office Management Software Resources

These resources are provided solely as a reference and are not intended to be a comprehensive list of all software or services that are available. The authors and publisher have not reviewed and do not endorse or make any representation or warranty regarding any of these products or services or the accuracy of the information provided.

ARES Development Group, LLC
Torrance, CA
(310) 782-7700
http://www.aresdg.com

Comput-a-Search, Inc.
Sarnia, Ontario, Canada
(519) 383-8383 (for product info.)

Constellation Data
Fairfield, Iowa
(515) 472-3199
(800) 214-3494

Decisions, Inc.
Sequim, Washington
(800) 397-0260

East Point Systems
Andover, CT
(860) 742-1019
http://www.eastpointsystems.com

GUI Software Systems, Inc.
Markham, Ontario, Canada
(905) 477-0244
(888) GUI-8623
http://www.guisoftware.com

The Lucero System for Real Estate Office Management
Show Low, AZ 85901
(800) 862-8193 (sales)
(520) 537-1300 (corporate offices)
http://www.lucero.com

Moore Data Management
Services
Minneapolis, Minnesota
(612) 661-1000
(800) 996-6547
http://www.mdms.com

Powermate Software
San Jose, California
(408) 977-1058
(800) 581-1943
http://
www.powermatecorp.com

REAL/Easy
Milwaukee, Wisconsin
(800) 732-5327
http://realeasy.com

Realty Executives of Phoenix
Phoenix, AZ 85018
(602) 912-1575

Realty Express
Fountain Valley, California
(714) 857-0606

Rocky Mountain Consulting
and Training Group, Inc.
Highlands Ranch, CO
(800) 791-5161

Transaction Programs
Nevada City, California
(530) 478-0512

United Data Systems, Inc.
Augusta, Georgia
(706) 823-9723
(800) 241-2404
http://www.udsnet.com

Whisky Hill Software
Woodside, CA 94062-0466
(650) 851-8702
http://
www.woodsideca.com/
clientrac/
(650) 851-8702

Worksware
Sherman Oaks, California
(818) 989-2298

GLOSSARY

Accounts payable Liabilities that represent amounts owed to creditors, usually for goods or services that were purchased.

Accounts receivable Claims against debtors, usually for goods or services that were delivered to the debtors.

Agency A relationship in which one person (the principal or client) delegates authority to another (the agent) to act on behalf of the principal in certain business transactions. This creates a fiduciary relationship, which imposes certain responsibilities on the agent who acts in this capacity.

Agency contracts Written agreements that create an agency relationship between a principal and an agent. These include listing agreements such as an open listing, an exclusive agency and an exclusive-right-to-sell agreement and buyer agency contracts such as open agreements, exclusive agency buyer agency agreements and exclusive buyer agency contracts.

Agent A person authorized to act on behalf of the principal and who has fiduciary responsibilities to the principal. In a real estate transaction, the broker is normally considered to be the agent of the principal or client.

Affinity programs Enticements such as coupons, discounts and points used in marketing programs to attract consumers by giving them increased purchasing power for a wide range of products and services. Also known as *cross marketing programs*.

Americans with Disabilities Act (ADA)   A federal law enacted to eliminate discrimination against people with disabilities in employment, public accommodations, government services, public transportation and communications.

Andragogy   The process by which adults learn, which distinguishes the adult learning process from the child's. It recognizes differences in approaching and processing new information.

Antitrust laws   Federal and state laws enacted for the purpose of fostering competition and preventing anticompetitive practices. Antitrust violations include price fixing, certain types of boycotts, allocations of markets and tying agreements.

Arbitration   A nonjudicial proceeding in which a third party determines the resolution of a dispute between parties. The determinations of the arbitrator can be as enforceable as a decision rendered in court.

Autocratic style   Management style in which the manager dominates the organization and makes all decisions, but in a more humanistic or benevolent manner than the dictatorial manager. In the autocratic style of management there is greater concern for people, which enables them to feel more secure and comfortable, and the atmosphere is more relaxed. *See also* Dictatorial style; Laissez-faire style; Participative style.

Balance sheet   A financial statement that itemizes assets, liabilities and net worth.

Blockbusting   *See* Panic selling.

Brainstorming   A group discussion held for the purpose of having participants generate a variety of ideas relating to a selected issue or solutions to a specific problem. Management uses brainstorming to encourage people to participate in the organization and utilizes their creativity and talents, rather than making unilateral decisions without the benefit of staff input.

Branch office   A secondary office or place of business of a brokerage firm, normally required to be registered, licensed and supervised according to the real estate licensing laws of the state.

Broker   A party, being a person, a corporation or a partnership, that is properly licensed as a broker under the real estate licensing laws within the jurisdiction where the individual or entity serves as a special agent to others in the brokerage of real property.

Brokerage   The specialty in the real estate business that is concerned with bringing parties together in the sale, lease or exchange of real property.

Budget   A statement of estimated income and expenses; a forecast to guide the financial operations of a business.

Business plan   A long-range blueprint, typically covering three to five years, that includes the mission statement, general objectives, goals and strategies of the company.

Buyer's broker   A broker who represents a buyer in a fiduciary capacity in a real estate transaction.

Caveat emptor   The Latin term meaning "let the buyer beware," denoting that a buyer purchases at his or her own risk. This ancient doctrine is replaced today by a more consumer-oriented approach; that is, the seller or the seller's agent has a duty to disclose any factors that might influence a buyer's decision.

Certificate of occupancy   A certificate or permit issued by a government authority indicating that the building is fit for use or occupancy according to the laws that the authority enforces.

Chain of command   The hierarchy of authority, which normally begins with upper levels of management and filters down to lower levels of management.

Clayton Antitrust Act   A federal statute that prohibits price discrimination, exclusive dealing arrangements and interlocking directives.

Client   The person who employs an agent to perform certain activities on his or her behalf, also known as the *principal* under the law of agency.

Client trust account   An account set up by a broker in which clients' monies are segregated from the broker's general business accounts. Individual states' real estate licensing laws prescribe specific requirements for the manner in which these accounts must be administered. Also known as *earnest money* or *escrow accounts* in some states.

Closing   The consummation of a real estate transaction, in which the seller delivers title to the buyer in exchange for payment of the purchase price by the buyer.

Code of ethics   A standard of ethical conduct, normally committed to writing. Any organization can establish a code of conduct for its members, such as the code of ethics of the National Association of REALTORS® and other professional organizations.

Commingling   Mixing or mingling monies; for example, depositing client funds in the broker's personal or business account. Licensees who do this are subject to disciplinary action by the regulatory body that enforces a state's real estate license laws. Some states' laws do permit brokers to deposit a small amount of business or personal funds in trust accounts to cover fees or other deposit requirements of a bank or savings institution.

Company dollar   Funds remaining from gross income after the cost of sales has been deducted. The cost of sales includes the commissions paid to the salespeople and other brokers cooperating in transactions, overrides to the manager, and sales fees, such as MLS, franchise, and referral or relocation fees.

Comparative market analysis   A value analysis of a seller's property compared with other similar properties and their sales prices to arrive at an anticipated sale price for the subject property.

Comprehensive Environmental Response Compensation and Liability Act   A federal law that imposes liability on owners, lenders, occupants and operators for correcting environmental problems on a property. Superfund statutes establish a fund to clean hazardous waste sites and respond to spills and releases on properties.

Computerized loan originations (CLOs)   Automated systems that enable a purchaser/borrower to locate a lender, submit a mortgage application and obtain a conditional loan commitment right in the real estate office. With CLOs, consumers can comparison shop the various mortgage lenders and all of their loan products. CLOs must comply with the requirements of the Real Estate Settlement Procedures Act. *See also* Real Estate Settlement Procedures Act (RESPA).

Conciliation agreement   A settlement or compromise agreement. Under the fair housing laws a respondent in a discrimination complaint can agree to a settlement rather than having the case resolved by judicial proceedings.

Consumer price index   A statistical measure prepared by the Bureau of Labor and Statistics that indicates changes in the prices of consumer goods.

Contingency A provision in a contract that requires the completion of certain acts or requires certain events to happen before the contract is binding.

Contingency plans Alternative goals and strategies that a company can implement in case certain events happen. These may be events that could affect a company's operations but have not yet occurred (and may never occur) when the company develops its business plan. Contingency plans provide a course for the organization to follow if these situations arise.

Contract A legally enforceable agreement between competent parties who agree to perform or refrain from performing certain acts for a consideration.

Controlled business arrangements (CBAs) Networks of interrelated companies that offer real estate services associated with a real estate transaction. They offer convenience to consumers and enhance the broker's service because the broker has control over all phases of the transaction.

Cooperating broker A broker who assists another broker to complete a real estate transaction. The cooperating broker may act as a subagent of the other broker's principal, as the agent of his or her own principal or have no fiduciary obligation to anyone in a transaction.

Corporation A legal entity created under a state's law that is an association of one or more individuals and has the capacity to act as an individual. A corporation is usually governed by a board of directors elected by the shareholders.

Cost of sales Commissions paid to the salespeople, to other brokers cooperating in real estate transactions, overrides to the manager, and sales fees, such as MLS, franchise, and referral or relocation fees. Also included are *transaction fees,* which are monies brokers are collecting separate from commissions to cover administrative costs associated with processing sales transactions.

Cross-marketing programs   Enticements, such as coupons, discounts and points, used in marketing programs to attract consumers by giving them increased purchasing power for a wide range of products and services. Also known as *affinity programs*.

Customer service surveys   A tool to find out what customers and clients think about the services that the company and its personnel provide. Information gathered from these surveys enables the company to monitor and improve the quality of its services where necessary.

Decentralized organization   An organization in which there are fewer levels of management and authority, giving each level greater authority and control over the activities of its departments or divisions.

Demographics   The profile of the population in an area, considering such characteristics as age, education, income, employment and household structure.

Desk cost   Reflects the amount of the company's expenses that can be attributed to each salesperson who works for the brokerage firm. It is calculated by dividing the expenses of the firm by the number of salespeople and can be used as a guide to determine the amount of expense each salesperson's production should cover.

Dictatorial style   Management style in which the manager has absolute and total control over all decisions. Nothing is delegated, only orders are issued, and there is little interaction with the people being supervised and little concern for them as human beings or for their capabilities. *See also* Autocratic style; Laissez-faire style; Participative style.

Discrimination   Making a distinction against or in favor of a person because of the group or class of people with whom the person is identified. Illegal discrimination is the failure to treat people equally under the fair housing or equal opportunity laws because of the group with which they are identified.

Disparate impact   The fact that an action has a significant impact on people in a protected class. This determines that the action is discriminatory, that is, the effect of an action is discriminatory without regard to the intent of the action.

Dispute resolution   Mediation and arbitration services for resolving disputes; a speedy and affordable alternative to resolving disputes in civil court.

Dual agency   Representing two principals with opposite interests in the same transaction. State law normally specifies whether a real estate licensee is permitted to provide dual agency. In states where it is permitted, the laws require that both principals must provide written consent for the dual representation.

Earnest money   A cash deposit made by a prospective buyer as evidence of good faith to perform on a sales contract. It is also known as *deposit money, hand money* or a *binder*.

Earnest money account   *See* Client trust account.

Employee   A person who works under the supervision and control of another. For income tax purposes, an independent contractor is distinguished from an employee. *See also* Independent contractor.

Equal employment opportunity laws   Laws that provide for equal employment for all qualified individuals regardless of their race, color, religion, sex, age, disability, marital or family status, or nationality.

Equity with the competition The comparison of a company's compensation or commission program in relation to competitors' programs.

Ethics A system of moral principles or rules and standards of conduct. *See also* Code of ethics.

Exclusive agency A written listing agreement that gives an agent the sole right to sell or lease a property within a specified time period, with the exception that the owner can sell or lease the property himself or herself without being liable to the agent for compensation.

Exclusive agency buyer agency The buyer contracts with a sole agent for locating a property that meets certain specifications, *with the exception* that the buyer is relieved of any obligation to the agent if the buyer locates the property without the assistance of the agent or another broker.

Exclusive buyer agency The buyer contracts with a sole agent for locating a property that meets certain specifications. The buyer owes 100 percent loyalty to the agent and is obligated for a commission, regardless of whether the buyer, the agent or another broker locates the property.

Exclusive listing A written listing in which an owner of a property contracts with a sole agent to sell or lease a property. It may be an *exclusive agency* or an *exclusive-right-to-sell* agreement.

Exclusive-right-to-sell A written listing giving an agent the sole right to sell or lease a property within a specified time period. The owner is liable to the agent for a commission regardless of whether the agent, the owner or another broker sells or leases the property.

Facilitator A person who assists a buyer or seller to reach an agreement in a real estate transaction. A facilitator does not represent or have fiduciary obligations to either party.

Federal Fair Housing Act   Title VIII of the Civil Rights Act of 1964, as amended. It protects people against discrimination in housing because of their race, color, religion, sex, handicap, familial status or national origin.

Federal Trade Commission (FTC)   A federal agency responsible for investigating and eliminating unfair and deceptive trade practices and unfair methods of competition.

Fictitious business name (FBN)   A business name, other than the name of a person, under which the business is registered to conduct business.

Foreign Investment in Real Property Tax Act (FIRPTA)   A federal law that subjects nonresident aliens and foreign corporations to U.S. income tax on their gains from the disposition of an interest in real property.

Franchise   The formal privilege or contractual right to conduct a business using a designated trade name and the operating procedures of the company that owns the franchise.

Fraud   An *intentional* deceptive act or statement with which one person attempts to gain an unfair advantage over another. It may be either a *misstatement* or *silence* about a defect.

General objectives   Major aspirational objectives an organization intends to accomplish to fulfill its mission.

General partnership   A form of business organization in which two or more owners engage in business. All of the general partners share full liability for the debts of the business.

Goals   The end results that a company wants to achieve. Goals break down the aspirational or futuristic nature of the general objectives into specific, measurable, short-term accomplishments and show how the organization intends to achieve its general objectives.

Gross income　The total income derived from doing business before any costs or expenses are deducted.

Group boycotting　An antitrust violation in which two or more competitors band together to exert pressure on another competitor for the purpose of eliminating competition. It may involve withholding goods, services or patronage that are essential to the competitor's economic survival or dealing only on unfavorable terms with the competitor. Group boycotting is a *per se* offense if it is done for the express purpose of reducing or eliminating competition.

Hazardous substance　Any material that poses a threat to the environment or to public health.

Hazardous waste　Materials that are dangerous to handle and dispose of, such as radioactive materials, certain chemicals, explosives or biological waste.

Home officing　A term in business referring to the practice of people working primarily from their homes. This is an increasingly popular trend in business, made possible by technology.

Human resources　The people or personnel of an organization.

Income statement　*See* Profit and loss statement.

Independent contractor　A person retained to perform certain acts or achieve certain results without control or direction of another regarding the methods or processes used to accomplish the results.

Intellectual property　Assets that are original works; the product of an individual's creative efforts, such as manuscripts and art. With the emergence of the Internet intellectual property has gained new meaning as individuals create Web sites and display their wares, including listings.

Internal equity   A comparison of compensation plans within a company that prescribes that all people who work in the same class of jobs within an organization be paid at the same rates and that people with greater experience or productivity or specialized jobs be compensated at higher rates.

Job description   Precisely defines the responsibilities as well as the activities of a position. This ensures that both the company and the worker know exactly what a person in a specific position is expected to do.

Laissez-faire style   A management style in which the manager adopts a hands-off, do-nothing approach, characterized by nonintervention and indifference. This creates a chaotic environment because the manager doesn't exercise any authority. *See also* Autocratic style; Dictatorial style; Participative style.

Law of agency   The common-law doctrine that pertains to the relationship created when one person or entity is authorized to act on legal matters for the benefit of another.

Lead poisoning   Illness caused by high concentrations of lead in the body. Common sources are lead that was used in paint prior to 1978 and water contamination from lead pipes and solder containing lead.

License referral company   Separate subsidiary of a brokerage company that some companies use as an alternative to accommodate licensees who do not meet their criteria for full-time salespeople, but whom the company wants to capture because of the business that these people may be able to refer to it.

Licensee   A person who is issued a valid real estate license by the licensing body in the jurisdiction in which the person provides real estate services as prescribed by law.

Limited liability company (LLC)   An alternative business entity with characteristics of a limited partnership and an S corporation. Investors are members rather than partners or shareholders in the business and hold membership interests rather than stock in the company. An LLC has advantages over corporations and partnerships because personal liability and taxes are different.

Limited partnership   A partnership in which one person or group, known as the general partner, organizes, operates and is responsible for the partnership venture. Other individual members are merely investors and are responsible for potential liabilities only to the extent of their original investments.

Line authority   The authority given to the people who are responsible for contributing *directly* to the achievement of the company's objectives, such as the sales office or the property management, leasing or new construction departments.

Listing agreement   A written employment agreement between an owner of real estate and a broker that authorizes the broker to find a suitable buyer or tenant for the property. There are several types of contracts, including an open listing, an exclusive agency and an exclusive-right-to-sell listing.

Lockbox   Small, secure box affixed to a property that enables only certain authorized individuals to access its contents, usually a key to the property.

Management   The activity of guiding or directing the financial and human resources of an organization. There are various management philosophies that attempt to define the way in which organizations function and managers use their authority and make decisions. The common theme in current management trends is the participative style, which emphasizes the value of people and their contribution to the organization.

Manager   Individuals who are responsible for guiding or directing the financial and human resources of an organization. The prevailing theory in management today is that managers inspire, energize and support the people they supervise rather than controlling or dominating them.

Market   The geographic area in which a company does business or the specific consumers the company seeks to serve with its products or services.

Mediation   An alternative to arbitration and judicial proceedings, in which parties can resolve disputes between themselves using an impartial third party to moderate the proceedings and help them find a mutually acceptable resolution. If the parties are unsuccessful in mediation, they may proceed to arbitration or civil court.

Misrepresentation   False statements or concealment of a *material fact*, that is, information deemed to be pertinent to a decision. Misrepresentations may be motivated by an attempt to deceive though, unlike fraud, they are limited to a fact that is material to the transaction.

Mission statement   States what a company's purpose is for doing business, specifically what the business does and where the organization intends to be in the future.

Monolithic organization   A highly centralized operation that functions as a single (mono) unit, even though it normally consists of a number of work groups, with authority being highly controlled at the top of the organization.

Monthly operating budgets   Monthly budgets constructed from the annual operating budget. By dividing the annual gross income and operating expenses by 12, the company has monthly projections to use as benchmarks for monitoring income and expenses during the year.

Multiple listing service (MLS)   Information systems that provide their members with a variety of information including mortgage loan information, competitive market analysis data, sample contracts, worksheets for qualifying buyers and estimating ownership and closing costs, investment analysis and online mapping and tax records, in addition to listing inventory.

Net income   The sum arrived at after deducting the expenses of operation from gross income.

Niche marketing   Services directed to specialized segments of the consumer population. Niche marketing appeals to consumers because it satisfies their demand for specialized knowledge.

Online services   Commercial computer networks providing a wide variety of information that subscribers to the services can access. Commercial online services include CompuServe, Prodigy, GEnie, MCI and America Online.

Open-ended questions   Questions that begin with *How, What, Who, When* or *Where,* and require explanations, as opposed to closed-ended questions that can be answered only "Yes" or "No." Open-ended questions solicit feedback and information in a way not possible with closed-ended questions.

Open listing   A listing in which the owner of the property gives the right to sell or lease a property to a number of brokers, who then can work simultaneously to effect a sale or lease. Compensation is owed to the broker who procures a ready, willing and able buyer or tenant.

Operating expenses   Recurring fixed expenses, such as rent, dues and fees, salaries, taxes and license fees, insurance and depreciation (funding for depreciation on equipment, buildings and automobiles the company owns), and variable expenses such as advertising and promotion, utilities, equipment and supplies and cost of sales.

Operating strategy   The methodology employed by an organization to accomplish its goals. A strategy defines how the organization plans to use its financial and human resources.

Organization chart   The structure of an organization that identifies the various business units, divisions or departments within the firm and the line of authority or chain of command for each manager of the units.

Override   A method of calculating managerial compensation based on a percentage of the gross commission (before the agents' shares are deducted), a percentage of commission after the sales and listing commissions are deducted, or a percentage of the office's net profits.

Panic selling   Efforts to sell real estate in a particular neighborhood by generating fear that real estate values are declining because people in a protected class are moving into or out of a neighborhood, which has nothing to do with the intrinsic value of the real estate itself. Panic selling violates the fair housing laws.

Participative style   A humanistic management style in which the manager creates a democratic environment that promotes initiative and recognizes the value of the human resources. Participative management utilizes the talents and insight of people to a greater extent than is common in other styles of management. *See also* Autocratic style; Dictatorial style; Laissez-faire style.

Performance criteria   The basis on which people will be evaluated in a performance review. Criteria include production quotas and other performance-based issues that are considered to be important in the performance of a person's job.

Performance reviews   An evaluation of a worker's progress in which the manager and the worker or salesperson can meet one-on-one and discuss a variety of issues about the job and the salesperson's career.

Per se rule   Decision by the U.S. Supreme Court that identifies certain antitrust activities that cannot be defended as being reasonable under any circumstances because they are so destructive to competition that their anticompetitive effect is automatically presumed. These include activities such as price fixing, certain kinds of boycotts, territorial assignments and tying agreements.

Personal success plans   A salesperson's business plan that converts the salesperson's aspirations for success into action with specific or measurable goals and strategies to guide him or her along the way. A personal success plan is a holistic approach to defining what a person intends to accomplish as a professional salesperson, in addition to a production quota.

Policy and procedures manual   A document that tells people how they are to conduct business for the company. It includes the general business philosophy and business ethics and prescribes procedures for handling a multitude of details of the company's operations.

Polychlorinated biphenyls (PCBs)   Used in the manufacture of electrical products (such as transformers, switches, voltage regulators), paints, adhesives, caulking materials and hydraulic fluids. PCBs can cause birth defects and cancer and other diseases.

POSDC   A management model that groups various activities involved in the operation of a business by functions. These functions include planning, organizing, staffing, directing and controlling.

Profit and loss statement   A detailed statement of the income and expenses of a business, commonly known as a P & L, operating statement or income statement.

Profit center   A business unit within a company that is expected to produce enough income to cover its cost of operation plus make a profit for the firm.

Radon   A radioactive gas produced by the natural decay of other radioactive substances, which is suspected to be a cause of cancer.

Real Estate Settlement Procedures Act (RESPA)   A federal law enacted with the goal of encouraging home ownership. It intends to protect consumers from practices that are considered abusive as well as to see that consumers are provided with more complete information about certain lending practices and closing and settlement procedures.

Referral networks   Formally structured organizations that enable a broker to refer buyers and sellers to brokers in other geographic areas or to brokers who specialize in other types of real estate services. There are independent networks as well as those connected with national franchises and corporations.

Relocation networks   Formal organizations that may be part of or in addition to referral networks to provide relocation services. There are corporate relocation management companies, otherwise known as third-party equity contractors, who enter into agreements with large corporations to handle their employee transfers.

Residential Lead-Based Paint Hazard Reduction Act   Sets forth procedures for disclosing the presence of lead-based paint in the sale of residential properties built before 1978.

Salesperson   A licensed individual employed by a licensed broker, either as an employee or independent contractor, to perform certain acts as defined by the real estate license laws of the state.

S corporation   A kind of corporation that allows a business to operate as a corporation but not pay corporate tax. Each shareholder is taxed on his or her individual share of the corporation's income, which avoids the double taxation feature of corporations. There are limitations on the number of shareholders and the sources of corporate income.

Sexual harassment   According to the federal Equal Employment Opportunity Commission, unwelcome sexual advances, requests for sexual favors and other verbal or physical conduct of a sexual nature when submission is either explicitly or implicitly a term or condition of a person's employment, used as the basis for employment decisions affecting a person or has the purpose or effect of unreasonably interfering with a person's work performance or creating an intimidating, hostile or offensive working environment.

Sherman Act   An antitrust law intended to curtail large trusts, cartels or monopolies that are perceived to threaten healthy competition and the growth of businesses. The theory is that competitive forces must be allowed to function, with the ultimate result being the lowest prices, highest quality and greatest progress in the marketplace.

Signature   The words, graphics and colors that create an identity for the company.

Single agency   The practice of representing either the buyer/tenant *or* the seller/landlord, but never both in the same transaction.

Sole ownership   A method of owning a business in which one person owns the entire business and is solely responsible and liable for all activities and debts of its operation. Business may be conducted under the name of the owner or a fictitious name. Also known as a *sole proprietorship.*

Staff authority The authority given to the people who are responsible for support services, the work groups that provide administrative support. They contribute *indirectly* to the achievement of the company's objectives by providing such services as accounting, marketing and advertising, training, purchasing (materials for the operation of the business) and maintenance.

Steering The illegal practice of channeling homeseekers to particular areas or neighborhoods. When another person, such as a licensee, does this, the act has the effect of limiting a homeseeker's choices by restricting the person's ability to choose the neighborhood in which she or he will live.

Stigmatized properties Those that individuals consider to be "psychologically impacted" because certain events have occurred that people may find offensive or that provoke emotional reactions. These include events such as a suicide, murder or other felony, paranormal activities (ghosts), a lingering illness or death.

Strategies The methodology that will be used to accomplish a specific goal or objective. Long-range planning is otherwise known as *strategic planning* because it provides not only goals but also the strategic methodology for accomplishing them.

Subagent An agent of a person authorized to act as the agent of the principal under the law of agency.

Target market The specific audience or consumers for the company's products or services.

Team-building The process of mobilizing the collective efforts of people to work toward the goals of the organization and at the same time satisfy themselves.

Telecommuting   Using technology to conduct business from any location in which computers can be linked to the base office through the telephone network. *See* Home officing; Virtual office.

Telephone Consumer Protection Act   FCC regulations that govern the use of telephone lines for commercial solicitation and advertisement to protect telephone subscribers who do not wish to receive unsolicited live "cold called," autodialed, prerecorded or artificial voice messages and fax machine solicitations.

Territorial assignments   An antitrust violation in which competitors agree to divide the market geographically or by some other criterion, which destroys competition when the purpose of segregating the market is to establish power in that market.

Text telephone (TT)   Typewriterlike unit that displays conversation on a screen that can be read so a person who is deaf or hearing-impaired can communicate via telephone. A TT "talks" with another text telephone or a computer. Formerly known as *TDDs*.

Transaction expenses   *See* Cost of sales.

Tying agreement   An arrangement in which a party agrees to sell one product only on the condition that the buyer also purchases a different or *tied* product. Frequently the tied product is less unique or desirable than the *tying* product. The courts have concluded that the only purpose of a tying arrangement is to extend the market power of the tying product and have declared these agreements to be *per se* illegal.

Urea formaldehyde   A chemical used in building materials in the 1970s, particularly in insulation. Urea formaldehyde foam insulation (UFFI) has been targeted because of the formaldehyde gases that leach out of the insulation.

Variable expense budgets   Specific budgets prepared to identify individual expenditures within categories of certain general variable expenses, such as advertising and promotion, utilities, equipment and supplies and cost of sales.

Virtual office   A relatively new term used to refer to the fact than an office can exist anywhere people can use technology.

BIBLIOGRAPHY

Americans with Disabilities Act of 1990. Public Law 101-336, U.S. Code, vol. 42, sec. 12101.

Belasco, James A. *Teaching the Elephant to Dance.* New York: Crown Publishing Co., 1990.

Bennis, Warren. *On Becoming a Leader.* New York: Addison-Wesley, 1989.

Burley-Allen, Madelyn. *Listening, the Forgotten Skill.* New York: John Wiley & Sons, 1995.

Covey, Stephen R. *Principle-Centered Leadership.* New York: Fireside, Simon & Schuster, 1991.

Covey, Stephen R. *The Seven Habits of Highly Effective People.* New York: Fireside, Simon & Schuster, 1990.

de Heer, Robert. *Real Estate Contracts.* Chicago: Real Estate Education Company, 1995.

de Heer, Robert. *Realty Bluebook®.* 32nd ed. Chicago: Real Estate Education Company, 1998.

de Heer, Robert. *Risk Management.* 2nd ed. Chicago: Real Estate Education Company, 1998.

Dennison, Mark S. *Environmental Considerations in Real Estate Transactions.* Chicago: Real Estate Education Company, 1994.

Dooley, Thomas W., and Charles M. Dahlheimer. *Real Estate in the 90s, A Whole New World Ahead.* St. Louis: North American Consulting Group, Inc., 1989.

Dooley, Tom, Stefan I. Swanepoel, Michael A. Abelson. *Real Estate Confronts Reality: Consumers, Computers, Confusion.* Chicago: Real Estate Education Company, 1998.

Drucker, Peter E. *Innovation and Entrepreneurship.* New York: Harper & Row, 1985.

Fair Housing Act. Public Law 90-284, U.S. Code, vol. 42, secs. 3600-20, 1989.

Finley, David L. *Agency Plus.* Chicago: Real Estate Education Company, 1994.

Harlan, Don, Gail Lyons and John Reilly. *Consensual Dual Agency: A Practical Approach to the In-House Sale.* Chicago: Real Estate Education Company, 1994.

Harris, Philip R. and Robert T. Moran. *Managing Cultural Differences.* Houston: Gulf Publishing Company, 1996.

Kami, Michael J. *Trigger Points.* New York: McGraw-Hill, 1988.

Keigher, Patrick J., and Joyce A. Emory. *Professional Real Estate Development.* Chicago: Real Estate Education Company, 1994.

Labovitz, George and Victor Rosansky. *The Power of Alignment: How Companies Stay Centered and Accomplish Extraordinary Things.* New York: John Wiley & Sons, Inc., 1997.

Levi, Donald R. *How to Teach Adults.* 2nd ed. Chicago: Real Estate Educators Association, 1996.

Lyons, Gail, and Don Harlan. *Buyer Agency.* 3rd ed. Chicago: Real Estate Education Company, 1997.

Lyons, Gail G., Donald D. Harlan, John Tuccillo. *The Future of Real Estate: Profiting from the Revolution.* Chicago: Real Estate Education Company, 1996.

O'Toole, James. *Leading Change: The Argument for Values-Based Leadership.* New York: Ballantine Books, 1996.

Peters, Tom, and Robert H. Waterman, Jr. *In Search of Excellence.* New York: Warner Books, 1992.

Pivar, William H. and Donald L. Harlan. *Real Estate Ethics, Good Ethics = Good Business.* Chicago: Real Estate Education Company, 1995.

Reilly, John. *Agency Relationships in Real Estate.* 2nd ed. Chicago: Real Estate Education Company, 1994.

Ritchie, Ingrid, and Stephen J. Martin. *The Healthy Home Kit.* Chicago: Real Estate Education Company, 1995.

Rules and Regulations, "ADA Accessibility Guidelines," *Federal Register* 56, no. 44 (28 July 1991).

Rules and Regulations, "Fair Housing Accessibility Guidelines," *Federal Register* 56, no. 44 (6 March 1991): 9497–9506.

Rules and Regulations, "Fair Housing Act," *Federal Register* 56, no. 13 (23 January 1989): 3232–3317.

Rules and Regulations, "Fair Housing Advertising" *Federal Register* 54, No. 13 (23 January 1989): 3308–11.

Sence, Peter M. *The Fifth Discipline.* New York: Doubleday/ Currency, 1990.

Seraydarian, Patricia E. *Writing for Business Results.* Burr Ridge, Ill.: Business One Irwin/Mirror Press, 1994.

Sewell, Carl, and Paul B. Brown. *Customers for Life, How to Turn That One-Time Buyer into a Lifetime Customer.* New York: Pocket Books/Simon & Schuster, 1990.

Tuccillo, John. *The Eight New Rules of Real Estate: Doing Business in a Consumer-Centric, Techno-Savy World.* Chicago: Real Estate Education Company, 1999.

Tuccillo, John, Buddy West and Betsey West. *Targeting the Over-55 Client: Your Guide to Today's Fastest Growing Market.* 2nd ed. Chicago: Real Estate Education Company, 1998.

Wheatley, Margaret J. *Leadership and the New Science.* San Francisco: Berrett-Koelhler Publishers, 1992.

Whitworth, Laura, Henry Kimsey-House and Phil Sandall. *Co-Active Coaching.* Palo Alto: Davies-Black Publishing, 1998.

Williams, Martha R., and Marcia L. Russell. *ADA Handbook: Employment and Construction Issues Affecting Your Business.* Chicago: Real Estate Education Company, 1993.

This is only a sample of the publications available to inform, inspire or guide the leaders and managers of real estate brokerage organizations.

INDEX